Words and Phrases Legally Defined

Words and Phrases Legally Defined

SUPPLEMENT 2023

David Hay MA, LLM
of the Inner Temple, Barrister

LexisNexis®

LexisNexis® UK & Worldwide

United Kingdom — RELX (UK) Limited trading as LexisNexis®, 1-3 Strand, London WC2N 5JR

LNUK Global Partners — LexisNexis® encompasses authoritative legal publishing brands dating back to the 19th century including: Butterworths® in the United Kingdom, Canada and the Asia-Pacific region; Les Editions du Juris Classeur in France; and Matthew Bender® worldwide. Details of LexisNexis® locations worldwide can be found at www.lexisnexis.com

Published by LexisNexis®

A CIP Catalogue record for this book is available from the British Library.

ISBN for this volume: 9781474325400

Printed in Great Britain by Hobbs the Printers Ltd, Totton, Hampshire

Visit LexisNexis at http://www.lexisnexis.co.uk

Preface

This supplement contains a further selection of definitions from case law and statute.

The law as indicated is that existing at 18 September 2023.

This is the fifth Supplement to the Fifth Edition to be published. Editorial notes have been revised, particularly reference to Halsbury's Laws of England where volumes have been reissued, or issued for the Fifth Edition.

The style follows that used in the main volumes, which should be consulted first. Notes of statutory repeals or amendments and any other editorial comments are shown in square brackets.

LexisNexis

September 2023

A

AARHUS CAP

'[6] … Lang J by order dated 31 January 2018, which I discuss in para [8] below, accepted that [the appellant's] claim fell within the scope of art 9 of the UNECE Convention on Access to Information, Public Participation in Decision-Making and Access to Justice in Environmental Matters adopted at Aarhus, Denmark on 25 June 1998 ("the Aarhus Convention"). As a result, CPRE-Kent obtained protection under CPR Pt 45 against adverse costs by means of a cap of £10,000 ("the Aarhus cap").' *CPRE Kent v Secretary of State* [2021] UKSC 36, [2022] 1 All ER 847 at [6], per Lord Hodge DP

ABANDONMENT

Of distress

[For 62 Halsbury's Laws of England (5th Edn) (2016) para 282 see now 62 Halsbury's Laws of England (5th Edn) (2022) para 305.]

Of goods

[For 80 Halsbury's Laws of England (5th Edn) (2013) para 848 see now 80 Halsbury's Laws of England (5th Edn) (2020) para 848.]

ABATEMENT

Of legacy

[For 103 Halsbury's Laws of England (5th Edn) (2010) para 1086 see now 103 Halsbury's Laws of England (5th Edn) (2021) para 1090.]

ABODE

See PLACE OF ABODE

ABEYANCE

Of peerage

[For 79 Halsbury's Laws of England (5th Edn) (2014) para 832 see now 79 Halsbury's Laws of England (5th Edn) (2020) para 830.]

ACCEPTANCE

Of bill of exchange

[For 49 Halsbury's Laws of England (5th Edn) (2015) paras 235–248 see now 49 Halsbury's Laws of England (5th Edn) (2021) paras 199–212.]

Of offer

[For 22 Halsbury's Laws of England (5th Edn) (2012) para 251 see now 22 Halsbury's Laws of England (5th Edn) (2019) para 51.]

ACCESSION

[For 80 Halsbury's Laws of England (5th Edn) (2013) para 823 see now 80 Halsbury's Laws of England (5th Edn) (2020) para 823.]

ACCIDENT

In insurance policy

[For 60 Halsbury's Laws of England (5th Edn) (2011) para 545 see now 60 Halsbury's Laws of England (5th Edn) (2018) para 522.]

ACCOMMODATION BILL

[For 49 Halsbury's Laws of England (5th Edn) (2015) para 266 see now 49 Halsbury's Laws of England (5th Edn) (2021) para 230.]

ACCORD AND SATISFACTION

[For 22 Halsbury's Laws of England (5th Edn) (2012) para 605 see now 22 Halsbury's Laws of England (5th Edn) (2019) para 396.]

ACCRETION

[For 100 Halsbury's Laws of England (5th Edn) (2009) para 39 see now 100 Halsbury's Laws of England (5th Edn) (2018) para 46.]

ACT OF GOD

[For 22 Halsbury's Laws of England (5th Edn) (2012) para 478 see now 22 Halsbury's Laws of England (5th Edn) (2019) para 269.]

ACTION (LEGAL)

[For 11 Halsbury's Laws of England (5th Edn) (2015) para 117 see now 11 Halsbury's Laws of England (5th Edn) (2020) para 121.]

ADDUCE

Canada [Criminal Code, RSC 1985, c C-46, ss 276, 278.1, 278.92 to 278.94.] '76 The parties and interveners disagree about the meaning of "adduce" in ss 278.92(1), 278.93(2) and 278.93(4). The disagreement focuses on whether "adduce" only includes entering evidence as an exhibit at trial, or if it applies as well to the use of the information contained within the record for the purposes of cross-examination. Justice Côté in dissent would adopt the narrow interpretation. In contrast, our interpretation of "adduce" is not limited to circumstances where evidence is entered as an exhibit. Instead, we adopt a purposive approach that includes references to the content of a record made in defence submissions or the examination and cross-examination of witnesses. Specifically, under the record screening regime, the accused must screen records when they seek to use information during a hearing that they specifically learned from those records. If they have independent knowledge of the information, gathered from sources that do not rely on the complainant's private records, they may use this information without invoking the record screening regime (subject to other applicable evidentiary rules and trial procedures).

'77 We reject the narrow interpretation of "adduce" for several reasons. …

…

'81 In conclusion, the use of the word "adduce" in the impugned provisions captures the content of the record that is referenced by the accused during the trial, even if the record is not formally entered as an exhibit.' *R v JJ* [2022] SCJ No 28, 2022 SCC 28 at paras 76–77, 81, per Wagner CJ and Moldaver J

ADEMPTION

[For 60 Halsbury's Laws of England (5th Edn) (2011) para 455 see now 60 Halsbury's Laws of England (5th Edn) (2018) para 433.]

[For 102 Halsbury's Laws of England (5th Edn) (2010) para 155 see now 102 Halsbury's Laws of England (5th Edn) (2021) para 157.]

ADMINISTRATION

[For 103 Halsbury's Laws of England (5th Edn) (2010) para 607 see now 103 Halsbury's Laws of England (5th Edn) (2021) para 609.]

ADOPT

[Insolvency Act 1986, Sch B1 para 99(5).] '[70] I should first deal with a preliminary argument that para 99(5) is simply inapplicable in the current situation. Ms Toube QC indicated that some commentators in the market apparently take the view that since Lord Browne-Wilkinson had identified that correction of the mischief in *Nicoll v Cutts* [[1985] BCLC 322, CA] was the reason for the introduction of the forerunner to para 99(5) in the 1986 Act, and since the only identified mischief in *Nicoll v Cutts* was that employees might render services in the insolvency without payment, para 99(5) should be read as having no application whatever unless employees actually rendered services to the company in administration. Hence, so the argument goes, a contract which provides for an employee to be furloughed could never be adopted by administrators under para 99(5).

'[71] I reject that argument. It is certainly true that the mischief in *Nicoll v Cutts* involved an employee not being paid for services that they had rendered in an insolvency. But if Parliament had wanted to limit super-priority for wages and salary to cases where services are actually rendered to a company in administration, it could have said so simply and directly. Instead it chose to deploy the concept of adoption of the contract of employment itself, and to persist with that concept when making subsequent amendments to the Insolvency Act (first by the Insolvency Act 1994 and secondly by the Enterprise Act 2002 when introducing Sch B1), long after any difficulties with that concept had become apparent.

'[72] Moreover, even in normal circumstances not involving COVID-19 or furlough, there are situations in which an administrator might, without committing any breach or repudiation of an employee's contract of employment, not require the employee to work for a period during the administration, but where it would nevertheless be entirely appropriate for the administrator to be required to continue to pay their wages or salary. To give one example, take an employee who has particular skills or know-how regarding the company's business which would, if available to a competitor, devalue the business which the administrator was seeking to sell. Even if there was no new work for the employee to do in the administration until it was known whether the business could be sold, it would be commercially important for the administrator not to terminate the employee's contract. In that way, the employee would continue to be available to the purchaser of the business, the restrictive covenants in his contract would continue in effect, and the maximum post-termination period of restraint would be available for the potential benefit of the purchaser. Given those benefits to the administration, even if, with the permission of the administrator, the employee were not required to attend the premises to work, it would be wrong if they were not entitled to payment of their wages or salary.

'[73] Moreover, although the coronavirus and the concept of furlough were obviously not foreseen by Parliament when it enacted and amended the relevant insolvency legislation, or by the House of Lords when *Paramount* [*Powdrill v Watson*] was decided, it is very clear from Lord Browne-Wilkinson's speech ([1995] 2 All ER 65 at 76 and 79, [1995] 2 AC 394 at 441–442 and 445) that promotion of the rescue culture is an important consideration when interpreting the Insolvency Act. In the instant case, a conclusion that because furloughed employees could not provide services, their contracts of employment could not be adopted under para 99(5) would have the unwelcome result that the main statutory provision dealing with the issue of employment in administrations would have no application and would not enable furloughed wages or salary to be paid as the Scheme plainly envisages. That would be entirely contrary to the rescue culture in the current situation in which such an approach may be needed more than ever before.

'[74] I therefore see no reason whatever to strive to reach a conclusion that para 99(5) is wholly inoperable in the current situation. Instead, if it is possible to do so, para 99(5) should be interpreted to permit the Scheme to be given effect, and thus support the rescue culture and the Government's efforts to deal with the economic consequences of the COVID-19 pandemic.' *Re Carluccio's Ltd (in administration)* [2020] EWHC 886 (Ch), [2020] 3 All ER 291 at [70]–[74], per Snowden J

[Insolvency Act 1986, Sch B1 para 99(5).]

'[53] … When Lord Browne-Wilkinson referred [in *Powdrill v Watson* ('*Paramount*')] at [1995] 2 All ER 65 at 83, [1995] 2 AC 394 at 449 to "some conduct by the administrator or receiver which amounts to an election to treat the continued contract of employment as giving rise" to super-priority, he was not introducing as a relevant factor the intentions of the administrator, even if objectively determined. He did not, as Mr Smith submitted, require the conduct of the administrator to evidence an election by the administrator. It is a question of law: is the conduct of the administrator such that he must be taken to have to accept that the relevant amounts falling due under the employment contract enjoy super-priority? It is a wholly objective question, focussed entirely on the conduct of the administrator. As Lord Browne-Wilkinson repeatedly said, the issue is whether the office-holder has "continued" the employment of the relevant employees. This is the essence of the test propounded by him. If the office-holder has continued their employment, in other words has taken active steps to continue their employment, that necessarily results in super-priority for the relevant liabilities under the contracts of employment. As earlier noted, and by contrast, doing nothing involves no continuation by the administrators of the employment.

'[54] We agree with the way in which Laddie J summarised the effect of *Paramount* on the meaning of adoption in *Re Antal International Ltd (in admin)* [2003] EWHC 1339 (Ch), [2003] 2 BCLC 406, [2003] BPIR 1067 (at [7]):

> "What Lord Browne-Wilkinson was pointing out was that it was important to find some conduct on behalf of the administrator or receiver which could be treated as an election or could be regarded as … him exercising a choice as to whether or not the contracts of employment were to be adopted".
>
> And again at [12] where he said:
>
> "It is necessary to look at the facts and to decide whether there has been some conduct by the administrator or receiver which can legitimately be treated as an election to continue the contract of employment".'

Re Debenhams Retail Ltd (in administra-

tion) [2020] EWCA Civ 600, [2020] 3 All ER 319 at [53]–[54], per David Richards LJ

ADOPTION

Of child

[For 9 Halsbury's Laws of England (5th Edn) (2012) para 361 see now 9 Halsbury's Laws of England (5th Edn) (2017) para 399.]

ADULTERY

[For 72 Halsbury's Laws of England (5th Edn) (2015) para 399 see now 72 Halsbury's Laws of England (5th Edn) (2019) para 394.]

ADVANCEMENT

[For 98 Halsbury's Laws of England (5th Edn) (2013) para 516 see now 98 Halsbury's Laws of England (5th Edn) (2019) para 489.]

ADVERSE

Adverse possession

[For 68 Halsbury's Laws of England (5th Edn) (2016) para 1076 see now 68 Halsbury's Laws of England (5th Edn) (2021) para 1180.] 12 Halsbury's Laws of England (5th Edn) (2015) para 851

Adverse witness

[For 12 Halsbury's Laws of England (5th Edn) (2015) para 851 see now 12 Halsbury's Laws of England (5th Edn) (2020) para 843.]

AFFILIATES

[Settlement agreement, cl 8 provided for the 'Parties' Affiliates' to be able to enforce the terms of cll 2 and 3 of the agreement in accordance with the Contracts (Rights of Third Parties) Act 1999.] '[51] "Affiliate" is defined in the Settlement Agreement in such a way as to include a person's "Employee", and the definition of "Employee" encompasses, among others, "any former … officers … and agents". The JAs [joint administrators] contend that, as administrators of REL, Properties and Askwith, they were both "officers" and "agents" of those companies and so are their "Affiliates" for the purposes of the Settlement Agreement. In that connection, Mr Tom Smith QC, who appeared for the JAs with Ms Hannah Thornley, pointed out that para 69 of Sch B1 to the 1986 Act states in terms that, "[i]n exercising his functions under this Schedule the administrator of a company acts as its agent". Citing *Re X Co Ltd* [1907] 2 Ch 92, *Re Home Treat Ltd* [1991] BCLC 705, [1991] BCC 165, *Re Powertrain Ltd (in lid)* [2015] EWHC 3998 (Ch), [2017] 1 BCLC 95, [2016] BCC 216 and *R (on the application of Palmer) v Northern Derbyshire Magistrates' Court, R (on the application of Forsey) v Northern Derbyshire Magistrates' Court* [2021] EWHC 3013 (Admin), [2022] ICR 531, Mr Smith said that the authorities show that administrators are also "officers".

'[52] For his part, Mr Davies argued that an administrator is imposed on a company, acts primarily in the interests of its creditors and would not normally be referred to as an "affiliate" of the company in question. In the present case, Mr Davies said, the JAs were recognised not to be in the same camp as REL, Properties and Askwith and so the draftsman of the Settlement Agreement could be expected to have identified them specifically as "Affiliates" of those companies had they been intended to be such.

'[53] In my view, however, the Judge was right to regard the JAs as "Affiliates" within the meaning of the Settlement Agreement. The simple fact is that the JAs were both officers and agents of REL, Properties and Askwith and so they naturally come within the definition of "Employee" and, hence, those of "Affiliate" and "Released Parties". Nor is it odd to speak of the JAs as having been "affiliated" to REL, Properties and Askwith. After all, they had charge of the companies' affairs and acted on their behalf. It was, moreover, crucial to Barclays' protection against "ricochet" claims that the JAs are "Affiliates" and so "Released Parties". Were the position otherwise, there would be nothing at all in the Settlement Agreement to prevent REL, Properties or Askwith from bringing proceedings against the JAs or the JAs from claiming contribution from Barclays. In particular, neither the second sentence of cl 3.2 of the Settlement Agreement nor cl 3.4 would have any application. Since the JAs would not be "Affiliates", the obligation on each "Party" to ensure that its "Affiliates" do not bring proceedings would not bite, and such proceedings therefore not being "contrary to clause 3.2" cl 3.4 could not be in point either.' *Schofield v Smith; Rhino Enterprises Properties Ltd v Clyde & Co LLP* [2022] EWCA Civ 824, [2023] 1 All ER 480 at [51]–[53], per Newey LJ

AFTER-CARE SERVICES

[Mental Health Act 1983, s 117.] '[38] As discussed, in interpreting a statutory provision it is not sufficient to consider the ordinary meanings of the words used and how the same words are used elsewhere in the Act: it is necessary to identify the purpose of the provision, read in its context. The clear purpose of s 117 is to arrange for the provision of services to a person who has been, but is not currently being, provided with treatment and care as a hospital patient. That purpose is implicit in the very expression "after-care", which is used not only in the heading but throughout the body of s 117 in the phrase "after-care services". It is further articulated by the definition of "after-care services" in s 117(6). As specified in s 117(6)(b), to constitute after-care services, the services must have the purpose of "reducing the risk of a deterioration of the person's mental condition (and, accordingly, reducing the risk of the person requiring admission to a hospital again for treatment for mental disorder)". That purpose is only capable of being fulfilled if the person concerned is not currently admitted to a hospital at which he or she is receiving treatment for mental disorder.

...

'[42] On the facts of the present case there is neither any need nor any scope for the claimant to be provided with "after-care services". As he remains in the care of the hospital and its staff even when he goes on the bus trips for which he is granted leave of absence, no question or possibility of "after-care" arises. Nor can it possibly be said in these circumstances that any services provided to the claimant during the trips have the purpose of "reducing the risk of the person requiring admission to a hospital again for treatment for mental disorder", as required by s 117(6)(b). This is not and could not be their purpose because the claimant's return to the hospital at the end of each trip is not a risk which it is the aim of the trip to reduce: it is inevitable, being one of the terms on which leave of absence is granted. In any case, the claimant does not require "admission to a hospital again for treatment" at the end of each trip, as I interpret those words, as he has remained admitted to the hospital for treatment throughout the trip. I would accept that the phrase "admission to a hospital" as it is used in s 117(6), like the phrase "leave hospital" in s 117(1), has to be read in light of the purpose of the provision, and is capable of applying to a person living in the community on leave of absence who is then recalled to hospital. But there is no basis in either the language or the purpose of s 117(6)(b) for regarding a person who returns from a trip during which he has never left the custody of hospital staff as requiring re-admission to the hospital for treatment. That is all the more so when, as noted earlier, one of the very purposes of the leaves of absence granted to the claimant in this case, recorded on the forms signed by the responsible clinician, is "treatment". In other words, the trips are part of the treatment which the hospital is providing to the claimant. Accordingly, the services provided to the claimant in taking him on escorted day trips do not and cannot constitute "after-care services" within the meaning of s 117.

...

'[44] The inescapable conclusion is that the claimant does not "cease to be detained" or "leave hospital" within the meaning of s 117(1) when he is escorted on day trips and is therefore not a person to whom s 117 applies. Moreover, even if this were wrong, I think it clear that the services provided during the trips do not constitute "after-care services" within the meaning of s 117(6) because it is not their purpose to reduce the risk of the claimant requiring admission to a hospital again for treatment for mental disorder; they are part of the treatment which he is currently receiving as a hospital patient. The claimant has at all times remained in the hospital's care.' *R (on the application of CXF (by his mother, his litigation friend)) v Central Bedfordshire Council* [2018] EWCA Civ 2852, [2019] 3 All ER 20 at [38], [42], [44], per Leggatt LJ

AGENT—AGENCY

[For 1 Halsbury's Laws of England (5th Edn) (2017) para 1 see now 1 Halsbury's Laws of England (5th Edn) (2022) para 1.]

General agent

[For 1 Halsbury's Laws of England (5th Edn) (2017) para 11 see now 1 Halsbury's Laws of England (5th Edn) (2022) para 11.]

Of necessity

[For 1 Halsbury's Laws of England (5th Edn) (2017) para 24 see now 1 Halsbury's Laws of England (5th Edn) (2022) para 24.]

Special agent

[For 1 Halsbury's Laws of England (5th Edn) (2017) para 11 see now 1 Halsbury's Laws of England (5th Edn) (2022) para 11.]

AGISTMENT

[For 2 Halsbury's Laws of England (5th Edn) (2017) para 18 see now 2 Halsbury's Laws of England (5th Edn) (2022) para 19.]

AGREED

[Limitation Act 1980, s 10(4): contribution under the Civil Liability (Contribution) Act 1978, s 1, in the case of a settlement is treated as accruing on the 'earliest date on which the amount to be paid … is agreed'.] '[26] … It is important to approach the section on the basis that ss 10(3) and (4) are, upon their true construction, intended to be mutually exclusive. I agree with Rix LJ that there can only be one trigger date to start time running under s 10; namely either:
26.1 the date of the judgment or award requiring a payment in cases where such issue is the subject of a judicial or arbitral determination; or
26.2 the date of the agreement to make the payment in a case where the issue is compromised.

'[27] Since there can only be one trigger event, it follows that time cannot start to run where the parties reach an unenforceable agreement as to payment. In such a case the litigation or arbitration remains on foot and time will only start to run under s 10(4) from the date of the subsequent formal agreement or, if the matter cannot be agreed, under s 10(3) from the date of the judgment or award.

'[28] In my judgment Mr Walker QC is right therefore to submit that the proper construction of s 10(4) is that time only starts to run from the date of a binding agreement as to the amount of the compensation payment.

…

'[32] [I]t is open to the parties to reach an immediately binding agreement as to the settlement payment, but leave for later agreement details as to payment terms … or any liability for costs …. In such cases, time will start to run from the date of the agreement as to the amount of the payment. Equally, it is open to the parties to agree that, to use an expression much used in connection with the current Brexit negotiations, nothing is agreed until everything is agreed. If so, time will not start to run until the date of the subsequent binding agreement as to the payment or, should agreement prove impossible, the judgment or award.' *RG Carter Building Ltd v Kier Business Services Ltd (formerly Mouchel Business Services Ltd)* [2018] EWHC 729 (TCC), [2018] 4 All ER 456 at [26]–[29], [32], per Edward Pepperall QC

AGRICULTURAL HOLDING

[For 1 Halsbury's Laws of England (5th Edn) (2017) para 423 see now 1 Halsbury's Laws of England (5th Edn) (2022) para 323.]

AID AND ABET

[For 25 Halsbury's Laws of England (5th Edn) (2016) para 53 see now 25 Halsbury's Laws of England (5th Edn) (2020) para 76.]

ALIEN

[For 4 Halsbury's Laws of England (5th Edn) (2011) para 411 see now 4 Halsbury's Laws of England (5th Edn) (2019) para 411.]

Australia [Commonwealth Constitution, s 51(xix).] '[73] The Commonwealth's concern, that to hold that its legislative power does not extend to treating an Aboriginal Australian as an alien is to identify a race-based limitation on power, is overstated. It is not offensive, in the context of contemporary international understanding, to recognise the cultural and spiritual dimensions of the distinctive connection between indigenous peoples and their traditional lands, and in light of that recognition to hold that the exercise of the sovereign power of this nation does not extend to the exclusion of the indigenous inhabitants from the Australian community.

'[74] The conclusion is not to deny that an attribute of every sovereign state is the power to decide whether an alien is admitted to membership of the community and to expel an alien whom it chooses not to suffer to remain. As Gleeson CJ observed in *Re Minister for Immigration and Multicultural Affairs; Ex parte Te*

[(2002) 212 CLR 162; 193 ALR 37; [2002] HCA 48], the exercise of the power is vital to the welfare, security and integrity of the nation. The position of Aboriginal Australians, however, is sui generis. Notwithstanding the amplitude of the power conferred by s 51(xix) it does not extend to treating an Aboriginal Australian as an alien because, despite the circumstance of birth in another country, an Aboriginal Australian cannot be said to belong to another place.

...

'[373] Aboriginal Australians have a unique connection to this country; it is not just ancestry or place of birth or even both. It is a connection with the land or waters under Indigenous laws and customs which is recognised under Australian law. The Australian Citizenship Act has not removed or modified that connection. Nor has the Parliament removed or modified that connection by other legislation. Whether the Parliament could remove or modify that connection need not be decided.

'[374] It is a connection to this country that means that Aboriginal Australians are not foreigners within the constitutional concept of alien under s 51(xix). And it is a connection which means that even if an Aboriginal Australian's birth is not registered and as a result no citizenship is recorded, or an Aboriginal Australian is born overseas without obtaining Australian citizenship, they are not susceptible to legislation made pursuant to the aliens power or detention and deportation under such legislation.' *Love v Commonwealth* [2020] HCA 3, (2020) 375 ALR 597 at [73]–[74], per Bell J and at [373]–[374], per Gordon J

Australia [Australian Citizenship Act 2007 (Cth), s 36B: cessation of citizenship on terrorism-related grounds; Commonwealth Constitution, s 51(xix).] '[27] Section 51(xix) of the Constitution empowers the Commonwealth Parliament to make laws with respect to "naturalization and aliens". The defendants confined their arguments in support of s 36B as a valid exercise of the legislative power of the Commonwealth to reliance upon s 51(xix).

'[28] Mr Alexander submitted that s 36B is not supported by s 51(xix) in its application to him because, as a person who became an Australian citizen at birth by virtue of s 10 of the 1948 Citizenship Act, he could not thereafter be regarded as an "alien". Mr Alexander's contention is that once a person attains the status of an Australian citizen, the operation of s 51(xix) is "spent" so that Parliament cannot make a law that would transform a non-alien into an alien.

...

'[33] While alienage, describing a lack of formal legal relationship with the community or body politic, is a constitutional concept, the Constitution leaves it to Parliament to decide who shall be granted the status of citizenship and what that status may mean in terms of the rights, privileges, immunities and duties of citizens. In this regard, s 51(xix) of the Constitution empowers the Parliament to "create and define the concept of Australian citizenship", to select or adopt the criteria for citizenship or alienage and to attribute to any person who lacks the qualifications prescribed for citizenship "the status of alien". In *Chetcuti* [*Chetcuti v Commonwealth* (2021) 95 ALJR 704; 392 ALR 371; [2021] HCA 25 at [12]], Kiefel CJ, Gageler, Keane and Gleeson JJ said that "the aliens power encompasses both power to determine who is and who is not to have the legal status of an alien and power to attach consequences to that status".

'[34] It has been said in this Court that the terms "citizen" and "alien" are antonyms. Recently, the majority of this Court in *Love* [*Love v Commonwealth* (2020) 270 CLR 152; 375 ALR 597; [2020] HCA 3 at [81]] held that Aboriginal Australians who satisfy the tripartite test in *Mabo v Queensland* [(1992) 175 CLR 1; 107 ALR 1] constitute a separate category of non-citizen, non-alien, and that "non-citizen" is not inevitably and always synonymous with "alien". But in *Chetcuti*, Kiefel CJ, Gageler, Keane and Gleeson JJ observed that this Court's decision in *Shaw* [*Shaw v Minister for Immigration and Multicultural Affairs* (2003) 218 CLR 28; 203 ALR 143; 77 ALD 251; [2003] HCA 72] (from which the holding of the majority in *Love* does not depart, except in respect of an Aboriginal Australian according to the tripartite test in *Mabo*) establishes that the aliens power supports a law of the Commonwealth which determines who shall have the status of Australian citizenship, and which provides that persons who do not share that status are aliens.

'[35] In *Pochi* [*Pochi v Minister for Immigration and Ethnic Affairs* (1982) 151 CLR 101 at 109; 43 ALR 261 at 267], Gibbs CJ said that "Parliament cannot, simply by giving its own definition of 'alien', expand the power under s 51(xix) to include persons who could not possibly answer the description of 'aliens' in the ordinary understanding of the word". It does not stretch the ordinary understanding of the expression "alien" to include within that category an individual who has engaged in conduct exhibiting such extreme enmity to Australia as to warrant being excluded from membership of the Australian community. The Parliament has the power under s 51(xix) to attribute the constitutional status of alien to a person who has lost the statutory status of citizenship. By the same power, Parliament can define the circumstances in which that occurs.

...

'[38] ... As a general principle, where the Parliament may confer rights by the exercise of legislative power, it may also take them away. Once it is accepted, as it must be, that the statute conferring citizenship is the source of Mr Alexander's rights as a citizen, it must also be accepted that (the present version of) that statute may limit those rights, including by providing for the circumstances in which they may be lost. A person who has forfeited the rights of citizenship is no less accurately described as an alien than a person who has never enjoyed those rights.

...

'[63] In summary in relation to the first issue, it should be held that it is open to the Parliament under s 51(xix) to create a status of citizenship that allows for the exclusion of persons from membership of the body politic. It is not an abuse of language to say that a person whose conduct is inimical to Australia's interests may, by a law of the Commonwealth, forfeit the rights of citizenship conferred by the Parliament, and thereby become an alien. The withdrawal of citizenship from an individual who voluntarily engages in the conduct described in s 36B(5)(h) cannot be said to pursue an eccentric understanding of the meaning of "aliens" in s 51(xix) of the Constitution.' *Alexander (by his litigation guardian Alexander) v Minister for Home Affairs* [2022] HCA 19, (2022) 401 ALR 438 at [27]–[28], [34]–[35], [38], [63], per Kiefel CJ, Keane and Gleeson JJ (footnotes omitted)

Alien enemy

[For 3 Halsbury's Laws of England (5th Edn) (2011) para 195 see now 3 Halsbury's Laws of England (5th Edn) (2019) para 157.]

ALLEGIANCE

[For 20 Halsbury's Laws of England (5th Edn) (2014) para 37 see now 20 Halsbury's Laws of England (5th Edn) (2023) para 32.]

ALLOTMENT

Garden

[For 1 Halsbury's Laws of England (5th Edn) (2017) para 649 see now 1 Halsbury's Laws of England (5th Edn) (2022) para 524.]

ALLUVION

[For 29 Halsbury's Laws of England (5th Edn) (2014) para 177 see now 29 Halsbury's Laws of England (5th Edn) (2019) para 182.]

ALTERNATIVE DISPUTE RESOLUTION

[For 2 Halsbury's Laws of England (5th Edn) (2017) para 504 see now 2 Halsbury's Laws of England (5th Edn) (2023) para 604.]

ALWAYS SPEAKING

[Limitation Act 1980, s 32(1)(c).] '[218] It is debatable, but ultimately does not matter, whether this question should be approached by focusing specifically on the "always speaking" principle, as counsel for the bank did in *Kleinwort Benson* [*Kleinwort Benson Ltd v Lincoln City Council* [1998] 4 All ER 513, [1999] 2 AC 349]. That somewhat vague expression is commonly used in connection with statutory terms which change in their connotations over time, such as "family" (*Fitzpatrick v Sterling Housing Association Ltd* [1999] 4 All ER 705, [2001] 1 AC 27). The case of *R v Ireland, R v Burstow* [1997] 4 All ER 225, [1998] AC 147, cited by counsel in *Kleinwort Benson*, was of a similar kind. The question was whether the words "bodily harm", in the Offences Against the Person Act 1861, should be interpreted in the light of contemporary knowledge as applying to psychiatric injury. The "always speaking" principle is also invoked where the question arises whether a statutory expression should be interpreted as including a novel invention or activity which does not naturally fall within its meaning, and was not envisaged at the time of its enactment, but which may nevertheless fall within the scope of its original intention. Examples of the latter kind of case include *Victor Chandler International v Customs and Excise Comrs* [2000] 2 All ER 315, [2000] 1 WLR 1296, which concerned the question whether a teletext fell within the scope of the statutory term "document", and *R (on the application of Quinta-valle) v Secretary of State for Health* [2003] UKHL 13, [2003] 2 All ER 113, [2003] 2 AC 687, which concerned the question whether an embryo created by the novel technique of cloning, rather than by the traditional method of fertilisation, fell within the scope of the statutory expression "embryo where fertilisation is complete". …

'[219] The question in the present case is not of precisely the same kind. The cause of action recognised in *Kleinwort Benson* undoubtedly falls within the scope of the language used in s 32(1)(c), if that language is given its ordinary meaning. A mistake of law was understood to be a "mistake" in 1939, and in 1980, just as much as it is today. Nevertheless, the decision taken in *Kleinwort Benson* to recognise a cause of action for the recovery of money paid under a mistake of law could not have been foreseen in 1939 or 1980. The question therefore arises whether s 32(1)(c) applies to those unforeseen circumstances: a question which ultimately boils down to the same issue as arises when considering the "always speaking" principle, and indeed in all cases concerned with statutory interpretation: what is the construction of the provision which best gives effect to the policy of the statute as enacted?'

…

'[269] The guidance regarding the ambit of the "always speaking" doctrine is in fact concerned with the fundamental underlying issue of whether Parliament can be taken to have intended by a statutory provision passed at one point in time, using language directed to the circumstances at that time, to cover a new set of circumstances which has come into existence since then. … The issue of how broadly one should construe the language of the statutory provision to cover new matters arising after its enactment necessarily involves consideration of what inferences can be drawn from the language used and the circumstances of the enactment as to Parliament's policy intention in promulgating the provision. If the inference can be drawn that Parliament's policy intention was broad and the new matters are aligned with that broad intention and are covered by it, a court will be justified in concluding that the provision applies; conversely, if there is not sufficient congruence between the policy issues raised by the new matters and Parliament's intention as expressed when it enacted the provision, the provision does not apply.

'[270] … In certain contexts it may be improper to give an extended interpretation to a word or phrase to treat it as applying to something outside Parliament's contemplation at the time of enactment. As Lord Steyn pointed out in *R v Ireland, R v Burstow* [1997] 4 All ER 225 at 233, [1998] AC 147 at 158 with reference to *The Longford* (1889) 14 PD 34, "[s]tatutes dealing with a particular grievance or problem may sometimes require to be historically interpreted" '. *Test Claimants in the Franked Investment Income Group Litigation v Revenue and Customs Comrs* [2020] UKSC 47, [2021] 1 All ER 1001 at [218]–[219], per Lord Reed P and Lord Hodge DP and at [269]–[270], per Lords Briggs and Sales JJSC

AMBIGUITY

Latent ambiguity

[For 102 Halsbury's Laws of England (5th Edn) (2010) para 219 see now 102 Halsbury's Laws of England (5th Edn) (2021) para 222.]

Patent ambiguity

[For 102 Halsbury's Laws of England (5th Edn) (2010) para 219 see now 102 Halsbury's Laws of England (5th Edn) (2021) para 222.]

AMOTION

[For 24 Halsbury's Laws of England (5th Edn) (2010) para 364 see now 24 Halsbury's Laws of England (5th Edn) (2019) para 464.]

ANIMAL

[For 2 Halsbury's Laws of England (5th Edn) (2017) paras 1, 5, 7 see now 2 Halsbury's Laws of England (5th Edn) (2023) paras 1, 6, 8.]

Domestic animal

[For 2 Halsbury's Laws of England (5th Edn) (2017) paras 1, 5, 7, 35 et seq see now 2 Halsbury's Laws of England (5th Edn) (2023) paras 1, 6, 8, 36 et seq.]

AMOUNT OF THE BILL

[Solicitors Act 1974, s 70.] '[19] Section 70(9) of the 1974 Act provides, subject to two conditions that are irrelevant here, "the costs of an assessment shall be paid according to the event of the assessment, that is to say, if the amount of the bill is reduced by one fifth, the solicitor shall pay the costs, but otherwise the party chargeable shall pay the costs". Section 70(10) of the 1974 Act provides that the "costs officer may certify to the court any special circumstances relating to the bill or to the assessment of a bill, and the court may make such order as respects the costs of the assessment as it may think fit".

...

'[31] ... The only question we have to decide is as to the proper meaning of the words "the amount of the bill" in s 70(9). The question of whether a statutory bill properly needs to state the base costs from which the amount ultimately charged is derived is a separate one.

...

'[49] I have, however, decided that the proper question for the court to ask in determining "the amount of the bill" under s 70(9) is, in respect of the category or categories of costs being assessed, "what is the total sum that the bill is demanding be paid to the Solicitors, whether or not all or part of that total sum has actually been paid".' *Karatysz v SGI Legal LLP* [2022] EWCA Civ 1388, [2023] 3 All ER 135 at [19], [31], [49], per Sir Geoffrey Vos MR

ANNUITY

[For 80 Halsbury's Laws of England (5th Edn) (2013) para 675 see now 80 Halsbury's Laws of England (5th Edn) (2020) para 803.]

[For 58 Halsbury's Laws of England (5th Edn) (2014) paras 549, 557 see now 99 Halsbury's Laws of England (5th Edn) (2018) paras 152, 159–160.]

ANOTHER PARTY

New Zealand [Funding agreement: by cl 3.2.2, where another party agreed to fund the proceedings, Blue Chip was to procure that party to repay the Funding and to pay the Fee.] '[61] Remember, the Liquidators acted as agent of Blue Chip. Any reference in the Agreement to "the company" incurring an obligation of necessity includes a reference to the Liquidators as agent of the company, with the authority under sch 6 of the Companies Act to conduct the business of the company. In that context, we note that:

(a) it is "the company and [explicitly] the Liquidators" who are to give Commercial Factors the first option;
(b) it is the company, and hence implicitly the Liquidators, who agree not to enter a Funding Agreement "with another party" on any less favourable terms without first reoffering the funding opportunity to Commercial Factors; and
(c) it is the company, and hence implicitly the Liquidators, who contract to procure the funder to pay "before the proceedings are filed or any funding for the proceedings is made available to the company or the liquidators".

'[62] In our view, therefore, when cl 3.2 refers to "another party" it is referring to a party other than the company or the Liquidators. We place particular reliance on the opening words of cl 3.2 in reaching that conclusion. That is, it is the Liquidators who will endeavour to obtain funding for proceedings and it is the Liquidators who, under s 301 of the Companies Act, actually take the proceedings. It would, in those circumstances, be unusual to regard the Liquidators as "another party" for the purposes of cl 3.2.2.' *Commercial Factors Ltd v Meltzer* [2018] NZCA 505, [2019] 2 NZLR 484 at [61]–[62], per Clifford J

ANY

Any appropriate relief

[Cross-Border Insolvency Regulations 2006, SI 2006/1030, Sch 1, art 21.] '[1] This appeal raises important questions about the proper scope of the powers conferred on the English court by the Cross-Border Insolvency Regulations 2006, SI 2006/1030, (the "CBIR") to order a stay of proceedings in this jurisdiction in support of a foreign insolvency proceeding.

...

'[84] It is clear, to my mind, that the present case does not involve an issue of jurisdiction in the former, or what one might call the "strict", sense. The application was made by a foreign representative of a foreign proceeding, duly recognised as such in this jurisdiction under the CBIR. Furthermore, the foreign proceeding was still in progress both when the application was made and when it was determined by the

High Court. As Mr Bayfield made clear, the application is made under art 21(1)(a) and (b), which expressly empower the court, "where it is necessary to protect … the interests of the creditors", to "grant any appropriate relief" at the request of the foreign representative, including a stay of the commencement or continuation of individual actions or proceedings concerning the debtor's assets, rights, obligations or liabilities, or a stay of execution against the debtor's assets to the extent that there has not already been an automatic stay under art 20(1)(a) and (b). As a matter of jurisdiction in the strict sense, the application seems to me to fall squarely within the clear wording of art 21. In particular, I would reject a submission made by Mr Moss that the only purpose of art 21(1)(a) and (b) is to enable the court, upon reorganisation of a foreign *non-main* proceeding, to grant equivalent relief to that automatically conferred by the corresponding paragraphs of art 20(1) in the case of a foreign *main* proceeding. That is no doubt an important function of art 21(1)(a) and (b), but I can see no warrant in the wide language of the paragraphs for confining their scope so narrowly.' *Re OJSC International Bank of Azerbaijan; Bakhshiyeva v Sberbank of Russia* [2018] EWCA Civ 2802, [2019] 2 All ER 713 at [1], [84], per Henderson LJ

Any person

New Zealand [Oranga Tamariki Act 1989, s 15.] '[57] Section 15 of OTA (as it was prior to 1 July 2019 amendments) provided:

> Any person who believes that any child or young person has been, or is likely to be, harmed (whether physically, emotionally, or sexually), ill-treated, abused, neglected, or deprived may report the matter to the chief executive or a constable.

'[58] Presuming (for present purposes) that "any person" includes a person employed by MSD [Ministry of Social Development] or MoE [Ministry of Education], s 15 imposes no duty to report. Rather, as this Court noted in *R v Strawbridge* [[2003] 1 NZLR 683, CA], it confers a "right" to report where the requisite belief is genuine. Meanwhile, as noted by the appellant, s 16 protects the reporter from civil, criminal or disciplinary proceedings, in relation to the disclosure.

…

'[61] The s 19 process is more formal and supervision of it is closer and more prescriptive. We accept that this section is designed for use by state agencies. The procedural requirements in subs (1A) reflect this. But ss 15 and 19 should not be mutually exclusive. A key purpose of the Act is to protect tamariki from harm. The Act's multiple reporting pathways should be construed liberally so as to be consistent with that purpose. There is no reason to read s 15 as if employees of MSD or MoE do not fit the description "any person". On the contrary, this is good reason to construe the phrase as applying to such employees if that would better provide for the safety of tamariki. We think it would. We conclude therefore that both ss 15 and 19 may be used by MSD and MoE employees to report to OT or the police any concerns they may have for the safety of tamariki.' *Attorney-General v J* [2019] NZCA 499, [2020] 2 NZLR 176 at [57]–[58], [61], per Williams J

APOTHECARY

[The passage from 74 Halsbury's Laws of England (5th Edn) (2011) para 5 is not reproduced in 74 Halsbury's Laws of England (5th Edn) (2019).]

APPARENT

[For 102 Halsbury's Laws of England (5th Edn) (2010) para 82 see now 102 Halsbury's Laws of England (5th Edn) (2021) para 83.]

APPOINTMENT

[For 9 Halsbury's Laws of England (5th Edn) (2012) para 80 see now 9 Halsbury's Laws of England (5th Edn) (2017) para 79.]

APPRENTICE

[For 39 Halsbury's Laws of England (5th Edn) (2014) para 112 see now 39 Halsbury's Laws of England (5th Edn) (2021) para 111.]

APPROACHING

[International Regulations for Preventing Collisions at Sea 1972, r 7.] '[55] Rule 7(d)(i) provides that a risk of collision shall be deemed to exist if the compass bearing of an approaching vessel does not appreciably change. In this context "approaching" simply means getting nearer. It does not necessarily mean heading towards each other. For example, a vessel being overtaken may be heading directly away from the overtaking vessel, but if they are each on a steady bearing from the other there is nonetheless a risk of collision because they are getting nearer to each other. Rule 7(d)(i) does not make a steady compass bearing the only indicator of a risk of collision: see eg r 7(a), (b) and (d)(ii). But nor is it merely a rebuttable presumption. Wherever it applies, the risk of collision must be taken to exist.' *Nautical Challenge Ltd v Evergreen Marine (UK) Ltd; The Alexandra 1 and Ever Smart* [2021] UKSC 6, [2021] 4 All ER 1113 at [55], per Lord Briggs and Lord Hamblen JJSC

ARBITRATION

[For 2 Halsbury's Laws of England (5th Edn) (2017) para 501 see now 2 Halsbury's Laws of England (5th Edn) (2023) para 501.]

ARBITRATOR

[For 2 Halsbury's Laws of England (5th Edn) (2017) para 526 et seq see now 2 Halsbury's Laws of England (5th Edn) (2023) para 626 et seq.]

ARCHITECT

[For 6 Halsbury's Laws of England (5th Edn) (2018) para 424 see now 6 Halsbury's Laws of England (5th Edn) (2023) para 527.]

ARMS

Court of Chivalry

[For 79 Halsbury's Laws of England (5th Edn) (2014) paras 884, 878–882 see now 79 Halsbury's Laws of England (5th Edn) (2020) paras 880, 874–878.]

ARREST

[For 84 Halsbury's Laws of England (5th Edn) (2013) para 485 see now 84 Halsbury's Laws of England (5th Edn) (2019) para 450.]

ARRESTS, RESTRAINTS AND DETAINMENTS

[For 60 Halsbury's Laws of England (5th Edn) (2011) para 330 see now 60 Halsbury's Laws of England (5th Edn) (2018) para 309.]

ARSON

[For 25 Halsbury's Laws of England (5th Edn) (2016) para 392 see now 25 Halsbury's Laws of England (5th Edn) (2020) para 436.]

ARTICLES

[For 91 Halsbury's Laws of England (5th Edn) (2013) para 529 see now 91 Halsbury's Laws of England (5th Edn) (2019) para 429.]

AS A RESULT OF

Australia '[9] Whether a benefit can be said to be obtained "as a result of" knowing participation in a breach of fiduciary duty by another contrary to the principles of equity is a question of causation or contribution that depends on "a precise examination of the particular facts" of the case, rather than upon attempts to refine the expression "as a result of" as if that phrase has some determinate operation of its own that may be discerned and applied independently of the equitable principle of which it is part. The equitable disgorgement principle with which we are concerned is a "prophylactic rather than a restitutionary principle". It is sufficient to show that the profit would not have been made but for dishonest wrongdoing. Further, whatever may be the position for wrongdoing that is not marked by dishonesty, a defendant cannot avoid liability to disgorge profits dishonestly made by showing that those profits might have been made honestly. …' *Ancient Order of Foresters in Victoria Friendly Society Ltd v Lifeplan Australia Friendly Society Ltd* [2018] HCA 43, (2018) 360 ALR 1 at [9], per Kiefel CJ, Keane and Edelman JJ

AS OF RIGHT

[For 32 Halsbury's Laws of England (5th Edn) (2012) para 23 see now 32 Halsbury's Laws of England (5th Edn) (2019) para 23.]

ASCERTAIN

[For 91 Halsbury's Laws of England (5th Edn) (2013) para 303 see now 91 Halsbury's Laws of England (5th Edn) (2019) para 304.]

ASSAULT

[For 25 Halsbury's Laws of England (5th Edn) (2016) para 134 see now 25 Halsbury's Laws of England (5th Edn) (2020) para 187.]

[For 97 Halsbury's Laws of England (5th Edn) (2015) para 528 see now 97A Halsbury's Laws of England (5th Edn) (2021) para 127.]

ASSETS

[For 17 Halsbury's Laws of England (5th Edn) (2011) para 630 see now 17 Halsbury's Laws of England (5th Edn) (2017) para 569.]

Canada '**1** At issue in this appeal is whether the interest that the appellant, SA, has in a trust that was set up for her care and maintenance should be treated as an "asset", which would negatively affect her eligibility to participate in a rental subsidy program offered by her landlord, the respondent, Metro Vancouver Housing Corporation ("MVHC").

'**40** The next issue that must be addressed is the meaning of the word "assets" as it is used in the Assistance Application, which is the source of SA's obligation to supply MVHC with information supporting the valuation of her assets if she wishes to be considered for rental assistance. To be clear, the issue in this appeal is not the meaning of the word "assets" *in the abstract*, but rather how that word should be understood in the specific context of MVHC's Rental Assistance Program. In this respect, I agree with the Court of Appeal that the Chambers Judge erred in analyzing this issue at least in part through the lens of the Tenancy Agreement: "[t]he critical document to determine whether to grant rental assistance is the Assistance Application" (para 52).

…

'**46** If the definition in [the Asset Ceiling] policy does not apply, what should the word "assets" be understood to mean? The words in the Assistance Application must be given their ordinary and grammatical meaning in light of the specific context in which they were used (*Sattva* [*Sattva Capital Corp v Creston Moly Corp* 2014 SCC 53, [2014] 2 SCR. 633], at paras 47–48; *Ledcor Construction Ltd v Northbridge Indemnity Insurance Co* 2016 SCC 37, [2016] 2 SCR 23, at para 27). With this in mind, I would observe that the word "asset" is ordinarily used to denote valuable property that a person can use to discharge debts and other liabilities. One of the definitions of the word "asset" in the Oxford English Dictionary (online) is "an item of value owned; spec. an item on a balance sheet representing the value of a resource, right, item of property, etc., placed under an appropriate heading. Frequently coupled with *liability*". Similarly, Merriam-Webster (online) defines the plural word "assets" as "the entire property of a person, association, corporation, or estate applicable or subject to the payment of debts" and the singular word "asset" as "an item of value owned". The Chambers Judge referred to a similar definition from *Black's Law Dictionary* (6th ed 1990), at p 117 (Chambers Judge's Reasons, at para 50):

> Property of all kinds, real and personal, tangible and intangible, including inter alia, for certain purposes, patents and causes of action which belong to any person including a corporation and the estate of a decedent. The entire property of a person, association, corporation, or estate that is applicable or subject to the payment of his or her or its debts.

…

'**56** A careful reading of documents relevant to the resolution of this appeal leads me to conclude that the word "assets", as it is used in the Assistance Application, is not broad enough to encompass SA's interest in the Trust. Given that the discretion over distributions lies exclusively in the Trustees' hands, SA's interest in the trust property is in the nature of a mere hope of receiving some or all of that property in the future. Unless and until the Trustees actually decide to make distributions in SA's favour, that interest is not in practice something on which she can rely to pay the rent (or to offset other debts and liabilities).' *SA v Metro Vancouver Housing Corp* [2019] SCJ No 4, [2019] 1 SCR 99 at paras 1, 40, 46, 56, per Côté J

ASSIGNMENT

[For 22 Halsbury's Laws of England (5th Edn) (2012) para 333 see now 22 Halsbury's Laws of England (5th Edn) (2019) para 135.]

AT AND FROM

[For 60 Halsbury's Laws of England (5th Edn) (2011) para 249 see now 60 Halsbury's Laws of England (5th Edn) (2018) para 228.]

AT WORK

'**100** … An employee is "at work", for the purposes of both the Management Regulations [Management of Health and Safety at Work Regulations 1999, SI 1999/3242] and the PPE Regulations [Personal Protective Equipment at Work Regulations 1992, SI 1992/2966], throughout the time when she is in the course of her employment: section 52(1)(b) of the [Health and Safety at Work etc Act 1974]. The point is illustrated by the facts of *Robb v Salamis (M & I) Ltd* [2007] ICR 175. Miss Kennedy in particular, as a home carer, was "at work" when she was travelling between the home of one client and that of another in order to provide them with care. Indeed, travelling from one client's home to another's was an integral part of her work. The meaning of the words "while at work" in regulation 4(1) of the PPE Regulations (and of the equivalent words, "whilst they are at work", in regulation 3(1) of the Management Regulations) is plain. They mean that the employee must be exposed to the risk during the time when she is at work, that is to say, during the time when she is in the course of her employment. They refer to the time when she is exposed to the risk, not to the cause of the risk.' *Kennedy v Cordia (Services) LLP* [2016] UKSC 6, [2016] ICR 325 at para 100, per Lord Reed and Lord Hodge JJSC

ATTAINDER

[For 24 Halsbury's Laws of England (5th Edn) (2012) para 643 see now 24A Halsbury's Laws of England (5th Edn) (2019) para 43.]

ATTEST

[For 102 Halsbury's Laws of England (5th Edn) (2010) para 70 et seq see now 102 Halsbury's Laws of England (5th Edn) (2021) para 70 et seq.]

ATTORNEY

[For 65 Halsbury's Laws of England (5th Edn) (2015) para 435 see now 22 Halsbury's Laws of England (5th Edn) (2020) para 397.]

ATTORNMENT

[For 62 Halsbury's Laws of England (5th Edn) (2016) para 3 see now 62 Halsbury's Laws of England (5th Edn) (2023) para 3.]

AUCTION

[For 4 Halsbury's Laws of England (5th Edn) (2011) para 1 see now 4 Halsbury's Laws of England (5th Edn) (2020) para 1.]

AUCTIONEER

[For 4 Halsbury's Laws of England (5th Edn) (2011) para 2 see now 4 Halsbury's Laws of England (5th Edn) (2020) para 1.]

AUTREFOIS CONVICT

[For 27 Halsbury's Laws of England (5th Edn) (2015) para 369 see now 27 Halsbury's Laws of England (5th Edn) (2021) para 375.]

AVERAGE

[For 7 Halsbury's Laws of England (5th Edn) (2011) paras 606–608 see now 7 Halsbury's Laws of England (5th Edn) (2020) paras 553–555.]

General average

[For 60 Halsbury's Laws of England (5th Edn) (2011) para 386 see now 60 Halsbury's Laws of England (5th Edn) (2018) para 364.]

Particular average

[For 60 Halsbury's Laws of England (5th Edn) (2011) para 399 see now 60 Halsbury's Laws of England (5th Edn) (2018) para 377.]

AWARE OF

[Taxes Management Act 1970, s 29(5): 'discovery assessment' allowed where officer could not have been reasonably expected, on the basis of the information made available to him before a specified time, to be 'aware of' the situation mentioned in s 29(1).] '[27] In *Revenue and Customs Comrs v Lansdowne Partners Ltd Partnership* [[2011] EWCA Civ 1578, [2012] STC 544, 81 TC 318], when considering the meaning of "be aware of" for the purposes of s 29(5), it was said that "awareness" was a matter of perception not conclusion and that it was possible to say that an officer was "aware of" something even when he could not at that stage resolve points of law and even though he was not then aware of all of the facts which might turn out to be relevant. Although the word "discover" and the phrase "be aware of" cannot be treated as synonyms, we consider that if it is possible to be aware of something when one does not know all of the relevant facts and one cannot foretell how relevant points of law will be resolved, it cannot be said to be premature for an officer to "discover" that same something even when he knows he is not in possession of all of the relevant facts and does not know how relevant points of law will be resolved.' *Anderson v Revenue and Customs Commissioners* [2018] UKUT 159 (TCC), [2018] 4 All ER 338 at [27], per Morgan J and Judge Berner

B

BAILMENT

[For 4 Halsbury's Laws of England (5th Edn) (2011) paras 101, 106 see now 4 Halsbury's Laws of England (5th Edn) (2020) paras 101, 106.]

BAIRD PRINCIPLE

'[8] But a series of 19th century cases beginning with *Coverdale v Charlton* (1878) 4 QBD 104 and culminating in the decision of the House of Lords in *Mayor of Tunbridge Wells v Baird* [1896] AC 434, [1895–9] All ER Rep Ext 2006, established that the successive statutory provisions for the automatic vesting of proprietary interests in highways in the bodies responsible for their maintenance and repair operated in a much more limited way than would a simple conveyance or transfer of the freehold. First, it was a determinable, rather than absolute, fee simple, which would end automatically if the body responsible for its repair ceased to be so responsible (eg if the road ceased to be a public highway): see *Rolls v Vestry of St George the Martyr, Southwark* (1880) 14 Ch D 785. Secondly it was inalienable, for so long as that responsibility lasted. Thirdly, and most importantly for present purposes, statutory vesting conferred ownership only of that slice of the land over which the highway ran, viewed in the vertical plane, as was necessary for its ordinary use, including its repair and maintenance. Following the example of counsel, I shall call this "the Baird principle".

'[9] That slice of the vertical plane included, of course, the surface of the road over which the public had highway rights, the subsoil immediately beneath it, to a depth sufficient to provide for its support and drainage, and a modest slice of the airspace above it sufficient to enable the public to use and enjoy it, and the responsible authority to maintain and repair it, and to supervise its safe operation. That lower slice was famously labelled 'the top two spits' in *Tithe Redemption Commission v Runcorn Urban DC* [1954] 1 All ER 653 at 661, [1954] Ch 383 at 407. A spit is a spade's depth. Although colourful, that phrase says nothing about the necessary airspace above the surface. Again following counsel's example, I prefer the phrase "zone of ordinary use".

'[10] It is common ground that the zone of ordinary use is a flexible concept, the application of which may lead to different depths of subsoil and heights of airspace being vested in a highway authority, both as between different highways and even, over time, as affects a particular highway, according to differences or changes in the nature and intensity of its public use. A simple footpath or bridleway might only require shallow foundations, and airspace of up to about ten feet, to accommodate someone riding a horse. By contrast a busy London street might require deep foundations to support intensive use, and airspace sufficient to accommodate double-decker buses, and even the overhead electric power cables needed, in the past, by trolley buses and, now, by urban trams.

'[11] The Baird principle was developed so as to limit, in the vertical plane, the defeasible freehold interest automatically vested in the body responsible for the repair of a highway. This was because, in a series of leading judgments, the court regarded this statutory vesting as a form of expropriation of private property rights without compensation, and was therefore concerned to limit its effect strictly to that which was necessary to achieve the Parliamentary objective, that is conferring upon highway authorities sufficient property to enable them to perform their statutory duties of the repair, maintenance and operation of highways. …' *Southwark London Borough Council v Transport for London* [2018] UKSC 63, [2019] 2 All ER 271 at [8]–[11], per Lord Briggs

BARONET

[For 79 Halsbury's Laws of England (5th Edn) (2014) para 861 see now 79 Halsbury's Laws of England (5th Edn) (2020) para 857.]

BARRATRY

[For 60 Halsbury's Laws of England (5th Edn) (2011) para 333 see now 60 Halsbury's Laws of England (5th Edn) (2018) para 312.]

BASE FEE

[For 87 Halsbury's Laws of England (5th Edn) (2017) para 160 see now 87 Halsbury's Laws of England (5th Edn) (2022) para 128.]

BASED ON

Australia [Criminal code (Qld), s 304(3): defence of sudden provocation not to apply in respect of a domestic relationship if the sudden provocation is 'based on' certain factors.] '[12] In his dissenting reasons, McMurdo JA focussed on the expression "sudden provocation", a term of art, which his Honour observed is concerned with, and related to, the accused's temporary loss of self-control, as distinct from the provocative conduct which caused that condition. Given that the expression "sudden provocation" is to be understood as having a uniform meaning in each of subss (1), (2), (3) and (5), McMurdo JA rejected that the connection in subs (3) between the sudden provocation and an act done to change the relationship is between the conduct of the deceased and a thing done to change the relationship. The relevant connection, in McMurdo JA's view, consistent with the content of the expression "sudden provocation", is between the conduct of the deceased and the accused's loss of self-control, and the necessary connection is that the former must have caused the latter. For the reasons to be given, McMurdo JA's conclusion, that the words "based on" signify a relation of causation simpliciter between the sudden provocation and the thing done by the deceased to change the relationship, is the preferable construction.

...

'[14] It may be accepted that unlike the words "caused by" in subs (1), the words "based on" in subs (3) are capable of conveying a wider connection than one of causation simpliciter. There are, however, good reasons for not assigning that wider meaning to the phrase in this statutory setting. ...

'[15] As earlier explained, "sudden provocation" is a compendious expression which conveys the accused's loss of self-control induced by the deceased's conduct. The preclusion of the defence in a case in which the loss of self-control is "based on", in the sense of caused or induced by, anything done by the deceased to change the relationship gives workable and coherent operation to subs (3). The construction does not require reading the provision as if the words "based on" are taken to mean "*immediately* caused by": there may be an interval between the thing done by the deceased to change the relationship and the emotional response to that conduct. All that is required is that the thing done by the deceased to change the relationship induced the loss of self-control. It is a construction that coheres with the concept of "sudden provocation" that informs the defence. The defence reduces an accused person's liability for murder to manslaughter where the person kills in a state of lost self-control induced by the deceased's conduct. In the case of an accused who kills his or her domestic partner the defence is excluded where that conduct consists of anything done to change the relationship.' *Peniamina v R* (2020) 385 ALR 367, [2020] HCA 47, BC202012190 at [12], [14]–[15], per Bell, Gageler and Gordon JJ

BATTERY

[For 25 Halsbury's Laws of England (5th Edn) (2016) para 134 see now 25 Halsbury's Laws of England (5th Edn) (2020) para 187.]

BED

Of minerals

[For 76 Halsbury's Laws of England (5th Edn) (2013) para 14 see now 76 Halsbury's Laws of England (5th Edn) (2019) para 14.]

Of river

New Zealand [Resource Management Act 1991, s 2.] '[2] This appeal is primarily concerned with the proper interpretation of "bed", as it relates to a river, under s 2 of the RMA. Relevantly, "bed" is defined as "the space of land which the waters of the river cover at its fullest flow without overtopping its banks". The Council contends that the High Court's interpretation (given on appeal from the District Court) was incorrect.

...

'[10] The second judgment was appealed to the High Court where Gendall J considered that

Judge Hassan applied the wrong legal test to determining the bed of a river for the purposes of the RMA. The correct legal test was regarded as the "bank to bank" test outlined in *Kingdon v Hutt River Board* (1905) 25 NZLR 145, SC, which stands for the proposition that the bed of a river extends only from bank to bank, and more specifically, is the area within the banks covered by water during the rainy season.

'[11] The High Court held that the words "usual or non-flood" should be implied and read into the RMA definition of "bed" before the words "fullest flow". "Fullest flow" for the purpose of the definition was therefore to be regarded as:

> … the river's fullest usual flow over a reasonable period of years of river activity cycles, and not including flood waters that would flow onto the margins and flood plain adjacent to the river.

…

'[36] Of relevance is the fact that the terms "fullest flow" and "banks", used in the definition of "bed" in s 2(1), are not defined in the RMA.

…

'[38] In the present context, the terms "bed" and "river" are used in connection with statutory restrictions on the uses of beds of rivers. …

…

'[51] To assist the analysis in this case, the following principles emerge from the above common law authorities:

(a) The description of a river or watercourse includes as essential features the channel (or bed) and its banks.
(b) The bed comprises the space between the banks occupied by the river at its fullest flow.
(c) Ascertaining the bed in a given case will require consideration of all relevant geographical, meteorological and hydrological features such as banks, channels, shores, seasonal flows, as well as unseasonable wet weather events which produce a flood where the water overflows the banks and spreads into the surrounding areas.
(d) The bed of a river is not limited to the portion between the banks through which the water flows only in dry weather. Equally, though a river or watercourse is dry for part (even the greater part) of the year, it is nonetheless a river or watercourse.
(e) The bank of a river is the outermost part of the bed and comprises an acclivity or elevation of land above the level of the adjacent land or water, which creates a boundary sufficient to prevent the water from flowing into the neighbouring land.
(f) The banks of some rivers may often be indistinct or indefinite and liable to constant changes, as are the waters or currents in their beds.
(g) All the water contained in the riverbed, between the two banks, or their high-water line on the shore, is river.
(h) Ascertaining the dividing line between the banks and the bed cannot be determined by reference only to the ordinary high water mark or the ordinary low water mark. The task requires examining the banks and the bed and finding where the presence and action of the water are common or usual as apply in ordinary years. Also relevant are the nature of the soils of the bed and the banks and the surrounding vegetation.
(i) The bed of a river is a natural object to be determined not by abstract rules, but by the distinctive appearances they present, particularly in respect of the banks and their soils and vegetation.

…

'[77] It follows that we also agree with the view of Gendall J that a river's "fullest flow" for the purposes of the definition of "bed" must be something less than the point where it floods.

'[78] It was at this point of his analysis that Gendall J invoked the principle (correctly in our view) that the bed of a river comprises those lands covered by water during the ordinary rainy season, but contained within the banks of the river and extending from bank to bank. Such an approach is entirely consistent with the common law and the principles set out in the treatises discussed above.

'[79] Accordingly, we consider that the determination of the "bed" of a river, as defined in s 2(a)(ii), will depend not only on the position of the banks of the river, but also on the water coverage measure as determined by the river's fullest flow which occurs within those banks. This latter criterion is qualified by the words "without overtopping its banks". This qualifying term serves to exclude flows or inundations arising from major storms where the water extends temporarily beyond the banks.

'[80] We would not exclude from consideration in particular cases those features identified in principles (c), (d) and (h) in [51] above. These factors are all endorsed by the common law cases and we see no basis for excluding them in the wording of the s 2 definition of "bed".

...

'[99] For all the above reasons we uphold the interpretation of Gendall J in the High Court as to the meaning of "bed" in relation to a river in s 2(a)(ii) of the RMA definition of "bed".' *Canterbury Regional Council v Dewhirst Land Co Ltd* [2019] NZCA 486, [2020] 2 NZLR 10 at [2], [10]–[11], [36], [38], [51], [77]–[80], [99], per Stevens J

BEDROOM

[Housing Benefit Regulations 2006, SI 2006/213, reg B13(5).] '[2] The issue for consideration in this appeal is: what is a "bedroom" for the purpose of reg B13(5)? The size criteria pursuant to B13(5) entitle an HB claimant to "one bedroom for each of the following categories of person" in occupation of the property. The categories are listed (a) to (e) as at the relevant time of the first respondent's determination.

...

'[37] The methodology of the regulations is that the bedroom is used as a proxy for need. The size criteria/bedroom criteria are a means of quantifying cash entitlement. A "bedroom" does not represent a precise proxy. The Secretary of State accepts that it is an imprecise means of measuring need but it serves the purpose because all persons in housing need a bedroom and thus it is useful. It is also accepted that mismatches can arise but can be met, for example, by DHPs.

'[38] "Bedroom" is an ordinary word which is neither defined nor qualified in the regulations. The word has to be construed and applied in its context having regard to the underlying purposes of the legislation. The underlying purpose of the regulations is to limit HB entitlement to those occupying social housing. The language of the regulations demonstrates that the criteria identified as limiting such benefit is the entitlement of a tenant to a bedroom for persons listed in sub-paras (5) and (6). The assessment is to be carried out by the relevant authority in respect of a notionally vacant house. A point accepted by the first respondent. It is also accepted by the first respondent that B13(5) depersonalises the assessment to be performed such that the characteristics of the particular individuals are irrelevant. It follows that such an assessment is an objective one.

'[39] There is nothing in the regulations to indicate that any such assessment is required to take account of how a property and, in particular, the bedrooms in the property would be used by a particular family unit. Were that to be so, the purpose underlying the legislation would be frustrated as a tenant could, by use of the property, change the objective classification so as to reduce the relevant number of bedrooms. This further demonstrates the objective nature of the assessment and, with it, the interpretation of "bedroom" within B13(5).

...

'[41] For the reasons given I find that pursuant to the size criteria (reg B13(5) of the Housing Benefit Regulations 2006, which entitles the housing benefit claimant to "one bedroom for each of the following categories of person" in occupation of the property) the word "bedroom" should be interpreted as meaning a room capable of being used as a "bedroom" by any of the listed categories and not a room capable of being used as a "bedroom" by the particular claimant. In holding that the correct interpretation was a room capable of being used as a "bedroom" by the particular claimant, the UT erred in law and its decision was wrong.' *Hockley v Secretary of State for Work and Pensions* [2019] EWCA Civ 1080, [2020] 2 All ER 20 at [2], [37]–[39], [41], per Nicola Davies LJ

BENEVOLENT

[For 8 Halsbury's Laws of England (5th Edn) (2015) para 93 see now 8 Halsbury's Laws of England (5th Edn) (2019) para 93.]

BEQUEST

[For 102 Halsbury's Laws of England (5th Edn) (2010) para 286 see now 102 Halsbury's Laws of England (5th Edn) (2021) para 286.]

BET

[For 67 Halsbury's Laws of England (5th Edn) (2016) para 281 see now 67 Halsbury's Laws of England (5th Edn) (2021) para 296.]

BETH DIN

Australia '[1] On 14 December 2017, the primary judge, Sackar J, found the appellants guilty of two charges of criminal contempt on the basis that they had threatened the second respondent, Mr Reuven Barukh, with religious sanctions if he did not submit to the jurisdiction of the Sydney Beth Din, a religious court that administers Halacha, or Jewish law: *Live Group Pty Ltd v Ulman* [2017] NSWSC 1759.

...

'[6] According to the appellants, the Beth Din has authority to determine civil disputes between observant Jews, its jurisdiction deriving from the interpretation of Jewish law by the Rabbis who constitute themselves as a Beth Din. In other words, "*their ultimate authority comes from themselves in the sense that as a community of Dayan ... they interpret as best they can ... the Halachic law*". *Ulman v Live Group Pty Ltd* [2018] NSWCA 338, (2018) 367 ALR 95 at [1], [6], per Bathurst CJ and Beazley P

BILL

[For 96 Halsbury's Laws of England (5th Edn) (2012) para 767 see now 96 Halsbury's Laws of England (5th Edn) (2018) para 376.]

Hybrid bill

[For 96 Halsbury's Laws of England (5th Edn) (2012) para 625 see now 96 Halsbury's Laws of England (5th Edn) (2018) para 225.]

BILL OF LADING

[Delete the entry referenced to 91 Halsbury's Laws of England (5th Edn) (2012) para 377; and for 7 Halsbury's Laws of England (5th Edn) (2015) paras 314, 324 see now 7 Halsbury's Laws of England (5th Edn) (2020) paras 428, 440.]

BILL OF SALE

[For 49 Halsbury's Laws of England (5th Edn) (2015) para 403 see now 49 Halsbury's Laws of England (5th Edn) (2021) para 367.]

BIOMETRIC DATA

In this Act: 'biometric data' means personal data resulting from specific technical processing relating to the physical, physiological or behavioural characteristics of an individual, which allows or confirms the unique identification of that individual, such as facial images or dactyloscopic data. (Data Protection Act 2018, s 205(1))

BLASPHEMY

[Delete the entry referenced to 11(1) Halsbury's Laws of England (4th Edn 2006 Reissue) para 826.]

BLOCKADE

[For 85 Halsbury's Laws of England (5th Edn) (2012) para 614 see now 85 Halsbury's Laws of England (5th Edn) (2020) para 714.]

BOARDING HOUSE

[For 68 Halsbury's Laws of England (5th Edn) (2016) paras 648, 661 see now 68 Halsbury's Laws of England (5th Edn) (2021) paras 664, 677.]

BODY

Corpse

[For 24 Halsbury's Laws of England (5th Edn) (2010) para 83 see now 24 Halsbury's Laws of England (5th Edn) (2019) para 272.]

Of note

[For 49 Halsbury's Laws of England (5th Edn) (2015) para 304 see now 49 Halsbury's Laws of England (5th Edn) (2021) para 268.]

BONA VACANTIA

[For 29 Halsbury's Laws of England (5th Edn) (2014) para 149 see now 29 Halsbury's Laws of England (5th Edn) (2019) para 154.]

[For 102 Halsbury's Laws of England (5th Edn) (2010) para 513 see now 102 Halsbury's Laws of England (5th Edn) (2021) para 514.]

BOND

[For 6 Halsbury's Laws of England (5th Edn) (2018) para 382 see now 6 Halsbury's Laws of England (5th Edn) (2023) para 484.]

BOOTY

[For 85 Halsbury's Laws of England (5th Edn) (2012) para 605 see now 85 Halsbury's Laws of England (5th Edn) (2020) para 705.]

BOUNDARY

[For 4 Halsbury's Laws of England (5th Edn) (2011) para 301 see now 4 Halsbury's Laws of England (5th Edn) (2020) para 301.]

BREAKING AND ENTERING

Australia [Crimes Act 1900 (NSW), s 112(1): offence committee by a person who 'breaks and enters any dwelling-house or other building and commits any serious indictable offence therein'.] '[36] This difficult case illustrates the complexities of the concept of "break and entry", the meaning of which was established in historical circumstances quite different from contemporary society, including when domestic and family violence was generally not treated as criminal. In other jurisdictions, "breaking and entering" as an element of housebreaking and burglary offences has been replaced with trespass or unlawful or unauthorised entry in response to these complexities, while avoiding the extension of those offences to lawful entries.

...

'[56] There was no dispute that the apartment was a "dwelling-house". There was also no dispute that the appellant committed a "serious indictable offence therein" in circumstances of aggravation. The focus of this appeal was upon the word "break". That word is not defined in the Crimes Act, but it was, properly, common ground on this appeal that the provisions of Div 4 of Pt 4 of the Crimes Act, including the word "break", were to be interpreted in light of their lengthy legislative histories and judicial interpretation of the predecessor provisions.

'[57] Section 112 has a long legislative history, recorded by Leeming JA in *Ghamrawi [Ghamrawi v R* (2017) 95 NSWLR 405; [2017] NSWCCA 195 at [50]–[51], [66]–[73]], and commencing in New South Wales with the incorporation into New South Wales law by the Imperial Criminal Acts Adoption Act 1828 (NSW) (9 Geo 4 No 1) of the Larceny (England) Act 1827 (7 & 8 Geo 4 c 29) (the 1827 UK Act). In England, the precursor statutory "breaking and entering" offences go back at least as far as 1547.

'[58] The original offences, which were the precursors to the seven offences contained in Div 4 of Pt 4 of the Crimes Act, were described by Coke as requiring a break and entry, with the intention to commit a felony, into "a mansion house of another". The cases consistently recognised some complexity around the outer limits of the concept of a "break". The "break" (*fregit*) needed to be a break "in law" as well as a break "in fact". For centuries, it was established that breaking and entering required both of these elements of law and fact.

'[59] A break "in law" was "every entry into the house by a trespasser", although it included an act done *in fraudem legis* ("in fraud of law"). This requirement underscored that there must, of course, be an "entry" in addition to a break to constitute the crime of burglary (*fregit et intravit*). The requirement of entry was satisfied upon "any part of the body be[ing] within the house". For example, a single finger being placed inside a window would constitute entry. The essence of the break "in law" requirement was therefore "unlawful entry on the possession of another", which would support an action in trespass *quare clausum fregit*. The trespass was also the foundation of the need for an indictment to state with accuracy "to whom the mansion belongs", with ownership of the dwelling-house being "neither referable altogether to the legal title, nor to the possession, but partaking sometimes of one sometimes of the other, as well as of both".

'[60] A break "in fact" required some "substantial and forcible irruption" although opening a lock with a key or "lifting up the latch of a door or unloosing any other fastening which the owner has provided" was sufficient. Although the element of a break "in fact" could involve a minimal physical action, that physical action with felonious intent was still necessary, "otherwise it is only a trespass". In other words, a trespassory entry by an open door or window was not sufficient without more for the requirements of breaking and entering.

'[61] The effect of the trespass requirement of a break "in law" was that it was well established that a person with a right of immediate possession of a premises could not commit burglary by entering the premises. In that sense it was said that "it cannot be burglary [for a person] to break open [their] own house". An owner residing in the same house would not commit burglary by breaking the chamber of an inmate having the same outer doo, and nor could a person by breaking into any part of a dwelling-house which they occupy with another. Further, a landlord would not commit burglary by stealing from the room of a travelling guest because the landlord "might go into the room when he pleased, and would be no trespasser to the guest". And the same was true of any contractual right to entry or occupation that did not amount to a right of exclusive possession. For example, if a person was a paid lodger at an inn — and therefore had contractual permission to enter and leave the inn — they could not be convicted of burglary if they stole from the inn. The position was different if the owner or landlord had no right of immediate possession, such as where there was said to be a "lease of the room".

'[62] This long history of breaking and entering as requiring a trespass by the accused person has been consistently reiterated. As earlier noted, in some jurisdictions, the element of breaking and entering has been simplified in analogous statutory offences by removing the requirement of a break "in fact" and replacing the element with that of trespass or unlawful or unauthorised entry, consistently with the established understanding that trespass is a core element of a break.

'[63] Against this long history, the Crown identified no authority to suggest a different meaning of the word "breaks" in the compound phrase "breaks and enters" in s 112. Nor is there any reason of principle that it should bear a different meaning. Thus, for example, an owner of a house who breaks a window to gain entry, having lost their keys, does not "break" the premises within the meaning of s 112. Likewise, a tenant who breaks a window in the same circumstances does not "break" the premises within the meaning of s 112 in the absence of some term of the relevant lease or residential tenancy agreement that limits their right or authority to enter the premises in that way.

...

'[65] It is unnecessary to consider the history or meaning of other provisions of Div 4 of Pt 4 of the Crimes Act such as ss 109, 110 and 111 because once "breaks and enters" is read in the manner explained above, it will necessarily confine the scope of "any dwelling-house" that could be broken and entered into by a person to those dwelling-houses in respect of which the person has no right, authority or permission to enter.' *BA v R* [2023] HCA 14, (2023) 409 ALR 41 at [36], [56] [63], [65], per Gordon, Edelman, Steward and Gleeson JJ

BRIBE

Australia '[52] The publishers argued that imputation 3 was not conveyed. In particular they relied on what White J had said in *Hockey v Fairfax Media Publications Pty Ltd* (2015) 237 FCR 33; 332 ALR 257; [2015] FCA 652 (*Hockey*) at [94], namely:

> The word "bribe" does not have a precise meaning as it is capable of encompassing more than one form of dishonest conduct by, or in relation to, a public official. However, **I consider that the ordinary reasonable reader would understand that a bribe usually involves the elements of a payment to a public official personally or to someone else on the official's behalf; a reasonably close relationship between the payment, on the one hand, and an expected decision or action by the public official, on the other; and the payment being made to secure or induce a benefit to the payer from the decisions or action in question**. The word bribe is not in ordinary understanding used to refer to the payments made by donors to political parties, or to political candidates, **which are unconnected** with any particular executive decision making, even if the motivation of the donors is to promote goodwill by the recipient towards themselves.
>
> (emphasis added)

...

[55] ... The concept of buying access and influence falls within the natural and ordinary meaning of a "bribe". The *Oxford English Dictionary* online defines "bribe" as: "a sum of money, gift, or other inducement which is given to another person in order to influence his or her behaviour, especially to persuade him or her to act in one's favour". The *Macquarie Dictionary* online defines "bribe" as "anything of value, as money or preferential treatment, privilege, etc, given or promised for corrupt behaviour in the performance of official public duty, anything given or serving to persuade or induce". Of course, in *Hockey*, White J was dealing with a different publication and explaining how he had arrived at his findings about it, not laying down general propositions of law as to how an ordinary reasonable person would understand all publications.' *Chau v Australian Broadcasting Corp (No 3)* [2021] FCA 44, (2021) 386 ALR 36, BC202100414 at [52], [55], per Rares J

BRIBERY

[For 1 Halsbury's Laws of England (5th Edn) (2017) para 94 see now 1 Halsbury's Laws of England (5th Edn) (2022) para 94.]

[Delete the entry referenced to 26 Halsbury's Laws of England (5th Edn) (2016) para 529.]

BROKER

[For 1 Halsbury's Laws of England (5th Edn) (2017) para 13 see now 1 Halsbury's Laws of England (5th Edn) (2022) para 13.]

[For 91 Halsbury's Laws of England (5th Edn) (2012) para 43 see now 91 Halsbury's Laws of England (5th Edn) (2019) para 42.]

BROUGHT

[Limitation Act 1980, ss 2, 5.] '[25] Section 2 of the Limitation Act 1980 provides that "[a]n action founded on tort shall not be brought after the expiration of six years from the date on which the cause of action accrued". Section 5 of the same Act states that "[a]n action founded on simple contract shall not be brought after the expiration of six years from the date on which the cause of action accrued". The question arises: when is an action "brought" for the purposes of the Act?

'[26] As explained by Peter Jackson LJ in *Hayes v Butters (No 2)* [2021] EWCA Civ 252, [2021] 4 All ER 1185 (at [23](3)), in an ordinary case an action is brought within the limitation period if a claim form is issued by the court within that period. However, where the claim form is received in the court office on a date earlier than the date on which it is actually issued by the court, the claim is "brought" for the purposes of the Limitation Act 1980 on that earlier date: see *Barnes v St Helens Metropolitan BC* [2006] EWCA Civ 1372, [2007] 3 All ER 525, [2007] 1 WLR 879. …

…

'[29] Although the wording of the test has varied slightly from case to case, I am content to adopt the formulation of Warby J (as he then was) in *Bhatti [Bhatti v Ashgar* [2016] EWHC 1049 (QB), [2016] 3 Costs LR 493] to the effect that, in order to take advantage of this principle, a claimant must have done all that he or she reasonably could do to bring the matter before the court in the appropriate way (and, I would add, at the appropriate time). In a case like this, a claimant must do what is necessary and sufficient to cause the court to issue the proceedings.

…

'[50] As noted above, the limitation position is frozen, and time stops to run, when an action is "brought". *Barnes* [above] and *Page v Hewetts [Page v Hewetts Solicitors* [2012] CP Rep 40] are authority for the proposition that the date the proceedings were "brought" for the purposes of the Limitation Act can be earlier than the actual date of the issue of the claim form. That position is also reflected in Practice Direction 7A, para 5.1, which provides:

> "Proceedings are started when the court issues a claim form at the request of the claimant (see rule 7.2) but where the claim form as issued was received in the court office on a date earlier than the date on which it was issued by the court, the claim is 'brought' for the purposes of the Limitation Act 1980 and any other relevant statute on that earlier date".'

Chelfat v Hutchinson 3G UK Ltd [2022] EWCA Civ 455, [2023] 1 All ER 461 at [25]–[26], [29], [50], per Coulson LJ

BROUGHT BEFORE

Australia [Extradition Act 1988 (Cth), s 15(1): a person who is arrested under an extradition arrest warrant must be brought as soon as practicable before a magistrate or eligible judge.] [136] … On the day of his arrest, 20 August 2020, Mr Pauga was brought before a magistrate as required by s 15(1) by reason of being legally represented at that hearing.

'[170] While the basis for a person accused of a criminal offence being able to appear by counsel or solicitor is both in common law and statute, that also reflects the practicalities of such litigation. Extradition is required to be no less practical. There is nothing in the text of s 15, let alone s 15(1), that requires appearance in person, as opposed to an appearance in the legal sense. A person the subject of an extradition proceeding may be brought before a magistrate either by appearance in person, or by being legally represented.' *Pauga v Chief Executive of Queensland Corrective Services* [2023] FCAFC 58, (2023) 408 ALR 56 at [136], [170], per Wigney , Bromwich and Abraham JJ

BULLYING

[Ministerial Code, para 1.2: 'Harassing, bullying or other inappropriate or discriminating behaviour wherever it takes place is not consistent with the Ministerial Code and will not be tolerated'.] '[50] Secondly, there is within the different departmental policies and documents in evidence before us, a broad consensus that conduct will fall within the description of "bullying" if it can be characterised as (1) offensive, intimidating, malicious or insulting behaviour or (2) abuse or misuse of power in ways that undermine, humiliate, denigrate or injure the recipient. That is provided for in the Guide which sets the standards that government departments are expected to follow. The definition reflects that used by the Arbitration, Conciliation and Advisory Service. Furthermore, none of the departmental policies that we were shown expressly required that the person responsible for engaging in conduct falling within the first limb above had to be aware of, or intend, the harm or offence caused. Some did expressly say that it was not the intention of the perpetrator that was relevant rather it was the perception of the individual who was the subject of the conduct which mattered. Conduct may fall within the first limb of the definition, and so constitute bullying (within the meaning of para 1.2 of the Ministerial Code) whether or not the perpetrator is aware or intends, that the conduct is offensive, intimidating, malicious or insulting.

'[51] There are some policies which, in relation to the second limb, refer to the abuse or misuse of power being intended to undermine, humiliate, denigrate or injure the recipient. That is in truth a reflection of that type of conduct. An example discussed in argument was a decision to take away some of a particular civil servant's responsibilities or duties. That may be a legitimate management choice. It may, however, be done with the aim (or, expressed differently, the intention) of denigrating or humiliating the person concerned. Only in the latter case would that type of conduct be regarded as bullying and so within para 1.2 of the Ministerial Code.' *R (on the application of the FDA) v Prime Minister and Minister for the Civil Service* [2021] EWHC 3279 (Admin), [2022] 3 All ER 675 at [50]–[51], per Lewis LJ

BUSINESS CONDUCTED

Canada [Income Tax Act, RSC 1985, c 1 (5th Supp), s 95.] '3 … We are tasked only with interpreting the precise words of the arm's length requirement – "the business (other than any business conducted principally with persons with whom the affiliate does not deal at arm's length)" – found in the financial institution exception, in accordance with the ordinary rules of statutory interpretation. When these words are read in their grammatical and ordinary sense, in harmony with their context and the *ITA*'s objects, it becomes clear that they do not encompass an assessment of capital contributions or corporate oversight.

…

'44 … Our task is to discern what the Parliament of Canada intended by the words "other than any business conducted principally with persons with whom the affiliate does not deal at arm's length". The Crown has failed to provide any persuasive reason why the Barbados Parliament's understanding of international banking business is in any way reflective of the Parliament of Canada's understanding of conducting business. As I said above, we must discern the Parliament of Canada's intent by examining the text of the *ITA* in its entire context and in its grammatical and ordinary sense, alongside the statute's scheme and objects.

'45 The Crown also argues that conducting business should be given a wide meaning based on s 248 of the *ITA*, which defines "business" in broad terms as including "a profession, calling, trade, manufacture or undertaking of any kind whatever" (AF, at para 71). I agree that the definition of "business" in s 248 is broad and not restricted to income-generating activities. However, we are not concerned with the word "business" alone. In my view, an ordinary and grammatical reading of the words "business conducted" conveys a different meaning than the word "business" alone. The addition of the verb "conducted" emphasizes Parliament's intent to focus on the active carrying out of the business rather than on the establishment of prerequisite conditions that enable a foreign affiliate to conduct business.

…

'61 I again reiterate that if taxpayers are to act with any degree of certainty, then full effect should be given to Parliament's precise and unequivocal words. The grammatical and ordinary meaning of the words "business conducted", read in the context and in light of the purpose of the FAPI regime, clearly shows that Parliament did not intend capital injections to be considered. Again, this is a view that the CRA itself previously shared. …' *Canada v Loblaw Financial Holdings Inc* [2021] SCJ No 51, 2021 SCC 51 at paras 3, 44–45, 61, per Côté J

BY 7 DAYS

[Unless order: 'Unless by 7 days of this order the claimant comply with paragraph 6 of the order of 27 September 2018 … the claim and defence to counterclaim shall be struck out automatically without any further order of the court'.] '[18] The question on ground 2 of the appeal is the true interpretation of the order. Counsel for Poule contends that the time for compliance with the unless order, so as to avoid its sanction, was 7 days from the date of service of the order. …

'[19] The defendants contend the correct meaning is that the period runs for 7 days from the date the order was made. …

'[20] Taking the order at face value, I would hold that the words "by 7 days of this order" mean that the 7 day period runs from the date of the order, in other words the date the order was made. That date appears on the document itself. There is a possible ambiguity between 28 November (date of making) and 29 November (date of sealing) but in this case that makes no difference.' *Poule Securities Ltd v Howe* [2021] EWCA Civ 1373, [2022] 4 All ER 887 at [18]–[20], per Birss LJ

BY ORDER

Australia '[748] Ground One of the appeal was that the primary judge erred in determining that the reference in cl 3(c) to a closure "by order of a competent government, public or statutory authority" means a closure "required by" the relevant order as opposed a closure "caused by" it (PJ [1102]).

…

'[755] The primary judge was correct to conclude that the context in which the expression "by order" was used indicates that it was intended to be narrower than "caused by". In cl 3(a) where the expression "damage by any insured event" is used, it can legitimately be said that "by" means "caused by". However, where the expression is "by order", as it is in cl 3(c) and (d), it signifies that the cause of the closure is to be required by the order itself. As the primary judge concluded (PJ [1102]), the expression "by order" incorporates the requirement that the nature of the order is one mandating the closure, in and of itself, in the sense that it must require the closure of the premises. To read "by order" as simply meaning "caused by" would elide the requirement that the closure or evacuation of the premises be "by" the order. It would, as her Honour observed, have the consequence that the closure may occur as a result of a voluntary decision of the insured in response to some order of an authority which did not actually require the premises to be closed. Were that to be so, it would afford the insured great latitude as to from when the policy would operate and an insurer would face considerable difficulties in going behind the insured's motivation for closing the premises. Mr Slattery QC submitted that this was ameliorated because the order must be the proximate cause of the closure. However, on the construction which he proffered, the causal connection would necessarily be indirect given that it is filtered through the insured's subjective thoughts. It is also wrong to describe the nexus of "caused by" as connoting proximate cause.

…

'[759] It follows that the meaning of the disputed part of cl 3(c) is that the closure or evacuation of all or part of the premises must be the result of an order of a relevant authority which both mandates that the closure occurs and, in fact, causes that to happen. EWT's submissions as to the meaning of "by order" in cl 3(c) must therefore be rejected.' *LCA Marrickville Pty Ltd v Swiss International SE* [2022] FCAFC 17, (2022) 401 ALR 204 at [748], [755], [759], per Derrington and Colvin JJ

BY REASON OF

New Zealand [Securities Act 1978, s 56(1).] '[129] If investors establish that they have invested on the faith of the prospectus, it will still be necessary for them to establish that they have sustained loss by reason of the untrue statement. We turn to that aspect of s 56(1) now.

'[130] The words "loss or damage [investors] may have sustained by reason of such untrue statement" indicate that there must be a nexus between the untrue statement and the loss sustained by the investor. The issue is what type of nexus is required. We consider that the words must be interpreted consistently with the meaning given to the concept of "untrue statement" in terms of s 55(a) (in particular the fact that it refers to an untrue statement, not a materially untrue statement) and the words "on the faith of [the] prospectus" in s 56(1) (particularly that those words do not require proof of actually having read and relied on the untrue statement and, indeed, do not require that an investor has read the prospectus).

'[131] Given our conclusion that s 55(a) deals with untrue statements, not just materially untrue statements, we see the "by reason of" requirement in s 56 as a mechanism for controlling the imposition of liability under s 56 (which is consistent with the courts' approach to "legal" causation in other areas).

…

'[134] We consider that the issue is rather whether loss or damage was sustained "by reason of" an untrue statement in a prospectus. This means that a court must determine whether the effect of the untrue statement was such that the market value of the securities for which the investor subscribed would have been lower than the price paid if the misleading statement had not been made or, put another way, if the prospectus had complied in all respects with the Securities Act and the Securities Regulations. If the price paid by the investor was greater than the price that would have been payable if adequate disclosure had been made in the prospectus, the investor will have suffered loss "by reason of" the untrue statement, assuming the investor has proved he or she invested on the faith of the prospectus in the sense described above.

'[135] In some cases, the untruth will be egregious and its impact obvious. In that type of case, subscribers may be able to obtain compensation equalling the full amount of their investment under s 56. Their argument would be that revelation of the truth would have revealed that the securities were, in truth, valueless or of such little value that investors would not have invested had the true position been known. In less serious cases, the inquiry will be on whether the revelation of the true position in the prospectus would have indicated the securities had a lower value than the offer price.' *Houghton v Saunders* [2018] NZSC 74, [2019] 1 NZLR 1 at [129]–[131], [134]–[135], per Elias CJ, Glazebrook, O'Regan, Arnold and Kós JJ

C

C.I.F.

[For 91 Halsbury's Laws of England (5th Edn) (2012) para 14 see now 91 Halsbury's Laws of England (5th Edn) (2019) para 15; and for 91 Halsbury's Laws of England (5th Edn) (2012) para 335 see now 7 Halsbury's Laws of England (5th Edn) (2020) para 387.]

CV FRAUD

[Proceeds of Crime Act 2002, s 6.] '[1] This appeal raises an important issue on the confiscation regime laid down by the Proceeds of Crime Act 2002 ("POCA"). It concerns what is often referred to as "cv fraud" ("cv" being shorthand for "curriculum vitae"). Typically, as in this case, this occurs where a fraudster includes lies on his or her application form for a job (for example, by including qualifications or experience which he or she does not have) and, as a result, is appointed to the job. The fraudster performs the agreed services satisfactorily and is paid the agreed salary until the fraud is discovered. On a conviction for fraud, should there be a confiscation order stripping the fraudster of his or her earnings (net of tax and national insurance)? In particular, would such a confiscation order be disproportionate under the proviso in s 6(5) of POCA?

…

'[56] Although we are not attempting to deal with all possible circumstances, the answer to the question certified (see para [2]) is that in cv fraud cases, where, focusing solely on the performance of services, the fraudster has given full value for the earnings received – and putting to one side where the performance of the services constitutes a criminal offence – it will normally be disproportionate under the proviso in s 6(5) to confiscate all the net earnings made. But it will be proportionate to confiscate the difference between the higher earnings made as a result of the cv fraud and the lower earnings that the defendant would have made had he or she not committed the cv fraud. In many situations of cv fraud, it will be appropriate, as a pragmatic approximation of that profit, simply to base it on the percentage difference between the fraudster's initial salary in the new job obtained by fraud and the fraudster's salary in his or her prior job. Moreover, there is no need for much time and effort to be expended in assessing, even in a broad-brush way, the difference between the earnings with and without the cv fraud if it is clear that, in any event, that difference will exceed the recoverable amount.' *R v Andrewes* [2022] UKSC 24, [2023] 1 All ER 443 at [1], [56], per Lord Hodge DP and Lord Burrows JSC

CAPTURE

[For 60 Halsbury's Laws of England (5th Edn) (2011) paras 328, 330 see now 60 Halsbury's Laws of England (5th Edn) (2018) paras 307, 309.]

CARGO

Deck cargo

[For 7 Halsbury's Laws of England (5th Edn) (2015) para 456 see now 7 Halsbury's Laws of England (5th Edn) (2020) para 253.]

CARRIAGE OF GOODS

[For 7 Halsbury's Laws of England (5th Edn) (2015) paras 7–27 see now 7 Halsbury's Laws of England (5th Edn) (2020) para 7.]

CARRIER

Private carrier

[For 7 Halsbury's Laws of England (5th Edn) (2015) paras 56–70 see now 7 Halsbury's Laws of England (5th Edn) (2020) paras 10–24.]

CARRY ON BUSINESS

Canada [Reciprocal Enforcement of Judgments Act, RSO 1990, c R5, s 3.] '40 I need not decide here whether the term "carrying on business" as it appears in *Van Breda* [*Club Resorts Ltd v Van Breda* 2012 SCC 17, [2012] 1 SCR 572] carries the same meaning as in the case law on traditional presence-based jurisdiction. However, it is safe to say that if the *Van Breda* standard is different, it is lower. In any event, the *Van Breda* requirements for "carrying on business" must also apply for the purposes of traditional presence-based jurisdiction. In *Chevron* [*Chevron Corp v Yaiguaje* 2015 SCC 42, [2015] 3 SCR 69], this Court recognized as much by quoting LeBel J's remark that "carrying on business requires some form of actual, not only virtual, presence in the jurisdiction, such as maintaining an office there", in describing what it means to "carry on business" for the purposes of presence-based jurisdiction.

'41 *Chevron* thus provided a clear definition of "carrying on business" as part of traditional presence-based jurisdiction at common law. For the reasons given above, this informs the interpretation of s 3(b) of the *REJA*. In sum, to determine whether a defendant is carrying on business in a jurisdiction, the court must inquire into whether it has some direct or indirect presence in the jurisdiction, accompanied by a degree of business activity that is sustained for a period of time. Whether or not a corporation is "carrying on business" is a question of fact, and in order to determine whether this definition is met, the court should consider the 10 *Adams* indicia listed above. And some kind of actual presence, whether direct or indirect, is required. A physical presence in the form of maintenance of physical premises will be compelling, and a virtual presence that falls short of an actual presence will not suffice.

'42 I am therefore unpersuaded by HMB's argument that the courts below erred in failing to interpret "carrying on business" in a "generous and liberal" manner in accordance with *Chevron*. *Chevron* itself affirms the test for carrying on business for the purposes of traditional presence-based jurisdiction. Section 3(b) of the *REJA* refers to the meaning of the term for those same purposes. As a result, the "generous and liberal" approach from *Chevron* does not modify the test for "carrying on business" in s. 3(b), as it is set out in *Chevron* itself.' *HMB Holdings Ltd v Antigua and Barbuda* [2021] SCJ No 44, 2021 SCC 44 at paras 40–42, per Wagner CJ

CASUAL PROFIT

[For 58 Halsbury's Laws of England (5th Edn) (2014) para 653 see now 99 Halsbury's Laws of England (5th Edn) (2019) para 233.]

CATASTROPHE

Australia [Indemnity insurance clause covering loss resulting from interruption of or interference with business in consequence of the action of a civil authority during a conflagration or other catastrophe for the purpose of retarding same; measures taken to control the spread of COVID-19.] '[343] LCAM submitted that the primary judge ought to have given the word "catastrophe" its ordinary meaning which, on the assumptions made, she had accepted would include a "pandemic" (PJ [333] citing *Star first instance* [*The Star Entertainment Group Ltd v Chubb Insurance Australia Ltd* (2021) 396 ALR 590; 156 ACSR 119; [2021] FCA 907] at [172]) as that would be the meaning given to it by a reasonable person in the position of the prospective insured.

'[344] That submission raises the issue of the meaning of the word "catastrophe" which the parties disputed on several levels. It is useful to first consider a number of dictionary definitions. The Oxford English Dictionary (online) provided the following:

> 3.b. *esp* in *Geology*. A sudden and violent change in the physical order of things, such as a sudden upheaval, depression, or convulsion affecting the earth's surface, and the living beings upon it, by which some have supposed that the successive geological periods were suddenly brought to an end.
>
> 4. A sudden disaster, wide-spread, very fatal, or signal. (In the application of exaggerated language to misfortunes it is used very loosely.)

'[345] Although LCAM acknowledged that many definitions identify suddenness as a characteristic of the word, it submitted that its ordinary usage extends much further and that an earlier version of the Oxford English Dictionary included an additional meaning, being an "event causing great damage or suffering".

'[346] The Macquarie Dictionary (online) gives the following meanings:

noun

1. a sudden and widespread disaster.

2. a final event or conclusion, usually an unfortunate one; a disastrous end.

3. (in a drama) the point at which the circumstances overcome the central motive, introducing the close or conclusion; the denouement.

4. a sudden violent disturbance, especially of the earth's surface; a cataclysm.

'[347] It is difficult to deny that common to a number of these definitions is the suddenness and magnitude of the event constituting the catastrophe as well as the implicit characteristic of a physical phenomenon. On the other hand, such temporal matters are relative and depend upon the circumstances. In the case of a novel disease which is highly contagious and virulent, it is possible that, at least, its initial appearance and spread amongst the population could be sufficiently sudden to satisfy any such requirement.

...

'[352] In the context of the particular policy, the words "or other" sufficiently connect the word "catastrophe" with "conflagration" with the result that "catastrophe" should be given a meaning which requires that the things within it have the essential characteristics of a conflagration, being a physical event of some magnitude causing widespread physical destruction or loss of life as a result of the unleashing of destructive forces. No error was shown to exist in this approach which was adopted by the primary judge.

...

'[356] Given the foregoing, the occurrence of a widespread outbreak of a disease, even if it amounts to a pandemic, does not necessarily fall within the concept of a "catastrophe" for the purposes of cl 9.1.2.5.

...

'[358] It follows that whether the expression "other catastrophe" is construed only in the context of cl 9.1.2.5 or, as would be appropriate, in the context of the whole of the policy, it did not extend to cover the consequences of a disease pandemic. The expression "catastrophe" requires the sudden onset of a physical event of substantial magnitude which results in widespread destruction or loss of life and necessitates physical action to retard it.' *LCA Marrickville Pty Ltd (ACN 601 220 080) v Swiss Re International SE* [2022] FCAFC 17, (2022) 401 ALR 204 at [343]–[347], [352], [356], [358], per Derrington and Colvin JJ

CAUSE OF ACTION

[For 11 Halsbury's Laws of England (5th Edn) (2015) para 115 see now 11 Halsbury's Laws of England (5th Edn) (2020) para 119.]

CHALLENGE

[For 61 Halsbury's Laws of England (5th Edn) (2010) para 825 see now 61A Halsbury's Laws of England (5th Edn) (2023) para 225.]

CHAMPERTY

[For 22 Halsbury's Laws of England (5th Edn) (2012) para 438 see now 22 Halsbury's Laws of England (5th Edn) (2019) para 229.]

CHARGE (NOUN)

[Equality Act 2010, s 165: taxi driver's duty 'not to make any additional charge' for carrying disabled person in wheelchair.] '[17] It is not in dispute between the parties that demanding payment from a wheelchair user for the time it takes to board the taxi would amount to the making of an additional charge for the purposes of s 165(4)(b) and s 165(7) of the EA 2010. ...

...

'[19] The main issue on this appeal is whether a "charge" was made by the Appellant by the act of him switching on his taximeter before Ms Vogelman and Ms Creek had boarded, even though Ms Vogelman never entered his taxi, no money was demanded (either expressly or by implication) and they ended up travelling in a different taxi.

...

'[29] The starting point is to note the precise language used in s 165(4)(b). The driver's duty is not "to make any additional charge" as a result of being hired by or on behalf of a disabled person. In this phrase the word "charge" is being used as a noun and not a verb. The online Oxford English Dictionary definitions of "charge" when used as a noun include "a price asked for goods or services" and also "a financial liability or commitment" (see https://en.oxforddictionaries.com/definition/charge).

'[30] The first of these meanings supports, to an extent, Mr Taylor's submission that the point in time when a driver makes an additional charge can only be at the end of the journey because it is then and only then that the precise fare can be ascertained, in other words, only is the price asked. On the other hand, the second definition supports Mr Patience's submission that in a taxi fitted with a taximeter the passenger's obligation is to pay whatever the meter shows at the end of journey, and so the moment the meter is switched on the passenger becomes financially liable for the fare, and it is thus at that point that the driver makes the charge.

'[31] In my judgment it is the second meaning which is to be ascribed to the word "charge" as used in s 165(4)(b), and a taxi driver makes a charge when he switches his taximeter on, and if he does this for a disabled passenger before the passenger and her wheelchair have been loaded into the taxi, there will be an additional charge and thus an offence under s 165(7) even if, for whatever reason, the driver never actually demands the fare.

…

'[35] In my judgment there can be no doubt that no later than the time a taximeter is switched on at the point of hire, an actual financial liability or commitment is imposed on the passenger to pay the amount shown on the meter when the hiring is terminated, and it is therefore at that point that the charge is made for the purposes of s 165(4)(b). …

…

'[42] For these reasons, in my judgment the words "make an additional charge" in s 165(4)(b) mean to impose an additional financial liability or commitment on a disabled wheelchair user as compared with an able bodied passenger, and such a liability or commitment is imposed no later than the point when a London taxi driver switches on his meter before such a person and their wheelchair have boarded the taxi.' *McNutt v Transport for London* [2019] EWHC 365 (Admin), [2020] 1 All ER 84 at [17], [19], [29]–[31], [35], [42], per Julian Knowles J

CHARITY—CHARITABLE PURPOSES

General meaning

[For 8 Halsbury's Laws of England (5th Edn) (2015) para 2 see now 8 Halsbury's Laws of England (5th Edn) (2019) para 2.]

[Charities Act 2011, s 6; Finance Act 2010, Sch 6 para 1: whether a community amateur sports club ('CASC') was a 'charity' for the purposes of the Value Added Tax Act 1994 Sch 8, which depended on whether the club was 'established for charitable purposes only' pursuant to the Finance Act 2010, Sch 6.] '[54] Section 6(1) CA 2011 (which provides that a registered sports club established for charitable purposes "is to be treated as not being so established, and accordingly cannot be a charity") is undoubtedly a deeming provision but there is nothing in the words of this section which limit or confine its effect in any way, still less to the operation of the CA 2011. The Club's case entails reading words into s 6(1) CA 2011 (such as "for the purposes of this Act"), words which are simply not there. Instead the language used is general and there is no ambiguity. As a statement of the general law it could not have been clearer: it applies without limitation, and therefore, for all purposes. No cross-reference between s 6 and [the Finance Act 2010,] para 1(1)(a) Sch 6 was necessary because, on the natural and ordinary meaning of the words used in s 6, its effect is that a CASC is for all purposes, and not just regulatory and administrative purposes, to be treated as not being established for charitable purposes and therefore cannot satisfy the charitable purpose condition in para 1 Sch 6 FA 2010. As a statement of the general law, there was no reason for s 6 to be directly or indirectly incorporated into the FA 2010. It stands on its own as a provision for all purposes unless disapplied.' *Eynsham Cricket Club v Revenue and Customs Commissioners* [2021] EWCA Civ 225, [2021] 3 All ER 369 at [54], per Simler LJ

CHARTER VALUES

Canada '61. As this Court explained in *Bell ExpressVu Limited Partnership v Rex*, 2002

SCC 42, [2002] 2 SCR 559, the "Charter values" interpretive principle serves a narrow purpose: when faced with two interpretations–one compliant with the Canadian Charter of Rights and Freedoms ("Canadian Charter"), the other infringing it–courts can apply the presumption of compliance with the Canadian Charter to read the statute in a manner respectful of the Charter value in question. This allows the statute to remain in force–untouched–and interpreted such that it complies with the Canadian Charter. This principle, however, does not allow the courts to generate in the name of Charter values an interpretation unsupported by the text of the statute (*Bell ExpressVu*, at para 62; *R v Clarke* 2014 SCC 28, [2014] 1 SCR 612, at para 12).' *Quebec (Commission des normes, de l'équité, de la santé et de la sécurité du travail) v Caron* [2018] SCJ No 3, [2018] 1 SCR 35 at para 61, per Rowe J

CHARTERPARTY

[For 7 Halsbury's Laws of England (5th Edn) (2015) paras 208, 211 see now 7 Halsbury's Laws of England (5th Edn) (2020) paras 162, 166.]

CHATTELS

Corporeal and incorporeal

[For 80 Halsbury's Laws of England (5th Edn) (2013) para 806 see now 80 Halsbury's Laws of England (5th Edn) (2020) para 806.]

Personal

[For 80 Halsbury's Laws of England (5th Edn) (2013) para 805 see now 80 Halsbury's Laws of England (5th Edn) (2020) para 805.]

Real

[For 80 Halsbury's Laws of England (5th Edn) (2013) para 804 see now 80 Halsbury's Laws of England (5th Edn) (2020) para 804.]

[For 87 Halsbury's Laws of England (5th Edn) (2017) para 3 see now 87 Halsbury's Laws of England (5th Edn) (2022) para 3.]

CHILD—CHILDREN

[For 9 Halsbury's Laws of England (5th Edn) (2012) para 142 see now 9 Halsbury's Laws of England (5th Edn) (2017) para 141.]

CHILDREN'S HOME

'[21] A "children's home" is defined in s 1(2) of the Care Standards Act 2000 as "An establishment [which] provides care and accommodation wholly or mainly for children" but this is subject to various qualifications in the Act and regulations which exclude certain types of accommodation from being classified as a "children's home". Thus, for example, s 1(3) provides that "an establishment is not a children's home merely because a child is cared for and accommodated there by a parent or relative of his or by a foster parent", s 1(4A) and (5) exclude hospitals and schools from the definition of a "children's home". Part II of the Care Standards Act makes provision for the registration and regulation of children's homes in England. The Children's Homes (England) Regulations 2015, SI 2015/541, in addition to excluding other types of accommodation from being classified as a "children's home", prescribe a range of quality standards for children's homes and make further wide-ranging provisions designed to ensure the safety and welfare of children in such establishments. …' *Re B (a child) (Association of Lawyers for Children intervening)* [2019] EWCA Civ 2025, [2020] 3 All ER 375 at [21], per Baker LJ

CHOSE IN ACTION

[For 80 Halsbury's Laws of England (5th Edn) (2013) para 806 see now 80 Halsbury's Laws of England (5th Edn) (2020) para 806.]

CHOSE IN POSSESSION

[For 80 Halsbury's Laws of England (5th Edn) (2013) para 806 see now 80 Halsbury's Laws of England (5th Edn) (2020) para 806.]

CHURCHWAY

[For 55 Halsbury's Laws of England (5th Edn) (2012) para 6 see now 55 Halsbury's Laws of England (5th Edn) (2019) para 8; and for 32 Halsbury's Laws of England (5th Edn) (2012) para 37 see now 32 Halsbury's Laws of England (5th Edn) (2019) para 37.]

CITIZENSHIP

Australia '[31] Citizenship, as formal membership of the national community, is a statutory concept. It is the grant of Australian citizenship that creates the status which attracts constitutional protections and engages federal and State legislation that confers or denies rights, privileges, immunities or duties. Relevantly for Mr Alexander, the status of Australian citizenship includes the right to enter and remain in Australia, the entitlement to an Australian passport, and the right and duty to vote in federal elections.

'[32] Citizenship is not a concept used in the Constitution (save for s 44(i), which is concerned with foreign citizenship). The Constitution, in contrast to the first clause of the Fourteenth Amendment to the Constitution of the United States, does not contemplate that individuals born here are citizens of Australia, much less that they are indelibly so. This Court's decisions in *Singh (an infant) (by her next friend Singh) v Commonwealth* [(2004) 222 CLR 322; 209 ALR 355; 79 ALD 425; [2004] HCA 43] and *Koroitamana v Commonwealth* [(2006) 227 CLR 31; 227 ALR 406; [2006] HCA 28] would be plainly misconceived if, as a matter of constitutional law, a person born in Australia has for that reason, and quite apart from any law of the Parliament, a right to live here. Mr Alexander's counsel made no attempt to challenge the correctness of *Singh* and *Koroitamana*.

...

'[34] It has been said in this Court that the terms "citizen" and "alien" are antonyms. Recently, the majority of this Court in *Love* [*Love v Commonwealth* (2020) 270 CLR 152; 375 ALR 597; [2020] HCA 3 at [81]] held that Aboriginal Australians who satisfy the tripartite test in *Mabo v Queensland* [(1992) 175 CLR 1; 107 ALR 1] constitute a separate category of non-citizen, non-alien, and that "non-citizen" is not inevitably and always synonymous with "alien". But in *Chetcuti*, Kiefel CJ, Gageler, Keane and Gleeson JJ observed that this Court's decision in *Shaw* [*Shaw v Minister for Immigration and Multicultural Affairs* (2003) 218 CLR 28; 203 ALR 143; 77 ALD 251; [2003] HCA 72] (from which the holding of the majority in *Love* does not depart, except in respect of an Aboriginal Australian according to the tripartite test in *Mabo*) establishes that the aliens power supports a law of the Commonwealth which determines who shall have the status of Australian citizenship, and which provides that persons who do not share that status are aliens.' *Alexander (by his litigation guardian Alexander) v Minister for Home Affairs* [2022] HCA 19, (2022) 401 ALR 438 at [31]–[32], [34], per Kiefel CJ, Keane and Gleeson JJ (footnotes omitted)

CIVIL COMMOTION

[For 60 Halsbury's Laws of England (5th Edn) (2011) para 571 see now 60 Halsbury's Laws of England (5th Edn) (2018) para 548.]

CIVIL LIST

[For 29 Halsbury's Laws of England (5th Edn) (2014) para 120 see now 29 Halsbury's Laws of England (5th Edn) (2019) para 125.]

CIVIL PARTNERSHIP

[For 72 Halsbury's Laws of England (5th Edn) (2015) para 3 see now 72 Halsbury's Laws of England (5th Edn) (2019) para 4.]

CLAIM

[Application for third party disclosure. CPR 31.17 – CPR PD 6B, para 3.1(20), which provides for service out of the jurisdiction with permission where a claim is made under an enactment which allows proceedings to be brought and those proceedings are not covered by any of the other grounds referred to in para 3.1.] '[31] Mr O'Leary's submission was that the word "claim" in para 3.1 of Practice Direction 6B refers to a claim to enforce a substantive as distinct from a procedural right; and that the term "proceedings" in gateway (20) refers to "claims or similar matters which are essentially freestanding", as distinct from applications (such as an application for third party disclosure) within such proceedings. He acknowledged that an application for pre-action disclosure would be a claim, but submitted that an application for pre-action disclosure was significantly different from an application for third party disclosure.

'[32] Jacobs J dealt with these submissions in considerable detail. He pointed out that there are circumstances in which proceedings in court may be originated by an application and that the definition of the term "claim" in CPR 6.2 is a broad one:

" 'claim' includes petitions and any application made before action or to commence proceedings and 'claim form', 'claimant' and 'defendant' are to be construed accordingly".

'[33] In the light of this definition, Jacobs J held that an application for third party disclosure is a "claim" for the purpose of gateway (20). …

'[34] I respectfully agree. The term "claim" in para 3.1 of Practice Direction 6B is not used in any restrictive or technical sense. It includes both an application for pre-action disclosure and an application for third party disclosure.' *Gorbachev v Guriev* [2022] EWCA Civ 1270, [2023] 2 All ER 809 at [31]–[34], per Males LJ

CLAIM … IN TORT

[CPR Practice Direction 6B, para 3.1(9): claimant may serve a claim form out of the jurisdiction with the permission of the court where a claim is made in tort where—(a) damage was sustained, or will be sustained, within the jurisdiction; or (b) damage which has been or will be sustained results from an act committed within the jurisdiction.] '[5] The Claimants submit that the contribution claim in respect of the torts of which both Samsung and LGD were found guilty by the Commission is a "*claim in tort*" within the meaning of PD 3.1(9). The Defendants submit that it is not, and that the only gateway available is the restitution gateway (and that the claim does not qualify for it).

…

'[11] I am persuaded that, notwithstanding the different wording used for the contract gateway, I should construe a "claim in tort" purposively in the light of the juridical history of the tort gateway, its proper assimilation to the Brussels Regulation and "in a broad internationalist spirit". I note that Lord Hoffmann in *FFSB* [*FFSB Ltd v Seward & Kissel LLP* [2007] UKPC 16, (2007) 70 WIR 20], though dealing with the old RSC wording, concluded at [22] that "there is no reason why it should matter whether the claim is made by the victim of the tort or by another tortfeasor seeking contribution". Similarly in the Scottish case of *Comex* [Comex Houlder Diving Ltd v Colne Fishing Co Ltd 1987 SC (HL) 85, (1987) Times, 20 March], the Lord President concluded 1987 SC (HL) 85 at 104, again on the basis of the RSC language, that "delict in Scotland forms the primary cause of this action (for contribution)". The claim, in my judgment, is a "claim in tort", albeit by a joint tortfeasor rather than by the original victim.' *Samsung Electronics Co Ltd v LG Display Co Ltd* [2021] EWHC 1429 (Comm), [2022] 1 All ER 717 at [5], [11], per Sir Michael Burton GBE

CLAIMANT

[For 11 Halsbury's Laws of England (5th Edn) (2015) para 117 see now 11 Halsbury's Laws of England (5th Edn) (2020) para 121.]

CLAIMS MANAGEMENT SERVICES

'[10] For present purposes, however, the critical part of the definition lies in the inclusion of "claims management services" in those which may be provided under a DBA [damages-based agreement]. That expression was itself defined by reference to s 4(2) of the Compensation Act 2006, the Preamble to which stated that it was "An Act … to make provision for the regulation of claims management services". By virtue of s 4(1) of the 2006 Act, "A person may not provide regulated claims management services unless—(a) he is an authorised person …". Section 4(2) then states that:

> "In this Part … (b) 'claims management services' means advice or other services in relation to the making of a claim …" …

[T]he definition of "claims management services" in s 4(2)(b) is extended by sub-s (3)(a)(i) to include "the provision of financial services or assistance".

…

'[87] The point which we have to decide is ultimately a short question of construction of the definition of "claims management services" in s 4(2) of the 2006 Act. Although on a literal, acontextual, reading of the extended definition, the words "the provision of financial services or assistance" "in relation to the making of a claim" could be read as including the provision of litigation funding by a third party which plays no part in the management of the claim, I consider that the Tribunal was correct to accept the submission of Mr Kirby for the RHA that those words are "to be interpreted as applying in the context of the management of a claim": see the main judgment at [41], quoted at [18] above. …' *PACCAR Inc v Road Haulage Association Ltd (Association of Litigation Funders of England and Wales intervening)* [2021] EWCA Civ 299, [2021] 4 All ER 737 at [10], [87], per Henderson LJ

CLASS

Gift to

[For 102 Halsbury's Laws of England (5th Edn) (2010) para 175 see now 102 Halsbury's Laws of England (5th Edn) (2021) para 177.]

CLASS CLOSURE ORDER

Australia [Civil Procedure Act 2005 (NSW), s 183.] '[33] The principal issue on the appeal was whether order 16 in the present case was within the power granted by s 183 of the Civil Procedure Act. So-called "class closure orders" have been endorsed by the Full Court of the Federal Court as being empowered by s 33ZF of the Federal Court Act, which is equivalent to s 183 of the Civil Procedure Act. The appellants submitted that ss 183 and 33ZF did not support an interpretation empowering the making of order 16 for the purpose of encouraging or facilitating a settlement. Further, it was submitted that even if there was power to make such an order, the discretion to make order 16 here miscarried.

...

'[62] Jargon abounds in cases arising under Pt 10 of the Civil Procedure Act. Order 16 describes itself as a "class closure order". "Class closure" is not a statutory term. Part 10 authorises a wide range of representative proceedings which may, but need not, concern an "open class". That is to say, Part 10 permits representative proceedings to be brought on behalf of Group Members who may (but need not necessarily) be identifiable on a list.

'[63] As it happens, practical considerations often result in representative proceedings being commenced on behalf of an open class, although that need not be so. Insofar as it was repeatedly submitted that "closure", whether at all or particularly before any settlement, was necessary, that is not so as a matter of demonstrable historical fact.

'[64] Critically, one of the few mandatory requirements in Pt 10 is for all Group Members to be given the right to "opt out" prior to the commencement of the initial hearing: s 162. That right is supported by requirements of notice: s 175(1)(a). But there is no requirement to "close" an open class before any hearing, including the hearing of common questions, even if that hearing about common questions also includes the hearing of claims for actual loss by the representative applicant and individual Group Members.

'[65] Part 10 deals expressly with the possibility of settlement but only by imposing an additional requirement of court approval: s 173(1). Part 10 says nothing about an obligation to "close" a class before a settlement is achieved or before mediation occurs.

'[66] That legislative framework tends strongly against an implication that there must be power to make an order extinguishing the rights of an unregistered Group Member in advance of any settlement being achieved (or even attempted) in order to facilitate settlement of the claims of Group Members who choose to register their claims.

'[67] Practical considerations may in many cases make it desirable to convert an "open" class to a "closed" or fully identified class of Group Members. This may occur in a number of ways. For very many years this occurred by courts permitting an amendment to the originating process so as to narrow the group definition so that it applied only to persons who in addition to having a claim against the defendant had also registered themselves or had retained the same firm of solicitors or agreed to a funding agreement with an external funder.

...

'[78] Of course, neither "class closure" nor "closed class" is a statutory term. Both terms describe the effect of amendments to originating process and pleadings or the operation of court orders upon the legal rights of Group Members in representative proceedings.

...

'[114] Nevertheless, order 16 in the present case is beyond the power conferred by s 183. This is not because settlement of proceedings is not a desirable aim. Plainly it is. I do not, however, accept as the respondents submitted that the "supplementary" power in s 183 was intended to provide a power of contingently extinguishing Group Members' claims so that "realistic settlement discussions may take place" by "seeking to crystallise the outer sum being claimed".

...

'[119] There are two significant matters to consider. The first is that the scheme of Part 10 is inconsistent with an interpretation of s 183 as empowering the Court to make orders for pre-settlement class closure. ...' *Haselhurst v Toyota Motor Corp Australia Ltd (t/a Toyota*

Australia) [2020] NSWCA 66, (2020) 379 ALR 556 at [33], [62]–[67], [78], [114], [119], per Payne JA

CLEARLY ABUSIVE

New Zealand [Immigration Act 2009, s 140(3): A refugee and protection officer may refuse to consider a subsequent claim for recognition as a refugee or a protected person if the officer is satisfied that the claim: (a) is manifestly unfounded or clearly abusive; or (b) repeats any claim previously made (including a subsequent claim).] '[58] Woodhouse J considered it preferable in approaching the issue of whether WK's fourth claim was "clearly abusive" to take "[a]ll relevant factors" into account, rather than to define that term by reference "to a set of circumstances" or "synonyms". The Judge accepted that a "clearly abusive" claim could include one that is lodged to prolong the appeal or deportation process, but that the circumstances in which a clearly abusive claim may arise were not exhaustive.

…

'[60] The RPO [Refugee and Protection Officer] concluded that WK's fourth claim was "clearly abusive". That finding rested on the history of WK's claims and the timing of his fourth claim. …

'[61] We consider that such a conclusion would not have been available to the RPO unless, as Woodhouse J observed, "[a]ll relevant factors" had been taken into account. In the circumstances of the present case, the relevant factors would necessarily include the particulars of the subsequent claim. The effect of the RPO's assessment was that WK's fourth claim based on his social media activities did not give rise to any essentially different risk of refoulement. It follows in those circumstances that, even on the test contended for by Mr Pidgeon, the RPO was permitted to draw an adverse inference from the timing of WK's fourth claim to conclude it was clearly abusive. This is particularly so when set against the history of his previous claims and the unmeritorious nature of WK's subsequent claim. In the circumstances, we, like Woodhouse J, consider that the RPO's finding was reasonably available to him.' *WK v Refugee and Protection Officer* [2018] NZCA 258, [2019] 2 NZLR 223 at [58], [60]–[61], per Mander J

CLOG

On equity of redemption

[For 77 Halsbury's Laws of England (5th Edn) (2016) para 320 see now 77 Halsbury's Laws of England (5th Edn) (2021) para 318.]

CODICIL

[For 102 Halsbury's Laws of England (5th Edn) (2010) para 1 see now 102 Halsbury's Laws of England (5th Edn) (2021) para 1.]

COLLIERY

[For 76 Halsbury's Laws of England (5th Edn) (2013) para 15 see now 76 Halsbury's Laws of England (5th Edn) (2019) para 15.]

COLLISION

Collision clause in marine policy

[For 60 Halsbury's Laws of England (5th Edn) (2011) para 336 see now 60 Halsbury's Laws of England (5th Edn) (2018) para 315.]

COMMERCIAL ACTIVITY

[Diplomatic Privileges Act 1964, Sch 1, art 31(1): commercial activity an exception to diplomatic immunity; exploiting a domestic worker.] '[15] It is not suggested that the alleged acts of Mr Basfar were a "professional" activity. The question is whether they were a "commercial activity exercised" by him within the meaning of art 31(1)(c) of the Diplomatic Convention.

…

'[27] Applying the general rule of interpretation set out in art 31(1) of the Treaties Convention [Vienna Convention on the Law of Treaties 1969] (see para [17] above), we agree with Mr Basfar's contention that employing a domestic worker does not itself constitute the exercise of a "commercial activity" by a diplomatic agent within the meaning of the exception.

'[28] We do not accept that this conclusion can be reached just by considering the ordinary meaning of the words used in art 31(1)(c) of the Diplomatic Convention. In particular, we cannot agree with the view expressed by Lord Sumption in *Reyes [Al-Malki v Reyes* [2017]

UKSC 61, [2018] 1 All ER 629, [2019] AC 735], at para [21](2), that the ordinary meaning of "exercising" a "commercial activity" is restricted to "carrying on a business" or "setting up shop". Certainly, the ordinary meaning of the words includes those concepts. But it is not limited to them. For example, it would be perfectly consistent with ordinary usage to describe a person who is employed as a shop assistant as "exercising a commercial activity" even though he or she is working in someone else's shop and is not carrying on a business. Nor do we understand the word "exercée" in the French text to have any materially different connotation from the English word "exercised".

'[29] As a matter of ordinary language, buying goods and services could be described as the exercise of a commercial activity, irrespective of the purpose for which they are purchased. The same could be said of entering into a contract of employment as an employer (or employee) and receiving (or supplying) personal services under such a contract. To support this proposition, we rely not just on dictionaries or our own understanding of the English language but on how similar language has been interpreted by courts in the United States and Canada in the context of state immunity.

...

'[34] Seen in this context, it would be contrary to the purpose of conferring immunity on diplomatic agents to interpret the words "any ... commercial activity" in art 31(1)(c) as including activities incidental to the ordinary conduct of daily life in the receiving state, such as purchasing goods for personal consumption or purchasing medical, legal, educational or domestic services privately. Immunity from the civil jurisdiction of the local courts is justified in relation to such activities to ensure that diplomatic agents and their families can live in the receiving state without the impediment arising from having to deal with civil claims against them.

...

'[42] The next step in Mr Basfar's argument is to contend that, seeing as the ordinary employment of a domestic worker by a diplomatic agent does not constitute the exercise of a commercial activity within the meaning of art 31(1)(c), the same must be true where a domestic worker is trafficked and exploited by a diplomat.

'[43] It is here that we part company with the argument. We cannot accept that exploiting a domestic worker by compelling her to work in circumstances of modern slavery is comparable to an ordinary employment relationship of a kind that is incidental to the daily life of a diplomat (and his family) in the receiving state. There is a material and qualitative difference between these activities. Employment is a voluntary relationship, freely entered into and governed by the terms of a contract. Subject to contractual provisions about notice, employees are free to leave when they please, and cannot be compelled to stay by injunction even if they leave in breach of contract. By contrast, the essence of modern slavery is that it is not freely undertaken. Rather, the work is extracted by coercion and the exercise of control over the victim. This usually involves exploiting circumstances of the victim which make her specially vulnerable to abuse. Those constraints generally make it impossible or very difficult for the worker to leave. That is why, on the assumed facts, we describe Ms Wong's departure from service with Mr Basfar as an "escape".

...

'[56] On any fair view of the matter, Mr Basfar has on the assumed facts made a substantial financial gain from his exploitation of Ms Wong's labour, albeit not in cash but in money's worth. The exploitation has been a systematic activity carried on over a significant period. It is accurately described as a commercial activity practised for personal profit.

...

'[97] It is sufficient that Mr Basfar's treatment of Ms Wong, on the assumed facts, amounted to a form of modern slavery, whether it was forced labour, servitude or trafficking. This shows that the relationship between them was not that of employment freely entered into, so as to be an ordinary part of Mr Basfar's daily life in the UK as a resident diplomat. And it shows that his conduct amounted to a commercial activity practised (in so far as it matters) for personal profit.' *Basfar v Wong* [2022] UKSC 20, [2022] 4 All ER 1 at [15], [27]–[29], [34], [42]–[43], [56], [97], per Lord Briggs and Lord Leggatt JJSC

COMMERCIAL PRACTICE

[Consumer Protection from Unfair Trading Regulations 2008, SI 2008/1277, reg 2(1); European Parliament and Council Directive 2005/29/EC (Unfair Practices Directive), art 2.]

'[41] [I]n my judgment, a commercial practice for the purposes of art 2(d) of the Directive (and thus reg 2(1) of the 2008 Regulations) may be constituted by or derived from a test purchase made of a product (including a service) that is generally promoted to and intended for purchase by consumers, even where the purchaser may not himself be a consumer. Specifically, the giving to the test purchaser of an invoice or other document incorporating false information as to a main characteristic of the product (including the execution of a service) that would mislead the average consumer into paying for services that he has not received (which he would not otherwise have done) is a commercial practice which is a misleading action for the purposes of regs 5 and 9 of the 2008 Regulations, being "directly connected with the promotion, sale or supply of a product to … consumers".' *Warwickshire County Council v Halfords Autocentres Ltd (Competition and Markets Authority intervening)* [2018] EWHC 3007 (Admin), [2019] 2 All ER 69 at [41], per Hickinbottom LJ

COMMODITY EXCHANGE

[Commercial Agents (Council Directive) Regulations 1993, SI 1993/3053, reg 2(2)(b): Regulations not to apply tp commercial agents when they operate on commodity exchanges or in the commodity market.] '[76] Taking first the concept of a "commodity exchange", I am unable to agree with the judge that an exchange in its historical and commercial sense is simply a place for sales to take place. No one, for example, would reasonably describe a supermarket as an exchange. Nor are the facts that the class of persons able to buy is restricted and the process of selling regulated sufficient to make a place where sales take place an exchange. An auction house, for example, where only people who satisfy specified criteria are permitted to bid and where sales are conducted in accordance with the auctioneer's rules would not be regarded in the commercial world as an exchange. The nature of an "exchange", as I believe the term would generally be understood, is a place where trading takes place among members of the exchange and subject to its rules. The corresponding phrases in the French and German text ("les bourses du commerce" and "Handelsbörsen") have a similar connotation. Thus, well known examples of commodity exchanges in the UK are the London Commodity Exchange, which in 1996 merged to become part of the London International Financial Futures Exchange ("LIFFE"), and the London Metal Exchange. Trading on such exchanges was traditionally conducted by open outcry, but now generally takes place electronically. Most of the trading on modern commodity exchanges is in futures and options but, like the judge, I see no reason to regard the availability of trading in such contracts as an essential characteristic. What would in my view be regarded as an essential feature of a commodity exchange is that the commodities (or rights to buy and sell commodities) which are traded on the exchange can be freely bought and sold among the participants.

…

'[85] I would accordingly hold that, in acting as a commercial agent for Pluczenik in negotiating purchases of rough diamonds from De Beers, Nagel was not operating on a commodity exchange or in the commodity market and that its activities were therefore within the scope of the Directive and the Regulations. It follows that on the termination of the agency contract Nagel was entitled to compensation from Pluczenik under reg 17." *W Nagel (a firm) v Pluczenik Diamond Co NV* [2018] EWCA Civ 2640, [2019] 2 All ER 194 at [76], [85], per Leggatt LJ

COMMODITY MARKET

[Commercial Agents (Council Directive) Regulations 1993, SI 1993/3053, reg 2(2)(b): Regulations not to apply tp commercial agents when they operate on commodity exchanges or in the commodity market.] '[77] I agree with the judge that the fact that the Directive [Council Directive 86/653/EEC on the co-ordination of the laws of member States relating to self-employed commercial agents] uses two different expressions ("commodity exchanges" and "the commodity market" in the English version) indicates that the two expressions must be intended to have different, even if overlapping, meanings. Thus, the phrase "the commodity market" must be wider than simply connoting the sum of all commodity exchanges; otherwise its inclusion would be superfluous. But equally, the phrase "the commodity market" must be given a meaning which does not make the inclusion of the reference to "commodity exchanges" superfluous. That is achieved, as it seems to me, by interpreting "commodity exchanges" as typical or paradigmatic instances of "the commodity market". Thus, transactions negotiated or concluded in the commodity market are transactions of a similar kind as those which are negotiated or concluded on a commodity exchange. So understood, the commodity market encompasses any general trading in commodities that takes place in the open market.

...

'[85] I would accordingly hold that, in acting as a commercial agent for Pluczenik in negotiating purchases of rough diamonds from De Beers, Nagel was not operating on a commodity exchange or in the commodity market and that its activities were therefore within the scope of the Directive and the Regulations. It follows that on the termination of the agency contract Nagel was entitled to compensation from Pluczenik under reg 17.' *W Nagel (a firm) v Pluczenik Diamond Co NV* [2018] EWCA Civ 2640, [2019] 2 All ER 194 at [77], [85], per Leggatt LJ

COMMON CARRIER

[For 7 Halsbury's Laws of England (5th Edn) (2015) para 3 see now 7 Halsbury's Laws of England (5th Edn) (2020) para 3.]

COMMUNITY BANK

Australia '[69] Bendigo contends that there are inconsistent findings as to the ordinary signification of the term "community bank" in the following paragraphs of the Judgment:

> [206] When used in combination the words "community" and "bank" convey the meaning of the provision of financial services to a group of people brought together by a common feature, for example geography, occupation or workplace. The use of these terms in conjunction is not so unique as to alter the meanings that "community" and "bank" possess individually.
>
> [207] There is no covert or skilful allusion to the Services provided by Bendigo. The combined words are directly descriptive of the Services offered, namely the provision of financial services to a community of people defined by geography.
>
> ...
>
> [233] The ordinary signification of the term "community bank" is a provider of banking services or financial institution that serves a particular community, whether defined by geography, workplace, trade or other feature. It is directly descriptive of the Services. Further, the evidence establishes that other traders, not actuated by improper motive, might, and indeed did as at the Priority Dates, legitimately desire to use those words for their ordinary signification.

'[70] We do not accept this submission. First, we do not accept that [207] of the Judgment is a finding as to the ordinary signification of the term "community bank". The language used in [207] is narrower than the other paragraphs — [206] and [233] contemplate the provision of services to communities that are defined by any common feature whereas [207] is limited to communities that are defined by geography. Yet these differences can be explained. At [207], it is clear that the primary judge is using the term "community bank" to describe the Services, as Bendigo provided the Services to local communities, rather than making a finding as to the ordinary meaning of the term.

'[71] We reach a similar conclusion in respect of [206] of the Judgment. When [206] is read in context alongside [207], it is apparent that even though the primary judge speaks of the meaning of the words used in combination, she is in fact using the words to describe the Services.

'[72] In any event, there is no inconsistency between [206] and [233] of the Judgment. Both paragraphs identify the recipients of services, namely a community defined by a common feature. The words "provision" ([206]) and "provider" ([233]) are cognate terms. The word "serves" in [233] is also used in the context of the earlier reference to "a provider of banking services or financial institution" and so, contrary to Bendigo's submissions, any question as to the nature of the services referred to in this paragraph is answered by the preceding words.

'[73] We are therefore satisfied that the primary judge's finding as to the ordinary signification of the term "community bank" is at [233] of the Judgment, and [206] and [207] are to be read as consistent variations of this meaning.

'[74] Bendigo's submissions raise the issue of whether the existence of more than one possible meaning of a term in the one context has the consequence that the term has no ordinary meaning at all.

...

'[80] The asserted ambiguities in the term "community bank" that Bendigo relies on are chiefly directed at how one might define a community. Bendigo submits that the potentially innumerable features that might define a particular community defeats any ordinary signification. However, the primary judge had already said that the community must be defined by a common feature and listed three possible features. The absence of any exhaustive list does not render the expression meaningless. Bendigo also submits that the primary judge's use of the expression "serves a particular community" in her finding at [233] of the Judgment provides no clear answers as to how and in what way a community bank serves the community. Yet as we have already observed, when read in context, the word "serves" is clearly referring to the provision of banking or financial services.

'[81] In any event, we do not see any basis for limiting the operation of the TM Act [Trade Marks Act 1995 (Cth)] in the way contended for by Bendigo. The practical effect of Bendigo's argument that "community bank" is not capable of ordinary signification is that, insofar as s 41 of the TM Act prevents the appropriation of ordinary language, its protections are limited to words and phrases that possess a singular meaning in the one context. Having regard to the cases outlined above we consider that such an approach would be unduly restrictive. As CFCU [Community First Credit Union] submits, establishing the ordinary signification of words is not so reductive a task as to exclude a word with more than one meaning or a potentially nuanced meaning.' *Bendigo and Adelaide Bank Ltd v Community First Credit Union Ltd* [2021] FCAFC 31, (2021) 389 ALR 196, BC202101578 at [69]–[74], [80]–[81], per Middleton and Burley JJ

COMPELLING CIRCUMSTANCES (VERY)

[Nationality, Immigration and Asylum Act 2002, s 117C(6): 'In the case of a foreign criminal who has been sentenced to a period of imprisonment of at least four years, the public interest requires deportation unless there are very compelling circumstances, over and above those described in Exceptions 1 and 2'.] '[51] There are two limbs to AEB's submissions on Ground 2. First, it is submitted that the sentence of 4 years was at the bottom of the range of sentences falling within s 117C(6) and that, therefore, it takes relatively little to amount to very compelling circumstances over and above those described in Exceptions 1 and 2. It is submitted that the UT failed to adopt this approach. Second, it is submitted that, since Exception 2 could be satisfied if the effect of an appellant's deportation would be unduly harsh on one qualifying child, it follows that the weight to be attributed to the effect of deportation being unduly harsh on three children should be correspondingly greater. In their written submissions Mr Chirico and Ms Griffiths submitted that the effect on three children should be given three times the weight that would be given in the case of only one. In oral submissions Mr Chirico retreated from this strictly mathematical proposition but maintained that the presence of additional children should be treated "incrementally". He submitted that the UT [Upper Tribunal] Judge failed to give incremental weight to the existence of the three children in this case and that this constituted a material error of law on the basis of which the UT's decision should be set aside.

'[52] I am unable to accept either limb of these submissions.

…

'[54] The general principles to be adopted emerge clearly from the words of the statute, which, in a case to which s 117C(6) applies, requires there to be "very compelling circumstances, over and above those described in Exceptions 1 and 2" before the public interest in deporting the foreign criminal is outweighed. The correct approach has been authoritatively established on high and binding authority and does not require substantial restatement here. …

'[55] *In HA (Iraq) [HA (Iraq) v Secretary of State for the Home Dept, RA (Iraq) v Secretary of State for the Home Dept* [2020] EWCA Civ 1176, [2021] 2 All ER 898; affd [2022] UKSC 22, [2023] 1 All ER 365] at [46]ff Lord Hamblen set out the approach to be adopted. At [51]–[52] he said:

> "[51] When considering whether there are very compelling circumstances over and above Exceptions 1 and 2, all the relevant circumstances of the case will be considered and weighed against the very strong public interest in deportation. As explained by Lord Reed in *Ali [Ali v Secretary of State for the Home Dept* [2016] UKSC 60, [2017] 3 All ER 20] at paras [24] to [35], relevant factors will include those identified by the European Court of Human Rights ('ECtHR') as being relevant to the art 8 proportionality assessment."

And, after summarising relevant factors as identified by the ECtHR (which include the nature and seriousness of the offence committed by the applicant and the applicant's family situation and the best interests of any children):

"[52] The weight to be given to the relevant factors falls within the margin of appreciation of the national authorities."

…

'[58] In the light of these authorities, I would accept that the effect on three children as opposed to one would be a material factor for the UT Judge to have considered in the present case. However, I am quite unable to accept that he did not do so, or that he applied the relevant principles in a manner that discloses a material error of law. …' *AEB v Secretary of State for the Home Department* [2022] EWCA Civ 1512, [2023] 3 All ER 319 at [51]–[52], [54]–[55], [58], per Stuart-Smith LJ

COMPLEMENTARITY

Canada '39. … As in all cases of statutory interpretation, the meaning of these words is a question of parliamentary intent. In the interpretation of a federal statute that uses concepts of property and civil rights, reference must be had to ss 8.1 and 8.2 of the *Interpretation Act*, RSC 1985, c I-21. …

'40. In other words, where Parliament uses a private law expression and is silent as to its meaning, courts must refer to the applicable provincial private law. This is known as the principle of complementarity. However, as both these sections also make clear, Parliament is free to derogate from provincial private law and create a uniform rule across all provinces (see R Sullivan, *Sullivan on the Construction of Statutes* (6th edn 2014), at pp 158–59).' *Canada v Canada North Group Inc* 2021 SCC 30, [2021] SCJ No 30 at paras 39–40, per Côté J

COMPOSITION

[For 5 Halsbury's Laws of England (5th Edn) (2013) para 856 see now 5 Halsbury's Laws of England (5th Edn) (2020) para 40, n 2.]

COMPUTER

Computer or data storage device

Australia [Crimes Act 1914 (Cth), s 3LA: constable may apply to a magistrate for an order requiring a specified person to provide any information or assistance that is reasonable and necessary to allow a constable to, among other things, access data held in, or accessible from, a computer or data storage device.] '[149] The Commissioner submits that having regard to the natural and ordinary meaning of the word "computer" as ordinarily understood in discourse, there can be no doubt that a modern smart phone is a "computer". The Commissioner referred to the definition in the Macquarie Dictionary and submits that a smart phone is "an apparatus for performing mathematical computations electronically according to a series of stored instructions called a program". He refers to the fact that the primary judge appeared to accept as much (at [185]).

…

'[154] Mr Luppino submits (correctly) that the magistrate made the Section 3LA Order on the basis that a mobile phone was a "computer or data storage device" and there is nothing in the material before the magistrate which suggests which of those distinct concepts he relied upon. He submits that the order was beyond the power conferred by s 3LA of the Crimes Act insofar as it related to the gold Samsung mobile phone because that device is not a computer or data storage device within the meaning of s 3LA of the Crimes Act. He submits that by "data storage device", the Crimes Act contemplates a concept quite different from a mobile phone. In that respect, he relies upon the Explanatory Memorandum for the 2010 Bill. Mr Luppino repeats the argument put to the primary judge that, although a mobile phone may contain data, a mobile phone is designed to contain data for use on the phone itself, not "for use by a computer" (unless, of course, the phone itself is a "computer"). He submits that the definition of "data storage devices" is purposive and the nature of the "thing" must be such that it contains data in order for it to be used by a computer.

'[155] Mr Luppino submits that the gold Samsung mobile phone is not a computer. He submits that the most common meaning of a computer as used in common parlance does not extend to a mobile phone, even a smart phone. He submits that a person who is asked whether they are carrying a computer does not mislead by answering "no" even if they are carrying their mobile phone. A smart phone is not a computer in ordinary parlance. …

'[156] In reply, the Commissioner submits that it was not the case that the common meaning of a computer as used in common parlance did not extend to a mobile phone, even a smart phone. He submits that the contemporary understanding of a smart phone is a mobile phone with access to the internet and the functionality of a personal computer. He submits that the ordinary and natural meaning of the term "computer" is to reflect the "contemporary Australian understanding" of the term (*Masson v Parsons* (2019) 266 CLR 554; 368 ALR 583; 59 Fam LR 503; [2019] HCA 21 at [29]). …

…

'[159] The dictionary definition of computer is set out above (at [149]). The definition of a smart phone in the Macquarie Dictionary (6th ed) is as follows:

> a mobile phone with access to the internet and the functionality of a personal computer.

…

'[168] Before leaving the merits of this ground, I should note a concession quite fairly and properly made by counsel for Mr Luppino. Mr Luppino submitted that the ordinary meaning of computer included a main frame computer, a desktop, laptop, or a personal computer. It does not include a mobile phone and perhaps not an iPad. It does not include the countless objects which have computers in them such as refrigerators and motor vehicles. The submission was that a computer does not, in ordinary parlance, mean a device that has the functionality of a computer, but is a "narrower subset" of a device which has the functionality of a computer. Counsel accepted that a weakness in his submission is that he is not able "to describe in terms that are wholly exhaustive and exclusive in terms of the meaning of computer in ordinary parlance".

'[169] The gold Samsung mobile phone was a computer, as that term is used in s 3LA. It might also be characterised as a data storage device. …' *Commissioner of Australian Federal Police v Luppino* [2021] FCAFC 43, (2021) 388 ALR 603, BC202102088 at [149], [154]–[156], [159], [168]–[169], per Besanko J

CONDITION (STIPULATION)

In lease

[For 62 Halsbury's Laws of England (5th Edn) (2016) para 126 see now 62 Halsbury's Laws of England (5th Edn) (2022) para 143.]

Conditions precedent and subsequent

[For 102 Halsbury's Laws of England (5th Edn) (2010) para 129 see now 102 Halsbury's Laws of England (5th Edn) (2021) para 131.]

CONDITIONAL DISCHARGE

[Mental Health Act 1983, s 73(2): tribunal must in specified circumstances direct conditional discharge of a patient who is subject to a restriction order.] '[28] The MHA is silent: it says nothing about the type or content of the conditions which may be imposed by the Secretary of State or the FtT [First-tier Tribunal]. In this respect it has remained unchanged since the 1959 Act. There are several possibilities: (1) that the FtT cannot impose a condition of detention in a hospital but the Secretary of State may do so; (2) that neither may do so; (3) that both may impose a condition of detention in a place which is not a hospital within the meaning of the MHA whether or not the patient consents; (4) that both may do so but only if the patient consents; and (5) that neither may do so.

'[29] There is of course the argument that a condition which amounts to a detention or deprivation of liberty could nonetheless serve the rehabilitative purpose of the power of conditional discharge. Just as there is nothing in the MHA which permits it, there is nothing in the MHA which prohibits it. The thinking of the experienced Upper Tribunal in *RB* [*Secretary of State for Justice v RB* [2010] UKUT 454 (AAC)] (para [21] above) is worthy of respect. The main textual argument in favour of a power to impose such a condition is that a conditionally discharged patient remains "liable to be detained" within the meaning of the MHA (see para [18] above). As such, he is more akin to a hospital patient who has been given leave of absence than to a patient who is subject to a community treatment order. "Discharge" therefore cannot mean "discharge from compulsion". Although it must mean "discharge from the hospital where he is currently detained", it need not mean any more than that, and so could encompass a range of possible arrangements. Furthermore, although it is clear that the FtT cannot impose a condition of detention in a hospital for treatment, because by definition the FtT is not satisfied that the grounds for such detention exist (para [10] above), the same is not true of the Secretary of State. He has power to discharge the patient conditionally irrespective of whether the grounds for detention in hospital still exist.' *Secretary of State for Justice v MM* [2018] UKSC 60, [2019] 2 All ER 749 at [28]–[29], per Lady Hale P

CONDUCT

Australia [Building and Construction Industry (Improving Productivity) Act 2016 (Cth), ss 83(2), 91; unlawful picketing.] '[109] Turning to the meaning of the word "conduct" in ss 83(2) and 91, in our opinion, the primary judge erred in concluding (at [60]–[61]) that the references in these provisions to "the same conduct" or "particular conduct" mean all of the physical and mental elements that go to making a person liable for a contravention of two laws at once. The word "conduct", in ordinary English, refers to what a person does or does not do. It does not encompass the mental element that accompanies a particular act or omission. That this is the sense that "conduct" is used in the Act is supported by the definition of "conduct" in s 5 of the Act. That section defines "conduct" as including an omission, which is inconsistent with the notion of a state of mind. It is further supported by the distinction drawn by ss 94 and 95 of the Act between conduct and states of mind. *Parker [Parker v Australian Building and Construction Commissioner* (2019) 270 FCR 39; 365 ALR 402; [2019] FCAFC 56], at the passages relied on by the Commissioner, does not stand for a contrary proposition.

'[110] Further, the words "the same conduct" and the "particular conduct" in ss 83(2) and 91 respectively refer to the actual conduct of the contravener rather than the elements of the statutory provisions that have been contravened. Otherwise, these provisions would be deprived of much of their operation and effect. While it is true that s 84 uses a different form of words ("founded on the same facts") we nevertheless consider that ss 83(2) and 91 are concerned with actual conduct rather than elements of statutory provisions, for the reasons we have given.

'[111] It follows that we consider that the primary judge was in error in determining, in relation to each individual appellant, that the conduct comprising the contraventions of ss 47(1) and 52(a) was different because the contravention of s 52(a) was committed with an intention to coerce Botany Cranes. That intention pertained to the individual appellants' states of mind in relation to their conduct. It did not form part of their "conduct" for the purposes of applying s 83(2).' *Construction, Forestry, Maritime, Mining and Energy Union (CFMMEU) v Fair Work Ombudsman* [2023] FCAFC 40, (2023) 409 ALR 656 at [109]–[111], per Bromberg, Moshinsky and Bromwich JJ

CONDUCT OF LITIGATION

[Legal Services Act 2007, s 14, Sch 2 para 4.] '[177] … Under the 2007 Act, the conduct of litigation includes functions which are ancillary to the commencement, prosecution, and defence of proceedings before any court in England and Wales.

…

'[191] In my judgment, the actions of the Respondents, both in relation to the claim form and particulars of claim and in relation to the reply and defence to counterclaim, amounted to the conduct of litigation, and so to reserved legal activities for the purposes of the 2007 Act.

…

'[198] I have, so far, considered whether the service of the reply and defence to counterclaim was the conduct of litigation. Moving on to the claim form and particulars of claim, in my judgment the reasoning of the Court of Appeal in *Ndole* [*Ndole Assets Ltd v Designer M&E Services UK Ltd* [2019] BLR 147] applies all the more clearly to the delivery of documents to the court as it does to the delivery of documents to the other party. If sending a pleading to the other side by way of service is the conduct of litigation, then sending a claim form or pleading to the court for issue in order to commence the proceedings must also amount to the conduct of litigation. …

…

'[200] The Court of Appeal in *Ndole* considered the entirety of the actions undertaken by the consultants in that case when deciding that the service of documents was the conduct of litigation. Applying the same approach to the current case, I am satisfied, to the criminal standard, that the filing of the claim form and particulars of claim, and the arrangements made for service of the reply and defence by the Respondents, amounted to the conduct of litigation.

'[201] As I have said, I am satisfied so that I am sure, on the evidence, that, in addition to filing the claim form and particulars of claim and serving the reply and defence to counterclaim, the Respondents carried out the following activities on behalf of Mr Persey: they gave legal advice; they drafted notices under s 8 and s 21 of the Housing Act 1988; they corresponded with the Claimant's solicitor; they drafted the claim form and particulars of claim; they paid the issue fees; an employee of the Second Respondent signed a certificate of service of the notice of issue; they gave instructions to an advocate for several hearings in the matter; they drafted witness statements; they drafted an application notice and draft order for the strike-out application; they drafted the reply and defence to counterclaim; and they drafted the case management summary for the [Case Management Conference].

Things that do not amount to the conduct of litigation

'[202] In my judgment, it is clear that several of these activities, taken in isolation, do not amount to the conduct of litigation for the purposes of the 2007 Act.

'[203] The giving of legal advice in itself does not amount to the conduct of litigation. This applies even if the legal advice is about the procedures that need to be followed in the proceedings. This was said in Agassi [*Agassi v Robinson (Inspector of Taxes) (Bar Council intervening)* [2006] 1 All ER 900], at para [56], and, in my view, it still holds good.

'[204] The drafting of the notices under ss 8 and 21 of the Housing Act 1988 do not amount to the conduct of litigation. These are not steps in court proceedings themselves, even though they are necessary precursors to such proceedings. In many, perhaps most, cases, the service of a s 8 and 21 notice will not lead to litigation. The matter will be resolved without the need to issue proceedings.

'[205] It is also unlikely, in my view, that the service of the notice of issue was, on its own, the conduct of litigation. Though it was a formal document, and one that contained a statement of truth, it was not a document that was required to be served as part of the proceedings, and it was not served on the court or on the other party to the proceedings: it was served on any other occupants of the property.

'[206] Furthermore, in light of the statutory language and the ruling in *Ndole*, no step that is taken prior to the issue or commencement of proceedings can amount to the conduct of litigation. …

'[207] In my judgment, however, this does not mean that the fact that a respondent has given legal advice or has taken steps before proceedings are issued, such as drafting the claim form and particulars of claim, is irrelevant to the question whether they are engaged in the conduct of litigation. It may contribute to the bigger picture and may, in particular, shed light on whether steps that were taken at a later stage in the proceedings were purely mechanical or clerical.

Should the court look in isolation at each particular action, or should the court consider the matter in the round?

'[208] In my judgment, the answer is that the court should look at the entirety of the activities undertaken by the Respondents to assist their client and then decide whether, taken in the round, they amount to the conduct of litigation. To do otherwise would be to lose sight of the context in which things are being done, and would lead to the risk of a misleading impression being gained. It would also run the risk of form being prioritised over substance.' *Baxter v Doble* [2023] EWHC 486 (KB), [2023] 3 All ER 395 at [177], [191], [198], [200]–[208], per Cavanagh J

CONFER

Confer any gratuitous benefit

[Inheritance Tax Act 1984, s 10: disposition not a transfer of value if it is shown that it was not intended, and was not made in a transaction intended, to confer any gratuitous benefit on any person.] '[61] The disponor's actual intention in making the disposition is, therefore, in point. That militates against an over-technical interpretation of what is meant by "confer any gratuitous benefit". To my mind, the approach taken by the majority in the Court of Appeal is essentially the correct one. The words "confer" and "benefit" have to be given their ordinary meaning, and the dictionary definitions (see Newey LJ's para [88], quoted at para [40] above) show that they import the idea of granting or bestowing some advantage on the recipient. Like Newey LJ, I do not think it is appropriate to speak of a disposition having been intended to confer any gratuitous benefit if the recipient of the benefit was intended to receive no more than he would have had in any event. It is necessary, therefore, to ask whether the disponor was intending, by the overall effect of the disposition, to put the recipient in a better position, or, to borrow from what Newey LJ said at para [88], putting things broadly, to ask whether the disposition was being used to improve someone's position on a gratuitous basis. The exercise is not, however, simply a matter of asking the disponor whether or not he or she intended to confer benefit, as Miss Wilson submits would be all that was required under the appellants' test. I go so far with HMRC as to accept that it is not possible to consider whether a disposition was intended to improve someone's position without taking into account what rights the recipient had, in law, before and after the disposition. This legal context will permit a more rigorous evaluation of whether the requisite absence of intention has been shown. But this legal analysis of the rights is a factor in the evaluation, not the be all and end all of the consideration. I do not accept, for example, that the mere fact that the rights are to be enjoyed in a different legal form after the disposition means that they are necessarily a gratuitous benefit. Furthermore, I cannot accept the return to zero analysis, whereby the existing set of rights must necessarily be treated as ending immediately prior to the disposition, with a new set commencing which, in comparison to the void left by the ending of the pre-existing rights, can then be described as beneficial. There must, as I see it, be more attention paid to the practical reality of the legal situation than that wholly artificial analysis permits.

'[62] It would probably be unwise to attempt to define further what is meant by "intended … to confer any gratuitous benefit", particularly as it is unnecessary to do so to resolve the instant case. Instead, I hope that by turning to the facts of the case, I can demonstrate the way in which it seems to me the section should be interpreted.' *Revenue and Customs Commissioners v Parry* [2020] UKSC 35, [2021] 1 All ER 365 at [61]–[62], per Lady Black JSC

CONFUSION

[For 80 Halsbury's Laws of England (5th Edn) (2013) para 824 see now 80 Halsbury's Laws of England (5th Edn) (2020) para 824.]

CONSIDERATION

[Value Added Tax: whether overpayments in respect of parking at 'pay and display' car parks, where a customer who did not have correct change paid more than the stipulated amount, were consideration.] '[6] Article 1(2) of Council Directive 2006/112/EC on the common system of value added tax ("the Principal VAT Directive") explains that the principle of the common system of VAT "entails the application to goods and services of a general tax on consumption exactly proportional to the price of the goods and services". Amongst the transactions subject to VAT are "the supply of services for consideration within the territory of a Member State by a taxable person acting as such" (art 2(1)(c)). By art 73, in respect of a supply of goods or services:

> "the taxable amount shall include everything which constitutes consideration obtained or to be obtained by the supplier, in return for the supply, from the customer or a third party …"

'[7] Provisions to similar effect are to be found in the Value Added Tax Act 1994. Under s 4(1), VAT is to be charged on "any supply of goods or services made in the United Kingdom, where it is a taxable supply made by a taxable person in the course or furtherance of any business carried on by him". "Supply" includes "all forms of supply, but not anything done otherwise than for a consideration" (s 5(2)(a)).

'[8] The word "consideration", which features in both arts 2(1)(c) and 73 of the Principal VAT Directive and s 5(2)(a) of the 1994 Act, does not in the VAT context refer to what might be deemed "consideration" for the purposes of domestic contract law but has an autonomous EU-wide meaning (see eg *Staatssecretaris van Financiën v Coöperative Aardappelenbewaarplaats* (Case 154/80) EU:C:1981:38, [1981] ECR 445, [1981] 3 CMLR 337 ("the *Dutch potato* case"), at para 9 of the judgment of the Court of Justice). "[T]he concept of the supply of services effected for consideration within the meaning of art 2(1) of the Sixth Directive [ie the predecessor of the Principal VAT Directive] presupposes the existence of a direct link between the service provided and the consideration received" (*Apple and Pear Development Council v Customs and Excise Comrs* (Case 102/86) EU:C:1988:120, [1988] 2 All ER 922, [1988] ECR 1443, at para 12 of the Court of Justice"s judgment; see also eg *Commission of the European Communities v Finland* (Case C-246/08) EU:C:2009:671, [2009] ECR I-10605, at para 45 of the Court of Justice's judgment). A supply of services is effected "for consideration", and hence is taxable, "only if there is a legal relationship between the provider of the service and the recipient pursuant to which there is reciprocal performance, the remuneration received by the provider of the service constituting the value actually given in return for the service supplied to the recipient" (*Tolsma v Inspecteur der Omzetbelasting Leeuwarden* (Case C-16/93) EU:C:1994:80, [1994] STC 509, [1994] ECR I-743, at para 14 of the Court of Justice's judgment; see also eg *Geemente Borsele v Staatssecretaris van Financiën, Staatssecretaris van Financiën v Geemente Borsele* (Case C-520/14) EU:C:2016:334, [2016] STC 1570, at para 24 of the Court of Justice's judgment).

'[9] The authorities also show that "consideration" is a "subjective value" in the sense that "the basis of assessment for the provision of services is the consideration actually received and not a value assessed according to objective criteria" (the *Dutch potato* case, at para 13 of the judgment). In *Campsa Estaciones de Servicio SA v Administración del Estado* (Case C-285/10) EU:C:2011:381, [2011] STC 1603, the Court of Justice explained in para 28 of its judgment:

> "According to settled case law ..., the taxable amount for the supply of goods or services for consideration is the consideration actually received for them by the taxable person. That consideration is thus the subjective value, that is to say, the value actually received, and not a value estimated according to objective criteria."

...

'[11] In the present case, the UT [Upper Tribunal], upholding the FTT's [First-tier Tribunal's] decision, considered that in the hypothetical example set out in para [3] above the taxable amount and consideration for VAT purposes was the full £1.50 actually paid rather than the £1.40 tariff for up to an hour's parking. ...

...

'[18] English law, of course, generally adopts an objective approach when deciding what has been agreed in a contractual context. Here, it seems to me that, taken together, the tariff board and the statement that "overpayments" were accepted and no change given indicated, looking at matters objectively, that NCP was willing to grant an hour's parking in exchange for coins worth at least £1.40. In the hypothetical example, the precise figure was settled when the customer inserted her pound coin and 50p piece into the machine and then elected to press the green button rather than cancelling the transaction. The best analysis would seem to be that the contract was brought into being when the green button was pressed. On that basis, the pressing of the green button would represent acceptance by the customer of an offer by NCP to provide an hour's parking in return for the coins that the customer had by then paid into the machine. At all events, there is no question of the customer having any right to repayment of 10p. The contract price was £1.50.

'[19] This is the contractual analysis in the hypothetical example where the customer has only a pound coin and a 50p piece, and therefore has no alternative but to pay £1.50 if she wishes to park in the car park. However, the analysis is the same even if it is possible for the customer to obtain the right coins, for example by obtaining change from another user of the car park. If the customer nevertheless chooses to insert £1.50 and presses the green button, it remains the case that she has accepted the offer to provide an hour's parking at that price.

...

'[22] In the circumstances, I agree with the UT and FTT that, in the hypothetical example, the consideration and taxable amount was £1.50. Like the UT, I consider that, "[i]f a customer pays £1.50, that amount is the value given by the customer and received by the supplier in return for the right to park for up to an hour". That means that NCP's present appeal should be dismissed.' *National Car Parks Ltd v Revenue and Customs Commissioners* [2019] EWCA Civ 854, [2019] 3 All ER 590 at [6]–[9], [11], [18]–[19], [22], per Newey LJ

CONSPIRACY

[For 25 Halsbury's Laws of England (5th Edn) (2016) para 78 see now 25 Halsbury's Laws of England (5th Edn) (2020) paras 104–105.]

CONSTITUTIONAL LAW

[For 20 Halsbury's Laws of England (5th Edn) (2014) para 1 see now 20 Halsbury's Laws of England (5th Edn) (2023) para 1.]

CONSTRUCTION ESTABLISHMENT

[Industrial Training Act 1982, s 11(2); Industrial Training Levy (Construction Industry Training Board) Order 2015, SI 2015/701, art 5(2). Company providing freelance operatives to clients in the construction industry.] '[62] It is common ground that if an employer is in the construction industry but does not have a qualifying construction establishment, there can be no assessment to levy. For an assessment there must therefore be a relevant "construction establishment"; that is to say, an establishment of the employer "engaged wholly or mainly in the construction industry during the necessary period". It is also common ground that this question resolves to whether construction activities take place "from" the Bridlington head office so that it is a "construction establishment" within the meaning of art 5(2) of the 2015 Order.

...

'[72] The 2015 Order, not least arts 5(4) and 7(1) and (2), envisages persons employed (in the extended sense) "at or from" a relevant construction establishment. The ordinary case will be one in which workers doing construction work carry it out *at* the construction establishment at which they are employed. However, the legislation has a wider reach and plainly extends also to cover people who are not employed to do their work *at* a construction establishment, but who are employed *from* a different place (or base) to that at which they do their work activities, reflecting the wide range of circumstances deemed to be employment and workers who are treated as employees for levy purposes under the 1982 Act.

...

'[76] In my judgment, both as a matter of law and on the facts I have summarised, the Employment Tribunal was entitled to conclude that Hudson's operatives are employed *from* the head office at Bridlington which is a construction establishment accordingly, and Lambert J was correct to reject this ground of appeal. ...' *Hudson Contract Services Ltd v Construction Industry Training Board* [2020] EWCA Civ 328, [2020] 4 All ER 1007 at [62], [72], [76], per Smiler LJ

CONTEMPT OF COURT

[For 22 Halsbury's Laws of England (5th Edn) (2012) para 2 see now 24 Halsbury's Laws of England (5th Edn) (2019) para 2.]

CONTEXT

Australia '[27] The modern approach to statutory interpretation, as Sir Anthony Mason observed more than 35 years ago in *K & S Lake City Freighters Pty Ltd v Gordon & Gotch Ltd* (1985) 157 CLR 309 at 315; 60 ALR 509 at 514; 2 MVR 289 at 292, "insists that the context be considered *in the first instance*, especially in the case of general words, and not merely at some later stage when ambiguity might be thought to arise" (emphasis added). The importance of context has routinely been emphasised by the High Court in cases concerned with statutory interpretation ....

...

'[30] It has also been emphasised that "context" is to be understood in a broad sense and not confined to the immediate context supplied by other provisions in a statute of which one or more provisions are the subject of the immediate inquiry by the Court. Context extends to include the existing state of the law, legislative purpose and any mischief which the statute was intended to remedy: see, for example, *CIC* [*CIC Insurance Ltd v Bankstown Football Club Ltd* (1997) 187 CLR 384; 141 ALR 618] at CLR 408; ALR 635; *Maloney* [*Maloney v R* (2013) 252 CLR 168; 298 ALR 308; [2013] HCA 28] at [324]; *SZTAL* [*SZTAL v Minister for Immigration and Border Protection* (2017) 262 CLR 362; 347 ALR 405; [2017] HCA 34] at [14].

'[31] Words, whether used in a statute or more generally, always exist in and take their meaning from the particular context in which they are used. That context may expose any mischief which a statute is directed towards redressing and may reveal the purpose underpinning the enactment. That purpose, in turn, guides the preferred meaning to be given to the words being construed. The process of statutory interpretation may thus be seen as a holistic one or, as Campbell JA has identified both judicially and extra-judicially, as one involving something akin to hermeneutic reasoning: see *Thomas v New South Wales* (2008) 74 NSWLR 34; [2008] NSWCA 316 at [22]; *Waugh Hotel Management Pty Ltd v Marrickville Council* (2009) 171 LGERA 112; [2009] NSWCA 390 at [118]; *AVS Group of Companies Pty Ltd v Commissioner of Police* (2010) 78 NSWLR 302; [2010] NSWCA 81 at [133]–[137]; and J Campbell and R Campbell, "Why Statutory Interpretation is Done as it is Done" (2014) 39 *Australian Bar Review* 1.' *Sydney Seaplanes Pty Ltd (t/a Sydney Seaplanes) v Page* [2021] NSWCA 204, (2021) 393 ALR 485 at [27], [30]–[31], per Bell P

CONTRACT

[For 22 Halsbury's Laws of England (5th Edn) (2012) para 201 see now 22 Halsbury's Laws of England (5th Edn) (2019) para 1.]

Contract of record

[For 22 Halsbury's Laws of England (5th Edn) (2012) para 215 see now 22 Halsbury's Laws of England (5th Edn) (2019) para 11.]

Contract made by deed

[For 22 Halsbury's Laws of England (5th Edn) (2012) para 216 see now 22 Halsbury's Laws of England (5th Edn) (2019) para 12.]

Executed contract

[For 22 Halsbury's Laws of England (5th Edn) (2012) para 205 see now 22 Halsbury's Laws of England (5th Edn) (2019) para 6.]

Executory contract

[For 22 Halsbury's Laws of England (5th Edn) (2012) para 205 see now 22 Halsbury's Laws of England (5th Edn) (2019) para 6.]

Illegal contract

[For 22 Halsbury's Laws of England (5th Edn) (2012) para 452 see now 22 Halsbury's Laws of England (5th Edn) (2019) para 243.]

Simple contract

[For 22 Halsbury's Laws of England (5th Edn) (2012) para 218 see now 22 Halsbury's Laws of England (5th Edn) (2019) para 14.]

Void contract

[For 22 Halsbury's Laws of England (5th Edn) (2012) para 207 see now 22 Halsbury's Laws of England (5th Edn) (2019) para 4.]

Voidable contract

[For 22 Halsbury's Laws of England (5th Edn) (2012) para 207 see now 22 Halsbury's Laws of England (5th Edn) (2019) para 4.]

CONTRIBUTION

Insurance

[For 60 Halsbury's Laws of England (5th Edn) (2011) paras 233–234 see now 60 Halsbury's Laws of England (5th Edn) (2018) paras 212–213.]

CONTRIBUTORY

[For 17 Halsbury's Laws of England (5th Edn) (2011) para 661 et seq see now 17 Halsbury's Laws of England (5th Edn) (2017) para 599 et seq.]

CONTROL

Canada [Income Tax Act, RSC 1985, c 1 (5th Supp), s 111; if control of corporation is acquired, non-capital losses from before acquisition cannot be carried over.] '**80** First, the text of s 111(5) references "control". While control is not expressly defined within the provision or the Act, this Court concluded in *Duha Printers* [*Duha Printers (Western) Ltd v Canada*, [1998] 1 SCR 795] that it refers to *de jure* control. The general test for de jure control is "whether the controlling party enjoys, by virtue of its shareholdings, the ability to elect the majority of the board of directors" (*Duha Printers*, at para 36; R Taylor and M-C Marcil, "Duha Printers Revisited: Issues Regarding Corporate Control" (2022), 70 *Can Tax J* 495, at pp 504–507; G Lord et al, *Les principes de l'imposition au Canada* (13th ed 2002), at s 3.3; *Explanatory Notes*, at pp 502–504; at common law, see *Buckerfield's Ltd v Minister of National Revenue* [1965] 1 Ex CR 299). The power to select a majority of directors generally means the power to choose those who manage the affairs of the corporation, subject, in particular, to the constating documents or a unanimous shareholder agreement (*Duha Printers*, at para 85; see also *Canada Business Corporations Act*, RSC 1985, c C-44 ("*CBCA*"), ss 2(3) and 102(1); *Business Corporations Act*, RSO 1990, c B16, ss 1(5) and 115(1); Business Corporations Act, CQLR, c S-31.1, ss 2 "to control" and 112; *Civil Code of Québec*, arts 310, 335 and 336). I will return to the concept of *de jure* control, in contrast to *de facto* control, below.

...

'**113** In light of the foregoing, the object, spirit and purpose of s 111(5) is to prevent corporations from being acquired by unrelated parties in order to deduct their unused losses against income from another business for the benefit of new shareholders. Parliament sought to ensure that a lack of continuity in a corporation's identity was accompanied by a corresponding break in its ability to carry over non-capital losses. This is the rationale underlying the provision and properly explains why Parliament enacted s 111(5).

…

'**116** In s 111(5), Parliament has clearly chosen a test for control: *de jure* control. *De jure* control was a reasonable marker for the situations in which a corporation's identity has changed. This being so, it is primarily a means of giving effect to Parliament's aim, rather than a complete encapsulation of the aim itself. As with any provision, Parliament had to select a general test for s 111(5) among the options available: it had good reason to select the *de jure* control test over a broad *de facto* control test, which would have captured a variety of conduct unrelated to Parliament's aims. Again, the test to apply on the straightforward application of s 111(5) is not in dispute. However, *de jure* control does not, in itself, explain what was concerning to Parliament, as is amply demonstrated by a careful analysis of the intrinsic and extrinsic evidence. Respectfully, my colleague's reasons conflate the means found within a provision's text (in this case, *de jure* control) with the provision's underlying rationale; this approach would have implications for a variety of provisions involving a control test, such that the GAAR would effectively not apply.

…

'**170** In short, Iacobucci J in *Duha Printers* took a purposive approach to interpreting the word "control". Interpreted literally, "control" could mean any type of influence over a corporation (para 35). Nevertheless, Iacobucci J concluded that the "general purpose" of s 111(5) – preventing the transfer of non-capital losses from one corporation to another – does not expand the meaning of *de jure* control (para 88). Therefore, even prior to the adoption of the GAAR [Income Tax Act], one thing was clear: Parliament intended the acquisition of *de jure* control – and only the acquisition of *de jure* control – to trigger the application of s 111(5). To this day, Parliament continues to rely upon the distinction between *de jure* and *de facto* control. And despite my colleague's suggestion to the contrary, the GAAR cannot eliminate this distinction.' *Deans Knight Income Corp v Canada* [2023] SCJ No 16, 2023 SCC 16 at paras 80, 113, 116, 170, per Rowe J

CONVICTION

[Forfeiture Act 1982, s 2(3): 'In any case where a person stands convicted of an offence of which unlawful killing is an element, the court shall not make an order under this section modifying the effect of the forfeiture rule in that case unless proceedings for the purpose are brought before the expiry of the period of three months beginning with his conviction'.] '[34] In my judgment, where there is an initial conviction followed by an appeal, and then a subsequent conviction, it is the *subsequent* conviction which is the relevant one for the purposes of s 2(3) of the Act and the time-limit provided for. So, for these reasons, I respectfully disagree with the passage cited from *Rossdale* [Dew, Bedworth and Beer*Rossdale: Probate and Administration of Estates* (5th edn, 2016) 295].

'[35] I return therefore to the question of the actual event or events which constitutes or constitute the 'conviction' for the purposes of s 2(3). The word "conviction" may mean different things in different contexts. …

…

'[40] The question before me is what the word "conviction" means in s 2(3) of the 1982 Act. As I have said, it appears that HHJ Norris QC in *Re Land* [*Re Land (decd), Land v Land* [2006] EWHC 2069 (Ch), [2007] 1 All ER 324] assumed without argument that it meant the occasion of the guilty plea by the defendant in the case, rather than the occasion on which the court sentenced the defendant to a term of imprisonment. …

…

'[43] It is clear from [the Criminal Law Act 1967, s 6(2), (5)] that the defendant to a murder charge may plead guilty to manslaughter, and, if she is convicted of manslaughter on that plea, she is automatically acquitted of murder. It is also clear that, for this purpose, "convicted" cannot simply refer to the making of the plea by the defendant. It is necessary that the court should *accept* the plea, and that is a formal step in the proceedings. …

'[44] This means that there is in fact a third candidate for the meaning of "conviction" in s 2(3) of the 1982 Act, which is the occasion on which the court accepts the plea of guilty to manslaughter. In the present case, the claimant pleaded not guilty to murder and tendered a plea of guilty to manslaughter on 5 April 2019. The Crown indicated that it was willing to accept the guilty plea to manslaughter and not guilty plea to murder on 29 May 2019. But it was not until 7 June 2019 that there was a hearing before the court at which the plea of guilty to manslaughter was accepted by the court and she was sentenced. So in the present case it does not matter whether "conviction" means the occasion when the plea of guilty to manslaughter was accepted by the court or the occasion on which the claimant was sentenced, since in this case they occurred on the same day.

'[45] In my judgment, the word "conviction" in s 2(3) of the 1982 Act does not refer to the occasion of the plea of guilty to manslaughter, but to the occasion (if they are at the same time) when the plea is accepted and the defendant is sentenced. On the facts of the present case, it is not strictly necessary for me to decide which is the relevant occasion if the plea is accepted and the defendant is sentenced on different days. However, the reasoning of the Court of Criminal Appeal in *R v Cole* [[1965] 2 All ER 29, [1965] 2 QB 388] in deciding that the court retains a discretion to refuse to accept a plea to a lesser offence is based on the proposition that the defendant may with the consent of the judge change his plea at any time *up until sentence is passed*.' *Re Challen (deceased); Challen v Challen* [2020] EWHC 1330 (Ch), [2021] 2 All ER 738 at [34]–[35], [40], [43]–[45], per Judge Paul Matthews sitting as a Judge of the High Court

COOKIE

'[10] … . A "cookie" is a small block of data that is placed on a device when the user visits a website. A "third party cookie" is a cookie placed on the device not by the website visited by the user but by a third party whose content is included on that website. Third party cookies are often used to gather information about internet use, and in particular web pages visited over time, to enable the delivery to the user of advertisements tailored to interests inferred from the user's browsing history.' *Lloyd v Google LLC* [2021] UKSC 50, [2022] 2 All ER 209 at [10], per Lord Leggatt JSC

COPARCENARY

[For 87 Halsbury's Laws of England (5th Edn) (2017) paras 192–193 see now 87 Halsbury's Laws of England (5th Edn) (2022) paras 192–193.]

CORONAVIRUS

In this Act: 'coronavirus' means severe acute respiratory syndrome coronavirus 2 (SARS-CoV-2); 'coronavirus disease' means COVID-19 (the official designation of the disease which can be caused by coronavirus)' (Coronavirus Act 2020, s 1(1))

Coronavirus test device

See also MEDICAL DEVICE

'Coronavirus test device' means an *in vitro* diagnostic medical device for the detection of the presence of a viral antigen or viral ribonucleic acid (RNA) specific to severe acute respiratory syndrome coronavirus 2 (SARS-CoV-2). (Medical Devices Regulations 2002, SI 2002/618, reg 2(1) (as amended by SI 2021/910))

CORPORATION

Corporation aggregate

[For 24 Halsbury's Laws of England (5th Edn) (2010) para 312 see now 24 Halsbury's Laws of England (5th Edn) (2019) para 412.]

Corporation sole

[For 24 Halsbury's Laws of England (5th Edn) (2010) para 314 see now 24 Halsbury's Laws of England (5th Edn) (2019) para 414.]

CORROBORATION

[For 28 Halsbury's Laws of England (5th Edn) (2015) para 539 see now 28 Halsbury's Laws of England (5th Edn) (2021) para 552.]

COSTS

[For 29 Halsbury's Laws of England (5th Edn) (2014) para 310 see now 29 Halsbury's Laws of England (5th Edn) (2019) para 310.]

[For 12A Halsbury's Laws of England (5th Edn) (2015) paras 1688, 1702, 1704 see now 12A Halsbury's Laws of England (5th Edn) (2020) paras 1653, 1667, 1669.]

Of appeal

[For 12 Halsbury's Laws of England (5th Edn) (2015) para 1737 et seq see now 12A Halsbury's Laws of England (5th Edn) (2020) para 1645 et seq.]

Of reference to arbitration

[For 2 Halsbury's Laws of England (5th Edn) (2017) para 570 et seq see now 2 Halsbury's Laws of England (5th Edn) (2023) para 670 et seq.]

COUNTERCLAIM

[For 11 Halsbury's Laws of England (5th Edn) (2015) para 367 et seq see now 11 Halsbury's Laws of England (5th Edn) (2020) para 361 et seq.]

COUNTY PALATINE

[For 20 Halsbury's Laws of England (5th Edn) (2014) para 135 see now 20 Halsbury's Laws of England (5th Edn) (2023) para 134.]

COURT

[For 24 Halsbury's Laws of England (5th Edn) (2010) para 606 see now 24A Halsbury's Laws of England (5th Edn) (2019) para 6.]

[Third Parties (Rights against Insurers) Act 2010, s 2(6): where the court makes a declaration under s 2, the effect of which is that the insurer is liable to the claimant, the court may give the appropriate judgment against the insurer; whether employment tribunal a 'court'.] '[17] Unlike the High Court, [Employment Tribunals] have no inherent jurisdiction. They exercise jurisdiction only in cases where statute confers it. ETs have exclusive jurisdiction in many areas, including unfair dismissal and discrimination in the course of employment. ETs also have concurrent jurisdiction with civil courts in respect of equal pay claims and certain contractual claims brought under Employment Tribunals Extension of Jurisdiction (England and Wales) Order 1994, SI 1994/1623 and the Scottish equivalent (SI 1994/1624). Claims under the 2010 Act are not among those listed in the 1994 Extension of Jurisdiction Orders.

...

'[23] The authorities indicate that whether a tribunal is to be treated as a "court" for the purposes of a statute or rule depends on context. We were referred to a number of reported cases.

...

'[32] The two authorities on whether an ET is a "court" which featured most prominently in argument were *Peach Grey v Sommers* [*Peach Grey & Co (a firm) v Sommers* [1995] 2 All ER 513], relied on by Mr Gray-Jones, and *Brennan v Sunderland* [*Brennan v Sunderland City Council* [2012] ICR 1183], relied on by Mr Mitchell. Despite the eminence of the presiding judges in each case, neither of these cases is binding on us, the first being a decision of a Divisional Court and the second a decision of the EAT. I entirely agree with all the reasons given by Rose LJ in *Peach Grey* for holding that an ET should be regarded as a court for the purposes of the contempt jurisdiction. They are, in my view, of general application.

...

'[39] Like Kerr J, I do not accept the argument that the ET's lack of enforcement powers is a reason why it should not be considered a "court" within s 2(6). Parliament has provided that enforcement of ET judgments for the payment of money is dealt with by county courts in order to avoid the perceived inefficiency of creating a separate division of ET staff including bailiffs and the like, not because it regards the ET as too lowly or inadequate to exercise such powers. The county court has no discretion to revisit the decision of the ET and, as I understand it, applications for enforcement are dealt with administratively without a hearing.

'[40] I also reject, as Kerr J did, the suggestion that Parliament could not have intended ETs to deal with questions of insurance law. ETs regularly have to deal with difficult questions of law across a variety of topics, not confined to what would be regarded as mainstream employment law. ...

...

'[42] Accordingly, despite the series of points which Mr Mitchell deployed with skill and ingenuity, I am in no doubt that an ET is a "court" within the meaning of s 2(6) of the 2010 Act.' *Watson v Hemingway Design Ltd* [2021] EWCA Civ 67, [2021] 4 All ER 805 at [17], [23], [32], [39]–[40], [42], per Bean LJ

Court of a State

Australia [Commonwealth Constitution, Ch III; Judiciary Act 1903 (Cth), s 39.] '[172] As was apparent from the summary of the submissions which I have set out above, each of the parties approached the question of whether the Tribunal [New South Wales Civil and Administrative Tribunal] was a "court of a State" for the purpose of Ch III of the Constitution in a somewhat different fashion. The applicant and the Commonwealth approached it as a matter of construing the legislation which established the body, while the contradictors suggested that, if all the indispensable features of a "court" were present, then it was a "court of a State" for the purpose of Ch III of the Constitution irrespective of whether the State legislature intended to create it as such.

'[173] In the present case, I do not think that the different approaches yield different results.

It will be unusual to find that the legislature created a body with all the essential characteristics of a "court" for the purpose of Ch III of the Constitution while not intending it to be a "court" in some other sense.

'[174] In *Pompano* [*Assistant Commissioner Condon v Pompano Pty Ltd* (2013) 252 CLR 38; 295 ALR 638; [2013] HCA 7] at [125], the majority stated that "independence and impartiality are defining characteristics of all of the courts of the Australian judicial system". Similarly, Gageler J emphasised at [182]–[183] that, for a court to be able to act judicially, it "must have institutional integrity: it must 'be and appear to be an independent and impartial tribunal'", citing *Forge* [*Forge v Australian Securities and Investments Commission* (2006) 228 CLR 45; 229 ALR 223; 59 ACSR 1; [2006] HCA 44] at [78]; *Bradley* [*North Australian Aboriginal Legal Aid Service Inc v Bradley* (2004) 218 CLR 146; 206 ALR 315; [2004] HCA 31] at [29].

'[175] However, there are three things to be noted in this context. The first is that, as was pointed out in *Bradley* at [30], "no exhaustive statement of what constitutes [the minimum standard] in all cases is possible". The second is that it is clear that a "court of a State" does not have to be solely constituted by judges with the same terms of appointment as s 72 of the Constitution provides for judges of federal courts: see *Commonwealth v Hospital Contribution Fund of Australia* (1982) 150 CLR 49 at 61; 40 ALR 673 at 682 (*Hospital Contribution Fund*); *Forge* at [40]–[41].

'[176] The third matter is this. The fact that the Tribunal has some of the "trappings" or features of a court does not necessarily mean it is a "court of a State" for the purpose of Ch III of the Constitution. …

…

'[184] Applying these principles to the present case, I am of the view that, although the Tribunal has many of the features of a "court" and can, in a number of areas, exercise State judicial power, it is not a "court of a State" for the purpose of Ch III of the Constitution. My reasons are set out below. While none of these may be decisive individually, in combination, they lead to the clear conclusion that the Tribunal is not a "court of a State".

…

'[190] The combination of these factors means that, in my view, the State legislature did not intend the Tribunal to be a "court of a State" for the purpose of Ch III of the Constitution and that the Tribunal did not have the necessary degree of independence and impartiality to constitute such a court. Thus, irrespective of the approach adopted, the same conclusion is reached.

…

'[192] In these circumstances, I am of the opinion that the Tribunal was not a "court of a State" for the purpose of Ch III of the Constitution or s 39 of the Judiciary Act 1903 (Cth).' *Attorney-General (NSW) v Gatsby (2018 of 66655)* [2018] NSWCA 254, (2018) 361 ALR 570 at [172]–[176], [184], [190], [192], per Bathurst CJ

COURT MARTIAL

[For 3 Halsbury's Laws of England (5th Edn) (2011) paras 633, 638 see now 3 Halsbury's Laws of England (5th Edn) (2019) paras 534, n 1, 534, 538.]

COVENANT

[For 32 Halsbury's Laws of England (5th Edn) (2012) para 448 see now 32 Halsbury's Laws of England (5th Edn) (2019) para 448.]

[For 62 Halsbury's Laws of England (5th Edn) (2016) para 125 see now 62 Halsbury's Laws of England (5th Edn) (2022) para 142.]

For quiet enjoyment

[For 62 Halsbury's Laws of England (5th Edn) (2016) para 404 see now 62 Halsbury's Laws of England (5th Edn) (2022) para 438.]

CRIME

[For 25 Halsbury's Laws of England (5th Edn) (2016) para 1 see now 25 Halsbury's Laws of England (5th Edn) (2020) para 1.]

CRIMINAL CAUSE OR MATTER

[Senior Courts Act 1981, s 18(1)(a): no appeal to Court of Appeal from any judgment of the High Court in any 'criminal cause or matter'; appeal against refusal of judicial review of decision to discontinue prosecutions.] '[22] In my opinion, it is wholly plain that the judgment below was in a "criminal cause or matter". That being so, by reason of the provisions of s 18(1) of the 1981 Act no appeal lies to this court.

'[23] It does no harm first to view the matter without reference to authority. In the present case, there had been ongoing criminal proceedings in the Crown Court. The decision of the CPS was to discontinue those criminal proceedings. How, it may be asked, can a judgment upholding such a decision be anything other than in a criminal matter? Mr Schama could give no sensible answer.

...

'[25] At all events, what cannot here validly be maintained is that there is no criminal cause or matter involved simply and solely because the decision under challenge is a decision of the executive sought to be challenged on public law grounds in judicial review proceedings. Such an approach most emphatically is not the law.' *R (on the application of Thakrar) v Crown Prosecution Service* [2019] EWCA Civ 874, [2020] 1 All ER 704 at [22]–[23], [25], per Davis LJ

CRIMINAL ORGANIZATION

Canada [Criminal Code, RSC 1985, c C-46, s 467.1(1).] '**12** ... Section 467.1(1) of the *Criminal Code* defines a "criminal organization" as follows:

criminal organization means a group, however organized, that:

(a) is composed of three or more persons in or outside Canada; and

(b) has as one of its main purposes or main activities the facilitation or commission of one or more serious offences that, if committed, would likely result in the direct or indirect receipt of a material benefit, including a financial benefit, by the group or by any of the persons who constitute the group.

It does not include a group of persons that forms randomly for the immediate commission of a single offence.

...

'**76** Not every group of three or more persons that facilitates or commits a serious offence for a material benefit is a criminal organization. This Court in *Venneri* [*R v Venneri*, 2012 SCC 33, [2012] 2 SCR 211] interpreted Parliament's direction in s 467.1(1) of the Criminal Code that a criminal organization be "organized" in some fashion as requiring the group to have "some form of structure and degree of continuity" before the "exceptional regime" of the organized crime provisions of the Criminal Code is engaged (para 29).

...

'**78** The purpose of the *Criminal Code*'s criminal organization regime is to identify and undermine groups that pose an enhanced threat to society due to the institutional advantages of structure and continuity (*Venneri*, at para 40). Structured and continuous criminal entities offer advantages to their members by consolidating and retaining knowledge; sharing customers and resources; developing specializations; dividing labour; fostering trust and loyalty; and developing reputations in the community, including for violence (para 36). These same advantages enable criminal organizations to elude law enforcement more effectively.

'**79** To counteract these advantages, Parliament has enacted not only substantive criminal organization offences but also heightened investigative, procedural and penal consequences where a criminal organization is involved or alleged to be involved in an offence. These include greater police powers for certain authorizations and warrants (ss 185(1.1), 186(1.1), 186.1, 492.1(6)(a) and (b) and 492.2(5)(a) and (b)) and a reverse onus for bail (s 515(6)(a)(ii)). At sentencing, involvement in a criminal organization is an aggravating factor (s 718.2(a)(iv)), conditional sentences are unavailable (s 742.1(d)), and parole ineligibility can be delayed (s 743.6(1.1)). Sentences for certain criminal organization offences must be served consecutively to other sentences arising from the same event (s 467.14). Murder is elevated to first degree murder where the death is caused for the benefit of, at the direction of, or in association with a criminal organization (s 231(6.1)).

'**80** The enhanced threat to society posed by criminal organizations by virtue of their structure and continuity explains why the criminal organization regime is considered exceptional. Groups of individuals acting in concert, where they lack structure and continuity, do not pose the same enhanced threat to society constituted by criminal organizations (*Venneri*, at paras 27, 29 and 40). As Fish J explained in *Venneri*:

> Stripped of the features of continuity and structure, "organized crime" simply becomes all serious crime committed by a group of three or more persons for a material benefit. Parliament has already criminalized that activity through the offences of conspiracy, aiding and abetting, and the "common intention" provisions of the *Code* (see, eg, ss 21 and 465(1)). [para 35]

Identifying a group as a criminal organization when it lacks the requisite qualities of structure and continuity "would cast a net broader than that intended by Parliament" and subject the group to the exceptional procedural and substantive consequences of the criminal organization regime (paras 31 and 35).

...

'**84** I agree with the appellant and the intervener, the Criminal Lawyers' Association of Ontario, that careful consideration of a group's structure and continuity is needed to guard against improper reasoning in identifying a criminal organization. This is needed to avoid the risk that police, lawyers, juries, and judges could identify a group as a criminal organization based on shared characteristics such as ethnicity, cultural background, neighbourhood, religion, language, or dialect. While such characteristics may indicate a common social or cultural identity among persons who commit offences, they are irrelevant in identifying the existence of a criminal organization. To view such characteristics as indicative of organized crime is to depart from Parliament's intention and to do so in a way that undercuts a key goal of Canadian society, cultural diversity.

'**85** The flexibility with which the definition of a criminal organization is applied must not become an invitation for irrelevant considerations or improper reasoning. The risk of improper reasoning is especially acute where an accused is a member of a marginalized community, underrepresented among police, lawyers, jurors, or the judiciary, and whose characteristics and practices may well be less familiar and possibly the subject of biases, prejudices, or stereotypes among those tasked with enforcing the law and passing judgment. The courts have recognized the risks of racial bias or stereotypical reasoning, including subconscious biases, in the criminal justice system (see, eg, *R v Williams* [1998] 1 SCR 1128, at paras 21–22; *Barton*, at paras 195–197). Just as the definition of a criminal organization must not be *limited* to stereotypical models of organized crime, care must also be taken not to identify a criminal organization merely *because* the group appears to satisfy some stereotypical model. The trier of fact's focus when tasked with identifying a criminal organization needs at all times to remain fixed on whether the *particular* group in question possesses the distinguishing qualities of a criminal organization, ie, structure and continuity.' *R v Abdullahi* [2023] SCJ No 19, 2023 SCC 19 at paras 12, 76, 78–80, 84–85, per Rowe J

CROSSING

[International Regulations for Preventing Collisions at Sea 1972, rr 15–17 (the crossing rules).] '[57] Rule 15 seeks to deal comprehensively with every other steady bearing collision situation, ie where the vessels are not overtaking or on reciprocal courses, but crossing courses. It provides as follows:

> "When two power-driven vessels are crossing so as to involve risk of collision, the vessel which has the other on her own starboard side shall keep out of the way and shall, if the circumstances of the case admit, avoid crossing ahead of the other vessel."

In this context "crossing" simply means that their courses are not parallel but intersecting: ie that the lines representing the probable future course of each will intersect at some point. That of itself may not create a risk of collision. The seas are full of vessels on crossing courses which come nowhere near each other. But if they are approaching each other and the bearings of each, taken from the other, do not appreciably change, then there will be a risk of collision. Unless one of them keeps clear of the other, the two vessels will be likely to meet each other and collide. That is what r 7(d)(i) provides in express terms. Although couched in terms of "deeming" this is not a deeming contrary to the facts. It is factually true as well. That is why it is described as an "infallible warning" of a risk of collision in *The Aracelio Iglesias* [[1968] 2 Lloyd's Rep 7, CA].' *Nautical Challenge Ltd v Evergreen Marine (UK) Ltd; The Alexandra 1 and Ever Smart* [2021] UKSC 6, [2021] 4 All ER 1113 at [57], per Lord Briggs and Lord Hamblen JJSC

CROWN EMPLOYMENT

[Employment Rights Act 1996, s 191.] '[23] Section 191(3) provides that "In this Act 'Crown employment' means employment under or for the purposes of a government department or any officer or body exercising on behalf of the Crown functions conferred by a statutory provision". Clearly, "employment" in this section cannot mean "employment under a contract" because it would then add nothing to the definition in s 230(3). The predecessor to s 191 was inserted into the Industrial Relations Act 1971 because historically Crown servants had not been seen to be employed under contracts of service and had not been able to complain of wrongful dismissal. The object was to enable them to complain of unfair dismissal and enjoy the other employment rights listed in s 191(2). Thus, argues the appellant, s 191 is apt to give her the protection of Pt IVA even if she is not employed under a contract.

'[24] The definition in s 191(3) has two limbs: employment under or for the purposes of a government department; and employment under or for the purposes of an officer or body exercising on behalf of the Crown functions conferred by a statutory provision. For the reasons given earlier, it is impossible to regard the judiciary as employed under or for the purposes of the Ministry of Justice. They are not civil servants or the equivalent of civil servants. They do not work for the ministry. It is slightly more plausible to regard them as working under or for the purposes of the Lord Chief Justice, who since the 2005 Act [Constitutional Reform Act 2005], has had statutory responsibilities in relation to the judiciary: under s 7 of that Act, he is responsible for the maintenance of appropriate arrangements for the welfare, training and guidance of the judiciary of England and Wales (within the resources provided by the Lord Chancellor) and for their deployment and the allocation of work within the courts. As already noted, he also shares some responsibility for appointments, discipline and removal with the Lord Chancellor. But it is difficult to think that, by conferring these functions upon the Lord Chief Justice, the 2005 Act brought about such a fundamental change in the application of s 191. Judges do not work "under and for the purposes of" those functions of the Lord Chief Justice but for the administration of justice in the courts of England and Wales in accordance with their oaths of office. Mutatis mutandis, the same reasoning would apply to the identical definition of crown employment in art 236(3) of the Employment Rights (Northern Ireland) Order 1996, SI 1996/1919.

'[25] It is perhaps worth noting that s 83(2) and (9) of the Equality Act 2010, passed since the 2005 Act, defines "employment" as covering "Crown employment" as defined in s 191 of the 1996 Act. But it also makes express provision, in ss 50 and 51, prohibiting discrimination in relation to, among other things, appointment to public offices. These are defined to include officers appointed by or on the recommendation of a member of the executive (such as the Lord Chancellor) or by the Lord Chief Justice or Senior President of Tribunals. Thus judicial office-holders are clearly protected by these provisions, which would have been quite unnecessary had they already been protected as persons in Crown employment. Sections 50 and 51 do not apply in Northern Ireland, but this does not affect the force of this point.' *Gilham v Ministry of Justice* [2019] UKSC 44, [2020] 1 All ER 1 at [23]–[25], per Lady Hale P

CRUEL

Canada [Canadian Charter of Rights and Freedoms 1982, s 12: everyone has the right not to be subjected to any cruel and unusual treatment or punishment.] '**1** This appeal requires this Court to decide whether s 12 of the *Canadian Charter of Rights and Freedoms* protects corporations from cruel and unusual treatment or punishment. Like our colleagues, we conclude that it does not, because corporations lie beyond s 12's protective scope. Simply put, the text "cruel and unusual" denotes protection that "only human beings can enjoy": *Irwin Toy Ltd v Quebec (Attorney General)* [1989] 1 SCR 927, at p 1004. The protective scope of s 12 is thus limited to human beings.

'**2** This Court's jurisprudence on s 12, in both its French and English versions, is marked by the concept of human dignity, as our colleagues have noted. And the existence of human beings behind the corporate veil is insufficient to ground a s 12 claim of right on behalf of a corporate entity, in light of the corporation's separate legal personality. Like our colleagues, and contrary to the majority at the Court of Appeal, we therefore reject the proposition that the effect of a corporation's bankruptcy on its stakeholders should be considered in determining the scope of s 12.

...

'**51** In my respectful view, s 12's purpose is to prevent the state from inflicting physical or mental pain and suffering through degrading and dehumanizing treatment or punishment. It is meant to protect human dignity and respect the inherent worth of individuals. Its intended beneficiaries are people, not corporations.

...

'**83** The *Oxford English Dictionary* defines "cruel", in relation to persons, as "[d]isposed to inflict suffering; indifferent to or taking pleasure in another's pain or distress, destitute of kindness or compassion; merciless, pitiless, hard-hearted" ((2nd ed 1989), vol IV, at p 78). It is also used to describe actions that are "proceeding from or showing indifference to or pleasure in another's distress" ("cruel", at p 78). When referring to conditions and circumstances, ie treatment or punishment, "cruel" means "[c]ausing or characterized by great suffering; extremely painful or distressing" (p 78).

'**84** Similarly, "cruelty" is defined in the *Oxford English Dictionary* as referring to:

1. The quality of being cruel; disposition to inflict suffering, delight in or indifference to the pain or misery of others; mercilessness, hard-heartedness: *esp.* as exhibited in action. Also, with *pl.*, an instance of this, a cruel deed; …
2. Severity of pain; excessive suffering; …
3. Severity, strictness, rigour; …

[p 79].

'**85** The term "*cruel*" is also defined in French by reference to the concept of suffering, which, as Chamberland JA noted, cannot be experienced by inanimate entities like corporations:

[TRANSLATION]

1. Taking pleasure in inflicting suffering, in witnessing suffering.
2. Denoting cruelty; showing the cruelty of humans.
3. Inflicting suffering through its harshness, its severity.
4. (Of persons). Without leniency, merciless.
5. (Of personified things). Inflicting suffering by manifesting a sort of hostility.
6. (Of persons). Indifferent, insensitive.

(Le Grand Robert de la langue française (2nd ed 2001), at pp 864–65)

'**86** In short, the ordinary meaning of the words cruel and unusual treatment or punishment centers on human pain and suffering. As Chamberland JA, eloquently stated:

> [TRANSLATION] It would completely distort the ordinary meaning of the words, in my view, to say that it is possible to be cruel to a corporate entity. Cruelty is inflicted on living beings of flesh and blood, be they human beings or animals. And not on corporations. Suffering, whether physical or mental, is unique to living beings, not corporate entities and inanimate objects without a soul or emotional life. [paras 53–56]

'**87** The fact that the word "everyone" is found in the text of s 12 cannot, by virtue of its literal meaning, expand the protection to corporations, without any regard for the purpose of the right as protecting *human* dignity. It is worth remembering that in *Irwin Toy*, this Court explained that "'[e]veryone' … must be read in light of the rest of the section and defined to exclude corporations and other artificial entities incapable of enjoying life, liberty or security of the person, and include only human beings" (p 1004).' *Quebec (Attorney General) v 9147-0732 Québec inc* [2020] SCJ No 32, 2020 SCC 32 at paras 1–2, per Brown and Rowe JJ and at paras 51, 83–87, per Abella J

CURTILAGE

Curtilage of a building

[Commons Act 2006, Sch 2, para 6.] '[1] This case concerns approximately 115 acres of land ("the Application Land"), which was registered with the First Respondent, Hampshire County Council ("HCC") as common land under the Commons Registration Act 1965 ("the 1965 Act"). The key issue is whether the Application Land met the statutory criteria for deregistration under para 6 of Sch 2 to the Commons Act 2006 ("the 2006 Act"). An Inspector appointed by the Second Respondent ("the Secretary of State") to determine the Appellant's application for deregistration decided that it did, and allowed the application. Holgate J quashed the Inspector's decision. In my judgment he was right to do so.

…

'[4] The issue turns on whether the Application Land, which forms the operational part of an airport, was "within the curtilage of a building" at and since the time when it was provisionally registered as common land. The building in question is a two-storey terminal building, with a footprint of about 360 m^2 and an overall floor area of about 760 m^2, which serves as the airport's operational hub.

'[5] If what is meant by "the curtilage of a building" is understood correctly, and all relevant factors are taken into account when determining whether the statutory requirements were satisfied in this case, the answer is no. This extensive area of operational airfield cannot properly be described as falling within the curtilage of the relatively small terminal building.

…

'[26] The ambit (or physical extent) of the curtilage of a building in any given case will be a question of fact and degree. Various factors may be helpful in resolving that question, including, where relevant, a consideration of the statutory consequences of a finding that land (or a building or other structure or object on it) falls within or outside of the curtilage of a building. In certain contexts, the Court may be slightly more generous in its application of the relevant factors to reach a particular result, bearing in mind the purposes of the governing statute; for example, when determining whether an ancillary structure falls within the curtilage of a listed building. But that does not mean that the concept of curtilage is different in listed building cases.

...

'[50] There are some words or expressions which are like an elephant; its essence is difficult to put into words, but you know it when you see it. "Curtilage" is a word of that nature. In *Barwick v Kent CC* (1992) 24 HLR 341, ("*Barwick*") Sir David Croom-Johnson made the following pertinent observation (at 346) with which I respectfully agree:

> "It is not possible to give a comprehensive definition of a curtilage. Indeed it would be most inadvisable. One can only describe a curtilage when one sees it and decides whether it was a curtilage, or not ..."

...

'[124] Holgate J was right to hold that the phrase "the curtilage of a building" in the 2006 Act requires the land in question to form part and parcel of the building to which it is related. The correct question is whether the land falls within the curtilage of the *building*, and not whether the land together with the building fall within, or comprise, a unit devoted to the same or equivalent function or purpose, nor whether the building forms part and parcel of some unit which includes that land. ...' *R (on the application of Hampshire County Council) v Secretary of State for Environment, Food and Rural Affairs (Blackbushe Airport Ltd and others, interested parties)* [2021] EWCA Civ 398, [2022] 1 All ER 524 at [1], [4]–[5], [26], [50], [124], per Andrews LJ

CUSTOM

[For 32 Halsbury's Laws of England (5th Edn) (2012) paras 1, 6 see now 32 Halsbury's Laws of England (5th Edn) (2019) paras 1, 6.]

Of country

[For 1 Halsbury's Laws of England (5th Edn) (2017) para 450 see now 1 Halsbury's Laws of England (5th Edn) (2022) para 350.]

CYNICAL BREACH

'[36] I interject here that the description of Millgate's behaviour as "highhanded and opportunistic" is what some commentators, especially in the context of breach of contract, have described as "cynical": see, for example, Peter Birks, 'Restitutionary Damages for Breach of Contract: *Snepp* and the Fusion of Law and Equity' [1989] LMCLQ 421. In line with this, I shall use the phrase "cynical breach" as a useful shorthand description of the conduct of Millgate in deliberately committing a breach of the restrictive covenant with a view to making profit from so doing.' Alexander Devine Children's *Cancer Trust v Housing Solutions Ltd* [2020] UKSC 45, [2021] 2 All ER 871 at [36], per Lord Burrows JSC

CY-PRÈS

Application to charity

[For 8 Halsbury's Laws of England (5th Edn) (2015) para 209 see now 8 Halsbury's Laws of England (5th Edn) (2019) para 207.]

Application to power of appointment

[For 80 Halsbury's Laws of England (5th Edn) (2013) para 4 see now 80 Halsbury's Laws of England (5th Edn) (2020) para 4.]

D

DAMAGE

[CPR Practice Direction 6B, para 3.1(9): requirement for suing a defendant who is outside the territorial jurisdiction of the English courts that 'damage was sustained … within the jurisdiction'. Road accident in Egypt, consequential damage in England.] '[49] … We are concerned here not with the completion of a cause of action in tort, a matter of substantive law, but with the scope of a jurisdictional rule which is intended to identify the appropriate forum for the adjudication of the resulting claim. In my view there is no justification in principle or in practice, for limiting "damage" in para 3.1(9)(a) to damage which is necessary to complete a cause of action in tort or, indeed, for according any special significance to a place simply because it was where the cause of action was completed. First, while damage is an essential element of many torts including negligence, many other torts, including trespass to the person and trespass to goods, are actionable per se, without proof of damage. There is therefore no warrant for reading para 3.1(9)(a), which is a rule of general application to claims in tort, in such a restrictive way.

'[50] Secondly, even in the case of those torts where actionability is conditional on proof of damage, the suggested link between damage completing a cause of action and the identification of an appropriate jurisdiction is unconvincing. …

'[51] Thirdly, damage is likely to be relevant to the identification of an appropriate jurisdiction for the adjudication of a claim in tort not because it may complete a cause of action but, more generally, because the damage actually suffered by the victim may, depending on all the circumstances of the case, serve to link the wrongdoing to a particular jurisdiction. In my view, therefore, there is no reason to read "damage" in para 3.1(9)(a) as limited to the damage which violates the claimant's right and which completes the cause of action. On the contrary, the word in its ordinary and natural meaning and when considered in the light of the purpose of the provision extends to the physical and financial damage caused by the wrongdoing, considerations which are apt to link a tort to the jurisdiction where such damage is suffered. Moreover, this reading is supported by the omission of the definite article in the current article of the rule, an amendment which was intended to reflect the decision in *Metall und Rohstoff* [*Metall und Rohstoff AG v Donaldson Lufkin & Jenrette Inc* [1989] 3 All ER 14, [1990] 1 QB 391] that it is sufficient that some significant damage has been sustained in the jurisdiction. (See *Brownlie I* [*Brownlie v Four Seasons Holdings Inc* [2017] UKSC 80, [2018] 2 All ER 91] per Lord Wilson at para [64], per Lord Clarke at para [68].)

…

'[81] For the reasons set out above, I consider that there is no sound reason to limit "damage" in gateway (9)(a) to damage which completes a cause of action. Furthermore, I can see no reason to apply within English domestic rules the distinction between direct and indirect damage which has now developed in the Brussels system. To my mind, the word "damage" in para 3.1(9)(a) of Practice Direction 6B simply refers to actionable harm, direct or indirect, caused by the wrongful act alleged. This reading reflects the ordinary and natural meaning of the word and is in accordance with the purpose of the provision and with principle. There is no need to limit its scope to direct as opposed to indirect damage, a distinction which in any event I consider obscure and likely to give rise to difficulty in its application. Furthermore, the Court of Appeal in *Metall und Rohstoff* was clearly correct in holding that a claimant may suffer damage within the meaning of the domestic tort gateway in more than one place.

'[82] The wider reading of damage within the meaning of the tort gateway, which I favour, does not confer on all claimants in personal injury cases a right to bring proceedings in the jurisdiction of their residence. The courts will be astute in ascertaining whether the dispute has its closest connection with this jurisdiction and the principle of forum non conveniens will provide a robust and effective mechanism for ensuring that claims which do not have their closest connection with this jurisdiction will not be accepted here.' *Brownlie v FS Cairo (Nile Plaza) LLC* [2021] UKSC 45, [2022] 3 All ER 207 at [49]–[51], [81]–[82], per Lord Lloyd-Jones JSC

[Data Protection Act 1988, s 13.] '[92] Two initial points can be made about the wording and structure of s 13. First, to recover compensation under this provision it is not enough to prove a breach by a data controller of its statutory duty under s 4(4) of the Act: an individual is only entitled to compensation under s 13 where "damage" – or in some circumstances "distress" – is suffered as a consequence of such a breach of duty. Second, it is plain from sub-s (2) that the term "damage" as it is used in s 13 does not include "distress". The term "material damage" is sometimes used to describe any financial loss or physical or psychological injury, but excluding distress (or other negative emotions not amounting to a recognised psychiatric illness): see eg *Watkins v Secretary of State for the Home Dept* [2006] UKHL 17, [2006] 2 All ER 353, [2006] 2 AC 395 (para [7]). Adopting this terminology, on a straightforward interpretation the term "damage" in s 13 refers only to material damage and compensation can only be recovered for distress if either of the two conditions set out in sub-s (2) is met.

...

'[138] ... I conclude that s 13 of the DPA 1998 cannot reasonably be interpreted as conferring on a data subject a right to compensation for any (non-trivial) contravention by a data controller of any of the requirements of the Act without the need to prove that the contravention has caused material damage or distress to the individual concerned.' *Lloyd v Google LLC* [2021] UKSC 50, [2022] 2 All ER 209 at [92], [138], per Lord Leggatt JSC

Pecuniary damage

[For 29 Halsbury's Laws of England (5th Edn) (2014) para 312 see now 29 Halsbury's Laws of England (5th Edn) (2019) para 312.]

DAMAGES

[For 29 Halsbury's Laws of England (5th Edn) (2014) para 304 see now 29 Halsbury's Laws of England (5th Edn) (2019) para 304.]

Aggravated damages

[For 29 Halsbury's Laws of England (5th Edn) (2014) para 322 see now 29 Halsbury's Laws of England (5th Edn) (2019) para 322.]

Liquidated damages

[For 29 Halsbury's Laws of England (5th Edn) (2014) para 311 see now 29 Halsbury's Laws of England (5th Edn) (2019) para 311.]

Liquidated damages and penalty distinguished

[For 29 Halsbury's Laws of England (5th Edn) (2014) para 551 see now 29 Halsbury's Laws of England (5th Edn) (2019) paras 550–551.]

Nominal damages

[For 29 Halsbury's Laws of England (5th Edn) (2014) paras 319–320 see now 29 Halsbury's Laws of England (5th Edn) (2019) paras 319–320.]

Prospective damages

[For 29 Halsbury's Laws of England (5th Edn) (2014) para 314 see now 29 Halsbury's Laws of England (5th Edn) (2019) para 314.]

Special damages

[For 29 Halsbury's Laws of England (5th Edn) (2014) para 317 see now 29 Halsbury's Laws of England (5th Edn) (2019) para 317.]

Statutory damages

[For 29 Halsbury's Laws of England (5th Edn) (2014) para 302 see now 29 Halsbury's Laws of England (5th Edn) (2019) para 302.]

DAMAGES-BASED AGREEMENT

[Courts and Legal Services Act 1990, s 58AA.] '[9] A DBA [damages-based agreement] is accordingly defined in s 58AA(3)(a) as an agreement between a person providing one of three specified types of services (advocacy, litigation or claims management) and the recipient of those services, which provides for the recipient to make a payment to the provider, the amount of which "is to be determined by reference to the amount of the financial benefit obtained". It is the latter aspect of the definition which makes the agreement "damages-based", in the sense that the stipulated remuneration for the services must take the form (broadly speaking) of a share of the damages recovered. That is the critical feature which distinguishes a DBA from a CFA [conditional fee agreement], under which a lawyer may stipulate for a success fee to become payable in specified circumstances, but not for a share of the damages recovered by the client.' *PACCAR Inc v Road Haulage Association Ltd (Association of Litigation Funders of England and Wales intervening)* [2021] EWCA Civ 299, [2021] 4 All ER 737 at [9], per Henderson LJ

(3) For the purposes of this section—
 (a) a damages-based agreement is an agreement between a person providing advocacy services, litigation services or claims management services and the recipient of those services which provides that—
  (i) the recipient is to make a payment to the person providing the services if the recipient obtains a specified financial benefit in connection with the matter in relation to which the services are provided, and
  (ii) the amount of that payment is to be determined by reference to the amount of the financial benefit obtained;
 (b) …

(Courts and Legal Services Act 1990, s 58AA(3) (s 58AA added by the Coroners and Justice Act 2009, s 154(1), (2)))

[Courts and Legal Services Act 1990, s 58AA(3).] '[1] In response to the recommendations in Jackson LJ's 2009 report on civil litigation costs, s 45 of the Legal Aid, Sentencing and Punishment of Offenders Act 2012 ("LASPO") made amendments to s 58AA of the Courts and Legal Services Act 1990 ("the 1990 Act"). These amendments, among other matters, legalised damages-based agreements ("DBAs") as a means of remuneration of a party's legal representatives in civil litigation. In consequence, it is now permissible for a claimant (which expression, for the purposes of this judgment, includes a counterclaiming defendant) to enter into an agreement with his solicitors to pay them a percentage of whatever he recovers from his opponent if he wins. However, in order to be enforceable, the DBA must strictly comply with the requirements of the relevant Regulations made by the Lord Chancellor pursuant to his powers under s 58AA(5) of the 1990 Act.

…

'[52] However, in my judgment the matter is put beyond doubt by the definition of "damages-based agreement" in s 58AA(3) of the primary statute. In order to qualify as a DBA, the agreement must provide for payment by the recipient of the services if he or she "obtains a specified financial benefit" from the litigation.

'[53] Mr Williams submitted that the primary legislation is neutral and can be interpreted as permitting defendants to enter into DBAs. The definition in s 58AA(3) refers to "the recipient" of the advocacy services, litigation services or claims management services. It is not limited to the provision of services to claimants. There was no reason why the dismissal of a claim in whole or in part should not be regarded as conferring 'a specified financial benefit' on the defendant. If he successfully defends the claim, he gains something of advantage, because he gets to keep his money or other property.

'[54] That submission ignores the fact that the successful defendant is financially no better off than he was at the start of the litigation. Indeed he may be considerably worse off, because he may have had to pay something to the claimant, even if the claim did not succeed in full. In Mr Wojakovski's case, he had to part with most of his shares in TGL.

'[55] In my judgment, the language of the statute is clear. I accept that the draftsman chose to refer to the "recipient of the services" rather than to the "claimant" – possibly to cater for the possibility that a DBA might be made in respect of what Mr Fulton described as an "outgoing" claim by a defendant, ie a counterclaim. I also accept that the phrase "specified financial benefit" is not confined to damages. Thus the expression "damages-based agreement" cannot be interpreted literally, as only applying to cases in which damages are paid (and not to debts or other forms of financial recovery). However, the word "obtains" envisages the litigant acquiring something that they do not already possess – by necessary implication, from the opposing party. That language is not apposite to describe a situation in which the defendant retains money or other assets of value, or is not required to make a payment or transfer of assets to the opposing party, even if this is the consequence of successfully resisting a claim for debt or damages, or a claim to those assets.' *Candey Ltd v Tonstate Group Ltd* [2022] EWCA Civ 936, [2023] 2 All ER 138 at [1], [52]–[55], per Andrews LJ

DANGEROUS DOG

[For 2 Halsbury's Laws of England (5th Edn) (2017) paras 221–229 see now 2 Halsbury's Laws of England (5th Edn) (2023) paras 231–239.]

DE BONIS NON

[For 103 Halsbury's Laws of England (5th Edn) (2010) para 793 see now 103 Halsbury's Laws of England (5th Edn) (20216) para 796.]

DEDICATION

[For 55 Halsbury's Laws of England (5th Edn) (2012) para 111 see now 55 Halsbury's Laws of England (5th Edn) (2019) para 142.]

DEED

[For 32 Halsbury's Laws of England (5th Edn) (2012) paras 201, 208 see now 32 Halsbury's Laws of England (5th Edn) (2019) paras 201, 208.]

DEED POLL

[For 32 Halsbury's Laws of England (5th Edn) (2012) para 203 see now 32 Halsbury's Laws of England (5th Edn) (2019) para 203.]

DEFAMATION

[For 32 Halsbury's Laws of England (5th Edn) (2012) paras 510, 543 see now 32 Halsbury's Laws of England (5th Edn) (2019) paras 509, 543.]

DEFEASANCE

[For 49 Halsbury's Laws of England (5th Edn) (2015) para 532 see now 49 Halsbury's Laws of England (5th Edn) (2021) para 495.]

DEFECT

[Council Directive 85/374/EEC; Consumer Protection Act 1987, s 3 ('CPA').] '[15] This appeal is unusual in that the legal issues concerning the application of the CPA are largely agreed. The basic principles may be summarised as follows:

(i) The Directive and the CPA have introduced a system of no-fault liability. The concept of "defect", introduced by the Directive and implemented by the CPA, is an autonomous one, defined in terms of failure of the product to meet an objective standard of safety that the court must evaluate.

(ii) The test of whether a product is defective is whether the safety of the product is not such as persons generally are entitled to expect. The test is not what is expected but one of entitled expectation. The test is an objective one. The standard of safety is measured by what the public at large is entitled to expect.

(iii) What persons generally are entitled to expect is assessed having regard to all the circumstances which are factually or legally relevant to the evaluation of safety, including the matters identified in s 3(2). This must be evaluated at the time when the product was supplied by its producer to another. The assessment of risks associated with a product, which might inform entitled expectations as to its safety, must be done at the time the product is supplied and not with the benefit of hindsight.

(iv) In determining whether a product met the level of safety persons generally were entitled to expect, the court is entitled to have regard to everything now known about it that is relevant to that enquiry, irrespective of whether that information was available at the time it was put on the market or has come to light subsequently.

(v) The burden of proof is on the consumer to establish a defect and a causal link to the injury. The standard and means of proof are matters for national law, subject to the principle of effectiveness.

(See *Wilkes v DePuy International Ltd* [2016] EWHC 3096 (QB), [2017] 3 All ER 589, [2018] QB 627 (paras [66], [76], [96]) per Hickinbottom J; *Gee v Depuy International Ltd* [2018] EWHC 1208 (QB) (paras [84]–[86], [98], [139]–[141]) per Andrews J; *NW v Sanofi Pasteur MSD SNC* (Case C-621/15) EU:C:2017:484, (2017) 158 BMLR 16, sub nom *W v Sanofi Pasteur MSD SNC* [2017] 4 WLR 171 (at paras 29, 37–38).)' *Hastings v Finsbury Orthopaedics Ltd* [2022] UKSC 19, [2023] 1 All ER 885 at [15], per Lord Lloyd-Jones JSC

DEL CREDERE AGENT

[For 1 Halsbury's Laws of England (5th Edn) (2017) para 13 see now 1 Halsbury's Laws of England (5th Edn) (2022) para 13.]

DELEGATION

[For 1 Halsbury's Laws of England (5th Edn) (2017) para 48 see now 1 Halsbury's Laws of England (5th Edn) (2022) para 48.]

DELIBERATE

Deliberate acts

'[5] The central issue on the appeal is whether the insurer is entitled to rely on an exclusion under the policy of "liability arising out of deliberate acts" of an employee.

...

'[44] ... It was said that "liability arising out of deliberate acts" addresses acts which the employee performs where the liability bears a relationship of proportionality to the employee's intention. Where the injury is death, the exclusion will only be triggered where the intention is one to cause serious injury. It was not, however, explained how this interpretation derives from the wording of the policy. The policy draws no distinction between injuries of differing seriousness nor does it require or refer to proportionality. Whilst one can understand an interpretation embracing an act causing "injury" or an act causing the "injury", there is simply no foundation in the policy wording for it to embrace an act causing "serious injury", an expression found nowhere in the policy.

'[45] For all these reasons, I would accept the insurer's argument that, in the context of the present case, "deliberate acts" in cl 14 of the policy means acts which are intended to cause injury.

'[46] Kenneth McBrearty QC for the insurer submitted that "deliberate", which qualifies "acts", and "wilful", which qualifies "neglect or default" should be interpreted as synonymous. He suggested that "neglect or default" referred to omissions and that the intention was to qualify both acts and omissions in the same way. The language used simply reflected the fact that in normal usage "deliberate" is the more natural adjective to describe a positive act, while "wilful" is more apt to describe an omission. He then relied on authorities in which "wilful" has been held to include recklessness to support a case that the same meaning should be given to "deliberate" in the context of cl 14. Both should therefore be interpreted as meaning an intention to cause injury, or recklessness as to whether injury will be caused.

...

'[51] I would reject the insurer's case on a number of grounds.

'[52] First, the starting point is the natural meaning of "deliberate" acts. This connotes consciously performing an act intending its consequences. It involves a different state of mind to recklessness. For reasons already stated, the relevant act in this case is that of causing injury, so its natural meaning in the present context is carrying out an act intending to cause injury.

'[53] Secondly, while the natural meaning of wilful includes deliberate, wilful is capable of having a wider meaning, depending on the context. ...' *Burnett or Grant v International Insurance Company of Hanover Ltd* [2021] UKSC 12, [2021] 3 All ER 503 at [5], [44]–[46], [51]–[53], per Lord Hamblen JSC

Deliberate inaccuracy

[Taxes Management Act 1970, s 118(7): 'references to a loss of tax or a situation brought about deliberately by a person include a loss of tax or a situation that arises as a result of a deliberate inaccuracy in a document given to Her Majesty's Revenue and Customs by or on behalf of that person'.] '[42] ... The question is whether [the phrase "deliberate inaccuracy" in s 118(7)] means (i) a deliberate statement which is (in fact) inaccurate or (ii) a statement which, when made, was deliberately inaccurate. If (ii) is correct, it would need to be shown that the maker of the statement knew it to be inaccurate or (perhaps) that he was reckless rather than merely careless or mistaken as to its accuracy.

'[43] We have no hesitation in concluding that the second of those interpretations is to be preferred, for the following reasons. First, it is the natural meaning of the phrase "deliberate inaccuracy". Deliberate is an adjective which attaches a requirement of intentionality to the whole of that which it describes, namely "inaccuracy". An inaccuracy in a document is a statement which is inaccurate. Thus the required intentionality is attached both to the making of the statement and to its being inaccurate.

...

'[47] It may be convenient to encapsulate this conclusion by stating that, for there to be a deliberate inaccuracy in a document within the meaning of s 118(7) there will have to be demonstrated an intention to mislead the Revenue on the part of the taxpayer as to the truth of the relevant statement or, perhaps, (although it need not be decided on this appeal) recklessness as to whether it would do so.' *Tooth v Revenue and Customs Commissioners* [2021] UKSC 17, [2021] 3 All ER 711 at [42]–[43], [47], per Lord Briggs and Lord Sales JJSC

DELIVERY

Of goods

[For 91 Halsbury's Laws of England (5th Edn) (2012) para 161 see now 91 Halsbury's Laws of England (5th Edn) (2019) para 164; and for 91 Halsbury's Laws of England (5th Edn) (2012) paras 161–193 see now 91 Halsbury's Laws of England (5th Edn) (2019) paras 164–196.]

Writ of delivery

[For 12A Halsbury's Laws of England (5th Edn) (2015) para 1383 see now 12A Halsbury's Laws of England (5th Edn) (2020) para 1357.]

DEMISE

[For 62 Halsbury's Laws of England (5th Edn) (2016) para 123 see now 62 Halsbury's Laws of England (5th Edn) (2022) paras 139–140.]

Of monarch

[For 29 Halsbury's Laws of England (5th Edn) (2014) para 11 see now 29 Halsbury's Laws of England (5th Edn) (2019) para 11.]

[For 20 Halsbury's Laws of England (5th Edn) (2014) para 49 see now 20 Halsbury's Laws of England (5th Edn) (2023) para 44.]

DEMURRAGE

[For 7 Halsbury's Laws of England (5th Edn) (2015) para 288 see now 7 Halsbury's Laws of England (5th Edn) (2020) para 332.]

'[1] Demurrage, as every shipping lawyer knows, is "a sum agreed by the charterer to be paid as liquidated damages for delay beyond a stipulated or reasonable time for loading or unloading, generally referred to as the laydays or laytime" (*Scrutton on Charterparties* (24th edn, 2020) article 170). The issue arising on this appeal is whether demurrage is liquidated damages for all the consequences of the charterer's failure to load or unload within the laytime, as Potter J held in *Richco International Ltd v Alfred C Toepfer International GmbH, The Bonde* [1991] 1 Lloyd's Rep 136, or only some of them, as Andrew Baker J held in this case.

...

'[21] It is now established that failure to complete cargo operations within the laytime is a breach of contract by the charterer for which demurrage is liquidated damages and that demurrage is not "money payable by a charterer as the consideration for the exercise by him of a right to detain a chartered ship beyond the stipulated lay days" (*President of India v Lips Maritime Corp, The Lips* [1987] 3 All ER 110 at 115, [1988] AC 395 at 422). However, this has not always been understood. In the Scots case of *Lilly & Co v DM Stevenson & Co* (1895) 22 R 278 Lord Trayner, reflecting earlier judicial statements, described days on demurrage as "just lay-days, but lay-days that have to be paid for". As Lord Brandon pointed out in *The Lips*, if that view of the meaning of demurrage had prevailed, a claim for demurrage would be a claim in debt and not for damages. As it was, it was not until the Court of Appeal decision in *Reidar v Arcos* [*Reidar, Aktieselskabet v Arcos Ltd* [1927] 1 KB 352, CA] in 1926 that it was finally determined in English law that demurrage is liquidated damages for breach unless the contract provides otherwise.

...

'[44] As we have already indicated, in our view the cases are inconclusive. However, as will be apparent from what we have said, we do not agree with the judge (at [88]) that "the preponderance of views evident in dicta" is that demurrage "serves to liquidate the loss of earnings resulting from delay" and nothing more. If anything, the balance tips the other way.

...

'[52] In circumstances where the cases do not provide a decisive answer and there is no clear consensus in the textbooks, we approach the issue as one of principle. Our conclusion is that, in the absence of any contrary indication in a particular charterparty, demurrage liquidates the whole of the damages arising from a charterer's breach of charter in failing to complete cargo operations within the laytime and not merely some of them. Accordingly, if a shipowner seeks to recover damages in addition to demurrage arising from delay, it must prove a breach of a separate obligation. ...' *K Line PTE Ltd v Priminds Shipping (HK) Co Ltd; The*

MV Eternal Bliss [2021] EWCA Civ 1712, [2022] 3 All ER 396 at [1], [21], [44], [52], per Males LJ

DENTAL SURGEON

[For 74 Halsbury's Laws of England (5th Edn) (2011) para 404 et seq see now 74 Halsbury's Laws of England (5th Edn) (2019) para 338 et seq.]

DEPENDENT RELATIVE REVOCATION

[For 102 Halsbury's Laws of England (5th Edn) (2010) para 108 see now 102 Halsbury's Laws of England (5th Edn) (2021) para 110.]

DEPOSIT

Of chattel

[For 4 Halsbury's Laws of England (5th Edn) (2011) para 111 see now 4 Halsbury's Laws of England (5th Edn) (2020) para 111.]

DEPRIVATION OF LIBERTY

[Mental Health Act 1983, s 17A: detained patient may in specified circumstances be discharged from hospital under a community treatment order ('CTO'); Human Rights Act 1998, Sch 1, Pt I, art 5 (right to liberty).] '[18] The Welsh Ministers are entirely correct in what they say about the legal effect of a CTO. But it does not follow that the patient has not in fact been deprived of his liberty as a result of the conditions to which he is subject. The European Court of Human Rights has said time and time again that the protection of the rights contained in the European Convention must be practical and effective. When it comes to deprivation of liberty, they and we must look at the concrete situation of the person concerned: has he in fact been deprived of his liberty? Otherwise, all kinds of unlawful detention might go unremedied, on the basis that there was no power to do it. That is the antithesis of what the protection of personal liberty by the ancient writ of habeas corpus, and now also by art 5 of the Convention, is all about.

'[19] Since the judgment in the Upper Tribunal, this case has proceeded on the basis that the factual circumstances in which PJ found himself under the CTO conditions did amount to a deprivation of liberty. Charles J found that the MHRT had applied the wrong test, but neither made the determination for himself nor sent the case back for the MHRT to do so. But it is enough for our purposes to proceed on the basis that there was a deprivation of liberty on the ground. The question is whether the RC has power, under the MHA, to impose conditions which have that effect.' *Welsh Ministers v PJ* [2018] UKSC 66, [2019] 2 All ER 766 at [18]–[19], per Lady Hale P

'[28] For what it is worth, in the case of *Secretary of State for the Home Dept v JJ* [2007] UKHL 45, [2008] 1 All ER 613, [2008] 1 AC 385, it was taken for granted that a curfew enforced by electronic tagging, clocking in and clocking out, and arrest or imprisonment for breach was a "classic detention or confinement" (para [59]). The only question was whether it was also a deprivation of liberty within the meaning of art 5 of the ECHR [European Convention on Human Rights], which leads on to the second issue.

'[29] Mr Tam makes an alternative argument in this Court which was not open to him in the courts below. This is that the concept of imprisonment for the purpose of the tort of false imprisonment should now be aligned with the concept of deprivation of liberty within the meaning of art 5 of the ECHR. The classic definition of this concept is taken from *Guzzardi v Italy* (App no 7367/76) (1980) 3 EHRR 333, [1980] ECHR 7367/76, at para 92:

> "In order to determine whether someone has been 'deprived of his liberty' within the meaning of article 5, the starting point must be his concrete situation and account must be taken of a whole range of criteria such as the type, duration, effects and manner of implementation of the measure in question."

'The ECHR distinguishes between the deprivation and restriction of liberty and the court emphasised that this was a matter of degree rather than nature or substance (para 93). This multi-factorial approach is very different from the approach of the common law to imprisonment.

'[30] In *Austin v Metropolitan Police Comr* [2007] EWCA Civ 989, [2008] 1 All ER 564, [2008] QB 660, the Court of Appeal held that "kettling" the claimants for several hours at Oxford Circus was indeed imprisonment at common law, but that it was justified by the common law principle of necessity; however, it was not a deprivation of liberty within the meaning of art 5, a conclusion with which both the House of Lords and the European Court of Human Rights agreed: [2009] UKHL 5, [2009] 3 All ER 455, [2009] AC 564, and *Austin v UK* (App no 39692/09) (2012) 32 BHRC 618, (2012) 55 EHRR 14. The trial judge's observation that there could be imprisonment at common law without there being a deprivation of liberty under art 5 and vice versa was cited by the Court of Appeal with apparent approval (para [87]). That observation was repeated by the Court of Appeal in *Walker v Comr of the Police of the Metropolis* [2014] EWCA Civ 897, [2015] 1 WLR 312, [2015] 1 Cr App Rep 283, where it was held to be false imprisonment for a police officer to stand in the front doorway of a house so as to prevent the claimant from leaving, even for a very short time, but it was not a deprivation of liberty within the meaning of art 5.

'[31] By contrast, when the *Bournewood* case [*R v Bournewood Community and Mental Health NHS Trust, ex p L* [1998] 3 All ER 289, [1999] AC 458, HL) reached the European Court of Human Rights, that court held that the patient had been deprived of his liberty within the meaning of art 5: *HL v UK* [(2004) 81 BMLR 131, (2004) 40 EHRR 761, ECtHR]. This is thought to be the only case going the other way. Imprisonment for the purpose of the tort of false imprisonment can take place for a very short period of time, whereas a number of factors are relevant to whether there has been a deprivation of liberty. On the other hand, imprisonment may be justified at common law in circumstances which are not covered by the list of possibly permissible deprivations of liberty in art 5(1) of the ECHR.

'[32] Mr Tam argues that the time has now come to align the two concepts: specifically to align the concept of imprisonment with the concept of deprivation of liberty. He says this because, in *Secretary of State for the Home Dept v JJ* [2007] UKHL 45, [2008] 1 All ER 613, [2008] 1 AC 385, while the House of Lords held, by a majority, that a 16-hour curfew was a deprivation of liberty, Lord Brown of Eaton-under-Heywood expressed the view that an eight-hour curfew, such as this, would not be such a deprivation.

'[33] It is, of course, the case that the common law is capable of being developed to meet the changing needs of society. In Lord Toulson's famous words in *Kennedy v Charity Commission* [2014] UKSC 20, [2014] 2 All ER 847, [2015] AC 455 (at [133]), "it was not the purpose of the [Human Rights Act 1998] that the common law should become an ossuary". Sometimes those developments will bring it closer to the ECHR and sometimes they will not. But what Mr Tam is asking this Court to do is not to develop the law but to make it take a retrograde step: to restrict the classic understanding of imprisonment at common law to the very different and much more nuanced concept of deprivation of liberty under the ECHR. The Strasbourg court has adopted this approach because of the need to draw a distinction between the deprivation and the restriction of physical liberty. There is no need for the common law to draw such a distinction and every reason for the common law to continue to protect those whom it has protected for centuries against unlawful imprisonment, whether by the State or private persons.

'[34] The Court of Appeal in Austin and in Walker were right to say that there could be imprisonment at common law without there being a deprivation of liberty under art 5. Whether they were also right to add 'and vice versa' may be open to doubt in the light of the *Bournewood* saga, but it is not necessary for us to express an opinion on the matter.' *R (on the application of Jalloh (formerly Jollah)) v Secretary of State for the Home Department* [2020] UKSC 4, [2020] 3 All ER 449 at [28]–[34], per Lady Hale

DEROGATION FROM GRANT

[For 32 Halsbury's Laws of England (5th Edn) (2012) para 258 see now 32 Halsbury's Laws of England (5th Edn) (2019) para 258.]

DESCENDANT

[For 102 Halsbury's Laws of England (5th Edn) (2010) para 339 see now 102 Halsbury's Laws of England (5th Edn) (2021) para 340.]

DESERTION

Matrimonial causes

[For 72 Halsbury's Laws of England (5th Edn) (2015) para 397 see now 72 Halsbury's Laws of England (5th Edn) (2019) para 392; and for 72 Halsbury's Laws of England (5th Edn) (2015) para 411 see now 72 Halsbury's Laws of England (5th Edn) (2019) para 406.]

DESIGN

[For 79 Halsbury's Laws of England (5th Edn) (2014) paras 711–712 see now 79 Halsbury's Laws of England (5th Edn) (2020) paras 648, 684.]

DESTRUCTION

Of will

[For 102 Halsbury's Laws of England (5th Edn) (2010) para 94 see now 102 Halsbury's Laws of England (5th Edn) (2021) para 96.]

DETAILED ASSESSMENT

[Order for costs to be the subject of detailed assessment if not agreed. CPR 44.3(4)(a), 44.6(1), (2), 45.29, Pt 47: whether 'subject to detailed assessment' could be read as providing for assessment of fixed costs.] '[40] The appellant's case rested on two central arguments. The first was that the use of the term "subject to detailed assessment" in the Order did not, or did not necessarily, indicate that the costs were to be assessed on the standard basis, particularly as the Order could have specified standard basis costs but did not do so. The appellant contended that the term "detailed assessment" was also apt to refer to the process of assessing the amount of fixed costs and, in particular, the quantum of disbursements, there being no other provision in the rules for the determination of the amount payable in the event of disagreement.

...

'[44] In my judgment, and contrary to the appellant's contention, there is no ambiguity whatsoever as to the natural and ordinary meaning of "subject to detailed assessment" in an agreement or order as to costs. The phrase is a technical term, the meaning and effect of which is expressly and extensively set out in the rules. It plainly denotes that the costs are to be assessed by the procedure in Pt 47 on the standard basis (unless the agreement or order goes on to provide for the assessment to be on the indemnity basis). The phrase cannot be read as providing for an "assessment" of fixed costs pursuant to the provisions of Pt 45 unless the context leads to the conclusion that the wrong terminology has been used (by the parties or by the Court) so that the phrase should be interpreted otherwise than according to its ordinary meaning.'

'[45] This is abundantly clear from consideration of the rules themselves:

(i) First and foremost, r 44.3(4)(a) expressly provides that, where an order for costs, or for assessment of costs, does not indicate the basis of assessment, the costs will be assessed on the standard basis. In other words, the effect of an order which provides for costs 'subject to detailed assessment' is, by simple and direct application of the rules, an order that costs will be assessed on the standard basis. An agreement to the same effect, intended to be embodied in an order, must have the same natural and ordinary meaning.

(ii) Second, r 44.6(1), in setting out the court's power to assess costs (either summarily or by way of a detailed assessment), expressly provides that such power does not relate to fixed costs. Fixed costs under Pt 45 are dealt with separately in r 44.6(2) and are stated to be recoverable 'in accordance with that Part'. It could not be clearer that an agreement or order for the detailed assessment of costs does not (unless something has 'gone wrong') relate to fixed costs.

(iii) Third, that same clear distinction is apparent from r 45.29 itself. In circumstances where the court will consider a claim for an amount of costs greater than fixed costs under r 45.29J, it may do so by assessing the costs (summarily or by way of detailed assessment). Such an assessment must necessarily be on the standard basis unless the court specifically directs that the indemnity basis should be used. Rule 45.29K then draws a distinction between the costs so assessed ('the assessed costs') and the fixed recoverable costs, requiring the court to award the latter unless the assessed costs are 20% greater. Again, it could not be clearer that costs assessed summarily or under Pt 47 are not the same as (and cannot include) fixed recoverable costs.

'[46] The clear distinction between assessed costs and fixed costs to be found in the rules (as set out above) was recognised in *Broadhurst [Broadhurst v Tan, Smith v Taylor* [2016] EWCA Civ 94, [2017] 2 All ER 60], Lord Dyson MR describing them at [30] as "conceptually different", a difference also recognised by Moore-Bick LJ in Solomon at [19]. Moore-Bick LJ went on, in the same paragraph, to state that the fixed costs regime does involve an assessment of some kind (particularly in relation to disbursements), but not one that is properly regarded as an assessment on the standard basis.' *Doyle v M&D Foundations & Building Services Ltd* [2022] EWCA Civ 927, [2023] 2 All ER 999 at [40], [44]–[46], per Phillips LJ

[CPR 44.11.] '[72] First, as to sub-rule (a) a Solicitor/Client Assessment is not a "summary assessment" (as defined). Whilst the costs of the Solicitor/Client Assessment might be summarily assessed, the costs being assessed in that Assessment cannot be summarily assessed. Moreover, in my judgment, a Solicitor/Client Assessment is not a "detailed assessment" within the meaning of that term in CPR 44.11. For the purposes of CPR Pts 44 to 46, "detailed assessment" is defined, in CPR 44.1(1), as "the procedure by which the amount of costs is decided by a costs officer in accordance with Part 47". A Solicitor/Client Assessment under the 1974 Act [Solicitors Act 1974] and CPR 46.9 and 46.10 is not such a procedure. Even if the procedure for a Solicitor/Client Assessment might, by default, incorporate in part some of the elements of CPR Pt 47 (as per the White Book commentary), it is not in itself a Pt 47 detailed assessment. (I address this further in paras [80] to [84] below.) In my judgment a CPR 46.9/46.10 assessment is not a "detailed assessment" as referred to in CPR 44.11(1)(a). Accordingly CPR 44.11(1)(a) does not apply to the costs the subject of a Solicitor/Client Assessment.' *John Poyser & Co Ltd v Spencer* [2022] EWHC 1678 (QB), [2023] 2 All ER 647 at [72], per Morris J

DETAINED

[Mental Health Act 1983, s 117: duty to provide after-care services to a patient who has ceased to be detained under s 3.] '[5] By s 117(1):

> "This section applies to persons who are detained under section 3 above … and then cease to be detained and (whether or not immediately after so ceasing) leave hospital."

It is the meaning of the final words of this provision which is at the centre of this dispute.

…

'[15] The first issue raised by the claim, and the main issue raised on this appeal, is whether, when he goes on an escorted day trip for which he is granted leave of absence under s 17, the claimant is a person to whom s 117 of the Act applies. This depends on whether, when he goes on such trips, the claimant "ceases to be detained and … leaves hospital" within the meaning of s 117(1).

…

'[32] I accept the starting point of the claimant's argument that the term "detained" as it is generally used in the Act refers to detention in a hospital. This is confirmed by the recent decision of the Supreme Court in *Secretary of State for Justice v MM* [2018] UKSC 60, [2019] 2 All ER 749, [2018] 3 WLR 1784, which held that there is no power under the Act to impose a condition of detention in a place which is not a hospital (save for the emergency powers under ss 135 and 136 to detain a person at a place of safety). But I do not accept that, as a matter of language, it is inappropriate to describe a patient who is permitted to leave the hospital premises to go on a short escorted trip and then return as a person who is still "detained" in the hospital. That description may reasonably be used to refer to the person's general situation, even if the person is not confined within the hospital premises at all times.

'[33] That the term "detained" not only can be but is actually used in the Act in this more general sense is confirmed by the decision of the Court of Appeal in *B v Barking, Havering and Brentwood Community Healthcare NHS Trust* [1999] 1 FLR 106, (1999) 47 BMLR 112.

…

…

'[35] I am not suggesting that the decision in the *B v Barking* case determines what is meant by the phrase "cease to be detained" in s 117(1) of the Act. But it does show that the term "detained" is capable of being used, and is used in at least one place in the Act, to encompass a person who is on leave of absence under s 17 from the hospital in which he or she is detained.

…

'[38] As discussed, in interpreting a statutory provision it is not sufficient to consider the ordinary meanings of the words used and how the same words are used elsewhere in the Act: it is necessary to identify the purpose of the provision, read in its context. The clear purpose of s 117 is to arrange for the provision of services to a person who has been, but is not currently being, provided with treatment and care as a hospital patient. That purpose is implicit in the very expression "after-care", which is used not only in the heading but throughout the body of s 117 in the phrase "after-care services". It is further articulated by the definition of "after-care services" in s 117(6). …

'[39] Interpreting s 117(1) in the light of this purpose, I readily accept that there will be cases in which a patient granted leave of absence from hospital under s 17 does "cease to be detained" and "leave hospital" within the meaning of s 117(1) so as to become eligible to receive after-care services during the period of their absence. I would also accept the submission made by Mr Wise QC that it is not necessary in order to trigger s 117 that the person concerned should have been "discharged" from hospital in either of the two senses, discussed in the *MM* case at paras [19]–[20], in which that term is used in the Act. I see no reason why s 117 should not apply to a person who is living in the community on leave of absence–either full-time or for part of the week like the claimant in the *Barking* case–without having been conditionally discharged from hospital under s 42(2) or 73(2) of the Act, let alone "absolutely" discharged from the liability to be detained.

…

'[44] The inescapable conclusion is that the claimant does not "cease to be detained" or "leave hospital" within the meaning of s 117(1) when he is escorted on day trips and is therefore not a person to whom s 117 applies. …' *R (on the application of CXF (by his mother, his litigation friend)) v Central Bedfordshire Council* [2018] EWCA Civ 2852, [2019] 3 All ER 20 at [5], [15], [32]–[33], [35], [38]–[39], [44], per Leggatt LJ

DETENTION

Liable to detention

[Immigration Act 2016, Sch 10, para 1(2): Secretary of State may grant a person immigration bail 'even if the person can no longer be detained, if … the person is liable to detention'.]. '[1] The main issue in this appeal is whether the Secretary of State has the power to place a person on bail under para 1(2) of Sch 10 to the Immigration Act 2016 ("the 2016 Act") in circumstances where it would be unlawful to detain them. …

…

'[66] First, the phrase "liable to detention", on its natural meaning, refers to a person who can in principle be detained: in other words that there exists a legal power to detain them. It does not say "liable to lawful detention". Nor does it say that the power to detain must not only exist but must be capable of being exercised lawfully.

'[67] Secondly, this is how the phrase "liable to detention" was interpreted by the House of Lords in *Khadir [R (on the application of Khadir) v Secretary of State for the Home Dept* [2005] UKHL 39, [2005] 4 All ER 114]. In my view, that was in a similar context to the present context, since it involved restrictions on what somebody who did not have leave to enter or remain could do while in this country. …' *R (on the application of Kaitey) v Secretary of State for the Home Department (Bail for Immigration Detainees intervening)* [2021] EWCA Civ 1875, [2022] 3 All ER 835 at [1], [66]–[67], per Singh LJ

DETERMINATION

[County Courts Act 1984, s 77(1); appeal if party is dissatisfied with the determination of a judge or jury.] '[15] Although s 77 of the 1984 Act refers to "the determination of a judge", there is no statutory definition of "determination". The table at para 3.5 of CPR PD 52A2 instead uses the word "decision", and provides that the destination of an appeal against any decision of a County Court Circuit Judge lies to the High Court. "Decision" is elsewhere defined as including "any judgment, order or direction of the High Court or the County Court". The House of Lords treated "decision" as being synonymous with "determination" in *Barder v Barder (Caluori intervening)* [1987] 2 All ER 440, [1988] AC 20. In addition, the White Book 2021 at 9A 59.3 correctly suggests that "determination" has the same meaning as "judgment or order".

'[16] In my view, the use of these different words in statute and statutory instruments may once have had an historic significance, but since the introduction of the CPR, those differences no longer matter: see, for example, the discussion in the White Book 2021 under r 40.1.1. Save in an exceptional case, there can be no practical difference between any of the possible formulations (namely "determination", "judgment", "order", or "direction"). If I was forced at gunpoint to say, I would venture the suggestion that "determination" is possibly the widest of them all.

'[17] What is much more important is that, however it may be labelled, an appeal can only lie against something which has been decided: a result, a conclusion, an outcome. It does not lie against any observation or comment by the judge along the way to that result. In this way, the winner cannot appeal against a finding or a reason for the judge's decision. A defendant whose defence is upheld by the judge cannot seek to appeal against a finding that he or she did not always tell the truth: see by analogy *Lake v Lake* [1955] 2 All ER 538, [1955] P 336, where the wife who had obtained an order entirely in her favour was not allowed to appeal the judge's finding that she had committed adultery. It is only the result that matters for the purposes of an appeal. That is why, although it is technically inaccurate (as this case demonstrates), judges are so fond of saying that "an appeal lies against an order, not a judgment".

. . .

'[24] The authorities to which I have referred in paras [17]–[20] above make it clear that a formal order is not a condition precedent to any appeal. There is no doubt that, in the present day, there will almost always be a sealed order and, if there is, a copy must be provided by the proposed appellant. But the authorities are clear that, in circumstances where there is no sealed order, but there is a determination under s 77 (or a decision or a direction or a judgment), the absence of a sealed order will not itself be a bar to an application for permission to appeal.' *Anwer v Central Bridging Loans Ltd* [2022] EWCA Civ 201, [2022] 4 All ER 1032 at [15]–[17], [24], per Coulson LJ

DEVASTAVIT

[For 103 Halsbury's Laws of England (5th Edn) (2010) para 1246 see now 103 Halsbury's Laws of England (5th Edn) (2021) para 1247.]

DEVIATION

Of ship

[For 60 Halsbury's Laws of England (5th Edn) (2011) para 313 see now 60 Halsbury's Laws of England (5th Edn) (2018) para 292.]

[For 7 Halsbury's Laws of England (5th Edn) (2015) para 249 see now 7 Halsbury's Laws of England (5th Edn) (2020) para 280.]

DEVOLVE—DEVOLUTION

[For 103 Halsbury's Laws of England (5th Edn) (2010) para 916 see now 103 Halsbury's Laws of England (5th Edn) (2021) para 919; and for 103 Halsbury's Laws of England (5th Edn) (2010) paras 916–954 see now 103 Halsbury's Laws of England (5th Edn) (2021) paras 919–958.]

Devolution issue

[Scotland Act 1988, Sch 6, para 1: which includes at para 1(f) 'any other question about whether a function is exercisable within devolved competence or in or as regards Scotland and any other question arising by virtue of this Act about reserved matters'. Whether the Scottish Parliament has power to legislate for the holding of a referendum to ask the question 'Should Scotland be an independent country?]

'[39] Construing para 1(f) according to the ordinary meaning of the words used is also consistent with the important function which para 1 plays in the overall scheme of the Scotland Act. It is by no means limited to defining the scope of references to this court. Devolution issues can arise in any civil or criminal proceedings in any court or tribunal in Scotland (Pt II of Sch 6), England and Wales (Pt III) or Northern Ireland (Pt IV), as well as being the subject of a reference by a Law Officer to this court (Pt V). The definition of a devolution issue in para 1 is the key to the raising before any court or tribunal, anywhere in the United Kingdom, of any question arising under the Scotland Act, other than (since 2013) a question in relation to a compatibility issue as defined by s 288ZA of the Criminal Procedure (Scotland) Act 1995, as amended (which concerns certain questions arising in criminal proceedings in relation to Convention rights, ie rights and freedoms guaranteed by the European Convention on Human Rights, and retained EU law).

. . .

'[42] In short, (1) the breadth of the language used by the United Kingdom Parliament in para 1(f), (2) the courts' general approach to the construction of the Scotland Act, (3) the apparent purpose that the provision should sweep up any questions arising under the Act about reserved matters which are not covered by paras 1(a) to (e), and (4) the critical role of para 1(f) in relation to justiciability, all incline us to construe para 1(f) in accordance with the ordinary meaning of the words used, rather than as being concerned only with the non-legislative powers of the Scottish Parliament and with the functions of United Kingdom ministers and cross-border public authorities.

. . .

'[47] For these reasons, we conclude that the question referred is a devolution issue, and that this court accordingly has jurisdiction to decide it.' *Re Scottish Independence Referendum Bill* [2022] UKSC 31, [2023] 1 All ER 961 at [39], [42], [47], per Lord Reed P, Lord Lloyd-Jones, Lord Sales, Lord Stephens and Lady Rose JJSC

DICTUM

[For 11 Halsbury's Laws of England (5th Edn) (2015) para 26 see now 11 Halsbury's Laws of England (5th Edn) (2020) para 26.]

DISCLAIMER

By trustee in bankruptcy

[For 5 Halsbury's Laws of England (5th Edn) (2013) paras 490–506 see now 5 Halsbury's Laws of England (5th Edn) (2020) paras 473–488.]

DISCLOSURE

[For 12 Halsbury's Laws of England (5th Edn) (2015) para 621 see now 12 Halsbury's Laws of England (5th Edn) (2020) para 614.]

DISCOVER

[For 59 Halsbury's Laws of England (5th Edn) (2014) para 2219 see now 99 Halsbury's Laws of England (5th Edn) (2018) para 672.]

[Taxes Management Act 1970, s 29 ('discovery assessment'): power to make an assessment if an inspector 'discovers' that tax which ought to have been assessed has not been assessed or an assessment to tax is insufficient or relief is excessive.] '[11] … In the present appeal, it is not in dispute that the concept of a "discovery" by an officer involves the application of a subjective test, as to the officer's state of mind, and an objective test as to whether it is open to an officer to have that state of mind.

…

'[28] … Having reviewed the authorities, we consider that it is helpful to elaborate the test as to the required subjective element for a discovery assessment as follows:

> "The officer must believe that the information available to him points in the direction of there being an insufficiency of tax."

That formulation, in our judgment, acknowledges both that the discovery must be something more than suspicion of an insufficiency of tax and that it need not go so far as a conclusion that an insufficiency of tax is more probable than not.

…

'[30] The officer's decision to make a discovery assessment is an administrative decision. We consider that the objective controls on the decision making of the officer should be expressed by reference to public law concepts. Accordingly, as regards the requirement for the action to be "reasonable", this should be expressed as a requirement that the officer's belief is one which a reasonable officer could form. It is not for a tribunal hearing an appeal in relation to a discovery assessment to form its own belief on the information available to the officer and then to conclude, if it forms a different belief, that the officer's belief was not reasonable.' *Anderson v Revenue and Customs Commissioners* [2018] UKUT 159 (TCC), [2018] 4 All ER 338 at [11], [28], [30], per Morgan J and Judge Berner

[Limitation Act 1980, s 32(1); postponement of the limitation period in cases of fraud, deliberate concealment or mistake.] '[1] The central question in this appeal is whether Gemalto's claims for loss arising from an unlawful cartel in which the defendants, Infineon and Renesas (together the defendants), participated are statute barred. The cartel related to the supply of Smart Card Chips ("SCCs"). The question turns on the proper approach to be adopted to the application of s 32(1) of the Limitation Act 1980 (s 32(1)). Bacon J ("the judge") ([2022] EWHC 156 (Ch)) identified two possible tests for the determination of whether the claimants' knowledge, more than 6 years before the commencement of the proceedings, was sufficient to amount to discovery for the purposes of s 32(1)(b).

'[2] The first was the so-called statement of claim test of whether the claimant had, or could with reasonable diligence have, obtained such knowledge as would allow it and its professional advisors properly to plead a claim that would not be liable to be struck out as unarguable or lacking a sufficient evidential basis (see the judgment at [50]). …

'[3] The second possible test was the so-called *FII* test adumbrated by the Supreme Court in a case concerning a mistake of law (*Test Claimants in the Franked Investment Income Group Litigation v Revenue and*

Customs Comrs [2020] UKSC 47, [2021] 1 All ER 1001, [2020] 3 WLR 1369 ("*FII*")). The *FII* test suggests that time should begin to run from the point when the claimant knows, or could with reasonable diligence know, that it has a worthwhile claim. The claimant must know about the mistake (or in this case the concealment) with sufficient confidence to justify embarking on the preliminaries to the issue of proceedings, such as submitting a claim to the proposed defendant, taking advice and collecting evidence. The Supreme Court in *FII* adopted that formulation from Lord Donaldson MR in *Halford v Brookes* [1991] 3 All ER 559 at 573–574, [1991] 1 WLR 428 at 443 ("Halford").

...

'[45] In my judgment, the parties were right to submit that, after *FII*, limitation begins to run in a deliberate concealment case when the claimant recognises that it has a worthwhile claim, and that a worthwhile claim arises when a reasonable person could have a reasonable belief that (in a case of this kind) there had been a cartel. Gemalto's four propositions overcomplicate the position. The *FII* test must be applied with common sense. As the judge held, there is unlikely in most cases, as in this case, to be a real difference between the application of the statement of claim test and the *FII* test. Indeed, the statement of claim test is, perhaps, little more than a gloss on the *FII* test. It is also worth noting that competition cases are not to be treated differently from other cases under s 32 (see *Arcadia* [*Arcadia Group Brands Ltd v Visa Inc* [2015] EWCA Civ 883, [2015] Bus LR 1362, [2015] 5 CMLR 846] at [51]).

'[46] First, the *FII* test makes clear that the claimant is not entitled to delay the start of the limitation period until it has any certainty about its claim succeeding. So, whilst in a fraud case, if there were an essential fact about the fraud that the claimant had not discovered, without which there would have been no fraud, it would make sense to say that the claimant had not discovered the fraud. But in concealment, what needs to have been discovered is just that, the concealment. Once the claimant knows objectively that a cartel has been concealed, it does not need to have certainty about its existence or about the details of that cartel. That is why the Supreme Court made clear that the claimant needs only sufficient confidence to justify embarking on the preliminaries to the issue of a writ, such as submitting a claim to the proposed defendant, taking advice and collecting evidence. The term "worthwhile claim" is also not to be construed as a deed. It requires a common sense application. A claim in respect of a concealed event would not be a worthwhile one if it were pure speculation, but it would be if, as in this case, an authoritative regulator had thought it sufficiently serious, having investigated all the evidence available, to lay charges or issue a statement of objections.

'[47] Secondly, the test adumbrated by the Supreme Court must be intended to operate in all situations in which there has been mistake, fraud or concealment, and to be consistent with the Limitation Act more generally. It would make no sense for the limitation period for a road traffic accident to start running when it happens (at which point the victim may know nothing about the circumstances of the accident that, for example, rendered them unconscious), but for s 32 to allow a claimant a lengthy period of investigation before it is said to have "discovered" that the facts relating to its claim have been concealed. The person who is run down knows that they have a worthwhile claim, even if they may eventually be shown to have been responsible for the accident by running in front of the vehicle. The claimant cannot postpone the start of the limitation period until it has had the time to investigate the details of the claim and the possible defences and to evaluate its prospects, any more than the road traffic victim is able to do so. That is what the 6-year limitation period is for. The question of whether a claim is worthwhile is not a complex balance of the chance of success as Mr Turner suggested. The limitation period is not postponed until the claimant can show that it is more likely than not to succeed. Of course, if the putative claim would be struck out as not disclosing a cause of action, it would be right to say that the claimant had not discovered that it had a worthwhile claim (see the comparisons with *Earl Beatty* [*Earl Beatty v IRC* [1953] 2 All ER 758 at 762, [1953] 1 WLR 1090 at 1095], *Paragon* [*Paragon Finance plc v DB Thakerar & Co (a firm), Paragon Finance plc v Thimbleby & Co (a firm)* [1999] 1 All ER 400 at 418, (1998) 1 ITELR 735 at 765], *Sephton* [*Law Society v Sephton & Co (a firm)* [2004] EWCA Civ 1627, [2005] QB 1013] and *Molloy* [*Molloy v Mutual Reserve Life Insurance Co* (1906) 94 LT 756] above at [37]). That is why I say that I am far from sure that there is a real difference between the statement of claim test and the *FII* test so far as concealment cases are concerned.

...

'[53] To summarise, therefore, the position after *FII* is that the proviso to s 32(1) has to be construed consistently as between mistake and deliberate concealment cases. Time begins to run in a deliberate concealment case when the claimant recognises that it has a worthwhile claim. In a case of this kind, a worthwhile claim arises when a reasonable person could have a reasonable belief that there had been a cartel. The claimant can embark on the preliminaries to the issue of a writ (and therefore the limitation has begun) once it knows that there may have been a cartel and the identity of the participants, without knowing chapter and verse about the details. It would not, however, know that it had a worthwhile claim if a claim pleaded on the basis of the details it knew would be struck out.' *Gemalto Holding BV v Infineon Technologies AG* [2022] EWCA Civ 782, [2023] 1 All ER 418 at [1]–[3], [45]–[47], [53], per Sir Geoffrey Vos MR

DISFRANCHISEMENT

[For 24 Halsbury's Laws of England (5th Edn) (2010) para 351 see now 7 Halsbury's Laws of England (5th Edn) (2019) para 451.]

DISMISS—DISMISSAL

[For 40 Halsbury's Laws of England (5th Edn) (2014) para 733 et seq see now 41 Halsbury's Laws of England (5th Edn) (2021) para 729 et seq.]

DISORDERLY HOUSE

[For 25 Halsbury's Laws of England (5th Edn) (2016) para 272 see now 25 Halsbury's Laws of England (5th Edn) (2020) para 546.]

DISPROPORTIONATELY SEVERE

See also CRUEL AND UNUSUAL PUNISHMENT; INHUMAN OR DEGRADING PUNISHMENT

New Zealand New Zealand Bill of Rights Act 1990, s 9: right not to be subjected to cruel, degrading, or disproportionately severe treatment or punishment.] '[170] As in the ICCPR [International Covenant on Civil and Political Rights], there are degrees of reprehensibility evident in ss 9 and 23(5). Section 9 is concerned with conduct on the part of the state and its officials which is to be utterly condemned as outrageous and unacceptable in any circumstances. Section 23(5), which is confined in application to persons deprived of their liberty, proscribes conduct which is unacceptable in our society but of a lesser order, not rising to a level deserving to be called outrageous.

'[171] All forms of conduct proscribed by s 9 are of great seriousness. Without attempting exhaustive definitions, they can be understood in the New Zealand context in the following way. The worst is torture, which involves the deliberate infliction of severe physical or mental suffering for a particular purpose, such as obtaining information. Treatment or punishment that lacks such an ulterior purpose can be characterised as cruel if the suffering that results is severe or is deliberately inflicted. In the s 9 context, treatment or punishment is degrading if it gravely humiliates and debases the person subjected to it, whether or not that is its purpose.

'[172] The last of the matters listed in s 9 is treatment or punishment that is "disproportionately severe". This expression has no counterpart in the overseas instruments discussed above, but must take its colour from the rest of s 9 and therefore from the jurisprudence under those overseas instruments. I have concluded that the words "disproportionately severe" must have been included to fulfil much the same role as "inhuman" treatment or punishment plays in art 7 of the ICCPR, and to perform the same function as the gloss of "gross disproportionality" does for s 12 of the Canadian Charter. There might not otherwise be a classification in s 9 to catch behaviour which does not inflict suffering in a manner or degree which could be described as cruel, and cannot be said to be degrading in its effect, but which New Zealanders would nevertheless regard as so out of proportion to the particular circumstances as to cause shock and revulsion.

...

'[176] It is therefore apparent that "disproportionately severe", appearing in s 9 alongside torture, cruelty and conduct with degrading effect, is intended to capture treatment or punishment which is grossly disproportionate to the circumstances. Conduct so characterised can, in my view, when it occurs in New Zealand, be fairly called "inhuman" in the sense given to that term in the jurisprudence under art 7 of the ICCPR.' *Taunoa v Attorney-General* [2007] NZSC 70, [2008] 1 NZLR 429 at [170]–[172], [176], per Blanchard J

DISQUALIFIED

[For 67 Halsbury's Laws of England (5th Edn) (2016) paras 5, 58 et seq see now 67 Halsbury's Laws of England (5th Edn) (2021) paras 5, 69 et seq; and for 89 Halsbury's Laws of England (5th Edn) (2011) paras 281–284 see now 90A Halsbury's Laws of England (5th Edn) (2022) para 812 et seq.]

DISTINCTIVE

[For 97A Halsbury's Laws of England (5th Edn) (2014) para 44 see now 97A Halsbury's Laws of England (5th Edn) (2021) para 448.]

DISTRESS

[For 32 Halsbury's Laws of England (5th Edn) (2012) para 901 see now 62 Halsbury's Laws of England (5th Edn) (2022) para 305 and note 2.]

DISTURB

New Zealand [Wildlife Act 1953, s 2: hunting or killing in relation to any wildlife includes pursuing, disturbing, or molesting.] '[69] In common usage, it is possible to disturb something without intending to do so. We agree with the Court of Appeal that, as with the word killing, disturbing is a word that prohibits a result and not an action. It follows that an intention to disturb need not be proved. While this imposes strict liability for a disturbance, we have already noted the imposition of strict liability is consistent with the overall statutory scheme, which clearly contemplates liability under s 63A for accidental acts.

'[70] Beyond that however, settling on a meaning for this word becomes more difficult. The *Oxford English Dictionary* lists among possible meanings:

(a) "To agitate and destroy (quiet, peace, rest); to break up the quiet, tranquillity, or rest of (a person, a country, etc); to stir up, trouble, disquiet."
(b) "To throw into a state of physical agitation, commotion, or disorder; to agitate."
(c) "To agitate mentally, discompose the peace of mind or calmness of (any one); to trouble, perplex."
(d) "To interfere with the settled course or operation of; to put out of its course; to interrupt, derange, hinder, frustrate."
(e) "To move anything from its settled condition or position; to unsettle."

...

'[72] We start from the premise that, as appears from the dictionary definition, the word "disturb" can carry many different meanings. We accept Shark Experience's argument that a definition of "disturb" which captures acts breaking up the peace or tranquillity of protected wildlife would cast too broad a net. It would result in criminalising actions such as walking through the bush, or swimming in the sea, since each of those will often result in startling wildlife, and some of that wildlife may be protected. Such conduct would be criminalised even though it carried with it no real risk of harm to the wildlife. We are confident it was not Parliament's intention to expose people to the risk of criminal liability in such circumstances.

'[73] That favours a narrower construction, as does the statutory context. The statutory purpose suggests a meaning for the word "disturbing" which prohibits conduct carrying a real risk of significant harm. If "disturbing" is construed to have a meaning closer to harm in this way, it fits both with the dictionary definition of disturbing and the purpose of the Act.

'[74] Construing the word in its statutory context and, in particular, placing it within the context of the list of the other prohibited actions, leads us to conclude that what is intended to be prohibited is action which physically or mentally agitates the protected wildlife to a level creating a real risk of significant harm. Such an interpretation is consistent with the meaning of the verb "disturb" in its common usage sense. It imbues the conduct thereby prohibited with a character in keeping with the other prohibited acts: conduct which carries a real risk of significantly harming a protected animal.

...

'[93] ... In the s 2(1) definition of "hunt or kill": "disturbing" means an action which physically or mentally agitates the protected animal to a level creating a real risk of significant harm.' *Shark Experience Ltd v PauaMAC5 Inc* [2019] NZSC 111, [2019] 1 NZLR 791 at [69]–[70], [72]–[74], [93], per Winkelmann CJ

DIVERT

[For 55 Halsbury's Laws of England (5th Edn) (2012) paras 811–813 see now 55 Halsbury's Laws of England (5th Edn) (2019) paras 831–833.]

DIVORCE

[For 72 Halsbury's Laws of England (5th Edn) (2015) para 396 et seq see now 72 Halsbury's Laws of England (5th Edn) (2019) para 391 et seq.]

DONATIO MORTIS CAUSA

[For 103 Halsbury's Laws of England (5th Edn) (2010) para 921 see now 103 Halsbury's Laws of England (5th Edn) (2021) para 924; and for 52 Halsbury's Laws of England (5th Edn) (2014) paras 271–272 see now 52 Halsbury's Laws of England (5th Edn) (2020) paras 271–272.]

DRAWBACK

[For 31 Halsbury's Laws of England (5th Edn) (2011) para 1105 see now 31 Halsbury's Laws of England (5th Edn) (2012) para 1105.]

DROP HANDS

'[74] … I cannot see how the offer of an admission of liability, still less a drop-hands offer (ie with each side paying their own costs) would have dissuaded the uninsured claimants from continuing to incur the cost of obtaining (in the event) default judgment, and summary judgment in relation to test claims C and D, once the insured claims had been settled and Travelers had withdrawn further funding.' *XYZ v Travelers Insurance Co Ltd* [2019] UKSC 48, [2020] 2 All ER 239 at [74], per Lord Briggs JSC

'[12] It was common ground before the judge, and also before this court, that the terms of the CFA [conditional fee agreement] meant that, if the Boshehs recovered nothing out of the litigation, Candey would not be entitled to anything by way of their costs. It was also agreed that, for these purposes, a settlement on a "drop hands" basis – with neither side recovering money from the other, and each side being responsible for its own costs – was a nil recovery and therefore meant that Candey would recover nothing from the Boshehs as a contribution towards the costs that they had incurred in acting pursuant to the CFA.' *Candey Ltd v Bosheh* [2022] EWCA Civ 1103, [2023] 3 All ER 26 at [12], per Coulson LJ

DURATION OF WORKING TIME

[Agency Workers Regulations 2010, SI 2010/93, regs 5, 6.] '[28] Mr Glyn's core submission, pleaded as ground (1) of the Grounds of Appeal and amplified by certain particular points pleaded as ground (2), was that the ET [Employment Tribunal] and the EAT [Employment Appeal Tribunal] had erred in law by failing to give reg 6(1)(b) what he said was its literal, natural and correct meaning. He contended that the phrase in reg 6(1) "terms and conditions relating to … duration of working time" naturally refers to any term dealing with the amount of time that a worker works and accordingly naturally covers the term in a contract that specifies the amount of work that the worker is both entitled and required to work. Accordingly, if the term of a comparator's contract of employment specified a 39-hour week the Claimant's entitlement under reg 5(1) to "the same … conditions" meant that he was entitled to work that number of hours. He submitted that that construction was consistent with the purpose of the Directive and in particular with the principle of equal treatment stated in art 5.

'[29] I do not accept either that that construction represents the natural meaning of the phrase "duration of working time" in reg 6(1)(b) or that it is consistent with the purpose of the legislation. My reasons are as follows.

'[30] I start with the words themselves. If one writes the definition of "working time" from para (5)(a) into para (1)(b), it reads:

> "… the duration of any period during which [the] individual is working, at the disposal of [his or her] employer … and carrying out [his or her] activity or duties".

There are elements of repetition or overlap in that definition and for present purposes I can shorten it to "the duration of any period during which the individual is working". (It would be possible to add in the other kinds of "working time" specified at para 5(b) and (c), but that would unnecessarily complicate the exercise.)

'[31] Even without any statutory context, I do not think it is natural to describe a term specifying the number of hours in the working week as relating to the "duration" of the "period" during which an individual is working. Mr Glyn referred us to the definition of "duration" in *Black's Law Dictionary* as "the length of time something lasts" or "the length of time; a continuance of time" and offered his own paraphrase "the time during which something continues". We need not be pinned to a specific definition, but I agree that "duration" connotes the length of a period of time. It seems to me to follow in the ordinary case that the period in question should be continuous, and indeed both the *Black*'s definition and Mr Glyn's incorporate that concept. That would mean that in this context the "periods" of time to whose duration reg 6(1)(b) refers are periods during which the worker is working continuously (ignoring rest-breaks), such as the working day or shift. Outside such a period the worker is neither working nor at the disposal of his or her employer nor carrying out any activity or duties. Regulation 5(1) would accordingly not apply to a term specifying a 39-hour working week, which will necessarily involve several discrete periods of work. Not only is that a correct use of language but it is in accordance with ordinary usage: you would not describe someone working full-time as working for a "period" of (say) 39 hours. At para 14 of his skeleton argument Mr Glyn summarises his position by adopting the shorthand "a quantity of time". But that is not accurate, because it does not incorporate the notion of a continuous period. It allows Mr Glyn to advance the apparently obvious proposition that 39 hours is "a quantity of time": no doubt in one sense it is, but it is not necessarily, and is not in this context, the duration of a period.

'[32] The position becomes clearer still when one takes into account the wider context. I have noted at para [17] above the correlations of heads (b)–(f) in reg 6(1) with the subject-matter, and language, of the WTR [Working Time Regulations 1998, SI 1998/1833]. In the light of that, it seems to me plain (subject to para [34] below) that reg 6(1)(b) is intended to refer to terms which set a maximum length for any such period, as the WTR does. …

'[33] That is how both the ET and the EAT read it: see para 49 of the ET's Reasons and para 44(a) and (b) of the EAT's judgment. I believe that they were right; and on that basis the Regulations do not entitle agency workers to work the same number of contractual hours as a comparator.' *Kocur v Angard Staffing Solutions Ltd* [2019] EWCA Civ 1185, [2020] 1 All ER 791 at [28]–[33], per Underhill VP

DURESS

[For 22 Halsbury's Laws of England (5th Edn) (2012) para 292 see now 22 Halsbury's Laws of England (5th Edn) (2019) para 92.]

[For 47 Halsbury's Laws of England (5th Edn) (2014) para 37 see now 47 Halsbury's Laws of England (5th Edn) (2021) para 37.]

DWELLING

[Housing Act 1985, ss 325, 326.] '[64] It has been recognised on the highest authority that "dwelling" is a normal English word which, in normal parlance, signifies the place where a person makes their home; and that a single room may in some circumstances qualify as a "dwelling". Where a person has exclusive possession of part and possession in common of other parts, it will be a question of fact and degree whether what was enjoyed in common was of such a character or of such significance as to preclude description of what was let as a separate dwelling. In making that assessment, distinctions have understandably and rightly been drawn between living rooms, such as bedrooms and kitchens, and ancillary offices, such as bathrooms and lavatories. Common enjoyment of the former but not the latter tend to weigh against recognition of the premises let as a separate dwelling ….

…

'[94] The question turns on whether the house is a "dwelling" as defined in s 343 HA 85. That section defines "dwelling" as "premises used or suitable for use as a separate dwelling". It was accepted by Mr Toby Vanhegan for the Appellant that the house was not "used … as a separate dwelling". He was clearly right about that: premises are only used as a separate dwelling if they are used for a single household. There is a very long history to the concept of a "separate dwelling'" familiar to all those who had to deal with the Rent Acts: see the account given by Lord Millett in *Uratemp* [*Uratemp Ventures Ltd v Collins* [2001] UKHL 43, [2002] 1 All ER 46, [2002] 1 AC 301] at [32]ff which traces the phrase "let as a separate dwelling" back to the first of the Rent Acts, the Increase of Rent and Mortgage Interest (War Restrictions) Act 1915, and the concept of a "separate dwelling" much further back to the reforms of the parliamentary franchise in 1832 and 1867.

'[95] It is not necessary to go over the history. The upshot of the long series of cases is that if premises are let to an occupier on terms that living accommodation is shared with others not in the same household, the occupier does not have a separate dwelling. For these purposes a kitchen is (generally) part of the living accommodation in a house so if, like the Appellant, the occupier of a bedroom has shared use of the kitchen, she does not have a separate dwelling. More significantly for present purposes, no one household occupies the house in which the Appellant lives as a whole. It is a house occupied by several different households. This is the very antithesis to a house let as a separate dwelling.' *Rowe v Haringey London Borough Council* [2022] EWCA Civ 1370, [2023] 2 All ER 1081 at [64], per Stuart-Smith LJ and at [94]–[95], per Nugee LJ

E

EASEMENT

[For 87 Halsbury's Laws of England (5th Edn) (2017) paras 731, 732, 734, 735, 737, 739 see now 87 Halsbury's Laws of England (5th Edn) (2022) paras 725, 726, 728, 729, 731, 733.]

New Zealand '[56] For an interest in land to be an easement, it must possess the following three characteristics:

(a) There must be a dominant tenement (the land deriving the benefit of the easement) and a servient tenement (the land over which the easement is exercisable). In this case, the dominant tenement is the Boatyard land and the servient tenement is the reserve.
(b) The right must accommodate (that is, confer a benefit on) the dominant tenement as opposed to a personal benefit on the owner of the dominant tenement.
(c) The right claimed must be capable of being the subject matter of the grant of an easement. This incorporates a number of requirements: that the easement be in sufficiently clear terms; that it is not so precarious that it is liable to be taken away by the servient owner; that it is not so extensive or invasive as to oust the servient owner from the enjoyment and control of the servient tenement; and that it does not impose on the servient owner an obligation to spend money or do anything beyond mere passivity.'

[Note: See *Re Ellenborough Park* [1956] Ch 131 at 163, CA (Eng). The additional requirement referred to in that case, that the owners of the dominant and the servient tenements must be different persons, is no longer a requirement in New Zealand: see the Land Transfer Act 2017, s 108(3). It is possible to have an easement in gross in New Zealand (that is, an easement in favour of a specified person, rather than specified land): see the Property Law Act 2007, s 291. Under that Act and the Land Transfer Act 2017, the terminology used in connection with easements is 'burdened land' rather than servient tenement and 'benefited land' rather than dominant tenement.]

Schmuck v Opua Coastal Preservation Inc [2019] NZSC 118, [2019] 1 NZLR 750 at [56], per O'Regan J

EDITION

[For 85 Halsbury's Laws of England (5th Edn) (2012) para 704, notes 2–3 see now 85 Halsbury's Laws of England (5th Edn) (2020) para 804.]

EDITOR

[For 85 Halsbury's Laws of England (5th Edn) (2012) para 732 see now 85 Halsbury's Laws of England (5th Edn) (2020) para 825.]

EFFECTED FOR THE PURPOSE OF

[European Convention for the Protection of Human Rights and Fundamental Freedoms 1950, art 5 (as set out in the Human Rights Act 1998, Sch 1); detention of a juvenile for his own protection or in his own interests under the Police and Criminal Evidence Act 1984, s 38.]

'[41] Against this background, the primary position for the appellant is simple: the appellant's detention was effected for the purpose of his own protection. Detention for that purpose is not permitted under art 5(1)(c), which only permits detention if its purpose is to bring the person before the court.

'[42] The respondent's counter-argument is said to require an interpretation of purpose that is divorced from the actual reason for detention. It is contrary to the plain and natural meaning of the phrase "effected for the purpose of", which must refer to the active reason for detention. Those words are to be construed according to their ordinary meaning in their context and in the light of the object and purpose of the provision from which they are drawn. The court is to have regard to the fact that the context of the provision is a treaty for the effective protection of individual human rights, taking into account any relevant rules and principles of international law applicable in relations between contracting states (see *Saadi v UK (App no 13229/03)* [2008] INLR 436, (2008) 47 EHRR 427 ("*Saadi*") at para 61). The respondent's interpretation requires an unnatural reading of the words and is inconsistent with the requirement to protect against arbitrary detention.' *Archer v Commissioner of Police of the Metropolis (Liberty and another intervening)* [2021] EWCA Civ 1662, [2022] 3 All ER 271 at [41]–[42], per Dame Victoria Sharp P

EFFECTS

In will: generally

[For 102 Halsbury's Laws of England (5th Edn) (2010) para 290 see now 102 Halsbury's Laws of England (5th Edn) (2021) para 290.]

EJUSDEM GENERIS

[For 32 Halsbury's Laws of England (5th Edn) (2012) para 435 see now 32 Halsbury's Laws of England (5th Edn) (2019) para 435.]

ELDEST

[For 102 Halsbury's Laws of England (5th Edn) (2010) para 335 see now 102 Halsbury's Laws of England (5th Edn) (2021) para 335.]

EMBLEMENTS

[For 1 Halsbury's Laws of England (5th Edn) (2017) para 466 see now 1 Halsbury's Laws of England (5th Edn) (2022) para 366.]

EMBRACERY

[For 26 Halsbury's Laws of England (5th Edn) (2015) para 369 see now 25 Halsbury's Laws of England (5th Edn) (2020) para 400.]

EMPLOYED FROM

[Industrial Training Act 1982, s 11(2); Industrial Training Levy (Construction Industry Training Board) Order 2015, SI 2015/701, arts 5(4), 7(1), (2). Company providing freelance operatives to clients in the construction industry.] '[74] So, what does employed *from* mean in this context, and does it cover Hudson's operatives in relation to the Bridlington head office? I do not accept Mr Maugham's argument that the concept of being employed *from* is limited to a situation where, for example construction industry tools and/or equipment are kept at a base (or yard) and workers go from the base or yard to a construction site. That too may be a paradigm example. However, it is not difficult to imagine many different kinds of self-employed, agency and labour-only workers in the construction industry, who may never go to a yard or base of any kind, but instead, go straight from home to the particular site at which they are then working. (The cleaning agency analogy adopted by the Tribunal is an example in a different industry; there are many others). It seems to me that in that situation, if an operative is employed (in the extended sense used in the 1982 Act) by a company, agency or entity with whom his or her only legal relationship is the contract they have entered into, and the company is based at its head office, then the operative may be employed *from* the head office too. That the company does not control, supervise or organise the worker's work from the head office (or at all) is irrelevant in the context of employment in this extended sense. Similarly, that the operative has no contact with head office staff and does not go there is also irrelevant in this context.

'[75] In reaching its conclusion that Hudson's operatives are employed *from* the Bridlington head office, the Tribunal relied on the following facts. Significantly, the contract made between Hudson and the operative (and indeed Hudson and the client) makes clear that Hudson steps into the shoes of the client and contracts with the operative on the terms negotiated between the operative and the client. The operative expressly agrees that he or she has no contract of any type whatsoever with the client. In these circumstances the fact that the contract is signed at the client's offices is nothing to the point – the client is merely acting as Hudson's agent – and the contract is returned to Hudson's head office since Hudson is the contracting counterparty. Further, Hudson knows (from the completed contract) the name of the operative, his trade and the client company, representative and address of the site where the contract is completed. Hudson is responsible for deducting tax and national insurance contributions and paying each operative from the Bridlington head office. If and to the extent that any status issue arises, it is dealt with from the head office by Hudson.

'[76] In my judgment, both as a matter of law and on the facts I have summarised, the Employment Tribunal was entitled to conclude that Hudson's operatives are employed *from* the head office at Bridlington which is a construction establishment accordingly, and Lambert J was correct to reject this ground of appeal. …' *Hudson Contract Services Ltd v Construction Industry Training Board* [2020] EWCA Civ 328, [2020] 4 All ER 1007 at [74]–[76], per Smiler LJ

EMPLOYEE

Casual employee

Australia [Fair Work Act 2009 (Cth), ss 86, 95, 106.] '[31] The meaning of casual employee as used in the expression "other than casual employees" in s 86 of the FW Act (dealing with entitlements to annual leave), s 95 of the FW Act (dealing with entitlements to personal/carer's leave) and s 106 of the FW Act (dealing with compassionate leave) was not in contest. It was accepted that in *Skene* [*WorkPac Pty Ltd v Skene* (2018) 264 FCR 536; 362 ALR 311; [2018] FCAFC 131], a Full Court of this Court (Tracey, Bromberg and Rangiah JJ) correctly determined that a casual employee is an employee who has no firm advance commitment from her or his employer to continuing and indefinite work according to an agreed pattern of work (**"firm advance commitment"**).' *WorkPac Pty Ltd v Rossato* [2020] FCAFC 84, (2020) 378 ALR 585 at [31], per Bromberg J

EMPLOYER IN THE CONSTRUCTION INDUSTRY

[Industrial Training Act 1982, s 11(2); Industrial Training Levy (Construction Industry Training Board) Order 2015, SI 2015/701, art 3(1). Liability to Construction Industry Training Board levy imposed on an 'employer in the construction industry'. Company providing freelance operatives to clients in the construction industry.] '[34] As already summarised above, the Employment Tribunal found that Hudson is an "employer in the construction industry" for two linked reasons. First, the Employment Tribunal concluded that what an employer does is to be determined by what its employees do. Secondly, since employees are defined by the 1982 Act to include self-employed contractors as well as directly employed employees, the question whether Hudson is an employer in the construction industry falls to be determined not just by reference to what its directly employed staff do, but also by reference to what the many thousands of self-employed operatives do. As the self-employed operatives are "in the construction industry", so too, the Employment Tribunal found, Hudson is also in the construction industry.

'[35] Lambert J's reasoning on the first issue was to similar effect: what Hudson does is to be answered not just by what the directly employed workforce do, but by what its 20,000 or more statutory employees do. As the Tribunal found, they are in the construction industry and therefore so is Hudson. …

…

'[61] … [I]n agreement with both the Employment Tribunal and Lambert J, on a proper construction of art 3(1) of the 2015 Order Hudson is an employer in the construction industry. …' *Hudson Contract Services Ltd v Construction Industry Training Board* [2020] EWCA Civ 328, [2020] 4 All ER 1007 at [34]–[35], [61], per Smiler LJ

EMPLOYERS' ASSOCIATION

[For 40 Halsbury's Laws of England (5th Edn) (2014) para 1079 see now 40 Halsbury's Laws of England (5th Edn) (2021) para 1073.]

EMPLOYMENT

[Double Taxation Relief (Taxes on Income) (South Africa) Order 2002, SI 2002/3138, arts 7, 14. If taxpayer was self-employed, by virtue of art 7, which applied to business profits, he was taxable in South Africa. If not, and the income was employment income, he was taxable in the UK by virtue of art 14. Income Tax (Trading and Other Income) Act 2005, s 15: in the case of a person who performs the duties of employment as a diver or diving supervisor in the UK or Continental Shelf, performance of the duties of employment is treated for income tax purposes as the carrying on of a trade in the United Kingdom.] '[11] So the first question is: what is the meaning of "employment" for the purposes of UK tax law? If UK tax law does not provide a complete answer then the second question is: what does "employment" mean under the general law of the UK?

'[12] For the purposes of UK taxation, s 4 of the Income Tax (Earnings and Pensions) Act 2003 ('the 2003 Act') contains a partial definition of "employment". It provides:

"In the employment income Parts 'employment' includes in particular–

(a) any employment under a contract of service,
(b) any employment under a contract of apprenticeship, and
(c) any employment in the service of the Crown."

'[13] Since this is not an exhaustive definition, but only an inclusive one, I consider that the meaning of the word "employment" has to be supplemented, where necessary, by the meaning of that word under the general law of England and Wales. This is expressly permitted by art 3(2) of the treaty. Although the partial definition of "employment" in the tax legislation prevails over the meaning of that word under the general law of England and Wales, where the definition is incomplete it is permissible to resort to other laws of the contracting state. For the purposes of the preliminary issue we must, I think, assume that Mr Fowler carried out his diving activities under a contract of service. On that assumption, his activities fell within the express definition of "employment".' *Fowler v Revenue and Customs Commissioners* [2018] EWCA Civ 2544, [2019] 1 All ER 717 at [11]–[13], per Lewison LJ (dissenting)

'[29] Like Lewison LJ and Marcus Smith J in the Upper Tribunal I have, with respect, reached the opposite conclusion. My reasons follow. The starting point is that the question which of arts 7 and 14 of the Treaty applies to Mr Fowler's diving activities depends upon the true construction of those articles, in the context of the Treaty as a whole and its purposes, with the meaning of terms within those articles ascertained as required by art 3(2) by reference to UK income tax law. The relevant terms are, in art 7, "profits" and "enterprise of a contracting state" and, in art 14, "salaries, wages and other similar remuneration" and "employment".

'[30] Nothing in the Treaty requires arts 7 and 14 to be applied to the fictional, deemed world which may be created by UK income tax legislation. Rather they are to be applied to the real world, unless the effect of art 3(2) is that a deeming provision alters the meaning which relevant terms of the Treaty would otherwise have. This much is confirmed by para 8(11) of the OECD Commentary quoted above, and it would be contrary to the requirement to treat the Treaty as a bilateral international agreement to do otherwise, as required by the dicta in the *Anson* case [*Revenue and Customs Comrs v Anson* [2015] UKSC 44, [2015] 4 All ER 288]. Were it not for s 15 of ITTOIA, there would be no doubt that art 14, not art 7, would apply to Mr Fowler's diving activities, at least on the necessary but as yet untested assumption that he really was an employee. The meaning of "employment" is laid down in s 4 of ITEPA, and his remuneration plainly constitutes employment income within ss 6 and 7. UK tax law would not regard him as making profits from a trade, or his business as being that of an establishment.' *Fowler v Revenue and Customs Commissioners* [2020] UKSC 22, [2021] 1 All ER 97 at [29]–[30], per Lord Briggs JSC

ENACTMENT

[For 96 Halsbury's Laws of England (5th Edn) (2012) para 609 see now 96 Halsbury's Laws of England (5th Edn) (2018) para 209.]

ENDOWMENT

Permanent endowment

(3) For the purposes of this Act, property is 'permanent endowment' if it is subject to a restriction on being expended which distinguishes between income and capital. (Charities Act 2011, s 353(3) (as substituted by the Charities Act 2022, s 9))

ENEMY

[For 3 Halsbury's Laws of England (5th Edn) (2011) para 194 et seq see now 3 Halsbury's Laws of England (5th Edn) (2019) para 462 et seq.]

ENFORCEMENT POWER

Provision is made under the Tribunals, Courts and Enforcement Act 2007 that applies where an enactment, writ or warrant confers power to use the statutory taking control of goods procedure ('the TCG procedure'). The power conferred by a writ or warrant of control to recover a sum of money, and any power conferred by a writ or warrant of possession or delivery to take control of goods and sell them to recover a sum of money, is exercisable only by using the TCG procedure. A power to use the TCG procedure to recover a particular sum is called an 'enforcement power'. Only an enforcement agent may take control of goods and sell them under an enforcement power. (12A Halsbury's Laws of England (5th Edn) (2020) para 1308)

ENTAILED INTEREST

[For 87 Halsbury's Laws of England (5th Edn) (2017) paras 111–112 see now 87 Halsbury's Laws of England (5th Edn) (2022) paras 111–112.]

ENTIRE CONTRACT

[For 6 Halsbury's Laws of England (5th Edn) (2018) para 209 see now 6 Halsbury's Laws of England (5th Edn) (2023) para 309.]

ENTITLED

In possession

[For 80 Halsbury's Laws of England (5th Edn) (2013) para 834 et seq see now 80 Halsbury's Laws of England (5th Edn) (2020) para 834 et seq.]

EQUITY—EQUITABLE

Equitable charge

[For 77 Halsbury's Laws of England (5th Edn) (2016) para 106 see now 77 Halsbury's Laws of England (5th Edn) (2021) para 106.]

Equitable execution

[For 12A Halsbury's Laws of England (5th Edn) (2015) para 1492 et seq see now 12A Halsbury's Laws of England (5th Edn) (2020) para 1463 et seq.]

Equity of redemption

[For 77 Halsbury's Laws of England (5th Edn) (2016) para 107 see now 77 Halsbury's Laws of England (5th Edn) (2021) para 107.]

Equitable interest

[For 87 Halsbury's Laws of England (5th Edn) (2017) para 100 see now 87 Halsbury's Laws of England (5th Edn) (2022) para 100.]

EQUIVALENT PERIOD OF COMPENSATORY REST

[Working Time Regulations 1998, SI 1998/1833 (WTR), reg 24: if the application of reg 12 (allowing a rest break of an uninterrupted period of not less than 20 minutes) was excluded by reg 21(f) (workers in railway transport), employer must wherever possible allow a worker to take 'an equivalent period of compensatory rest'.] '[42] I begin with the question whether it is necessary as a matter of law for an "equivalent period of compensatory rest" within the meaning of reg 24(a) to consist of an uninterrupted 20 minutes. …

'[43] The starting-point must be that reg 24 is only engaged because the WTR, following the Directive [Directive 2003/88/EC], provides that in the case of the kinds of work identified in reg 21 an employer is not required to afford workers rest breaks satisfying the requirements of reg 12. That being so, the description of the compensatory rest required under reg 24(a) as "equivalent" cannot be intended to import the identical obligation that would have applied under reg 12. Rather, the intention must be that the rest afforded to the worker should have the same value in terms of contributing to his or her well-being. That is what Lady Smith says at para [13] of her judgment in *Hughes* [*Hughes v Corps of Commissionaires Management Ltd (No 2)* [2011] EWCA Civ 1061, [2011] IRLR 915, [2012] 1 CMLR 649] (see para [36] above), with which I agree (subject to one immaterial caveat): it should be noted that she was sitting with (highly-experienced) lay members, and the views of the EAT on matters of this kind should be respected wherever possible. Although on the appeal only one aspect of the EAT's reasoning was formally in issue this Court certainly endorsed its view that the requirements of reg 12 and reg 24 cannot be identical. Indeed at para [23], albeit in a part of the judgment dealing with a different issue, Elias LJ said in terms:

> "… the concept of an equivalent period of compensatory rest under reg 24(a) cannot be a period identical to a reg 12 break. It is something given in place of that break."

'[44] Whether the rest afforded in any given case is "equivalent", in the sense explained by Lady Smith, must be a matter for the informed judgment of the (specialist) employment tribunal. There is no basis in principle for the proposition that only an uninterrupted break of 20 minutes can afford an equivalent benefit in that sense; and the provision for a collective or workforce agreement to make some different arrangement would be meaningless if that were so. I can see no reason why a single uninterrupted break of 20 minutes will always be better than, say, two uninterrupted breaks of 15 minutes one-third and two-thirds through the shift. The evidence referred to at para [28] above provides other illustrations of how different kinds of rest may be thought appropriate in particular cases.' *Crawford v Network Rail Infrastructure Ltd* [2019] EWCA Civ 269, [2019] 2 All ER 1095 at [42]–[44], per Underhill VP

ESCAPE

From prison

[For 26 Halsbury's Laws of England (5th Edn) (2016) para 806 see now 26 Halsbury's Laws of England (5th Edn) (2020) para 1009.]

ESCHEAT

[For 87 Halsbury's Laws of England (5th Edn) (2017) para 266 see now 87 Halsbury's Laws of England (5th Edn) (2022) para 266.]

ESCROW

[For 32 Halsbury's Laws of England (5th Edn) (2012) para 237 see now 32 Halsbury's Laws of England (5th Edn) (2019) para 237.]

ESPIONAGE

Australia '[109] The primary judge held that the applicant had used the word "espionage" in his imputation 5(a) in its ordinary and natural meaning, namely the practice of spying, or of employing spies, citing the *Oxford English Dictionary Online* and the *Macquarie Dictionary*. His Honour stated that—

> [A] spy is someone who spies upon, or watches, someone secretly or who is employed by a government to obtain information or intelligence relating to the military or naval or governmental affairs of one or more other countries, or to collect intelligence of any other kind.

'[110] His Honour held at [85]–[87] that paragraph 14(a) of the respondents' particulars might have been unobjectionable were it not accompanied by the alternative in (b), which is not a natural or ordinary meaning of "espionage". His Honour held that paragraph 14 was embarrassing because it sought to expand espionage to encompass vague and imprecise concepts which were not within the natural and ordinary meaning of the word "espionage". His Honour further observed that the activities alleged in paragraphs 15 to 17 of the particulars, such as the making of donations, offers, provision of trips, or access to persons of influence in China, were not within the ordinary meaning of the word "espionage" either. His Honour stated that he did not consider that the respondents could justify an imputation of "espionage" by redefining that word in their particulars and then using that bespoke sense to justify the imputation as redefined. However, his Honour stated that it was not necessary to decide the question, because his Honour considered that the particulars had more fundamental flaws.

...

'[172] Before the primary judge, the applicant submitted that "espionage" meant "spying". The primary judge accepted that submission, holding that "spying" was the natural and ordinary meaning of "espionage". His Honour did not say anything to suggest that there was any relevant ambiguity in the applicant's imputation 5(a) and its employment of the term "espionage". If his Honour had thought there was ambiguity, then he could have required the applicant to amend further the statement of claim to make the meaning of espionage explicit in the pleading. Before this Court, senior counsel for the applicant continued to submit that "espionage" in the applicant's imputation (a) meant "spying", and accepted that in confining the imputation to espionage in this way, the applicant had made a forensic choice.

'[173] The amendments made to the Criminal Code (Cth) by the National Security Legislation Amendment (Espionage and Foreign Interference) Act 2018 (Cth), to which the parties referred in argument, draw a distinction between espionage (Division 91), and foreign interference (Division 92). For the purposes of the Criminal Code, the content of both concepts is found in the statute, and they are different. In this case, we are not concerned with a statutory concept of "espionage", but with the content of the imputation alleged by the applicant. Whatever possible views there might be of the meaning of the word "espionage" generally, or in particular contexts, it is tolerably clear that for the purposes of the applicant's imputation (a), the applicant's case is that "espionage" has a meaning akin to "spying", and does not extend to the broader concepts such as those that were alleged by the respondents in their bespoke definition of "espionage" in paragraph 14(b) of their particulars which extend to influence, and attempted influence. We agree with the primary judge's opinion that the concepts into which the respondents sought to extend the meaning of espionage were vague and imprecise. In accordance with the relevant principles in *Sutherland v Stopes* [[1925] AC 47, HL], *Chakravarti [Chakravarti v Advertiser Newspapers Ltd* (1998) 193 CLR 519; 154 ALR 294; [1998] HCA 37], and *Hore-Lacy [Hore-Lacy v Cleary* (2007) 18 VR 562; [2007] VSCA 314], the respondents' defence of justification should be directed to the substance or sting of the applicant's meaning, or a permissible variant of it. We consider that there is a substantial difference between "espionage" as it is employed in the applicant's imputation 5(a), and the breadth of the respondents' case, with the consequence that the respondents' case relating to "espionage" is not responsive. The breadth of the respondents' case is manifested in paragraph 59(g) of their particulars which we set out at [111] above, which contains the only direct allegation of espionage by the applicant. That allegation is descriptive of political influence, and is far removed from the sense in which the applicant's imputation 5(a) is to be understood.' *Australian Broadcasting Corp v Chau Chak Wing* [2019] FCAFC 125, (2019) 371 ALR 545 at [109]–[110], [172]–[173], per Besanko, Bromwich and Wheelahan JJ

ESTATE

[For 87 Halsbury's Laws of England (5th Edn) (2017) para 2 see now 87 Halsbury's Laws of England (5th Edn) (2022) para 2.]

ESTOPPEL

Agency by

[For 1 Halsbury's Laws of England (5th Edn) (2017) para 25 see now 1 Halsbury's Laws of England (5th Edn) (2022) para 25.]

ESTRAYS

[For 29 Halsbury's Laws of England (5th Edn) (2014) para 286 see now 29 Halsbury's Laws of England (5th Edn) (2019) para 291.]

EVERYONE

Canada [Canadian Charter of Rights and Freedoms 1982, s 7: everyone has the right to life, liberty and security of the person and the right not to be deprived thereof except in accordance with the principles of fundamental justice.] **'96** That is, read as a whole, it appears to us that this section was intended to confer protection on a singularly human level. A plain, common sense reading of the phrase "Everyone has the right to life, liberty and security of the person" serves to underline the human element involved; only human beings can enjoy these rights. "Everyone" then, must be read in light of the rest of the section and defined to exclude corporations and other artificial entities incapable of enjoying life, liberty or security of the person, and include only human beings. …' *Irwin Toy Ltd v Quebec (Attorney General)* [1989] 1 SCR 927, [1989] SCJ No 36 at para 96, per Dickson CJ and Lamer and Wilson JJ.

EVICTION

[For 62 Halsbury's Laws of England (5th Edn) (2016) para 265 see now 62 Halsbury's Laws of England (5th Edn) (2022) para 288.]

EVIDENCE

[For 12 Halsbury's Laws of England (5th Edn) (2015) para 685 see now 12 Halsbury's Laws of England (5th Edn) (2020) para 680.]

Best evidence

[For 12 Halsbury's Laws of England (5th Edn) (2015) para 694 see now 12 Halsbury's Laws of England (5th Edn) (2020) para 689.]

Hearsay evidence

[For 12 Halsbury's Laws of England (5th Edn) (2015) para 697 see now 12 Halsbury's Laws of England (5th Edn) (2020) para 692.]

Secondary evidence

[For 12 Halsbury's Laws of England (5th Edn) (2015) para 695 see now 12 Halsbury's Laws of England (5th Edn) (2020) para 690.]

EXCEEDED

[Abortion Act 1967, s 1(1)(a): legal termination of pregnancy by a registered medical practitioner.] '[1] The issue in this case is the correct interpretation of the words, "the pregnancy has not exceeded its twenty-fourth week" in s 1(1)(a) of the Abortion Act 1967 ("the 1967 Act").

...

'[57] In my judgment the correct construction of the words "the pregnancy has not exceeded its twenty-fourth week" in s 1(1)(a) of the 1967 Act is that a woman will have exceeded her 24th week of pregnancy once she is 24 weeks + 0 days pregnant, or in other words, from midnight on the expiration of her 24th week of pregnancy, as stated in the Decision Letter [letter clarifying the Department of Health and Social Care's interpretation of the legal time limit].' *R (on the application of British Pregnancy Advisory Service) v Secretary of State for Health and Social Care* [2019] EWHC 1397 (Admin), [2019] 4 All ER 661 at [1], [57], per Supperstone J

'[70] In my view, the legal construction of the words "the pregnancy has not exceeded its twenty-fourth week" should be consistent with clinical practice, in particular as to the calculation of the gestational age of a foetus. It is necessary in order to provide certainty in respect of a penal statute, the interpretation of which has serious consequences for vulnerable women and medical practitioners.

'[71] Consistent with clinical practice, day 0 being the first day of the pregnancy and counting as one day, day 168 of the pregnancy occurs at week 23 + day 6. The 169th day is week 24 + 0 days and is the first day of the 25th week.

'[72] The appellant's case rests on the proposition that on week 24 + 0 days, 24 weeks of pregnancy have been "reached" but not "exceeded". I do not accept this to be correct. Once a period of time has elapsed, at every moment thereafter it has been exceeded; once the 24th week is complete the 25th week begins. Day 169 is the start of the 25th week. That is represented by a gestational age of the foetus of 24 weeks + 0 days.

'[73] In my judgment, the correct construction of the words "the pregnancy has not exceeded its twenty-fourth week" in s 1(1)(a) of the 1967 Act is that a woman will have exceeded her 24th week of pregnancy once she is 24 weeks + 0 days pregnant, which will commence from midnight on the expiration of 23 weeks + 6 days.

'[74] This construction is consistent with and reflects clinical practice. It accords with the construction of the phrase by Supperstone J. ...' *R (on the application of British Pregnancy Advisory Service) v Secretary of State for Health and Social Care* [2020] EWCA Civ 355, [2020] 4 All ER 1082 at [70]–[74], per Nicola Davies LJ

EXECUTION

Irregular or wrongful

[For 12A Halsbury's Laws of England (5th Edn) (2015) para 1372 et seq see now 12 Halsbury's Laws of England (5th Edn) (2020) para 1346 et seq.]

EXECUTOR

[For 103 Halsbury's Laws of England (5th Edn) (2010) para 606 see now 103 Halsbury's Laws of England (5th Edn) (2021) para 680.]

EXIT DAY

'"Exit day" means 31 January 2020 at 11 pm. ... In this Act references to before, after or on exit day, or to beginning with exit day, are to be read as references to before, after or at 11 pm on 31 January 2020 or (as the case may be) to beginning with 11 pm on that day.' (European Union (Withdrawal) Act 2018, s 20(1), (2) (amended by SI 2019/859 and SI 2019/1423)

EXONERATION

[For 5 Halsbury's Laws of England (5th Edn) (2013) para 674 see now 5 Halsbury's Laws of England (5th Edn) (2020) para 657.]

EXPENSES

Expenses incurred

[Political Parties, Elections and Referendums Act 2000, s 111(2): referendum expenses.] '[36] We turn to the question of what is meant by "expenses incurred" in the definition of "referendum expenses" in s 111(2) of PPERA quoted at para [26] above. The claimant's case is that in the definition the term "expense" means no more than an outflow of economic benefit and that to "incur" an expense simply means to bring upon oneself an expense or render oneself liable to an expense. Thus, "expenses" may be "incurred" by voluntarily making a payment which diminishes a person's assets as well as by assuming an obligation or liability to make such a payment. Counsel for the claimant submitted that this interpretation is consistent both with the ordinary dictionary meanings of the words and with the purpose of the legislation.

…

'[41] As a matter of ordinary English usage, the phrase "expenses incurred" is, we apprehend, most naturally understood in the broad sense contended for by the claimant. It is natural to describe a person as having incurred an expense whenever he or she has spent money or incurred a liability which in either case reduces his or her financial resources. This is also the sense in which accountants typically use the term – albeit with greater precision than in ordinary usage. For example, FRS 102, the Financial Reporting Standard applicable in the UK, defines "expenses" as "decreases in economic benefits during the reporting period in the form of outflows or depletions of assets or incurrences of liabilities that result in decreases in equity, other than those relating to distributions to equity investors". The concept is similarly defined in the Conceptual Framework for Financial Reporting issued by the International Accounting Standards Board. Under s 121 of PPERA, a permitted participant who incurs referendum expenses exceeding £250,000 during any referendum period is required to appoint an auditor to prepare a report on its return to the Electoral Commission. It would be reasonable to expect an auditor appointed for this purpose, unless otherwise instructed, to apply standard accounting concepts in verifying that the return gives a true and fair view of the expenses incurred by the permitted participant during the referendum period.

'[42] We do not accept that as a matter of ordinary language incurring an expense means the same as incurring a liability, as was argued on behalf of Vote Leave. An "expense" and a "liability" are different concepts. Certainly, someone who, for example, purchases goods under a contract and thereby incurs a liability to pay for them would naturally be said to have incurred an expense. But so too would someone who makes a donation to a charity. In the ordinary meaning of the words an expense can just as well be incurred by making a payment voluntarily without any obligation to do so as by undertaking an obligation to make a payment: the value of the person's assets is equally diminished in each case. It is also to be expected that, if the intention were to restrict the meaning of "referendum expenses" to expenses which there is a liability to pay, the legislation would say so expressly and that the word "liable" or "liability" would appear in the definition.' *R (on the application of the Good Law Project) v Electoral Commission (Vote Leave Ltd and another, interested parties)* [2018] EWHC 2414 (Admin), [2019] 1 All ER 365 at [36], [41]–[42], per Leggatt LJ

Expenses of a capital nature

[Corporation Tax Act 2009, s 1219.] '[59] I accept Mr Ewart's submission as to the correct interpretation of s 1219(3)(a) of the CTA 2009, that the reference to "expenses of a capital nature" must have the same meaning as "items of a capital nature" in s 53(1) of that Act … .

…

'[66] In my view, what Parliament did in 2004 is analogous. This indicates that Parliament intended that the phrase "expenses of a capital nature" should be interpreted in accordance with the meaning which it had acquired in the case law on what is materially the same phrase in other parts of the tax code.' *Centrica Overseas Holdings Ltd v Revenue and Customs Commissioners* [2022] EWCA Civ 1520, [2023] 3 All ER 148 at [59], [66], per Singh LJ

EXPLORE

Australia [Petroleum (Submerged Lands) Act 1982 (WA) and the Offshore Petroleum and Greenhouse Gas Storage Act 2006 (Cth) (collectively referred to as the Petroleum Acts).] '[31] Ultimately I did not find the dictionary meanings of great assistance to the process of construction in ascertaining the intended scope of those terms [explore/exploration] as they appear in the Petroleum Acts, because the natural and ordinary meaning of those terms do not decisively favour one construction over the other as a matter of textual analysis. Those terms are of sufficiently wide embrace in their ordinary and natural meaning to cover activities conducted for the purpose of evaluating the feasibility of recovering petroleum. To put it another way, an activity directed to "discovering" whether petroleum is recoverable does not require a departure from the ordinary and natural meaning of the verb "to explore" or the noun "exploration". Nor does the use of the preposition "for", as a matter of language, compel a different view. The word "for" in ordinary meaning means "with the object or purpose of" (see the *Macquarie Dictionary*) and as the word "explore" does not have a precise or rigid meaning as a matter of language, the expression "exploration for petroleum" is wide enough in meaning to include activities undertaken for the purpose of appraising the recovery of petroleum on a commercial basis as a matter of textual analysis.

…

'[52] The primary judge, in his consideration of the construction issue, observed as follows at [233]–[237]:

> …
>
> Having regard to the preceding matters, and adopting a contextual approach, the term "explore" as used in the [Petroleum Acts] should be interpreted to mean offshore activities undertaken to determine whether there is *recoverable* petroleum. Activities that might be connected in some way with exploration but are not undertaken in the area are not prohibited and are not the subject of the permission.

I agree and adopt those passages.' *Commissioner of Taxation (Cth) v Shell Energy Holdings Australia Ltd* [2022] FCAFC 2, (2022) 396 ALR 565 at [31], [52], per Davies J

EXTRAORDINARY CIRCUMSTANCES

[European Parliament and Council Regulation 261/2004/EC, art 5(3): carrier not liable to pay compensation if it could prove that cancellation of flight was caused by 'extraordinary circumstances which could not have been avoided even if all reasonable measures had been taken'.] '[1] Passengers whose flights are cancelled or significantly delayed are entitled to compensation under European Parliament and Council Regulation 261/2004/EC ("the Regulation"). The only way in which the air carrier can avoid paying such compensation is by demonstrating that the cancellation or significant delay was caused by "extraordinary circumstances". In the present case, the appellants' flight was cancelled because the captain did not attend for work due to illness. The respondent maintained that, because the captain became ill while he was off-duty, his non-attendance was an extraordinary circumstance within the meaning of the Regulation. Both the Deputy District Judge and the Circuit Judge accepted the respondent's argument. The appellants appeal to this court on the basis that the captain's non-attendance did not amount to an extraordinary circumstance, and that it cannot matter whether the captain became ill when he was on or off duty.

…

'[29] In my view, … the respondent has not made out a case of extraordinary circumstances on these facts. The non-attendance of the captain due to illness was an inherent part of the respondent's activity and operations as an air carrier, and could in no way be categorised as extraordinary.

'[30] As the CJEU emphasised at para 17 of their judgment in *Wallentin-Hermann* [*Wallentin-Hermann v Alitalia-Linee Aeree Italiane SpA* (Case C-549/07) [2009] Bus LR 1016], the expression "extraordinary circumstances" in art 5(3) of the Regulation must be given its usual meaning in everyday language. "Extraordinary circumstances" means something out of the ordinary: see *Sturgeon* [*Sturgeon v Condor Flugdienst GmbH, Böck v Air France SA* (Joined cases C-402/07 and C-432/07) EU:C:2009:716, [2010] 2 All ER (Comm) 983, [2009] ECR I-10923, ECJ] and *Jet2 v Huzar* [*Jet2.Com Ltd v Huzar* [2014] 4 All ER 581]. Staff illness, and the need to accommodate such illness on a daily basis, is a commonplace for any business. It is a mundane fact of commercial life: it is in no way out of the ordinary. To use the rather convoluted language of *Wallentin-Hermann* at para 44(1), the possibility of the captain's absence was, by its nature and origin, inherent in the normal exercise of the activity of the respondent. It was part of its operating system.

…

'[50] Accordingly, for all these reasons, I consider that the captain's non-attendance for work due to illness was inherent in the air carrier's activity and operations and was not an "extraordinary circumstance" within the meaning of art 5(3) of the Regulation. …' *Lipton v BA City Flyer Ltd* [2021] EWCA Civ 454, [2022] 1 All ER 120 at [1], [29]–[30], [50], per Coulson LJ

EXTRAORDINARY TRAFFIC

[In the final paragraph, for the words 'in the High Court or (where not exceeding £500) in the county court' substitute 'in the County Court'. For 55 Halsbury's Laws of England (5th Edn) (2012) paras 316–318 see now 55 Halsbury's Laws of England (5th Edn) (2019) paras 341, 345–347.]

F

FACILITIES FOR … RECREATION

[Ministry of Housing and Local Government Provisional Order Confirmation (Greater London Parks and Open Spaces) Act 1967, Sch 1, art 7(1)(a)(v): power for local authority in any open space to provide and maintain 'indoor facilities for any form of recreation whatsoever'; whether this included a day nursery for pre-school children.] '[21] Ms Wakefield supported the judge's interpretation of "recreation". She accepted that the children at the proposed nursery would engage in play and therefore in recreation, but the purposes of the interested party's facility were not so limited. At least for the purposes of sub-para (v) it was necessary to ask whether the purpose was wholly or mainly recreation. If one asked that question, the answer was that the interested party's nursery was obviously not within sub-para (v).

'[22] I agree with Ms Wakefield that, to come within sub-para (v), the facilities must be wholly or mainly for recreation. I would accept that a facility which is wholly or mainly for recreation is not disqualified because some necessary ancillary activity will also be carried on there. Thus an indoor recreational facility for children does not become disqualified under sub-para (v) because it is pointed out that children learn through play, and that the children are thereby being provided with a form of education. The purpose of the facility remains wholly or mainly recreational. It is not enough, however, that recreation occurs or may occur within the facility. So to construe art 7(1) would give the local authority free rein to provide any service to the public by means of an indoor facility in an open space provided they included a play area within the facility. Subparagraph (v) does not permit additional or different facilities which do not meet the description "recreation".

…

'[24] To my mind, therefore, the proposed facilities do not fall within sub-para (v) for essentially two reasons. Firstly, the proposed facility is more in the nature of a school than a recreational facility. … Secondly, the proposed facility will offer services which are not a necessary or inherent part of recreation and which go far beyond it, by providing all-day child care for pre-school children while their parents are at work or engaged elsewhere. …

…

'[26] … It is possible that there may be a penumbra around the terms "facilities for … recreation" in sub-para (v), but the meaning of the term itself is a question of law which the court can and must decide. Given the conclusion I have reached, the question of whether the proposed nursery school is wholly or mainly for recreation is, in my judgment, only capable of being answered in the negative.' *R (on the application of Muir) v Wandsworth Borough Council (Smart Pre-Schools Ltd, interested party)* [2018] EWCA Civ 1035, [2018] 4 All ER 422 at [21]–[22]. [24], [26], per Floyd LJ

FACTOR

[For 1 Halsbury's Laws of England (5th Edn) (2017) para 13 see now 1 Halsbury's Laws of England (5th Edn) (2022) para 13.]

FAIR (NOUN)

[For 71 Halsbury's Laws of England (5th Edn) (2013) paras 802–803 see now 71 Halsbury's Laws of England (5th Edn) (2020) paras 702–703.]

FAIR COMMENT

See now HONEST OPINION

[For 32 Halsbury's Laws of England (5th Edn) (2012) paras 637–638 see now 32 Halsbury's Laws of England (5th Edn) (2019) paras 637–638.]

Rolled-up plea

[For 32 Halsbury's Laws of England (5th Edn) (2012) see now 32 Halsbury's Laws of England (5th Edn) (2019).]

FAST AND LOOSE

[For 1 Halsbury's Laws of England (5th Edn) (2008) para 344 note 4 see now 2 Halsbury's Laws of England (5th Edn) (2023) para 349 note 4.]

FAMILY ARRANGEMENT

[For 91 Halsbury's Laws of England (5th Edn) (2012) paras 903, 906 see now 91 Halsbury's Laws of England (5th Edn) (2019) paras 789, 792.]

FEDERAL BOARD, COMMISSION OR OTHER TRIBUNAL

Canada [*Federal Courts Act*, RSC 1985, c F-7, s 2.] '18. The *Federal Courts Act* does not allow for judicial review of parliamentary activities. Indeed, ss 18 and 18.1 only grant the Federal Court jurisdiction to judicially review action taken by "any federal board, commission or other tribunal". A "federal board, commission or other tribunal" is defined in the Act, subject to certain exceptions, as a body exercising statutory powers or powers under an order made pursuant to a prerogative of the Crown (s 2; see also *Strickland v Canada (Attorney General)* 2015 SCC 37, [2015] 2 SCR 713, at para 64). Section 2(2) specifies that "federal board, commission or other tribunal" does not include "the Senate, the House of Commons, any committee or member of either House". Thus, I agree that s 2(2) is designed "to preclude judicial review of the legislative process at large" (CA reasons, at para 32). As I will explain further below, Cabinet and ministers do not act pursuant to statutory powers when developing legislation; rather, they act pursuant to powers under Part IV of the *Constitution Act, 1867*. As such, when developing legislation, they do not act as a "federal board, commission or other tribunal" within the meaning of s 2 (see *Shade v Canada (Attorney General)* 2003 FCT 327, 230 FTR.53, at para 34).' *Mikisew Cree First Nation v Canada (Governor General in Council)* [2018] SCJ No 40, [2018] 2 SCR 765 at para 18, per Karakatsanis J

FEE FARM RENT

[For 87 Halsbury's Laws of England (5th Edn) (2017) para 1046 see now 87 Halsbury's Laws of England (5th Edn) (2022) para 1041.]

FEE SIMPLE

[For 87 Halsbury's Laws of England (5th Edn) (2017) para 66 see now 87 Halsbury's Laws of England (5th Edn) (2022) para 66.]

FENCE

[For 4 Halsbury's Laws of England (5th Edn) (2011) para 350 see now 4 Halsbury's Laws of England (5th Edn) (2019) para 349.]

FIERI FACIAS

[Note that with effect from 6 April 2014, writs of fieri facias (except writs of fieri facias de bonis ecclesiasticis) have been renamed writs of control: see the Tribunals, Courts and Enforcement Act 2007, s 62(4)(a). See 12 Halsbury's Laws of England (5th Edn) (2020) para 1308.]

De bonis ecclesiasticis

[For 12A Halsbury's Laws of England (5th Edn) (2015) para 1380 see now 12A Halsbury's Laws of England (5th Edn) (2020) para 1354.]

FINANCIALLY INDEPENDENT

[Nationality, Immigration and Asylum Act 2002, s 117B(3).] '[51] Section 117B(3) of the 2002 Act … provides that it is in the public interest, and in particular in the interests of the economic well-being of the UK, that persons who remain here are "financially independent". Then the subsection proceeds to give two reasons why their financial independence is in the public interest.

…

'[55] The parties are correct to join in submitting to this court that financial independence in s 117B(3) means an absence of financial dependence upon the state. Why would it be "in the public interest" that they should not be financially dependent on other persons? Why would it in particular be "in the interests of the economic well-being of the United Kingdom" that they should not be dependent on them? Sales LJ suggested, at para [64], that the financial support provided to Ms Rhuppiah by her father and Ms Charles might cease, whereupon the obligation to maintain her would probably fall upon the state; but a cessation of a person's employment would probably have the same result. Indeed the present case is a good example of the sometimes flimsy distinction between employment and third party support. Anyone other than Ms Rhuppiah who provided extensive caring services to Ms Charles would need to be paid; and it is but an incident of their close friendship and of Ms Rhuppiah's legal inability to have taken employment prior to 9 February 2018 that instead the provision to her has taken the form of largely free board and lodging.

'[56] Regard must moreover be had to the first of the two reasons given in s 117B(3) for its statement as to where the public interest lay: "because such persons ... are not a burden on taxpayers". It was the view of Sales LJ at para [65] that, if the phrase "financially independent" referred to independence of the state, the quoted words were close to tautological. Had those words been part of the statement as to where the public interest lay, one might more readily have agreed with his view. But they are not part of the statement. They are part of the explanation for it and in my view they unequivocally support the construction of s 117B(3) now agreed between the parties.' *Rhuppiah v Secretary of State for the Home Department* [2018] UKSC 58, [2019] 1 All ER 1007 at [51], [55]–[56], per Lord Wilson JSC

FINE IN LIEU

Canada [Criminal Code, RSC 1985, c C-46, s 673.] '24 Before beginning my analysis, I should emphasize the special nature of a fine in lieu as a separate component of sentencing. Although a fine in lieu is technically part of a sentence pursuant to s 673 *Cr C*, such an order differs from the sentence imposed for the commission of a designated offence in that its purpose is to replace the proceeds of crime rather than to punish the offender (*R v Lavigne*, 2006 SCC 10, [2006] 1 SCR 392, at para 25). A fine in lieu is therefore, first and foremost, in the nature of a forfeiture order. It has consistently been held that the forfeiture inquiry is independent of the broader inquiry undertaken with respect to sentencing and the principles related thereto (*Lavigne*, at paras 25–26; *R v Craig*, 2009 SCC 23, [2009] 1 SCR 762, at paras 34–37; *R v Ouellette*, 2009 SCC 24, [2009] 1 SCR 818, at para 2; *R v Nguyen*, 2009 SCC 25, [2009] 1 SCR 826, at para 2). It is therefore imperative that, when calculating the amount of a fine in lieu, courts put aside the general principles of sentencing that are incompatible with the nature of this order.

...

'26 The imposition of a fine in lieu may be considered where forfeiture of the property that is proceeds of crime has become impracticable. In such a case, a court may, instead of ordering the forfeiture of the property, order the offender to pay a fine equal to the value of the property (s 462.37(3) Cr C). Although the use of the word "may" indicates that Parliament intended courts to have some discretion, I am of the view that this discretion does not allow them to limit the amount of a fine in lieu to the profit made from a criminal activity, even in cases where this would be consistent with the dual objective of deprivation of proceeds and deterrence. I will explain why.

...

'35 In summary, the discretion conferred on courts by s 462.37(3) Cr C does not allow them to limit the amount of a fine in lieu to the profit made from criminal activity. In accordance with the principles set out in *Lavigne*, judicial discretion applies first to the decision whether or not to impose a fine and second to the determination of the value of the property (para 35).' *R v Vallières* [2022] SCJ No 10, 467 DLR (4th) 1 at paras 24, 26, 35, per Wagner CJ

FINISHED OR MANUFACTURED INDIGENOUS TIMBER PRODUCT

New Zealand [Forests Act 1949, ss 2(1), 67C: swamp kauri may be exported if it constitutes any finished or manufactured indigenous timber product, regardless of the source of the timber used in the product.] '[52] Under para (a) of the definition of finished or manufactured indigenous timber product, whether a product is in its final form and ready for use or installation is judged by considering the product itself. Logs will almost always require modification before being ready for use or installation. Merely labelling a log a totem or temple pole does not change this. The definition must also be interpreted in light of its purpose. Two main (related) purposes of the introduction of Part 3A were to curtail the export of indigenous logs and woodchips and to ensure that value was added in New Zealand. Also relevant is the scheme of the Act which suggests that something more should be done after milling for a product to be exported under s 67C(1)(b).

'[53] Against that background a log cannot be a finished or manufactured indigenous timber product unless the work on it is so extensive that it has lost its identity as a log. Surface carving or decoration, however elaborate, is unlikely to cause such a loss of identity. In most cases, any value added in New Zealand by surface carving or decoration is likely to be minimal.

'[54] A slab of swamp kauri labelled a table top would not fit within para (a) of the definition. The use as a table could not be discerned from the product itself. Further, a table top is not a product in its own right and thus is not ready to be installed in a larger structure.

'[55] For similar reasons, we also accept NEPS' submission that a table top, exported as a timber slab without routing, legs, or fixings, does not fall within para (b). Further, an unfinished "table top", in the form of a rough sawn or dressed timber slab or similar, would in any event be excluded from the definition of finished or manufactured indigenous timber product by para (c). Paragraph (c) operates to limit the export of items that, whatever the label attached to them, are in reality unfinished timber and have not had the level of domestically added value that was the purpose of the export restrictions.

'[56] We do not, however, accept NEPS' submission that a complete table will be excluded by para (c) in all cases where the table top could be classified as dressed or rough sawn timber. Whether a complete (or kitset) table comes within the exclusion in paragraph (c) will depend on whether the table in question has a high degree of similarity to dressed or rough sawn timber or building materials in general.

'[57] This will be a factual question assessed by considering the product itself at the time of export. We do note that, where the adding of legs or other mountings can be seen as a device to avoid the exclusion clause, then it would be excluded by para (c) and may well not even come within para (a). At the other end of the scale, a crafted rustic bespoke table would clearly come within para (a) (or (b) if in kitset form) and would not come within the exclusion in para (c), even if the table had a table top that, considered alone, could be classified as rough sawn timber.' *Northland Environmental Protection Society Inc v Chief Executive of the Ministry for Primary Industries* [2018] NZSC 105, [2019] 1 NZLR 257 at [52]–[57], per Glazebrook J

FIRE

[For 60 Halsbury's Laws of England (5th Edn) (2011) para 566 see now 60 Halsbury's Laws of England (5th Edn) (2018) para 543.]

Loss by fire: marine insurance

[For 60 Halsbury's Laws of England (5th Edn) (2011) para 325 see now 60 Halsbury's Laws of England (5th Edn) (2018) para 304.]

FIRST USE

Australia [Income Tax Assessment Act 1997 (Cth), Div 40; deduction for depreciating asset allowed from time when taxpayer first uses it.] '[58] As Shell correctly submitted, Div 40 establishes a scheme identifying *what* deductions can be claimed (s 40-25 which provides that the deduction is for the "decline in value" of an asset), *when* deductions can start to be claimed (s 40-60, which provides that assets "decline in value" from their start date", ie from the time of first use or when it is installed ready for use), and *how much* can be deducted (s 40-65). In that scheme, s 40-80 is a provision which, where it applies, tells the taxpayer how much can be deducted in relation to that particular asset. It does not identify when an amount can be deducted — that is the function of s 40-60.

'[59] Shell argued that the scheme does not contemplate that the "start time" of an asset as stipulated in s 40-60(2) could be later than its "first use" since an asset's "start time" is when it is first used or first installed ready for use for any purpose. Shell also argued that the scheme does not contemplate the inverse, namely that the "first use" of an asset could be later than its "start time". Rather, it was submitted, the scheme contemplates that the "first use" time referred to in s 40-80(1)(a) corresponds with the "start time" referred to in s 40-60(2). This construction was said to be supported by the text, purpose and context of the provision, and is consistent with the decision of Siopis J at first instance in *Mitsui & Co (Australia) Ltd v Commissioner of Taxation (Cth)* (2011) 6 ATR 258; [2011] FCA 1423 (*Mitsui v Commissioner of Taxation*).

…

'[64] There is in my view a coherence in Shell's construction — s 40-80(1)(c) has the effect that the deduction is available only if "you satisfy" one of three conditions "as at the asset's start time". If the "first use" referred to in s 40-80(1)(a) and (b) corresponds with the "start time" as defined in s 40-60(2), all of the criteria in s 40-80(1) will occur, or not occur as the case may be, at the one time. Further, as Shell pointed out, notably the language used in s 40-80(1)(c) is "you satisfy" not "you satisfied", that is, the use of the present tense suggests that the "start time" for s 40-80(1)(c) purposes is intended to be no earlier than the time at which s 40-80(1)(a) and (b) are engaged. There is also a coherence with s 40-60 if the "first use" referred to in s 40-80(1)(a) corresponds with the "start time" referred to in s 40-60(2) and with the depreciation scheme as a whole on a purposive construction as once an asset starts to decline in value the taxpayer will be in a position to know which provision applies to determine that decline in value, one of the methodologies referred to in s 40-65 (prime cost or diminishing value) or the method referred to in s 40-80 (cost). It is understandable that the language of "first use" is employed in s 40-80(1)(a), in contradistinction to the reference to "start date" in s 40-80(1)(c), because "first use" is concerned with the nature of the use — ie "for exploration" — being the qualifying condition to obtain an immediate deduction for the cost of the asset whereas the function of s 40-80(1)(c) is different, namely to fix the point in time at which certain other criteria must also be satisfied.

'[65] Contrary to the Commissioner's submission, Shell's construction is further supported by case law to the effect that "passive use" may constitute "use" within the ordinary and natural meaning of that word: see eg *Goldsworthy Mining Ltd v Federal Commissioner of Taxation* (1975) 132 CLR 463 at 470; 5 ALR 139 at 144. …

Although those authorities concern a different statutory context, the point to make is that "use" is capable of being passive and the legislation does not prescribe that "use" must be active.' *Commissioner of Taxation (Cth) v Shell Energy Holdings Australia Ltd* [2022] FCAFC 2, (2022) 396 ALR 565 at [58]–[59], [64]–[65], per Davies J

FIXTURES

[For 62 Halsbury's Laws of England (5th Edn) (2016) para 167 see now 62 Halsbury's Laws of England (5th Edn) (2022) para 185.]

FLOTSAM

[For 29 Halsbury's Laws of England (5th Edn) (2014) para 185n see now 29 Halsbury's Laws of England (5th Edn) (2019) para 190 n 3.]

FOLDCOURSE

[For 13 Halsbury's Laws of England (5th Edn) (2017) see now 13 Halsbury's Laws of England (5th Edn) (2021).]

FOOT OR END

[For 102 Halsbury's Laws of England (5th Edn) (2010) paras 65–66 see now 102 Halsbury's Laws of England (5th Edn) (2021) paras 65–66.]

FOR ANY OTHER PURPOSE CONNECTED WITH ANY SUCH LAND

New Zealand [Reserves Act 1977,s 48(1)(f): administering body of the reserve, with the consent of the Minister of Conservation or their delegate, may grant rights of way and other easements over the reserve 'for any other purpose connected with' land not forming part of the reserve.] '[113] We conclude that the Court of Appeal was correct that there is no justification to read down the meaning of the phrase "for any other purpose connected with any such land" in s 48(1)(f) to exclude easements for commercial activities.' *Schmuck v Opua Coastal Preservation Inc* [2019] NZSC 118, [2019] 1 NZLR 750 at [113], per O'Regan J

FOR OR IN CONNECTION WITH THE PROVISION OF A DWELLING

[Defective Premises Act 1972, s 1: duty owed by a person taking on work 'for or in connection with the provision of a dwelling'.] '[38] In the present case the context includes the whole of s 1(1), not just the words: "A person taking on work for or in connection with the provision of a dwelling". This includes that the duty relates to how "the work which he takes on is done" and that it is done "with proper materials". The focus is therefore very much on the doing of work.

'[39] That work also has to relate to the "provision of a dwelling". This suggests the bringing of that dwelling into physical existence or its creation. This is consistent with how these words have been interpreted in other cases. For example, *Jacobs v Morton & Partners (a firm)* (1994) 43 ConLR 124 at 135, (1994) 72 BLR 92 at 105: "In my judgment, this phrase connotes the creation of a new dwelling" per Mr Recorder Jackson QC; *Saigol v Cranley Mansions Ltd* (6 July 1995) [1995] Lexis Citation 1860: "Mr Ticciati was in my view correct in submitting the 'provision' was a word which prima facie involved the creation of something new" per Hutchison LJ.

'[40] The emphasis is therefore on those who do work which positively contributes to the creation of the dwelling. That may include architects and engineers who prescribe how the dwelling is to be created, not just those who physically create it. It does not, however, include those whose role is the essentially negative one of seeing that no work is done which contravenes building regulations. Building control ensures that the dwelling is legal and properly certified, but it does not positively contribute to the provision or creation of that dwelling.

...

'[42] That an AI's [approved inspector's] function is far removed from the work of the provision or creation of the dwelling is borne out by the fact that an AI has no statutory power to order changes to be made to plans for works, or to building work which is ongoing or completed. The powers of the AI are confined to refusing to issue a plans certificate or final certificate in the face of non-compliant work. Moreover, unlike the local authority, the AI has no power to impose conditions or prescribe modifications to the works and the relevant enforcement powers are left entirely with the local authority.

'[43] An AI therefore has no statutory power to influence the design or construction of a building in any way, save to stipulate that it must comply with the law. In certifying, or refusing to certify, plans and works, the AI is not engaged in the positive role of the provision or creation of the relevant building, but performs the essentially negative regulatory role of checking for compliance against prescribed criteria.

'[44] For all these reasons, and those given by Mr Townend and the judge, I consider that the judge was correct to conclude that an AI performing statutory functions does not fall within s 1(1) DPA 1972 on its natural and ordinary meaning.' *Lessees and Management Company of Herons Court v Heronslea Ltd* [2019] EWCA Civ 1423, [2020] 2 All ER 145 at [38]–[40], [42]–[44], per Hamblen LJ

FORCED LABOUR

'[77] In the process of adopting the 1926 Slavery Convention, the Assembly of the League of Nations passed a number of resolutions, including one which effectively requested the ILO to take over responsibility for addressing forced labour, including "the best means of preventing forced or compulsory labour from developing into conditions analogous to slavery": League of Nations, Doc A.104.1926.VI, p 3. In 1930 the ILO adopted the Convention Concerning Forced or Compulsory Labour (No 29), which has been ratified by 179 states. Article 2(1) of this convention defines "forced or compulsory labour" as "all work or service which is exacted from any person under the menace of any penalty and for which the said person has not offered himself voluntarily".

'[78] Guidance given by the ILO supervisory bodies has helped to clarify each of the two elements of this definition: see eg ILO, "A Global Alliance against Forced Labour" (2005), paras 14–15 and Box 1.1. This guidance explains that the "menace of any penalty" can take many different forms. Arguably, its most extreme form involves physical violence or restraint. There can also be subtler forms of menace, sometimes of a psychological nature. Situations examined by the ILO have included threats to denounce victims to the police or immigration authorities when their employment status is illegal. Other penalties can be of a financial nature, including the non-payment of wages. Indicators that the work is not being performed voluntarily include physical confinement in the work location, deception or false promises about types and terms of work, retention of identity documents and withholding and non-payment of wages.' *Basfar v Wong* [2022] UKSC 20, [2022] 4 All ER 1 at [77]–[78], per Lord Briggs and Lord Leggatt JJSC

FORENSIC CHEATING

'[3] This utter disregard for the relevant guidance, procedure, and indeed orders is totally unacceptable. I struggle to understand the mentality of litigants and their advisers who still seem to think that guidance, procedure, and orders can be blithely ignored. … It should be understood that the deliberate flouting of orders, guidance and procedure is a form of forensic cheating, and should be treated as such. Advisers should clearly understand that such non-compliance may well be regarded by the court as professional misconduct leading to a report to their regulatory body.' *Xanthopoulos v Rakshina* [2022] EWFC 30, [2023] 1 FLR 388 at [3], per Mostyn J

FORTHWITH

Canada [Criminal Code, RSC 1985, c C-46, s 254(2)(b): demand to produce breath sample 'forthwith'.] '**1** This appeal concerns the interpretation of the immediacy requirement in what was, at the relevant time, s 254(2)(b) (now s 320.27(1)(b)) of the *Criminal Code*, RSC 1985, c C-46 ("*Cr C.*"). According to this provision, if a peace officer has reasonable grounds to suspect that a driver has alcohol in their body, the peace officer may, by demand, require the driver "to provide forthwith a sample of breath that, in the peace officer's opinion, will enable a proper analysis to be made" through an approved screening device ("ASD").

…

'**24** At the end of a statutory interpretation exercise, I am of the view that the Court of Appeal was correct in law in holding that, as a general rule, the word "forthwith" must be given an interpretation that reflects its ordinary meaning. This interpretation is consistent with the text, context and purpose of s 254(2)(b) *Cr C.* It is also in keeping with the decisions of this Court, from *R v Thomsen* [1988] 1 SCR 640, to *Woods* [*R v Woods* 2005 SCC 42, [2005] 2 SCR 205], in which the word "forthwith" has been interpreted in a manner consistent with its ordinary meaning, except in unusual circumstances.

…

'**29** It is important to consider the meaning of two words found in this provision: "provide" and "forthwith". "Provide" means to "supply" something to someone (*Canadian Oxford Dictionary* (2nd ed 2004), at p 1245). "Forthwith" means "immediately" or "without delay" (*Woods*, at para 13, quoting *Canadian Oxford Dictionary*, at p 585; see also *R v Grant* [1991] 3 SCR 139, at p 150).

'**30** According to the grammatical and ordinary meaning of these words, a driver detained under s 254(2)(b) *Cr C* must "supply" a breath sample to the peace officer "immediately" or "without delay". In addition, the provision states that the sample "will enable a proper analysis to be made" by means of an ASD.

'**31** Therefore, and contrary to what the Crown argues, the word "forthwith" qualifies the demand that drivers must obey. Stopped drivers "are bound by s 254(2) to comply immediately" (*Woods*, at para 45). They are not free to provide a sample when they see fit.

'**32** It is true that operational time is implicit in the word "forthwith", because the officer "has to ready the equipment and instruct the suspect on what to do" (*Bernshaw* [*R v Bernshaw* [1995] 1 SCR 254] at para 64). However, what is in issue in this case is not operational time, but rather the time needed for a device to be delivered to the scene.

…

'**35** Although a stopped driver is being detained at the first step of the detection procedure, the driver has no right to counsel; this right exists only at the second step (*Woods*, at para 31). This is the case because the word "forthwith" implicitly limits the right to counsel guaranteed by s 10(b) of the *Charter*. This is a condition for the application of s 254(2)(b) *Cr C*; since the detained driver must provide a breath sample forthwith, the driver may not consult counsel before doing so. The Court has recognized that this limit on s 10(b) of the *Charter* is justified under s 1 (*Thomsen* at p 653; *Woods*, at para 30) precisely because the detention is of very brief duration (*Bernshaw* at para 23). The more flexibly the word "forthwith" is interpreted, the less the recognized justification for limiting the right to counsel holds up.

'**36** Furthermore, as I said above, a driver who refuses or fails to comply with a demand is subject to criminal sanctions under s 254(5) *Cr C.* It is therefore not an offence to express an intention to refuse *once the ASD arrives at the* *scene*; refusing without reasonable excuse to *provide forthwith* a sample is what constitutes the offence (*Woods*, at paras 14 and 45). This suggests that compliance must actually be physically possible.

…

'**47** The ordinary meaning of the word "forthwith" is in keeping with the purpose of s 254(2)(b) *Cr C* and the context of this provision. Moreover, our Court has consistently interpreted this word by giving it this specific meaning, subject to unusual circumstances. For example, in *Grant*, this Court refused to interpret the word "forthwith" as allowing for a 30-minute delay for the delivery of an ASD to the scene (see also *Thomsen*, at pp 653–655; *Woods* at paras 13 and 43–44).' *R v Breault* [2023] SCJ No 9, 2023 SCC 9 at paras 1, 24, 29–32, 35–36, 47, per Côté J

FREE ON BOARD

[For 91 Halsbury's Laws of England (5th Edn) (2012) para 14 see now 91 Halsbury's Laws of England (5th Edn) (2019) para 15.]

FREEDOM OF INTERSTATE INTERCOURSE

Australia [Commonwealth Constitution (Cth), s 92: 'On the imposition of uniform duties of customs, trade, commerce, and intercourse among the States, whether by means of internal carriage or ocean navigation, shall be absolutely free'.] '[83] Section 92 of the Constitution emphatically and imperatively declares that "trade, commerce, and intercourse among the States … shall be absolutely free". The "riddle of s 92" lies in the question begged by the constitutional text: "absolutely free from what?"

'[84] Cutting through the debris left by some 140 earlier failed judicial attempts to resolve that riddle, *Cole v Whitfield* [(1988) 165 CLR 360, 78 ALR 42] provided a partial resolution. The partial resolution proceeded on the understanding that "[t]he notions of absolutely free trade and commerce and absolutely free intercourse are quite distinct and neither the history of [s 92] nor the ordinary meaning of its words require that the content of the guarantee of freedom of trade and commerce be seen as governing or governed by the content of the guarantee of freedom of intercourse".

'[85] *Cole v Whitfield* authoritatively determined that trade and commerce among the States is guaranteed by s 92 to be absolutely free from "discriminatory burdens of a protectionist kind". The guarantee of the trade and commerce limb is of absolute freedom from laws imposing differential burdens on interstate trade or commerce (in comparison to intrastate trade or commerce) which cannot be justified as a constitutionally permissible means of pursuing constitutionally permissible non-discriminatory legislative ends and which operate to the competitive advantage of intrastate trade or commerce. Subsequent cases on the trade and commerce limb of the guarantee eventually settled on the standard to be met for a differential burden on interstate trade or commerce to be justified as a constitutionally permissible means of pursuing a non-discriminatory legislative end. The standard, authoritatively determined in *Betfair* [*Betfair Pty Ltd v Western Australia* (2008) 234 CLR 418, 244 ALR 32, [2008] HCA 11], is that of "reasonable necessity".

'[86] What intercourse among the States is guaranteed by s 92 to be absolutely free from, *Cole v Whitfield* left to be resolved on another day. Left also for another day was the associated question of how the "intercourse limb" relates to the "trade and commerce limb" in respect of intercourse that occurs in trade or commerce. Subsequent cases touching on the intercourse limb have yielded no definitive answer.

…

'[96] The resolution of that part of the riddle of s 92 left unresolved by *Cole v Whitfield* was provided by Jeremy Kirk SC in an essay published on the eve of the onset of the pandemic. The argument presented in the essay was an elaboration of an argument put by the Attorney-General of the Commonwealth intervening in *Cole v Whitfield*. The argument was adopted by the Attorney-General of Queensland intervening in the present proceeding, and was ultimately accepted by the plaintiffs in reply. I am persuaded that the argument is sound.

'[97] The argument, which I accept, is to the effect that intercourse among the States is guaranteed by s 92 to be absolutely free from all discriminatory burdens. The guarantee of the intercourse limb is of absolute freedom from laws imposing differential burdens on interstate intercourse (in comparison to intrastate intercourse) which cannot be justified as a constitutionally permissible means of pursuing non-discriminatory legislative ends. The standard to be met for a differential burden on interstate intercourse to be justified as a constitutionally permissible means of pursuing a non-discriminatory legislative end, no differently from the standard to be met for a differential burden on interstate trade or commerce to be justified as a constitutionally permissible means of pursuing a non-discriminatory legislative end, is the standard of reasonable necessity.

'[98] Understood in that way, the guarantee of absolute freedom of interstate intercourse mirrors the guarantee of absolute freedom of interstate trade and commerce to the extent that: each invokes the same essential notion of discrimination as lying in "the unequal treatment of equals, and, conversely, in the equal treatment of unequals"; each posits the same essential comparison between that which is interstate and that which is intrastate; each demands "an acceptable explanation or justification for [any] differential treatment"; and each imposes, as the measure of justification for differential treatment, satisfaction of the same standard of reasonable necessity.

'[99] The guarantee of absolute freedom of interstate intercourse differs from the guarantee of absolute freedom of interstate trade and commerce only to the extent that absolute freedom of interstate intercourse extends to freedom from discriminatory burdens of any kind. That is to say, the guarantee of absolute freedom of interstate intercourse is infringed by any differential burden on interstate intercourse that cannot be justified. An unjustified differential burden on interstate intercourse need not operate to the competitive advantage of intrastate trade or commerce.' *Palmer v State of Western Australia* [2021] HCA 5, (2021) 388 ALR 180, BC202101051 at [83]–[86], [96]–[99], per Gageler J

FREIGHT

[For 7 Halsbury's Laws of England (5th Edn) (2015) para 568 et seq see now 7 Halsbury's Laws of England (5th Edn) (2020) para 352 et seq.]

Dead freight

[For 7 Halsbury's Laws of England (5th Edn) (2015) para 460 see now 7 Halsbury's Laws of England (5th Edn) (2020) para 374.]

FRUSTRATION

[For 22 Halsbury's Laws of England (5th Edn) (2012) para 468 see now 22 Halsbury's Laws of England (5th Edn) (2019) para 259.]

FUNCTUS OFFICIO

Canada '32 In concluding that it lacked jurisdiction to vary or set aside the relevant orders concerning court openness, the Court of Appeal relied, in part, on the doctrine of *functus officio*. The term *functus officio* – often rendered as "having performed his or her office" – has traditionally been understood to mean that once a judge decided a matter, they had discharged their office and did not have the ability to return to and correct their decision (A S P Wong, "Doctrine of *Functus Officio*: The Changing Face of Finality's Old Guard" (2020), 98 *Can Bar Rev* 543, at pp 546–547; see A Mayrand, *Dictionnaire de maximes et locutions latines utilisées en droit* (4th ed 2007), at p 193, who also uses the term *functa officio*).

'33 In its contemporary guise, *functus officio* indicates that a final decision of a court that is susceptible of appeal cannot, as a general rule, be reconsidered by the court that rendered that decision (see *Chandler v Alberta Association of Architects* [1989] 2 SCR 848, at p 860; *Reekie v Messervey* [1990] 1 SCR 219, at pp 222–223; *Doucet-Boudreau v Nova Scotia (Minister of Education)* 2003 SCC 62, [2003] 3 SCR 3, at paras 77–79). A court loses jurisdiction, and is thus said to be *functus officio*, once the formal judgment has been entered (*R v Adams* [1995] 4 SCR 707, at para 29; *R v Smithen-Davis* 2020 ONCA 759, 68 CR (7th) 75, at paras 33–34). After this point, the court is understood only to have the power to amend the judgment in very limited circumstances, such as where there is a statutory basis to do so, where necessary to correct an error in expressing its manifest intention, or where the matter has not been heard on its merits (*Chandler*, at p 861, citing *Paper Machinery Ltd v JO Ross Engineering Corp* [1934] SCR 186; *R v H (E)* (1997) 33 OR (3d) 202 (CA), at pp 214–215, citing *The Queen v Jacobs* [1971] SCR 92; see also *R v Burke* 2002 SCC 55, [2002] 2 SCR 857, at para 54).

'34 This rule serves goals of finality and, by stabilizing judgments subject to review, of an orderly appellate procedure (*Chandler*, at p 861; *H (E)*, at p 214). As Doherty JA wrote in *Tsaoussis (Litigation Guardian of) v Baetz* (1998) 41 OR (3d) 257 (CA), for the parties to litigation, finality meets both an economic and psychological need as well as serving as a practical necessity for the system of justice as a whole (pp 264–265). More specifically, if lower courts could continuously reconsider their own decisions, litigants would be denied a reliable basis from which to launch an appeal to a higher court (*Doucet-Boudreau*, at para 79; see also *Ayangma v French School Board* 2011 PECA 3, 306 Nfld & PEIR 103, at paras 11–12). The appeal record would be written on "shifting sand", ultimately inhibiting effective review (Wong, at p 548).'

'35 That said, *functus officio* is only one of several legal principles designed to promote the goal of finality. Indeed, given it is inherently tied to the entering of the formal judgment and its exceptions are relatively restrictive, this Court has described the doctrine of *functus officio* as narrow in scope (*Reekie*, at pp 222–223; see also Wong, at pp 555–556). So, while it is an important norm recognized in our jurisprudence to serve this necessary purpose, no one rule has a monopoly on finality.

'36 It is useful to distinguish between jurisdiction over the merits lost by operation of the doctrine of *functus officio* and jurisdiction that exists to supervise the court record. As I will endeavour to explain, even when a court has lost jurisdiction over the merits of a matter as a result of having entered its formal judgment, it retains jurisdiction to control its court record with respect to proceedings generally understood to be an ancillary but independent matter (see, eg, *GEA Refrigeration Canada Inc v Chang* 2020 BCCA 361, 43 BCLR (6th) 330, at paras 185–186).' *Canadian Broadcasting Corp. v. Manitoba* [2021] SCJ No 33, 461 DLR (4th) 635 at paras 32–36, per Kasirer J

FUNDAMENTAL

New Zealand [Crimes Act 1961, s 385(1)(c): appeal to be allowed if there was a miscarriage of justice.] '[25] Some errors are so serious that they cannot be saved by the proviso; put another way, in such a case the appeal will be allowed even if the appellate court is satisfied of the defendant's guilt. Such errors are characterised as "fundamental" or "radical" or said to go to "the root of the proceedings" or to "undermine the integrity of the trial" so that it has lost the character of a fair trial according to law. …

'[26] There exists no taxonomy of errors that are classified as fundamental; rather, incurability depends on the appellate court's assessment of the significance of the error in the context of the trial. In *Randall v R* [[2002] UKPC 19, [2002] 1 WLR 2237], Lord Bingham, delivering the judgment of the Privy Council, explained that:

> There will come a point when the departure from good practice is so gross, or so persistent, or so prejudicial, or so irremediable that an appellate court will have no choice but to condemn a trial as unfair and quash a conviction as unsafe, however strong the grounds for believing the defendant to be guilty.

'[27] This Court held in *Matenga* [*R v Matenga* [2009] NZSC 18, [2009] 3 NZLR 145] that the New Zealand Bill of Rights Act 1990 guarantees of a fair trial and an appeal do not require that an appeal should be allowed and a retrial ordered whenever there has been a miscarriage at the first trial. The Court cited *R v Condon* [[2006] NZSC 62, [2007] 1 NZLR 300], in which it adopted the passage just cited from *Randall* when discussing the requirements of a fair trial and held that a "fundamentally flawed" trial is an unfair trial for the purposes of s 25(a) of the Bill of Rights Act.

'[28] The language of fundamental error sets a deliberately high threshold to ensure the proviso can do the work for which it was designed. As this Court recognised in *Matenga*, it is a necessary, and usually sufficient, condition for use of the proviso that the appellate court be satisfied of the defendant's guilt:

> … the decision to confirm a jury verdict, despite something having gone wrong, depends upon whether the appellate court considers a guilty verdict was inevitable on the basis of the whole of the admissible evidence (including any new evidence).'

Lundy v R [2019] NZSC 152, [2020] 1 NZLR 1 at [25]–[28], per Miller J

FURNITURE

[For 63 Halsbury's Laws of England (5th Edn) (2016) para 715, note 2 see now 63 Halsbury's Laws of England (5th Edn) (2022) para 767, note 2.]

G

GALE

[For 76 Halsbury's Laws of England (5th Edn) (2013) para 614 see now 76 Halsbury's Laws of England (5th Edn) (2019) para 610.]

GAME (ANIMALS OF BIRDS)

[For 2 Halsbury's Laws of England (5th Edn) (2017) para 14 see now 2 Halsbury's Laws of England (5th Edn) (2023) para 15.]

GAMING

[For 67 Halsbury's Laws of England (5th Edn) (2016) para 258 see now 67 Halsbury's Laws of England (5th Edn) (2021) para 273.]

GARNISHEE PROCEEDINGS

[For 12A Halsbury's Laws of England (5th Edn) (2015) para 1406 see now 12A Halsbury's Laws of England (5th Edn) (2020) para 1380.]

GAVELKIND

[For 87 Halsbury's Laws of England (5th Edn) (2017) para 32 see now 87 Halsbury's Laws of England (5th Edn) (2022) para 32.]

GENDER DYSPHORIA

'[3] Gender dysphoria or GD is a condition where persons experience distress because of a mismatch between their perceived identity and their natal sex, that is, their sex at birth. Such persons have a strong desire to live according to their perceived identity rather than their natal sex.' *R (on the application of Bell) v Tavistock and Portman NHS Foundation Trust (University College London Hospitals NHS Foundation Trust intervening)* [2020] EWHC 3274 (Admin), [2022] 1 All ER 416 at [3], per Dame Victoria Sharp P, Lewis LJ and Lieven J

'[2] Gender dysphoria is a complex condition that occurs in both children and adults. It involves, in the simplest terms, a strong desire to be and to be treated as being of the gender other than their natal sex at birth. Those diagnosed with it suffer associated significant distress or impairment in function. A range of clinical interventions may be prescribed.' *R (on the application of Bell) v Tavistock and Portman NHS Foundation Trust (University College London Hospitals NHS Foundation Trust intervening)* [2021] EWCA Civ 1363, [2022] 1 All ER 416 at [2], per Lord Burnett CJ

GENETIC DATA

In this Act … 'genetic data' means personal data relating to the inherited or acquired genetic characteristics of an individual which gives unique information about the physiology or the health of that individual and which results, in particular, from an analysis of a biological sample from the individual in question. (Data Protection Act 2018, s 205(1))

GIFT

Class gift

[For 102 Halsbury's Laws of England (5th Edn) (2010) para 175 see now 102 Halsbury's Laws of England (5th Edn) (2021) para 177.]

Inter vivos

[For 52 Halsbury's Laws of England (5th Edn) (2014) para 201 see now 52 Halsbury's Laws of England (5th Edn) (2020) para 201.]

GOLD

[For 49 Halsbury's Laws of England (5th Edn) (2015) para 25 see now 49 Halsbury's Laws of England (5th Edn) (2021) para 25.]

GOODS

New Zealand [Biosecurity Act 1993, s 116: power to seize and dispose of unauthorised goods.] '[21] Three key arguments were advanced to say that the trees subject to the notices and directions were not "unauthorised goods", and accordingly that the exercise of powers under s 116 was unlawful …

…

'[52] There is a further significant issue. The vast majority of the trees that are subject to the s 116 notice are now growing in the ground. Some have reached their second or third season. This calls into question whether they can be now subject to the exercise of power under s 116. The unauthorised goods, or goods that have been in contact with other authorised goods, must be "goods" as defined. The definition in s 2 is:

> **goods** means all kinds of moveable personal property.

'[53] As Mr Greig submitted, s 116 should be contrasted with other terminology used in other sections of the Act. For example, the powers of examination in s 121 covers organisms, organic material, as well as other goods or material. The words "organic material" and "organism" are subject to their own clear definitions in s 2. The more restricted use of the concept of "goods" in s 116 is significant. It shows that the text, in light of the scheme and purpose of the Act, is intended to have its limits.

'[54] The distinction between personal property and real property is subject to a rich vein of case law. As a general proposition, trees planted in the ground are not treated as moveable property. On this basis any trees that remained in pots, or in other equivalent containment, would be goods but any such trees that had been planted would not be. There is the further complexity here that some of the trees in the ground are dug up and transported once sold by a nursery.

'[55] I accept the argument of Mr Fong that the meaning to be given to "goods" or "moveable property" will be highly dependent on the context. He challenged the idea that the reach of s 116 could turn on the arbitrary actions of the owner of the tree. But Parliament has provided limits on when property can be traced from unauthorised goods for the purposes of s 116. Here a large number of trees are now planted in the land and producing fruit. In some cases, those trees have been in the environment for years. There may have been other trees in the vicinity of these trees. In most cases the situation here seems to be beyond the outer limits of the reach of s 116. So I do not accept that the point made by the applicants is a technicality. Rather it goes to the heart of the intended reach of s 116. It is the Ministry that is pushing its application beyond its technical limits.' *Waimea Nurseries Ltd v Director-General for Primary Industries* [2018] NZHC 2183, [2019] 2 NZLR 107 at [21], [52]–[55], per Cooke J

In marine insurance policy

[For 60 Halsbury's Laws of England (5th Edn) (2011) para 287 see now 60 Halsbury's Laws of England (5th Edn) (2018) para 266.]

GOODWILL

[For 80 Halsbury's Laws of England (5th Edn) (2013) paras 807, 810 see now 80 Halsbury's Laws of England (5th Edn) (2020) paras 807, 810.]

GOVERNMENT

[For 20 Halsbury's Laws of England (5th Edn) (2014) para 5 see now 20 Halsbury's Laws of England (5th Edn) (2023) para 5.]

GOVERNMENT POLICY

[Planning Act 1980, s 5(8).] '[105] The principal question for determination is the meaning of "Government policy" in s 5(8) of the PA 2008. We adopt a purposive approach to this statutory provision which expands upon the obligation in s 5(7) that an NPS give reasons for the policy set out in it and interpret the statutory words in their context. The purpose of the provision is to make sure that there is a degree of coherence between the policy set out in the NPS [national policy statement] and established Government policies relating to the mitigation of and adaptation to climate change. The section speaks of "Government policy", which points toward a policy which has been cleared by the relevant departments on a government-wide basis. In our view the phrase is looking to carefully formulated written statements of policy such as one might find in an NPS, or in statements of national planning policy (such as the National Planning Policy Framework), or in government papers such as the Aviation Policy Framework.

For the subsection to operate sensibly the phrase needs to be given a relatively narrow meaning so that the relevant policies can readily be identified. Otherwise, civil servants would have to trawl through Hansard and press statements to see if anything had been said by a minister which might be characterised as "policy". Parliament cannot have intended to create a bear trap for ministers by requiring them to take into account any ministerial statement which could as a matter of ordinary language be described as a statement of policy relating to the relevant field.

'[106] In our view, the epitome of "Government policy" is a formal written statement of established policy. In so far as the phrase might in some exceptional circumstances extend beyond such written statements, it is appropriate that there be clear limits on what statements count as "Government policy", in order to render them readily identifiable as such. In our view the criteria for a "policy" to which the doctrine of legitimate expectations could be applied would be the absolute minimum required to be satisfied for a statement to constitute "policy" for the purposes of s 5(8). Those criteria are that a statement qualifies as policy only if it is clear, unambiguous and devoid of relevant qualification: see for example *R v Board of Inland Revenue, ex p MFK Underwriting Agencies Ltd* [1990] 1 All ER 91 at 110, [1990] 1 WLR 1545 at 1569 per Bingham LJ; *R (on the application of Davies) v Revenue and Customs Comrs, R (on the application of Gaines-Cooper) v Revenue and Customs Comrs* [2011] UKSC 47, [2012] 1 All ER 1048, [2011] 1 WLR 2625 (at [28] and [29]) per Lord Wilson of Culworth, delivering the judgment with which the majority of the court agreed, and para [70] per Lord Mance. The statements of Andrea Leadsom MP and Amber Rudd MP (para [72] above) on which the Court of Appeal focused and on which Plan B Earth particularly relied do not satisfy those criteria. Their statements were not clear and were not devoid of relevant qualification in this context. They did not refer to the temperature targets at all and they both left open the question of how the Paris Agreement goal of net zero emissions would be enshrined in UK law. Andrea Leadsom went out of her way to emphasise that "there is an important set of questions to be answered before we do". The statements made by these ministers were wholly consistent with and plainly reflected the fact that there was then an inchoate or developing policy being worked on within Government. This does not fall within the statutory phrase.

'[107] We therefore respectfully disagree with the Court of Appeal in so far as they held (para [224]) that the words "Government policy" were ordinary words which should be applied in their ordinary sense to the facts of a given situation. We also disagree with the court's conclusion (para [228]) that the statements by Andrea Leadsom MP and Amber Rudd MP constituted statements of "Government policy" for the purposes of s 5(8).' *R (on the application of Friends of the Earth Ltd and another) v Secretary of State for Transport (Heathrow Airport Ltd, interested party)* [2020] UKSC 52, [2021] 2 All ER 967 at [105]–[107], per Lord Hodge DP and Lord Sales JSC

GRANT

Of watercourse

[For 87 Halsbury's Laws of England (5th Edn) (2017) para 918 see now 87 Halsbury's Laws of England (5th Edn) (2022) para 912.]

GRAVE

[Children Act 1989, s 33(3).] '[31] This court is now faced with determining whether the routine vaccination of healthy children in care is a matter which a local authority can properly consent to and arrange pursuant to its powers under s 33 CA 1989 or whether, where a parent opposes it, the issue is of such magnitude, seriousness or gravity that it necessitates an application to the High Court for leave to invoke its inherent jurisdiction.

...

'[81] During the course of argument, we indicated to Ms Grief QC on behalf of the local authority, that we did not think that the nomenclature attached to vaccinations mattered a great deal, that is to say whether they are categorised as "medical treatment" or as "preventative health care". The critical issue was, we suggested, whether immunisations are to be regarded as "grave" or "serious" in the context of the exercise of parental responsibility by a local authority such as to require the sanction of the court when a dispute arises.

...

'[85] I cannot agree that the giving of a vaccination is a grave issue (regardless of whether it is described as medical treatment or not). In my judgment it cannot be said that the vaccination of children under the UK public health programme is in itself a "grave" issue in circumstances where there is no contra-indication in relation to the child in question and when the alleged link between MMR and autism has been definitively disproved.

...

'[104] Pulling together the threads of this judgment, I have concluded that:

(i) Although vaccinations are not compulsory, the scientific evidence now clearly establishes that it is in the best medical interests of children to be vaccinated in accordance with Public Health England's guidance unless there is a specific contra-indication in an individual case.
(ii) Under s 33(3)(b) CA 1989 a local authority with a care order can arrange and consent to a child in its care being vaccinated where it is satisfied that it is in the best interests of that individual child, notwithstanding the objections of parents.
(iii) The administration of standard or routine vaccinations cannot be regarded as being a "serious" or "grave" matter. Except where there are significant features which suggest that, unusually, it may not be in the best interests of a child to be vaccinated, it is neither necessary nor appropriate for a local authority to refer the matter to the High Court in every case where a parent opposes the proposed vaccination of their child. To do so involves the expenditure of scarce time and resources by the local authority, the unnecessary instruction of expert medical evidence and the use of High Court time which could be better spent dealing with one of the urgent and serious matters which are always awaiting determination in the Family Division.
(iv) Parental views regarding immunisation must always be taken into account but the matter is not to be determined by the strength of the parental view unless the view has a real bearing on the child's welfare.'

Re H (a child) (parental responsibility: vaccination) [2020] EWCA Civ 664, [2021] 2 All ER 288 at [31], [81], [85], [104], per King LJ

GROUND RENT

[For 27(1) Halsbury's Laws of England (4th ed) para 212 at p 254, note 1 see now 62 Halsbury's Laws (5th Edn) (2022) para 264, note 1.]

GUARANTEE

[For 49 Halsbury's Laws of England (5th Edn) (2015) para 638 see now 49 Halsbury's Laws of England (5th Edn) (2021) para 601.]

GUARDIAN

[For 9 Halsbury's Laws of England (5th Edn) (2012) para 162 see now 9 Halsbury's Laws of England (5th Edn) (2017) para 161.]

GUARDIAN AD LITEM

[For 9 Halsbury's Laws of England (5th Edn) (2012) para 213 see now 9 Halsbury's Laws of England (5th Edn) (2017) para 225.]

H

HABEAS CORPUS

Ad testificandum or ad respondendum

[For 85 Halsbury's Laws of England (5th Edn) (2012) para 457, n 12 see now 85 Halsbury's Laws of England (5th Edn) (2020) para 455, note 12.]

HABITATION

Australia '[74] "Habitation" is a word in common English usage without any common law meaning. The references to "habitation" in the law of trespass or the law of burglary were never in the technical sense of a legal element to establish trespass or burglary. A holiday house or a second apartment in which the owner is not in present habitation is capable of being burgled. Conversely, a person in habitation did not always have a right to immediate possession sufficient at common law to support an indictment for burglary, as the mere fact of habitation does not necessarily create a right of exclusive possession. Further, at common law there would not be a burglary if the break and entry was to an inhabited building that was not a dwelling-house, such as a barn or warehouse.

'[75] The facts of "occupation" or "habitation" may be difficult to determine in the context of domestic or family violence, especially where one spouse or family member leaves or is ejected from or locked out of the family home. That person may be either a perpetrator or a victim of domestic or family violence who may seek to return to the family home in a multiplicity of circumstances. Cases of shared households may raise similar problems about whether or not a member or former member of the household is in occupation or habitation, and who has the right to exclude them. …' *BA v R* [2023] HCA 14, (2023) 409 ALR 41 at [74] [75], per Gordon, Edelman, Steward and Gleeson JJ

HABITUAL RESIDENCE

See RESIDE—RESIDENCE

HEIRLOOMS

[For 103 Halsbury's Laws of England (5th Edn) (2010) para 928 see now 103 Halsbury's Laws of England (5th Edn) (2021) para 931, and for 87 Halsbury's Laws of England (5th Edn) (2017) paras 17–18 see now 87 Halsbury's Laws of England (5th Edn) (2022) paras 17–18.]

HEREDITAMENT

[For 62 Halsbury's Laws of England (5th Edn) (2016) para 154 see now 62 Halsbury's Laws of England (5th Edn) (2022) para 171; and for 87 Halsbury's Laws of England (5th Edn) (2017) paras 8, 10 see now 87 Halsbury's Laws of England (5th Edn) (2022) paras 8, 10.]

Corporeal hereditament

[For 87 Halsbury's Laws of England (5th Edn) (2017) para 11 see now 87 Halsbury's Laws of England (5th Edn) (2022) para 11.]

Incorporeal hereditament

[For 87 Halsbury's Laws of England (5th Edn) (2017) para 12 see now 87 Halsbury's Laws of England (5th Edn) (2022) para 12.]

Real and personal hereditament

[For 87 Halsbury's Laws of England (5th Edn) (2017) para 13 see now 87 Halsbury's Laws of England (5th Edn) (2022) para 13.]

HIJACKING

See also **REVERSE DOMAIN NAME HIJACKING**

HIGHWAY

[For 55 Halsbury's Laws of England (5th Edn) (2012) paras 1–8 see now 55 Halsbury's Laws of England (5th Edn) (2019) paras 1–8.]

'[6] The word highway has no single meaning in the law but, in non-technical language, it is a way over which the public have rights of passage, whether on foot, on horseback or in (or on) vehicles. At common law, at least prior to 1835, there was, generally speaking, no necessary connection between those responsible for the maintenance and repair of a public highway and those with a proprietary interest in the land over which it ran. Prima facie the inhabitants of the parish through which the highway ran would be responsible for its repair, but they were not a corporate body suitable to hold ownership rights in relation to it: see Sauvain on Highway Law (5th edn, 2013) at para 3–05. As he puts it:

> "It was left to statute, therefore, to create an interest in land which was to be held by the body on whom the duty to repair had fallen."

Parliament began this task, in a rudimentary way, in s 41 of the Highways Act 1835, continued it in s 68 of the Public Health Act 1848, s 96 of the Metropolis Management Act 1855 and s 149 of the Public Health Act 1875. They all provided for a form of automatic vesting of a property interest in the land over which the highway ran in favour of the body responsible for its maintenance and repair.

…

'[31] The Court of Appeal concluded that "highway" as used in art 2 [of the GLA Roads and Side Roads (Transfer of Property etc) Order 2000, SI 2000/1552] and s 265 [of the Highways Act 1980] had a clear common law meaning, limited in the vertical plane to the zone of ordinary use. I respectfully disagree. The word "highway" is not a defined term, either in the 1980 Act, in the Transfer Order or in the GLA Act [Greater London Authority Act 1999]. There is a limited explanation, in s 328 of the 1980 Act that:

> "In this Act, except where the context otherwise requires, 'highway' means the whole or a part of a highway other than a ferry or waterway …"

This is largely circular so far as concerns the core meaning of "highway" and, in any event, subject to context. It does not follow that the interpreter is therefore required to find some uniform meaning of the word "highway" wherever it is used, either in the relevant legislation or, as the Court of Appeal thought, at common law.

'[32] There is in my view no single meaning of highway at common law. The word is sometimes used as a reference to its physical elements. Sometimes it is used as a label for the incorporeal rights of the public in relation to the locus in quo. Sometimes, as here, it is used as the label for a species of real property. When used within a statutory formula, as here, the word necessarily takes its meaning from the context in which it is used.

'[33] In agreement with counsel and with the Court of Appeal, I do consider that the meaning of art 2 is to be found by an examination of the meaning of the almost identically worded s 265. This is not merely because of the linguistic similarity between those two provisions, but because the whole of the structure for the transfer of property and liabilities in the Transfer Order is closely modelled on the pre-existing structure of the provisions in s 265 relating to trunk roads.

'[34] It is tempting but, in my view, wrong to assume that, where ss 263 and 265 both refer to "highway" as a label for real property rights which are to be vested in a highway authority, the word "highway" must therefore have precisely the same meaning in both sections. This is not merely because the word appears as part of two quite differently worded provisions. Rather, it is because, although now lying almost side by side in a consolidating statute, the two sections have completely different ancestry, and serve two very different purposes. As already noted, s 263 takes away from private ownership only those rights in the vertical plane of the highway which are necessary to enable the highway authority to perform its statutory functions of operation, maintenance and repair. By contrast, s 265 merely transfers rights in the vertical plane already owned by one public authority to a successor public authority, so that the successor can stand in the shoes of its predecessor so far as ownership is concerned. …' *Southwark London Borough Council v Transport for London* [2018] UKSC 63, [2019] 2 All ER 271 at [6], [31]–[34], per Lord Briggs

Highway constructed by a highway authority

[Highways Act 1980, s 36; path in a park.] '[22] In order to succeed in her contention that Wigan were under a duty to maintain the Path Ms Barlow has to prove one of two alternative cases. The first is that it was a "highway constructed by a highway authority" within the meaning of s 36(2)(a) of the 1980 Act. The second is that it was one of those highways which "immediately before the commencement of this Act were highways maintainable at public expense" within the meaning of s 36(1) of the 1980 Act.

...

'[43] The main issue under this heading is whether Ms Barlow has to show that, when Abram [Abram UDC] constructed the Path in the 1930s, they did so in their capacity as the local highway authority....

...

'[47] ... It may well be true that for the purposes of the law of contract a local authority is a single body corporate. But it does not follow that it is indivisible for all purposes. To take only one example, a council which is both housing authority and planning authority is not exempt from the need to obtain planning permission if it wishes to construct new housing. On the capacity issue under s 36(2)(a) of the 1980 Act I entirely agree with the reasoning and conclusions of Neuberger J [in *Gulliksen v Pembrokeshire County Council* [2002] QB 825 at 830: "To my mind, the notion of 'a highway constructed by a highway authority' means 'a highway constructed as a highway by a highway authority in its capacity as such"].

...

'[54] I therefore consider that Ms Barlow cannot succeed under s 36(2)(a) of the 1980 Act, because when Abram constructed the Path they were not acting in their capacity as the highway authority for the area. This makes it unnecessary to decide whether intention is a factor under s 36(2)(a), though the issue of intention crops up in a different form under the heading of dedication.

...

'[69] Neuberger J appeared to accept the submission made by counsel in *Gulliksen* that the interpretation he would give to s 36(2)(a) would involve the reading in of the words "as such" into that provision, in other words to make it clear that it only applies where a highway authority constructs a highway acting in its capacity as such. I do not consider that any words have to be read into the provision. In my view, it has the effect that Neuberger J thought it had, simply on its face. This is because, in my view, the words "highway authority" are used by Parliament to mean "an authority exercising its highway functions".' *Barlow v Wigan Metropolitan Borough Council* [2020] EWCA Civ 696, [2021] 3 All ER 223 at [22], [43], [47], [54], per Bean LJ and at [69], per Singh LJ

The highway, in so far as it is vested in the former highway authority

[The GLA Roads and Side Roads (Transfer of Property etc) Order 2000, SI 2000/1552, art 2(1)(a), which had been modelled on the Highways Act 1980, s 265, transferred to TfL 'the highway, in so far as it is vested in the former highway authority'.] '[29] In my judgment art 2(1)(a) transfers to TfL ownership of all that part of the vertical plane relating to a GLA road vested in the relevant council on the operative date, but only to the extent that ownership was then vested in the council in its capacity as former highway authority. That is, in my view, the true meaning of the phrase "the highway, in so far as it is vested in the former highway authority". ...' *Southwark London Borough Council v Transport for London* [2018] UKSC 63, [2019] 2 All ER 271 at [29], per Lord Briggs

HOMELESSNESS

[Housing Act 1996.] '[7] A person is homeless if he has no accommodation available for occupation by him and any person who normally resides with him as a member of his family or who might reasonably be expected to reside with him: see ss 175(1) and 176 of the 1996 Act. Section 175(3) of the 1996 Act provides that:

> "A person shall not be treated as having accommodation unless it is accommodation which it would be reasonable for him to continue to occupy."

'[8] Regard may be had to the general circumstances prevailing in relation to housing in the authority's area in determining whether it is reasonable for a person to continue to occupy accommodation: see s 177(2) of the 1996 Act. Section 177(1) provides that it is not reasonable to continue to occupy accommodation if it is probable that that would lead to a risk of domestic violence. The Secretary of State may prescribe other circumstances in which it is, or is not, reasonable to continue to occupy accommodation: see s 177(3) of the 1996 Act.

'[9] There are, therefore a number of situations in which a person may be regarded as homeless under the 1996 Act. They include circumstances where persons have no accommodation physically available to them at all. They also include situations where persons have some accommodation physically available to them but it is not reasonable for them to occupy it because, for example, it is overcrowded or may not address their needs. The accommodation, for example, may be on an upper floor of a block of flats and the person may have mobility issues. Or the person may have a disability and the property may not be adapted to meet their needs.

'[10] Furthermore, while it may be reasonable for the person and his family to continue to occupy accommodation for a short period, it may not be reasonable for them to continue to do so in the longer term. In those circumstances, the requirements of s 175(3) are met and the applicant and his family are still homeless for the purposes of Pt VII of the 1996 Act even though they are living in accommodation which is, at present, reasonable for them to occupy: see the speech of Baroness Hale, with whom the other members of the House of Lords agreed, *R (on the application of Ali) v Birmingham City Council* [2009] UKHL 36, [2009] 4 All ER 161, [2009] PTSR 1270, especially at paras [34] to [38].

'[11] A person is threatened with homelessness if it is likely that he will become homeless within 28 days (now amended by the 2017 Act to 56 days): see s 175(4) of the 1996 Act.' *R (on the application of Elkundi) v Birmingham City Council* [2022] EWCA Civ 601, [2022] 4 All ER 302 at [7]–[11], per Lewis LJ

HOMICIDE

[For 25 Halsbury's Laws of England (5th Edn) (2016) para 97 see now 25 Halsbury's Laws of England (5th Edn) (2020) para 124.]

HONEST OPINION

[For 32 Halsbury's Laws of England (5th Edn) (2012) paras 637–638 (on fair comment) see now 32 Halsbury's Laws of England (5th Edn) (2019) para 632.]

HOSPITIUM

[For 68 Halsbury's Laws of England (5th Edn) (2016) para 663 see now 68 Halsbury's Laws of England (5th Edn) (2021) para 679.]

HOTEL

[For 68 Halsbury's Laws of England (5th Edn) (2016) para 648 see now 68 Halsbury's Laws of England (5th Edn) (2021) para 664.]

HOTCHPOT

[For 91 Halsbury's Laws of England (5th Edn) (2012) para 825 see now 91 Halsbury's Laws of England
(5th Edn) (2012) para 718.]

HUMAN TRAFFICKING

'[81] In contrast to slavery and forced labour, international consensus on a definition of human trafficking is much more recent and was only arrived at in 2000 with the adoption of the Palermo Protocol, to which there are now 178 state parties. Article 3 of the Palermo Protocol defines "trafficking in persons" as meaning—

> "the recruitment, transportation, transfer, harbouring or receipt of persons, by means of the threat or use of force or other forms of coercion, of abduction, of fraud, of deception, of the abuse of power or of a position of vulnerability or of the giving or receiving of payments or benefits to achieve the consent of a person having control over another person, for the purpose of exploitation."

"Exploitation" is stated to include—

> "at a minimum, the exploitation of the prostitution of others or other forms of sexual exploitation, forced labour or services, slavery or practices similar to slavery, servitude or the removal of organs …"

Article 4(a) of the Council of Europe Anti-Trafficking Convention on Action against Trafficking in Human Beings (2005) defines "trafficking in human beings" in similar terms.

'[82] The definition of human trafficking has three elements:

(i) the act: recruitment, transportation, transfer, harbouring or receipt of persons;
(ii) the means (by which the act is done): threat or use of force, coercion, abduction, fraud, deception, abuse of power or vulnerability, or giving or receiving payments or benefits to a person to achieve the consent of a person who has control of the victim; and
(iii) the purpose: exploitation, which includes the purpose of forced labour or slavery or servitude.'

Basfar v Wong [2022] UKSC 20, [2022] 4 All ER 1 at [81]–[82], per Lord Briggs and Lord Leggatt JJSC

HUNT

New Zealand [Wildlife Act 1953, s 63A: offence to hunt or kill any absolutely or partially protected marine wildlife.] '[62] It is implicit in the prohibited act of "hunting" that the defendant intends to hunt. To hunt something, you must intend to catch or kill it. It is not possible to accidentally or unintentionally hunt an animal.

…

'[93] … In the s 2(1) definition of "hunt or kill": "hunting" means an intentional act committed if a person is proved to have had an intent to hunt.' *Shark Experience Ltd v PauaMAC5 Inc* [2019] NZSC 111, [2019] 1 NZLR 791 at [62], [93], per Winkelmann CJ

HUNT OR KILL

New Zealand [Wildlife Act 1953, s 63A: a specific offence to 'hunt or kill' certain marine wildlife (including great white sharks). Whether shark cage diving was hunting or killing.] '[29] As the parties acknowledge, the definition is particularly difficult to construe. Part of that difficulty lies in the use of the words "hunt" and "kill" in accordance with their usual meaning as part of an extended definition of the expression "hunt or kill". Part lies in the fact that the overall statutory scheme has been repeatedly amended over the course of the sixty-plus years since its enactment, causing the Act to lose some coherence.

'[30] Shark Experience maintains that the ordinary and grammatical reading of the s 2 definition is that the words "pursuing, disturbing, or molesting" are connected to, and qualified by, the words "hunt or kill". Ms Grey for Shark Experience argues that it is an available interpretation that all of the relevant actions, "pursuing, disturbing, or molesting", are to be read as connected to the words "to hunt or kill". On this reading, what is prohibited is disturbance of protected wildlife connected to hunting or killing, and pursuing or molesting protected wildlife in the course of hunting or killing.

…

'[33] It is helpful at this point to repeat the definition of "hunt or kill" in s 2:

> **hunt or kill**, in relation to any wildlife, includes the hunting, killing, taking, trapping, or capturing of any wildlife by any means; and also includes pursuing, disturbing, or molesting any wildlife, taking or using a firearm, dog, or like method to hunt or kill wildlife, whether this results in killing or capturing or not; and also includes every attempt to hunt or kill wildlife and every act of assistance of any other person to hunt or kill wildlife

'[34] On our analysis, the definition of "hunt or kill" operates on three levels as follows:

(a) The first level is "includes the hunting, killing, taking, trapping, or capturing of any wildlife by any means;". This describes the non-extended meaning of hunting, killing, trapping or capturing, actions that would be captured in accordance with common usage of these words.

(b) The second level is "and also includes pursuing, disturbing, or molesting any wildlife, taking or using a firearm, dog, or like method to hunt or kill wildlife, whether this results in killing or capturing or not;". We read this as extending the meaning of the expression "hunt or kill" beyond the common usage of those words to include both acts incidental to hunting or killing wildlife ("taking or using a firearm, dog, or like method to hunt or kill wildlife"), and also to other kinds of potentially harmful actions ("pursuing, disturbing, or molesting any wildlife") that are not necessarily connected to hunting or killing in a common usage sense.

(c) The third and final level is "and also includes every attempt to hunt or kill wildlife and every act of assistance of any other person to hunt or kill wildlife". As is common ground, this deals with attempts or the giving of assistance.

…

'[40] On our approach, the definition of "hunt or kill" can be seen as a list of prohibited actions relating to wildlife. The choice of the phrase "hunt or kill" as the defined term does not have any particular significance in determining the meanings of the items in the list. It might be thought improbable or unlikely that the phrase "hunt or kill" was chosen as a catch-all phrase for a collection of prohibited actions, some unrelated to hunting or killing in their common usage. But in other, later, Acts, the use of this phrase in just that manner is beyond question. …

…

'[92] To conclude this interpretative analysis, we are satisfied that the definition of "hunt or kill" captures within the s 63A offence conduct which is unconnected to the common usage meaning of hunting and killing, extending to pursuing, molesting and disturbing protected wildlife, whether or not those prohibited acts take place in the course of, or for the purpose of, hunting or killing or otherwise. We are satisfied that the overall statutory scheme supports this interpretation, as does the Act's purpose. This interpretation does not lead to incoherence in the statutory scheme, nor to over or indeterminate criminalisation. The nature of the prohibited acts, together with the availability of the s 68B and common law "no fault" defence, create a coherent framework from which exposure to criminal liability can be sufficiently predicted.

'[93] We summarise the nature of the prohibited acts as follows. In the s 2(1) definition of "hunt or kill":

(a) "hunting" means an intentional act committed if a person is proved to have had an intent to hunt;
(b) "killing" means causing the death of a protected animal. An intention to kill need not be proved;
(c) "pursuing" means to intentionally chase but does not include luring or attracting or merely following the animal at a safe distance;
(d) "disturbing" means an action which physically or mentally agitates the protected animal to a level creating a real risk of significant harm; and
(e) "molesting" means intentionally troubling, distressing or injuring a protected animal.

'[94] There is no requirement to prove an intent to commit the offence in s 63A. Aside from the prohibited act of "hunting", there is also no requirement to prove that any of the prohibited acts listed above are committed in the course of, or for the purpose of, hunting or killing in the ordinary usage sense of those words. Attempting any of the prohibited acts would also constitute an offence under s 63A.

...

'[123] The Court of Appeal's declaration that "Shark cage diving is an offence under s 63A Wildlife Act 1953" is set aside.' *Shark Experience Ltd v PauaMAC5 Inc* [2019] NZSC 111, [2019] 1 NZLR 791 at [29]–[30], [33]–[34], [40], [92]–[92], [123], per Winkelmann CJ

HYPOTHECATION

[For 7 Halsbury's Laws of England (5th Edn) (2012) para 506 see now 7 Halsbury's Laws of England (5th Edn) (2020) para 539.]

I

IP COMPLETION DAY

'IP completion day' means 31 December 2020 at 11 pm. … In this Act references to before, after or on IP completion day, or to beginning with IP completion day, are to be read as references to before, after or at 11 pm on 31 December 2020 or (as the case may be) to beginning with 11 pm on that day. (European Union (Withdrawal Agreement) Act 2020, s 39(1), (2))

IMAGING ORDER

'[177] For over a decade, it has been technically possible for forensic computer experts to take complete copies, referred to as "images", of the contents of storage media incorporated in or associated with computers, without affecting the data stored there. Over time, this capability has been extended to smart phones and cloud storage.

'[178] In the present context, imaging has both advantages and disadvantages. The key advantages are that (i) it is a relatively non-intrusive process which does not involve any removal of documents and (ii) it enables all digital evidence to be preserved for subsequent analysis. The key disadvantage is that imaging is, by its very nature, incapable of discrimination between information that is relevant to the issues in the proceedings and information that is irrelevant, or between business information and personal information, or between information that is subject to legal professional privilege and information that is not. Thus imaging can only ever be a preservation step, and it must be followed by proper consideration of the issues of disclosure and inspection of the documents preserved by the imaging process.

'[179] The availability of imaging has important consequences for search orders which in my experience have frequently been disregarded. The first is that, if what is needed is a remedy to preserve evidence in order to ensure that it cannot be altered, destroyed or hidden, then in many cases an order requiring the respondent to permit imaging of its digital devices and cloud storage ("an imaging order") will be the most effective means of achieving that objective. The second, which follows from the first, is that, if an imaging order is made, then that may well make a traditional search order unnecessary, or at least may enable the scope of the search order to be significantly restricted eg to articles as opposed to documents.'

…

'[181] Where an imaging order is made, it should be obvious that appropriate safeguards are required for the protection of respondents. Experience shows, however, that applicants and courts do not always give proper consideration to the safeguards that should be provided. By contrast with search orders, no standard form of imaging order has been developed. In my view this case demonstrates there is an urgent need for the Civil Procedure Rules Committee to promulgate a standard form of imaging order. Until such time as a standard form is available, however, it is incumbent upon solicitors and counsel representing applicants, and judges hearing applications, to give careful consideration to the provision of appropriate safeguards. …' *TBD (Owen Holland) Ltd v Simons* [2020] EWCA Civ 1182, [2021] 4 All ER 889 at [177]–[179], [181], per Arnold LJ

IMPLIED TERM

[For 22 Halsbury's Laws of England (5th Edn) (2012) paras 364–376 see now 22 Halsbury's Laws of England (5th Edn) (2019) paras 163–175.]

IMPRISONMENT

[Curfew imposed by Home Secretary on foreign national awaiting deportation; whether amounting to imprisonment.] '[1] The right to physical liberty was highly prized and protected by the common law long before the United Kingdom became party to the European Convention on Human Rights ("ECHR"). A person who was unlawfully imprisoned could, and can, secure his release through the writ of habeas corpus. He could, and can, also secure damages for the tort of false imprisonment. This case is about the meaning of imprisonment at common law and whether it should, or should not, now be aligned with the concept of deprivation of liberty in art 5 of the ECHR.

...

'[24] As it is put in *Street on Torts* (15th edn, 2018), by Christian Witting, p 259, "False imprisonment involves an act of the defendant which directly and intentionally (or possibly negligently) causes the confinement of the claimant within an area delimited by the defendant." The essence of imprisonment is being made to stay in a particular place by another person. The methods which might be used to keep a person there are many and various. They could be physical barriers, such as locks and bars. They could be physical people, such as guards who would physically prevent the person leaving if he tried to do so. They could also be threats, whether of force or of legal process. A good example is *R v Rumble* [2003] EWCA Crim 770, [2003] 1 Cr App Rep (S) 618, 167 JP 205. The defendant in a magistrates' court who had surrendered to his bail was in custody even though there was no dock, no usher, nor security staff and thus nothing to prevent his escaping (as indeed he did). The point is that the person is obliged to stay where he is ordered to stay whether he wants to do so or not.

'[25] In this case there is no doubt that the defendant defined the place where the claimant was to stay between the hours of 11 pm and 7 am. There was no suggestion that he could go somewhere else during those hours without the defendant's permission. ...

'[26] The fact that the claimant did from time to time ignore his curfew for reasons that seemed good to him makes no difference to his situation while he was obeying it. Like the prisoner who goes absent from his open prison, or the tunneller who gets out of the prison camp, he is not imprisoned while he is away. But he is imprisoned while he is where the defendant wants him to be.

'[27] There is, of course, a crucial difference between voluntary compliance with an instruction and enforced compliance with that instruction. The Court of Appeal held that this was a case of enforced not voluntary compliance and I agree. It is not to be compared with those cases in which the claimant went voluntarily with the sheriff's officer. There can be no doubt that the claimant's compliance was enforced. He was wearing an electronic tag which meant that leaving his address would be detected. The monitoring company would then telephone him to find out where he was. He was warned in the clearest possible terms that breaking the curfew could lead to a £5,000 fine or imprisonment for up to six months or both. He was well aware that it could also lead to his being detained again under the [Immigration Act 1971]. All of this was backed up by the full authority of the State, which was claiming to have the power to do this. The idea that the claimant was a free agent, able to come and go as he pleased, is completely unreal.' *R (on the application of Jalloh (formerly Jollah)) v Secretary of State for the Home Department* [2020] UKSC 4, [2020] 3 All ER 449 at [1], [24]–[27], per Lady Hale

IN

In a document

[Taxes Management Act 1970, s 118(7): 'references to a loss of tax or a situation brought about deliberately by a person include a loss of tax or a situation that arises as a result of a deliberate inaccuracy in a document given to Her Majesty's Revenue and Customs'.] '[48] The final question of construction of s 118(7) is as to the meaning of the phrase "in a document" as the place where the relevant deliberate inaccuracy is to be found. The Revenue submitted, and persuaded a majority of the Court of Appeal (Males and Patten LJJ), that it was enough if a deliberate inaccuracy could be found somewhere in the document, interpreted on its own and without regard to the rest of the contents of the document, always provided that it had the requisite causative effect in bringing about the insufficiency of tax or other relevant situation under s 29(1). By contrast Mr Tooth submitted, and Floyd LJ held in the Court of Appeal, that the accuracy or otherwise of the statement relied upon could only properly be assessed in the light of the whole of the document in which it was contained.

'[49] It almost goes without saying that the meaning of particular words or phrases in a document of any kind is generally to be ascertained by a contextual approach, that is by appraising the critical passage in the light of its context as part of the document read as a whole. There is no reason in principle why the same should not be true of a tax return. But in this respect the sheet anchor of the Revenue's case was the fact that, as the online tax return form clearly stated, the return would be read upon receipt at the Revenue by a computer rather than, initially at least, by a sentient, literate, human being. Computers, it was said, do not do contextual interpretation, but look at each part of, or box in, the return separately.

'[50] This is, with respect, a very unattractive argument. A document written in the English language (or any language other than computer language) does not have a different meaning depending upon whether it is read by a human being or by a computer. A choice by the recipient of such a document to have it machine-read cannot alter its meaning. Furthermore, the Revenue-approved online tax return form used by Mr Tooth and his advisors contained numerous "white spaces", that is, sections of blank white-coloured space, usually headed "Additional Information", within which the taxpayer is invited to add information using his own words and phrases, so as to ensure that the declaration required to be made and signed, namely that—

> "The information I have given on this Tax Return is correct and complete to the best of my knowledge and belief"

—is actually true.

'[51] The Revenue cannot in our view have it both ways. If they sensibly include ample white spaces in their approved form of online returns so as to ensure that the taxpayer is not constrained by the limitations of the boxes for figures from making a correct and complete return, then they cannot thereafter assert, for the purpose of advancing a non-contextual interpretation of one or more boxes, that their computer cannot read what is written on the white spaces. This must be a fortiori true where, as in the present case, the white space used by Mr Tooth to provide a full and frank explanation of the true meaning of the supposedly offending insertions in the partnership boxes was to be found immediately adjacent to those boxes.

'[52] It follows that the task of interpretation required by the need for the Revenue to prove that there was a deliberate inaccuracy in Mr Tooth's tax return was to interpret the meaning of each relevant part of the document by reference to its place in the context of the document as a whole, just as is normally done when interpreting any other document. This is not to say that the word "in" as part of the phrase "deliberate inaccuracy in a document" is to be ignored. It simply means that, rather than concluding that there is an inaccuracy by applying tunnel-vision to a particular part of the document, and ignoring the rest, the true meaning of that part is ascertained from a reading of the document as a whole.' *Tooth v Revenue and Customs Commissioners* [2021] UKSC 17, [2021] 3 All ER 711 at [48]–[52], per Lord Briggs and Lord Sales JJSC

IN ACCORDANCE WITH THE LAW

[European Convention for the Protection of Human Rights and Fundamental Freedoms (ECHR), art 8.] '[49] Mr Southey submitted that the [Child Sex Offender Disclosure Scheme Guidance] is unlawful because it fails to comply with standards of certainty, predictability in application and accessibility which are implicit in the concept of "law" as that concept is used in the ECHR and, in particular, in art 8(2). That is because it does not specify for every case whether representations should be sought from a subject but is flexible to allow for adaptation depending on the facts of particular cases. In our judgment, this submission is unsustainable for two reasons.

'[50] First, the Guidance does not purport to replace the underlying law which governs the circumstances in which a disclosure to the public may be made, that is to say (so far as is relevant for present purposes) the common law duty of fairness and the requirements inherent in art 8 itself (as applied by virtue of s 6(1) of the [Human Rights Act 1988]). That includes the requirement of proportionality and the right, where appropriate, to participate in a decision-making process. These requirements are explained fully in the case law of the European Court of Human Rights ("the Strasbourg Court") and the domestic courts. Mr Southey did not suggest that these legal regimes are defective by reference to the requirements of the concept of "law" in the ECHR. Clearly they are not. A police force which seeks to comply with its legal duties under these regimes, as the Guidance encourages it to do, will act "in accordance with the law" for the purposes of art 8(2).

'[51] Secondly, and in any event, the concept of "law" in the ECHR, including in art 8(2), does not imply a requirement that the domestic law relevant to a matter within the scope of a Convention right should be free from doubt as to its application and effect in particular cases. No system of law could possibly achieve that, and the ECHR does not require it. As the Strasbourg Court said in the landmark case of *Sunday Times v UK* (App no 6538/74) (1979) 2 EHRR 245, [1979] ECHR 6538/74 (para 49):

> "… a norm cannot be regarded as a 'law' unless it is formulated with sufficient precision to enable the citizen to regulate his conduct: he must be able – if need be with appropriate advice – to foresee, to a degree that is reasonable in the circumstances, the consequences which a given action may entail. Those consequences need not be foreseeable with absolute certainty: experience shows this to be unattainable. Again, whilst certainty is highly desirable, it may bring in its train excessive rigidity and the law must be able to keep pace with changing circumstances. Accordingly, many laws are inevitably couched in terms which, to a greater or lesser extent, are vague and whose interpretation and application are questions of practice."

See also, eg, *Silver v UK* (App nos 5947/72, 6205/73, 7052/75, 7061/75, 7107/75, 7113/75, 7136/75) (1983) 5 EHRR 347, [1983] ECHR 5947/72 (para 88), making the same point in the context of art 8.

'[52] … The most cursory review [of the authorities] shows that they do not support the submission Mr Southey makes that the Guidance is incompatible with art 8 by reason of the fact that there is a limited degree of imprecision in it. The "in accordance with the law" rubric in art 8(2) does not require the elimination of uncertainty, but is concerned with ensuring that law attains a reasonable degree of predictability and provides safeguards against arbitrary or capricious decision-making by public officials. Judged even on its own terms, the Guidance meets those standards.

'[53] We would add that it is established that a policy may make a contribution to meeting the 'in accordance with the law' requirement in some cases, by helping to provide a degree of predictability in the application of general discretionary provisions in statute (see eg *Silver v UK* (App nos 5947/72, 6205/73, 7052/75, 7061/75, 7107/75, 7113/75, 7136/75) (1983) 5 EHRR 347, [1983] ECHR 5947/72 (para 88)). However, it by no means follows that there is an obligation to have a policy in every case where a statute creates a discretionary power.' *R (on the application of A) v Secretary of State for the Home Department* [2021] UKSC 37, [2022] 1 All ER 177 at [49]–[53], per Lord Sales and Lord Burnett CJ

IN CONSEQUENCE OF

Australia '[779] This issue is a pure question of the proper construction of the expression "in consequence of" in the context in which it is used. It is used as the required nexus between the insured peril and the insured loss. For the reasons which have been set out previously there are logical grounds for requiring that the insured peril be "the efficient cause" of the loss, but it is undoubted that the parties may, by clear words, alter the presumption such that something less or more is required. In this matter, QBE supported the primary judge's interpretation and did not suggest that the expression was limited to the "proximate cause" of the loss. It can be accepted that the primary judge determined the issue as it was advanced by the parties despite the fact that it would not be unusual for the words "in consequence of" as used in cl 3 to impose a requirement of "proximate cause": *FCA v Arch [Financial Conduct Authority v Arch Insurance (UK) Ltd* [2021] AC 649] at [162].

'[780] In these circumstances, her Honour's conclusion as to the scope of the expression "in consequence of" can be accepted. Importantly, it is consistent with the authorities to which her Honour referred. The expression requires that there be an event which "follows as an effect or a result" of another, although it need not be the dominant cause: *Reseck v Federal Commissioner of Taxation* (1975) 133 CLR 45 at 51; 6 ALR 642 at 646, and although requiring causation, "the term 'consequence' — with its emphasis on effect — places less emphasis on the proximity of cause and effect than the term 'cause' may do in various contexts": *Container Handlers* [*Insurance Commission of Western Australia v Container Handlers Pty Ltd* (2003) 218 CLR 89; 206 ALR 335; 40 MVR 33; [2004] HCA 24] at [45]. So, in an insuring clause, although requiring that there be some causal nexus between the loss and the insured peril, that "nexus is less than a direct or proximate relationship as required by the words 'caused by'": *XL Insurance v BNY Trust Company* [(2019) 20 ANZ Ins Cas 62-211; [2019] NSWCA 215] at [62]. Whilst EWT relied on a number of other authorities in support of the broader interpretation, the meanings of the expression as used in taxation legislation: *McIntosh v Federal Commissioner of Taxation* (1979) 25 ALR 557: or social security legislation: *McAuliffe v Secretary, Department of Social Security* (1991) 23 ALD 284 at 295; *Director-General of Social Services v Hales* (1983) 47 ALR 281 at 300–301: are not especially persuasive.' *LCA Marrickville Pty Ltd v Swiss International SE* [2022] FCAFC 17, (2022) 401 ALR 204 at [779]–[780], per Derrington and Colvin JJ

IN THE PRESENCE OF

[For 102 Halsbury's Laws of England (5th Edn) (2010) para 70 see now 102 Halsbury's Laws of England (5th Edn) (2021) para 71.]

As a result of the challenges of the coronavirus pandemic, wills made on or after 31 January 2020 and on or before 31 January 2022 may be witnessed validly even though the testator is not in the physical presence of the two witnesses. They must be within sight of each other but not in their physical presence. During this period, in the requirement that the signature of the testator to the will be made or acknowledged by the testator in the presence of two or more witnesses present at the same time, and in the requirement that each witness attests and signs the will or acknowledges his signature in the presence of the testator, 'presence' includes presence by means of videoconference or other visual transmission. [See the Wills Act 1837, s 9(2) (added by the Wills Act 1837 (Electronic Communications) (Amendment) (Coronavirus) Order 2020, SI 2020/952.] (102 Halsbury's Laws of England (5th Edn) (2021) para 70)

INCAPACITATED FOR WORK OUTSIDE THE POLICE FORCE

Australia [Police Regulation (Superannuation) Act 1906 (NSW), s 10(1A)(b)(ii): superannuation amount commensurate with incapacity for work outside the police force.] '[17] As was observed at the outset, s 10(1A)(b)(ii) permits of a constructional choice. On one view of its terms, it provides for an "additional amount" of annual superannuation allowance for a "disabled member of the police force" who is incapacitated for work outside the police force regardless of the cause of the member's incapacity for work outside the police force. The alternative view is that it provides for an "additional amount" of annual superannuation allowance for a "disabled member of the police force" who is incapacitated for work outside the police force only if the incapacity for work outside the police force results from a specified infirmity of body or mind determined, in accordance with s 10B, to have been caused by the member having been hurt on duty when a member of the police force.

...

'[23] Turning next to s 10(1A)(c), the statutory exclusion of s 10(1A)(b) where s 10(1A)(c) applies, and vice versa, conveys that "incapacitated" in the expression "totally incapacitated for work outside the police force" in s 10(1A)(c) has the same meaning as "incapacity" in the expression "incapacity for work outside the police force" in s 10(1A)(b)(ii).

'[24] Contrary to the respondent's submissions, it is also apparent that "incapacitated for work outside the police force" in s 10(1A)(c) must mean incapacitated for work outside the police force from the specified infirmity of body or mind which rendered the member incapable of exercising the functions of a police officer and which was caused by being hurt on duty. That is implicit in the requirement in s 10(1A)(c)(ii) that the additional amount of between 12.25 and 27.25 per cent of attributed salary payable under s 10(1A)(c)(i) in respect of the disabled member's incapacity for work outside the police force be commensurate with the abnormality of the risks to which the member was exposed. As the chapeau to s 10(1A)(c) makes clear, the risks are those that cause the member to be hurt on duty. The provision thereby draws a clear link between the additional amount payable and the event of the member being hurt on duty.

...

'[29] Taking those considerations together conveys that the preferable view of s 10(1A)(b)(ii) is that, like s 10(1A)(c), it contemplates only one kind of incapacity for work outside the police force, being incapacity the result of the specified infirmity of body or mind determined to have been caused by the member being hurt on duty when a member of the police force.

...

'[40] In the result, it should be held that, upon the proper construction of s 10(1A)(b) of the Act, the expression "member's incapacity for work outside the police force" means the member's incapacity from a specified infirmity of body or mind determined pursuant to s 10B or on appeal to have been caused by the member being hurt on duty when he or she was a member of the police force. ...' *SAS Trustee Corp v Miles* [2018] HCA 55, (2018) 361 ALR 206 at [17], [23]–[24], [29], [40], per Kiefel CJ, Bell and Nettle JJ

INCAPACITY

OF CHILD

[For 9 Halsbury's Laws of England (5th Edn) (2012) para 5 see now 9 Halsbury's Laws of England (5th Edn) (2017) para 5.]

INCHMAREE CLAUSE

[For 60 Halsbury's Laws of England (5th Edn) (2011) para 335 see now 60 Halsbury's Laws of England (5th Edn) (2018) para 314.]

INCIDENTAL DEMAND

Canada [Civil Code of Québec ('CCQ'), art 3139: where a Québec authority has jurisdiction to rule on the principal demand, it also has jurisdiction to rule on an incidental demand or a cross demand.] '155 The Court must nevertheless bear in mind that art 3139 *CCQ* is a jurisdiction-*granting* provision, and that its operation assumes that, absent this provision, the court would not be competent, in the jurisdictional sense, to hear the "incidental demand or ... cross demand": Saumier [Saumier, Geneviève. "The Recognition of Foreign Judgments in Quebec — The Mirror Crack'd?" (2002), 81 *Can Bar Rev* 677], at p 703; *Spar* [*Spar Aerospace Ltd v American Mobile Satellite Corp* 2002 SCC 78, [2002] 4 SCR 205], at para 22 ("[t]hese rules [in Book Ten of the *CCQ*] cover a broad range of interrelated topics, including: the jurisdiction of the court (art 3136, 3139 and 3148 *CCQ*)" (emphasis added)). In my view, the term "incidental demand", as that term appears in art 3139 CCQ, is sufficiently broad to cover voluntary and forced intervention of third persons in the proceeding, including an incidental demand in warranty, and the consolidation of proceedings, whether or not they involve the same parties, and whether or not they arise from the same source or from related sources: see arts 184 to 190 and 210 of the new *Code of Civil Procedure*, CQLR, c C-25.01 ("new *CCP*"); see also Côté J's reasons, at paras 206 and 283 ("there is no doubt that [the precise meaning of 'incidental demand'] must be defined on the basis of Quebec procedural law"). Indeed, this point finds ample support in the Quebec doctrine. ...

...

'**157** Further, an "incidental demand" is not limited to a recourse in warranty: see, eg, art 184 para 3 of the new *CCP*. A *plaintiff* thus has the right to force the intervention of a third person in order to fully resolve the dispute: see *Bourdages v Québec (Gouvernement du) (Ministère des Transports)* 2016 QCCS 5066; *Fonds d'assurance responsabilité professionnelle du Barreau du Québec v Gariépy*, 2005 QCCA 60, at para 33. ...' *Barer v Knight Brothers LLC* [2019] SCJ No 13, [2019] 1 SCR 573 at paras 155, 157, per Brown J

INCUMBRANCE

[For 27(1) Halsbury's Laws (4th edn reissue) para 81 see now 62 Halsbury's Laws of England (5th Edn) (2022) para 113.]

INCUR

[Corporation Tax Act 2009, s 54: in calculating the profits of a trade, no deduction is allowed for—(a) expenses not incurred wholly and exclusively for the purposes of the trade.] '[34] By providing that references to expenses "do not imply that an amount has actually been ... paid", s 48(2) is therefore not restricted to amounts that either had been physically paid or had been incurred as enforceable obligations or had been included in accounts as provisions against what was likely to be spent in future years.

'[35] Section 54(1)(a), referring "in calculating the profits of a trade" to "expenses", is a provision to which s 48 applies. The construction advanced by HMRC, that the use of the word "incurred" to qualify "expenses" means that the expenses must have been incurred as a matter of legal liability or be a prospective liability for which a provision should be made, is thus at odds with the definitional effect of s 48(1) and (2).

'[36] For that reason, it is not a permissible construction, unless HMRC can rely on s 48(3) which provides that s 48 is "subject to any express provision to the contrary".

'[37] HMRC seek to extract out of the use of the word "incurred" in s 54 a provision to the contrary. The difficulty for HMRC is that it would not so much be a provision to the contrary as a provision that denies the effect of s 48(1) and (2) not for a restricted class of case but in all cases. It will be remembered that HMRC's case is that there is a two-stage test for an expense, involving satisfaction of both GAAP [generally accepted accounting practice] (ss 46 and 48) and their interpretation of "incurred" in s 54. But, if a general effect is given to s 54, as HMRC contend, it robs the definitional effect of s 48 of its purpose.

...

'[39] In my judgment, the UT [Upper Tribunal] was correct in its approach to ss 46 and 48 and to s 54. The combined effect of ss 46 and 48 is to define allowable expenses as those debits made in accordance with GAAP in calculating the profits of a trade. They do not require any further examination of whether such accounting debits were "expenses".' *NCL Investments Ltd v Revenue and Customs Commissioners* [2020] EWCA Civ 663, [2021] 1 All ER 319 at [34]–[37], [39], per David Richards LJ

INDEMNITY

[For 49 Halsbury's Laws of England (5th Edn) (2015) para 646 see now 49 Halsbury's Laws of England (5th Edn) (2021) para 609; and for 60 Halsbury's Laws of England (5th Edn) (2011) para 3 see now 60 Halsbury's Laws of England (5th Edn) (2018) para 3.]

INDENTURE

[For 32 Halsbury's Laws of England (5th Edn) (2012) para 203 see now 32 Halsbury's Laws of England (5th Edn) (2019) para 203.]

INDEPENDENT CONTRACTOR

[For 39 Halsbury's Laws of England (5th Edn) (2014) para 1 et seq see now 39 Halsbury's Laws of England (5th Edn) (2021) para 1 et seq.]

INDICTMENT

[For 27 Halsbury's Laws of England (5th Edn) (2015) para 315 see now 27 Halsbury's Laws of England (5th Edn) (2021) para 321.]

INDIRECT OR CONSEQUENTIAL LOSS OR DAMAGE

'[218] Clause 10.3 states:

> "Neither party shall be liable under this Agreement in connection with the supply of or failure to supply the Logistics Services for any indirect or consequential loss or damage including (to the extent only that such are indirect or consequential loss or damage only) but not limited to loss of profits, loss of sales, loss of revenue, damage to reputation, loss or waste of management or staff time or interruption of business."

...

'[222] The starting point is to consider the natural and ordinary meaning of the clause. The first part of the clause states: *"Neither party shall be liable under this Agreement in connection with the supply of or failure to supply the Logistics Services for any indirect or consequential loss or damage."* The clause is equally applicable to both parties. The exclusion covers liability for all contractual obligations in connection with performance of the Logistics Services. The exclusion is *"for any indirect or consequential loss or damage"*. The direct and natural result of the fire was the destruction of the goods and the warehouse, causing lost profits and business interruption losses to the claimants. Therefore, the claims in this case do not appear to fall within the scope of the exclusion.

'[223] Clause 10.3 is unhappily drafted and the second part of the clause, intended to provide an indication of the categories of loss excluded, is particularly unhelpful: *"including (to the extent only that such are indirect or consequential loss or damage only) but not limited to loss of profits, loss of sales, loss of revenue, damage to reputation, loss or waste of management or staff time or interruption of business"*. The effect of the words in parentheses is to negate the illustration intended by the words of inclusion. The only way in which these words can be given effect is to treat the reference to *"loss of profits ..."* and following categories of loss as losses that might or might not fall within the exclusion. As such, they are of no assistance in determining whether the losses claimed in this case fall within or without the exclusion.

...

'[241] In conclusion, cl 10.3 is unhappily worded but its meaning is reasonably clear on these facts. The loss of profits and business interruption costs claimed in this case do not constitute indirect or consequential loss or damage within the meaning of cl 10.3 of the Logistics Contract.' 2 *Entertain Video Ltd v Sony DADC Europe Ltd* [2020] EWHC 972 (TCC), [2021] 1 All ER 527 at [218], [222]–[223], [241], per O'Farrell J

INDORSEMENT

[For 49 Halsbury's Laws of England (5th Edn) (2015) para 191 see now 49 Halsbury's Laws of England (5th Edn) (2021) para 155.]

INELIGIBILITY PERIOD

Australia [Migration Act 1958 (Cth), s 494AA.] '[93] The "ineligibility period" is defined as "the period from the time of the unauthorised entry until the time when the person next ceases to be an unlawful non-citizen". So, like the operation of this term (differently defined) in s 494AB, the starting point for s 494AA, in terms of the time period, is when an individual enters Australia.

'[94] There is no meaning4 attributed by the statute to the term "ineligible". The applicant contends the use of a word such as "ineligible" connotes a temporal restriction. I do not agree. Eligibility, or ineligibility, in many statutory contexts, can fix on a person's characteristics or circumstances, on factual matters external to a person, or on periods of time. I accept it is a somewhat curious word to use as part of a definition in a privative clause, however Parliament has used it and the Court must strive to give it meaning. I consider it is clear enough from the context in which the compound phrase "ineligibility period" is used ("period" signalling a length of time) that, read with the prohibitions in s 494AA(1), the intention is to mark out, by reference to events occurring during a period of time, a category of proceeding that is "ineligible" for the exercise of jurisdiction by any Court except the High Court. As I say, it may not be the heights of drafting elegance, but I consider it is clear this is what is intended.' *DBE17 (by his litigation guardian Arthur) v Commonwealth* [2018] FCA 1307, (2018) 361 ALR 423 at [93]–[94], per Mortimer J

INFECTION

[For 85 Halsbury's Laws of England (5th Edn) (2012) para 625 see now 85 Halsbury's Laws of England (5th Edn) (2020) para 725.]

INFORMATION RELEVANT TO THE DECISION

[Mental Capacity Act 2005, s 3: inability to make decisions.] '[100] In summary, when considering whether, as a result of an impairment of, or disturbance in the functioning of, the mind or brain, a person is unable to understand, retain, or use or weigh information relevant to a decision whether to engage in sexual relations, the information relevant to the decision may include the following:

(1) the sexual nature and character of the act of sexual intercourse, including the mechanics of the act;
(2) the fact that the other person must have the capacity to consent to the sexual activity and must in fact consent before and throughout the sexual activity;
(3) the fact that P can say yes or no to having sexual relations and is able to decide whether to give or withhold consent;
(4) that a reasonably foreseeable consequence of sexual intercourse between a man and woman is that the woman will become pregnant;
(5) that there are health risks involved, particularly the acquisition of sexually transmitted and transmissible infections, and that the risk of sexually transmitted infection can be reduced by the taking of precautions such as the use of a condom.

'[101] There remains the question whether the information relevant to the decision whether to engage in sexual relations must always include all of the matters identified in the previous paragraph.

'[102] This is clearly a matter of considerable importance. In *NB* [*A local authority v NB* [2019] EWCOP 17], Hayden J held that an assessment of the information relevant to a decision to have sexual relations requires the incorporation of P's circumstances and characteristics according to the facts of the particular case. *NB* was not the first case in which this approach was adopted. As illustrated above, it was an approach I adopted myself in *Re TZ* [*A Local Authority v TZ (by his Litigation Friend, the Official Solicitor)* [2013] EWHC 2322 (COP), [2013] COPLR 477] when I observed in passing that the relevant information included the risks of pregnancy "if the relations are heterosexual".

'[103] It is important to note, however, that the question whether the information relevant to the decision whether to engage in sexual relations must always include all of the matters identified in para [100] above does not arise on the present appeal. Any observations we might make on the subject would therefore not be binding authority. The summary of the case law set out above illustrates that on several occasions judicial obiter dicta in this difficult area of the law have been initially followed by other judges, only to be rejected in later cases after hearing further argument. For that reason, it would be prudent for this Court to refrain from commenting until it has an opportunity to hear full argument on the point in a case where the issue arises on the appeal.' *A Local Authority v JB (by his litigation friend, the Official Solicitor)* [2020] EWCA Civ 735, [2021] 1 All ER 1103 at [100]–[103], per Baker LJ

INHERENT VICE

[For 60 Halsbury's Laws of England (5th Edn) (2011) para 344 see now 60 Halsbury's Laws of England (5th Edn) (2018) para 323.]

INJUNCTION

[For 12 Halsbury's Laws of England (5th Edn) (2015) para 1098 see now 12 Halsbury's Laws of England (5th Edn) (2020) para 1086.]

Interlocutory/Interim

[For 12 Halsbury's Laws of England (5th Edn) (2015) para 1101 see now 12 Halsbury's Laws of England (5th Edn) (2020) para 1089.]

Mandatory

[For 12 Halsbury's Laws of England (5th Edn) (2015) para 1099 see now 12 Halsbury's Laws of England (5th Edn) (2020) para 1087.]

Mareva injunction/Freezing injunction

[For 12 Halsbury's Laws of England (5th Edn) (2015) para 595 et seq see now 12 Halsbury's Laws of England (5th Edn) (2020) para 588 et seq.]

Perpetual

[For 12 Halsbury's Laws of England (5th Edn) (2015) para 1100 see now 12 Halsbury's Laws of England (5th Edn) (2020) para 1088.]

INN—INNKEEPER

[For 68 Halsbury's Laws of England (5th Edn) (2016) para 49 see now 68 Halsbury's Laws of England (5th Edn) (2021) para 665.]

INNUENDO

[For 32 Halsbury's Laws of England (5th Edn) (2012) para 547 see now 32 Halsbury's Laws of England (5th Edn) (2019) para 547.]

INSTALL

Australia '[66] … While the term "install" is normally applied to physical things, it is not inherently limited to those things, such as a program may be installed on a computer. While "install" implies the putting in place of something, neither the thing being installed nor the place of instalment need be a tangible use. The expression is capable of bringing within its scope Shell's acquisition of the additional proportional interest (once approved and registered) by reading "installed" as encompassing "putting in place", whether in a tangible or intangible sense. In practice, that means that a bundle of rights is installed ready for use once held for use.' *Commissioner of Taxation (Cth) v Shell Energy Holdings Australia Ltd* [2022] FCAFC 2, (2022) 396 ALR 565 at [66], per Davies J

INSTRUMENT

[For 32 Halsbury's Laws of England (5th Edn) (2012) para 340 see now 32 Halsbury's Laws of England (5th Edn) (2019) para 340.]

Under hand

[For 32 Halsbury's Laws of England (5th Edn) (2012) para 339 see now 32 Halsbury's Laws of England (5th Edn) (2019) para 339.]

INSURABLE INTEREST

[For 60 Halsbury's Laws of England (5th Edn) (2011) para 357 see now 60 Halsbury's Laws of England (5th Edn) (2018) para 336.]

INSURANCE

[For 60 Halsbury's Laws of England (5th Edn) (2011) para 2 see now 60 Halsbury's Laws of England (5th Edn) (2018) para 2.]

Contingency insurance

[For 60 Halsbury's Laws of England (5th Edn) (2011) para 746 see now 60 Halsbury's Laws of England (5th Edn) (2018) para 717.]

Double insurance

[For 60 Halsbury's Laws of England (5th Edn) (2011) para 229 see now 60 Halsbury's Laws of England (5th Edn) (2018) para 208.]

Industrial assurance

[For 60 Halsbury's Laws of England (5th Edn) (2011) para 479 see now 60 Halsbury's Laws of England (5th Edn) (2018) para 457.]

INTEREST (RETURN ON CAPITAL)

[For 49 Halsbury's Laws of England (5th Edn) (2015) para 90 see now 49 Halsbury's Laws of England (5th Edn) (2021) para 59.]

INTERPLEADER

[For 12A Halsbury's Laws of England (5th Edn) (2015) para 1404 see now 12A Halsbury's Laws of England (5th Edn) (2020) para 1378.]

INTERROGATORIES

[For 11 Halsbury's Laws of England (5th Edn) (2015) para 361 see now 11 Halsbury's Laws of England (5th Edn) (2020) para 355.]

INVENTOR

Australia [Patents Act 1990 (Cth), s 15(1); Patents Regulations 1991 (Cth), reg 3.2C(2)(aa). Whether an inventor may be other than a natural person; inventor claimed to be AI.] '[1] The central question in this appeal is whether a device characterised as an artificial intelligence machine can be considered to be an "inventor" within the meaning ascribed to that term in the Patents Act 1990 (Cth) and the Patents Regulations 1991 (Cth).

...

'[113] In our view, the reasoning of the primary judge regarding how it may be that Dr Thaler, as a matter of law, owns the work performed by DABUS, and that such ownership could entitle him to the grant of the application, does not arise, having regard to the view that we have taken to the construction of s 15(1) and reg 3.2C(2)(aa). It is not to the point that Dr Thaler may have rights to the output of DABUS. Only a natural person can be an inventor for the purposes of the Patents Act and Regulations. Such an inventor must be identified for any person to be entitled to a grant of a patent under s 15(1)(b)–(d).

...

'[115] Of course, the development of patent law since 1624 has not until now been confronted with the question of whether or not an inventor may be other than a natural person. However, as noted, the law to which we have referred has proceeded on the assumption that only a natural person could be an inventor. That assumption found expression in the different context considered by the High Court in *D'Arcy* [*D'Arcy v Myriad Genetics Inc* (2015) 258 CLR 334; 325 ALR 100; 115 IPR 1; [2015] HCA 35] where the majority (French CJ, Kiefel, Bell and Keane JJ) said of claims 1–3 in the patent then in suit at [6]:

> ... Despite the formulation of the claimed invention as a class of product, its substance is information embodied in arrangements of nucleotides. The information is not "made" by *human action*. It is discerned. That feature of the claims raises a question about how they fit within the concept of a "manner of manufacture". As appears from s 6 of the Statute of Monopolies, an invention is something which involves "making". It must reside in something. It may be a product. It may be a process. It may be an outcome which can be characterised, in the language of *NRDC*, as an "artificially created state of affairs". Whatever it is, *it must be something brought about by human action*. The requirement, in each claim, that the sequence in the isolate bear specified mutations or polymorphisms raises the same problem in a particular way. Satisfaction of that integer depends upon a characteristic of the human being from whom the nucleic acid is isolated, a characteristic which is not shared by all human beings. It has nothing to do with the *person* who isolates the nucleic acid bearing the mutant sequence.

(emphasis added and citations omitted)

'[116] The references to "human action" were deliberate. They pick up the requirement set out in *National Research Development Corporation v Commissioner of Patents* (1959) 102 CLR 252; [1960] ALR 114; (1959) 1A IPR 63 that a manner of new manufacture bring about an artificially created state of affairs: at CLR 276–7; IPR 64 (Dixon CJ, Kitto and Windeyer JJ). The assumption in both cases was that human agency was required in the development of the invention in suit. That approach accords with the legislative history to which we have referred, namely that the origin of entitlement to the grant of a patent lies in human endeavour, which is rewarded by the grant of a limited term monopoly.

'[117] Accordingly, having regard to the statutory language, structure and history of the Patents Act, and the policy objectives underlying the legislative scheme, we respectfully disagree with the conclusion reached by the primary judge. The Deputy Commissioner was correct to reach the conclusion that, by naming DABUS as the inventor, the application did not comply with reg 3.2C(2)(aa).' *Commissioner of Patents v Thaler* [2022] FCAFC 62, (2022) 401 ALR 551 at [1], [113], [115]–[117], per Allsop CJ, Nicholas, Yates, Moshinsky and Burley JJ

INVESTIGATION

Australia [Australian Crime Commission Act 2002 (Cth), s 7C.] '[96] The word "investigation" must, of course, be construed in the context of the Act read as a whole and in a manner consistent with the statutory purpose: *Project Blue Sky Inc v Australian Broadcasting Authority* (1998) 194 CLR 355; 153 ALR 490. In its ordinary meaning, the word may be understood as referring to an inquisitorial activity and so must have as its subject matter something that is capable of forming the basis of an inquiry. An investigation is something that is capable of generating material to be employed in the fulfilment of its stated purpose. However, in the particular statutory context, and in light of what is said below, the material need not necessarily be in the nature of "evidence" at least if that word is intended to refer to evidentiary material gathered solely to aid in the proof of a criminal charge.

'[97] It must also be accepted that the word "investigation", in context, must refer to an activity that is capable of producing outcomes of a kind that are contemplated by the Act: see s 7A(c) and (d); see also *XXVII* [*XXVII v Commonwealth* (2017) 265 A Crim R 519; [2017] FCA 320] at [119]–[120]. However, the Act does not require that an investigation have a "conclusion" in the sense of a fixed end date or pre-determined terminating event: *XXVII* at [117]–[124]; see also *XXVII* at [42] (Dowsett J), [77]–[89] (Wigney J) and [155] (Bromwich J). Moreover, by s 7C(3) and (4)(c) of the Act, it is apparent that the permissible purpose of an investigation will include the understanding, disrupting or preventing the criminal activity to which the investigation relates. These are words of broad import. There is nothing in the text or context of the provisions to suggest that "understanding, disrupting or preventing" the activity must be achieved by the sole means of gathering evidence for use in the trial of a criminal charge. The amendment to s 7C(3) of the Act (introduced after the High Court delivered judgment in *X7*), makes that clear.

'[98] As to the asserted requirement that an investigation have an organising principle, to my mind that should go without saying. However, to identify that requirement does little to inform the question of how wide or varied the subject matter of a single investigation may permissibly be.

'[99] In my view, the permissible scope of an investigation is not to be found in the meaning of the word "investigation". Rather, the permissible scope of an investigation must be discerned from the whole of the phrase "investigate matters relating to federally relevant criminal activity" as those are the words that the Legislature has used in s 7C(1)(c) to define the limits of the Board's authorisation function. The phrase must, of course, be construed in its statutory context (including in the context of the condition imposed by s 7C(3)). It is a defined phrase embedded with further terms that are themselves expressly and comprehensively defined.

…

'[102] With one qualification, on the proper construction of the Act the Board may authorise an investigation the subject matter of which is described in terms as wide as the language of the statute permits. The qualification is that the subject matter and scope of the investigation must be something in respect of which the mandatory condition in s 7C(3) can be fulfilled in a real and practical sense if the investigation is to be validly determined to be special. In other words, the matters to be investigated cannot be defined in such ephemeral or ill-defined terms that consideration cannot meaningfully be given, and a decision cannot meaningfully be made, as to whether ordinary police methods of investigation into the matters are likely to be effective at understanding, disrupting or preventing the federally relevant criminal activity to which the investigation relates. …' *CXXXVIII v Commonwealth of Australia* [2019]

FCAFC 54, (2019) 366 ALR 436 at [96]–[99], [102], per Charlesworth J

INVESTMENT TRUST

[Delete the entry.]

IRREPARABLE INJURY

[For 12 Halsbury's Laws of England (5th Edn) (2015) para 583 see now 12 Halsbury's Laws of England (5th Edn) (2020) para 576.]

IS TO

Australia [Crimes (Sentencing Procedure) Act 1999 (NSW), s 66.] '[72] It was then said that by dint of s 66(1), community safety must be the paramount consideration when the sentencing court is deciding whether to make an intensive correction order in relation to an offender, and that in any event by reason of s 66(2) the Court must consider whether making an intensive correction order is more likely to address the offender's risk of reoffending than a sentence of full-time imprisonment. I agree that that is the import of the statute. I also agree that the words "is to" in s 66(2) are words imposing an obligation upon the court. That is their natural meaning. The word "must" in s 66(3) is stronger and a clearer way of imposing an obligation, but I see no reason to depart from the ordinary meaning of "is to" in the present context, noting that "must *also*" in s 66(3) presupposes that "is to" connotes an obligation.' *Quinn v Director of Public Prosecutions (Cth)* [2021] NSWCA 294, (2021) 396 ALR 714 at [72], per Leeming JA

J

JETTISON

[For 60 Halsbury's Laws of England (5th Edn) (2011) para 332 see now 60 Halsbury's Laws of England (5th Edn) (2018) para 311.]

JOINTURE

[For 98 Halsbury's Laws of England (5th Edn) (2013) para 502 see now 91 Halsbury's Laws of England (5th Edn) (2019) para 524.]

JUDGMENT

Declaratory

[For 61 Halsbury's Laws of England (5th Edn) (2010) para 690 see now 61A Halsbury's Laws of England (5th Edn) (2023) para 107.]

In personam

[For 12A Halsbury's Laws of England (5th Edn) (2015) para 1600 see now 12A Halsbury's Laws of England (5th Edn) (2020) para 1565.]

In rem

[For 12A Halsbury's Laws of England (5th Edn) (2015) para 1597 see now 12A Halsbury's Laws of England (5th Edn) (2020) para 1562.]

JURISDICTION

[For 24 Halsbury's Laws of England (5th Edn) (2010) para 623 see now 24A Halsbury's Laws of England (5th Edn) (2019) para 23.]

JURISDICTIONAL FACT

Australia '[188] Judicial review for "jurisdictional fact" has been accompanied by an acute debate as to terminology. One aspect of that debate is whether a "jurisdictional fact" must have an objective existence in fact, as opposed to being a subjective state of mind. This was favoured by (among others) Spigelman CJ in *Timbarra Protection Coalition Inc v Ross Mining NL* (1999) 46 NSWLR 55; 102 LGERA 52; [1999] NSWCA 8 and Professor Aronson (see M Aronson, M Groves and G Weeks, *Judicial Review of Administrative Action and Government Liability* (Lawbook Co 2017), para [4.470]). However, the High Court has deployed the concept more broadly, including when the availability of a power is dependent upon a state of mind, such as an opinion, a state of satisfaction or a belief. See for example *Minister for Immigration and Multicultural and Indigenous Affairs v SGLB* (2004) 78 ALJR 992; 207 ALR 12; [2004] HCA 32 at [37]: "The satisfaction of the Minister is a condition precedent to the discharge of the obligation to grant or refuse to grant the visa, and is a 'jurisdictional fact' or criterion upon which the exercise of that authority is conditioned". As Basten JA said, with the agreement of Macfarlan and Meagher JJA, in *Trives v Hornsby Shire Council* (2015) 89 NSWLR 268; 208 LGERA 361; 326 ALR 541; [2015] NSWCA 158 at [52], the term "jurisdictional fact" is a "potentially confusing label for what is better described as a precondition to the engagement of a statutory power". This debate is merely definitional. No one has denied that if the exercise of a power is preconditioned upon a state of satisfaction, then it is open to challenge the validity of the power by challenging the legal sufficiency of the state of satisfaction.

'[189] This appeal raises a separate terminological debate. It is whether "jurisdictional fact" review is available in relation to the exercise of non-statutory power. It is as arid as the first. In order to expose why, it is helpful to return to first principle.

…

'[191] … As a matter of construction, the condition might have the legal consequence that the Secretary could not lawfully be satisfied of compliance unless the document contained certain things.

'[192] That is analogous to the "jurisdictional fact" analysis which is familiar as a matter of construction of powers conferred by legislation. The question is whether there is some objective, factual matter the existence of which is a precondition to the condition being satisfied, or whether all that matters is the subjective state of satisfaction of the Secretary.

...

'[201] In short, I see no reason why anything substantive should turn on whether the "power" is statutory or non-statutory. Indeed, the facts of this case suggest that the distinctions between "statutory" as opposed to "non-statutory", and "power" as opposed to "function", are inapt.' *Muswellbrook Shire Council v Hunter Valley Energy Coal Pty Ltd* [2019] NSWCA 216, (2019) 372 ALR 695 at [188]–[189], [191]–[192], [201], per Leeming JA

JURY

[For 61 Halsbury's Laws of England (5th Edn) (2010) paras 801–803 see now 61A Halsbury's Laws of England (5th Edn) (2023) paras 201–203.]

JUSTIFICATION

[For 32 Halsbury's Laws of England (5th Edn) (2012) para 582 see now 32 Halsbury's Laws of England (5th Edn) (2019) para 582.]

K

KNIGHT

[For 79 Halsbury's Laws of England (5th Edn) (2014) para 865 see now 79 Halsbury's Laws of England (5th Edn) (2020) para 861.]

Orders of knighthood

[For 79 Halsbury's Laws of England (5th Edn) (2014) paras 866–867 see now 79 Halsbury's Laws of England (5th Edn) (2020) paras 862–863.]

L

LAND

[For 87 Halsbury's Laws of England (5th Edn) (2017) paras 6–7 see now 87 Halsbury's Laws of England (5th Edn) (2022) paras 6–7.]

In lease

[For 62 Halsbury's Laws of England (5th Edn) (2016) para 154 see now 62 Halsbury's Laws of England (5th Edn) (2022) para 171.]

In mining law

[For 76 Halsbury's Laws of England (5th Edn) (2013) para 17 see now 76 Halsbury's Laws of England (5th Edn) (2019) para 17.]

LANDLORD

Landlord under a tenancy of housing

[Housing and Planning Act 2016, s 40; rent repayment order ('RRO').] '[24] The opening words of s 40(2) … identify as a person against whom an RRO can be made "the landlord under a tenancy of housing in England". A tenancy of housing consists of the grant by one person (or persons) to another person (or persons) of the right to occupy residential accommodation for a period (usually, and in the 2016 Act, called a term) in return for the payment of rent. At common law a tenancy is a grant of exclusive possession but the 2016 Act defines "tenancy" as including a licence … . The grantor under such a tenancy is called the landlord and the grantee is called the tenant. Thus in relation to a particular tenancy, the grantor is the landlord under that tenancy.

'[25] The landlord under a particular tenancy of housing will either be the freehold owner of the housing, or a tenant of it under a superior tenancy, which may include a number of housing units. …

…

'[28] This straightforward interpretation links the landlord with the tenancy that generates the relevant rent. It renders it artificial and unnatural to construe the opening words of s 40(2) as referring to any landlord other than the landlord under the tenancy which generates the relevant rent, that is the rent to be repaid under s 40(2)(a) and the rent in respect of which the universal credit is paid under s 40(2)(b). It excludes a superior landlord because it is not the 'landlord under' the tenancy which generates the rent.

'[29] Mr Fitzpatrick for the appellants sought to meet this difficulty in two alternative ways. First, he submitted that "landlord under a tenancy" was apt to include not merely the immediate landlord but any superior landlord in relation to the tenancy which generates the relevant rent. Secondly, he submitted that it was wrong to equate the tenancy under which the respondent was the landlord with the tenancy which generates the relevant rent. For the reasons already given, the first submission denies the ordinary and generally understood meaning of "landlord under a tenancy". The second submission flies in the face of the straightforward interpretation of the definitions of the two types of RRO when each is, as above, set out from end to end.

'[30] In our view, that straightforward exercise in interpretation of the words in s 40(2) indicates that the appeal should be dismissed; and that an RRO cannot be made against a superior landlord, that is, a landlord higher up the chain of tenancies than the immediate landlord under the tenancy which generates the relevant rent.' *Jepsen v Rakusen* [2023] UKSC 9, [2023] 3 All ER 95 at [24]–[25], [28]–[30], per Lord Briggs and Lord Burrows JJSC

LAPSE

Of testamentary gift

[For 102 Halsbury's Laws of England (5th Edn) (2010) para 160 see now 102 Halsbury's Laws of England (5th Edn) (2021) para 162.]

LARGE COAL MINING DEVELOPMENT

Australia [Environment Protection and Biodiversity Conservation Act 1999 (Cth), ss 24D, 24E: protection of water resources from coal seam gas development and large coal mining development.] '[1] This application raises a narrow issue of statutory construction, namely, what is the proper construction of the phrase "*involves*" or "*involving*" "*large coal mining development*" in ss 24D and 24E respectively of the Environment Protection and Biodiversity Conservation Act 1999 (Cth) (the EPBC Act) and the so-called "definition" of "*large coal mining development*" in s 528 of that Act.

...

'[47] Section 528 defines "*large coal mining development*" to mean:

> ... any coal mining activity that has, or is likely to have, a significant impact on water resources (including any impacts of associated salt production and/or salinity):
>
> (a) in its own right; or
>
> (b) when considered with other developments, whether past, present or reasonably foreseeable developments.

...

'[114] For the reasons set out above, the Minister's delegate erred in his construction of ss 24D and 24E of the EPBC Act and their relevant definitions, and thereby fell into legal error. Contrary to the delegate's view, an action will involve a large coal mining development for the purposes of the water trigger controlling provisions if the action is so closely associated with the mining of coal as to be integral to it. That being so, given the delegate's findings at [48] and [99] of the controlled action decision reasons (set out at [73] and [75] above), it follows that the operation of infrastructure for the harvesting and supply of water from the alternative location for the proposed 60-year period is properly characterised as integral to the conduct of mining operations at the Carmichael Coal Project. As such, the proposed action involves a coal mining activity within the "definition" of large coal mining development in s 528 of the EPBC Act, subject importantly to the questions of whether that development is likely to have the significant impact on water resources also required by the "definition" and satisfaction of the criteria in subs (1)(b) of ss 24D and 24E. The question of whether the particular action proposed by Adani Infrastructure meets the criteria for the water trigger in ss 24D and 24E so as to engage these controlling provisions must therefore be remitted to the Minister for decision.' *Australian Conservation Foundation Inc v Minister for the Environment* [2021] FCA 550, (2021) 390 ALR 157, BC202104268 at [1], [47], [114], per Perry J

LAW MERCHANT

[For 32 Halsbury's Laws of England (5th Edn) (2012) para 62 see now 32 Halsbury's Laws of England (5th Edn) (2019) para 62.]

LAWFUL OBJECT

[Explosive Substances Act 1883, s 4(1): 'Any person who makes or knowingly has in his possession or under his control any explosive substance, under such circumstances as to give rise to a reasonable suspicion that he is not making it or does not have it in his possession or under his control for a lawful object, shall, unless he can show that he made it or had it in his possession or under his control for a lawful object, be guilty of an offence'.] '[33] ... Experimentation and self-education, including to satisfy one's curiosity in relation to the subject of investigation, are lawful objects. As a matter of ordinary language, they are "objects" every bit as much as self-defence is an "object". That is true as a general proposition. It is particularly true in relation to s 4(1), enacted against the background of the 1875 Act, which in ss 4 and 5 recognised the lawfulness and legitimacy of individuals making or possessing quantities of explosives for the purposes of private experimentation and other "private use".

'[34] In the first part of para [42], the Court of Appeal rehearsed the analysis correctly set out in *Riding*'s case [*R v Riding* [2009] EWCA Crim 892, [2010] 1 Cr App Rep (S) 37]. But in the latter part of para [42], the court set the bar to be cleared by an accused under limb (2) of s 4(1) rather too high, when it said that he must "show that the way in which [the explosives in his possession] will be used is itself lawful". In my judgment, the accused does not have to identify precisely how the explosives will be used in future and that this will be lawful. To require that would be inconsistent with *Fegan*'s case [*R v Fegan* [1972] NI 80, NICA] and *A-G's Ref (No 2 of 1983)* [[1984] 1 All ER 988, [1984] QB 456], in which it was held that the accused only had to identify a relatively general object for which the explosive substances were to be used, which object was lawful (ie self-defence), and that it was in the reasonable contemplation of the accused that the explosive substances might be required for that purpose and could lawfully be used for that purpose. As noted above, the defendants in those cases could not demonstrate precisely how the substances might come to be used; nor could it be guaranteed that if and when they were used, such use would necessarily be lawful.

'[35] In my view, in para [43] the Court of Appeal erred by treating the statement in *Riding*'s case that "[m]ere curiosity simply could not be a lawful object in the making of a lethal pipe bomb" as, in effect, a proposition of law rather than a statement regarding the position on the facts in that case; and in rejecting the idea that experimentation or self-education can be objects for the purposes of s 4(1). In my judgment, they clearly can be "objects" for the purposes of that provision, as a matter of the ordinary use of language. The word "object" is synonymous with purpose, and similarly has a relatively general meaning. The object or purpose for which something is done is distinct from the precise conditions under which it might be done. Moreover, Parliament must have contemplated that that is how an accused or their spouse, speaking naturally when giving evidence pursuant to s 4(2) of the 1883 Act, would be likely to express themselves when giving an explanation in the witness box of the kind which it considered they should have the opportunity to present by way of defence under limb (2) of s 4(1).

'[36] In line with the approach in *A-G's Ref (No 2 of 1983)*, the word "object" is to be given its natural meaning as a matter of ordinary language. In *Berry*'s case [*R v Berry* [1984] 3 All ER 1008, [1985] AC 246], Lord Roskill, in giving the only substantive speech in the appellate committee, emphasised that the term "object" as used in s 4(1) is "an ordinary English word", and accordingly was to be given its ordinary meaning so that unlawful "object" is "synonymous with an unlawful purpose or an unlawful intent" ([1984] 3 All ER 1008 at 1012, [1985] AC 246 at 254).

'[37] There is nothing unlawful about experimentation and self-education as objects, in themselves, so they are capable of being "lawful objects" within the meaning of s 4(1). Further examples can be given to illustrate the intended meaning of "lawful object" in s 4(1): see para [40] below.

…

'[40] Section 4(1) has general application. It can apply in the case of a teacher in the chemistry department of a school or university, or a person in a commercial research laboratory, who makes explosive substances or has them in his possession. If a charge were brought against such a person under s 4(1) and the prosecution was able to surmount the relatively low hurdle in limb (1) of the provision, the accused would be entitled to defend himself under limb (2) by proving that his object in making or keeping the substances was experimentation, education or research. It is apt to describe each of those as an "object", as a matter of ordinary use of language. It might be the case that the accused had no developed and precise plan in mind as to how he proposed using the substance for those purposes, but that would not disable him from presenting a defence under limb (2). The absence of a precise plan as to how the substance was to be used in the course of pursuing those purposes might be a relevant matter to be taken into account at trial. But it would be for the jury to assess, on the evidence at trial, whether the defence was made out despite the absence of precise details as to proposed use. That view is supported by the approach taken to the lawful object of self-defence in *Fegan*'s case and *A-G's Ref (No 2 of 1983)*, as explained above.

'[41] For his defence under limb (2), the appellant only had to establish that he proposed using the HMTD [Hexamethylene Triperoxide Diamine] in his possession for the lawful objects of experimentation and self-education. The term "lawful object" in limb (2) does not require specification of the precise way in which the substance in question will be used by the accused. The appellant's proposed defence was that he intended to use the HMTD in small amounts to produce insignificant detonations of the order to be expected from a simple domestic firework, ie at a level which was lawful. It was possible that he could have achieved this, or that he genuinely believed that he could, as he had done using other explosive substances on previous occasions. Therefore his defence under limb (2) should have been allowed to be presented at trial, rather than being ruled out at the preliminary hearing.' *R v Copeland* [2020] UKSC 8, [2020] 4 All ER 173 at [33]–[37], [40]–[41], per Lord Sales JSC

'[56] These cases vividly reveal the difficulties that defendants may face when seeking to prove that they had a lawful object, in circumstances broadly similar to the present two sets of facts. We have had the advantage of being able to consider the evidence as it emerged at trial. Explosive substances – depending always on their nature and the quantities involved – unless handled and stored responsibly and with care, self-evidently pose a potential danger to people and property. Some of them, such as HMTD [Hexamethylene Triperoxide Diamine] and TATP [Triacetone Triperoxide], are inherently unstable; using explosive substances for experimentation rather than inert substances, particularly when detonating them, may well lead to damage to other people or their property, or cause a public nuisance; and the storage of these materials can be hazardous. It is a central element of the majority decision in *Copeland* [*R v Copeland* [2020] UKSC 8, [2020] 4 All ER 173] that an otherwise lawful objective (such as experimentation) which involves obvious risk to other people, or their property, from the use of the explosive substance will lead to the inference that the object of the accused was mixed, and therefore was not (wholly) lawful. Further, if the defendant knew that his or her proposed use of the explosive substance in his possession would injure others or cause damage to their property, or was reckless regarding this risk, the object would be tainted by that unlawfulness inherent in the way the object was being pursued, thereby rendering it impossible to establish the defence.

'[57] All cases differ on their facts, but we emphasise, therefore, that given the obvious risks with using explosive substances, any experimentation involving them which gives rise to a risk of harm to other people or their property, or other unlawfulness such as causing a public nuisance, will not be capable of coming within the scope of the lawful object defence.' *R v Flint; R v Holmes* [2020] EWCA Crim 1266, [2021] 3 All ER 158 at [56]–[57], per Fulford VP

LAY DAYS

[For 7 Halsbury's Laws of England (5th Edn) (2015) para 285 see now 7 Halsbury's Laws of England (5th Edn) (2020) para 328.]

LEASE

[For 62 Halsbury's Laws of England (5th Edn) (2016) para 67 see now 62 Halsbury's Laws of England (5th Edn) (2022) para 69.]

Agreement for lease

[For 62 Halsbury's Laws of England (5th Edn) (2016) paras 69, 76 see now 62 Halsbury's Laws of England (5th Edn) (2022) paras 71, 91.]

Mining lease

[For 76 Halsbury's Laws of England (5th Edn) (2013) para 321 see now 76 Halsbury's Laws of England (5th Edn) (2019) para 318.]

LEAVE HOSPITAL

[Mental Health Act 1983, s 117.] '[5] By s 117(1):

> "This section applies to persons who are detained under section 3 above … and then cease to be detained and (whether or not immediately after so ceasing) leave hospital."

It is the meaning of the final words of this provision which is at the centre of this dispute.

…

'[36] I also think it wholly unrealistic to suggest, as Mr Wise QC sought to do, that the expression "leave hospital" in s 117(1) necessarily applies to any absence from the hospital premises, irrespective of its length or nature. As Haddon-Cave LJ pointed out in the course of argument, there is a distinction in ordinary speech between the expressions "leave hospital" and "leave *the* hospital" (with a definite article). I agree with the judge when she said at para [40](ii) of her judgment:

> "As a matter of ordinary language, the phrase 'left hospital' is commonly used to refer to discharge from the care of a hospital, rather than simply leaving the premises for any period of time or any reason. If one person asks another 'have you left hospital yet?' they are not asking whether they have gone outside for a shopping trip. I note that, by contrast, s 17(4) refers to a patient on leave as 'absent from a hospital'. In short, a person may be 'absent from a hospital' (eg to go on a short trip outside the grounds), without having 'left hospital'."

'[37] Again, I would not go so far as to say that is impossible to use the phrase "leave hospital" in the narrow sense contended for by counsel for the claimant. But it is a perfectly ordinary and natural use of language to say that a patient who is allowed to leave the hospital in which he is detained to go on a short trip in the custody of hospital staff is not a person who has "left hospital".

'[38] As discussed, in interpreting a statutory provision it is not sufficient to consider the ordinary meanings of the words used and how the same words are used elsewhere in the Act: it is necessary to identify the purpose of the provision, read in its context. The clear purpose of s 117 is to arrange for the provision of services to a person who has been, but is not currently being, provided with treatment and care as a hospital patient. That purpose is implicit in the very expression "after-care", which is used not only in the heading but throughout the body of s 117 in the phrase "after-care services". It is further articulated by the definition of "after-care services" in s 117(6). …

'[39] Interpreting s 117(1) in the light of this purpose, I readily accept that there will be cases in which a patient granted leave of absence from hospital under s 17 does "cease to be detained" and "leave hospital" within the meaning of s 117(1) so as to become eligible to receive after-care services during the period of their absence. I would also accept the submission made by Mr Wise QC that it is not necessary in order to trigger s 117 that the person concerned should have been "discharged" from hospital in either of the two senses, discussed in the *MM* case [*Secretary of State for Justice v MM* [2018] UKSC 60, [2019] 2 All ER 749, [2018] 3 WLR 1784] at paras [19]–[20], in which that term is used in the Act. I see no reason why s 117 should not apply to a person who is living in the community on leave of absence–either full-time or for part of the week like the claimant in the *Barking* case [*B v Barking, Havering and Brentwood Community Healthcare NHS Trust* [1999] 1 FLR 106, (1999) 47 BMLR 112]–without having been conditionally discharged from hospital under s 42(2) or 73(2) of the Act, let alone "absolutely" discharged from the liability to be detained.

…

'[44] The inescapable conclusion is that the claimant does not "cease to be detained" or "leave hospital" within the meaning of s 117(1) when he is escorted on day trips and is therefore not a person to whom s 117 applies.' *R (on the application of CXF (by his mother, his litigation friend)) v Central Bedfordshire Council* [2018] EWCA Civ 2852, [2019] 3 All ER 20 at [5], [36]–[39], [44], per Leggatt LJ

LEGACY

[For 102 Halsbury's Laws of England (5th Edn) (2010) paras 118–120 see now 102 Halsbury's Laws of England (5th Edn) (2021) paras 120–122.]

Demonstrative legacy

[For 102 Halsbury's Laws of England (5th Edn) (2010) para 120 see now 102 Halsbury's Laws of England (5th Edn) (2021) para 122.]

Specific legacy

[For 102 Halsbury's Laws of England (5th Edn) (2010) para 118 see now 102 Halsbury's Laws of England (5th Edn) (2021) para 120.]

LEVY

Levy distress

[For 62 Halsbury's Laws of England (5th Edn) (2016) para 282 see now 62 Halsbury's Laws of England (5th Edn) (2022) para 305.]

Levy war

[For 25 Halsbury's Laws of England (5th Edn) (2016) para 419n see now 25 Halsbury's Laws of England (5th Edn) (2020) para 553 n 1.]

LIABLE TO DETENTION

[Immigration Act 2016, s 61(3), Sch 10, para 1(2), (5): whether statutory power existed to impose immigration bail on a person who could no longer be lawfully detained; meaning of 'liable to detention'.] '[39] Paragraph 1(2) gives the Secretary of State power to grant a person bail if the person is "liable to detention" under a provision mentioned in sub-para (1). Paragraph 1(3) gives the FTT [First-tier Tribunal] power, if an application is made to it, to grant bail in the same circumstances as are referred to in para 1(1).

'[40] Paragraph 1(4) provides that in Sch 10, references to the "grant of immigration bail", in relation to a person, are to the grant of bail to that person under any of sub-paras (1) to (3) of para 1 of Sch 10 (or under para 10(12) or (13) (release following arrest for breach of bail conditions)).

'[41] Paragraph 1(5) provides:

"A person may be granted and remain on immigration bail even if the person can no longer be detained, if—

(a) the person is liable to detention under a provision mentioned in sub-paragraph (1), or
(b) the Secretary of State is considering whether to make a deportation order against the person under section 5(1) of the Immigration Act 1971."

...

'[86] ... **Propositions**

1. The phrase "liable to detention" has the same meaning whether it is in a power to grant temporary admission or temporary release, or in a power to grant bail, because all of the relevant provisions are in the same series of statutes and there is an unbroken legislative line running through them.
2. The phrase has a broad meaning, as definitely decided in *Khadir* [*R (on the application of Khadir) v Secretary of State for the Home Dept* [2005] UKHL 39, [2005] 4 All ER 114, [2006] 1 AC 207]: a person is "liable to detention" whenever the detention power in question exists, whether or not the detention power can be lawfully exercised at that time.
3. When a court decided that the phrase had a narrower meaning, Parliament stepped in to reverse that decision by a substantial and unusual provision (s 67 of the 2002 Act [Nationality, Immigration and Asylum Act 2002]) that retrospectively specified that the phrase always had a broader meaning.
4. In the case of the temporary admission power then under consideration, this proved to have been unnecessary, because the phrase had always had a meaning even broader than provided by s 67.
5. When a court decided that a bail power could be exercised only within a narrower ambit, Parliament again stepped in to reverse that decision by a substantial and unusual provision (s 61(3) of the 2016 Act) that retrospectively specified that the bail power was always exercisable in wider circumstances. Parliament used the same phrase that had been in issue in Khadir and that had been the subject of the previous retrospective legislation (s 67), thus clearly intending the phrase to have had the same meaning in s 61(3) as was ultimately decided in *Khadir*.
6. The current bail powers are given effect by a provision (s 61(1)) in the same section as contained that legislative intervention, showing that when the phrase is used in the current bail powers, it must have been intended by Parliament to have the same meaning as in s 61(3).
7. If the Claimant and BID [Bail for Immigration Detainees] are correct in their contention that "liable to detention" must be interpreted as "liable to lawful detention", then s 61(3) and the corresponding provision in the current bail powers (s 61(5)) are otiose and meaningless.'

R (on the application of Kaitey) v Secretary of State for the Home Department (Bail for Immigration Detainees intervening) [2020] EWHC 1861 (Admin), [2021] 2 All ER 719 at [39]–[41], [86], per Elisabeth Laing J

LIBEL

[For 32 Halsbury's Laws of England (5th Edn) (2012) para 511 see now 32 Halsbury's Laws of England (5th Edn) (2019) para 510.]

LICENCE—LICENSE

[For 62 Halsbury's Laws of England (5th Edn) (2016) paras 7, 10, 13 see now 62 Halsbury's Laws of England (5th Edn) (2022) paras 7, 10, 13.]

LIEN

[For 68 Halsbury's Laws of England (5th Edn) (2016) paras 802–803 see now 68 Halsbury's Laws of England (5th Edn) (2021) paras 902–903.]

Equitable lien

[For 68 Halsbury's Laws of England (5th Edn) (2016) para 855 see now 68 Halsbury's Laws of England (5th Edn) (2021) para 956.]

Innkeeper's lien

[For 68 Halsbury's Laws of England (5th Edn) (2016) para 676 see now 68 Halsbury's Laws of England (5th Edn) (2021) para 692.]

Solicitor's lien

[For 66 Halsbury's Laws of England (5th Edn) (2015) para 768 see now 66 Halsbury's Laws of England (5th Edn) (2020) para 720.]

LIFE INTEREST

[For 87 Halsbury's Laws of England (5th Edn) (2017) paras 138–139 see now 87 Halsbury's Laws of England (5th Edn) (2022) paras 138–139.]

LIGHT

Right to light

[For 87 Halsbury's Laws of England (5th Edn) (2017) para 943 see now 87 Halsbury's Laws of England (5th Edn) (2022) para 937.]

LIKELY

Australia [Competition and Consumer Act 2010 (Cth), s 50: matters to be taken into account when determining whether acquisition would have the effect, or be likely to have the effect, of substantially lessening competition in a market.] '[105] The word "likely" is capable of more than one meaning. As discussed further below, it can mean more probable than not or it can mean a possibility that is real as opposed to remote. In the present case, the primary judge adopted the latter meaning. That aspect of his Honour's reasons is the subject of challenge in this appeal, and is considered below.

...

'[243] ... Strong arguments, based on the statutory text, can be made for construing the word "likely" to mean "probable". However, the word "likely" has been construed to mean a likelihood that is less than probable for 40 years (from *Tillmanns* [*Tillmanns Butcheries Pty Ltd v Australasian Meat Industry Employees' Union* (1979) 27 ALR 367; 42 FLR 331]) and there is no evidence of widespread inconvenience in the application of the law. To the contrary, the law has been amended on numerous occasions without any suggestion that the dual legal standard should be changed. ...

'[244] Similarly, if the meaning of the word "likely" was being considered for the first time, we would have been inclined to adopt the meaning probable, but there is insufficient reason to change course at this point in time. For those reasons, we reject ground 4 of Aurizon's amended notice of cross-appeal.

'[245] Nevertheless, substituting a synonym such as "real chance" for the statutory word "likely" creates the risk that the synonym may convey a different standard to the statutory language and may introduce a further element of uncertainty. As already noted, in *Tillmanns* Deane J observed that likelihood ought to be determined by reference to well-established standards of what could reasonably be expected to be the consequence of the relevant conduct in the circumstances. Similarly, in *AGL (No 3)* [*Australian Gas Light Co v Australian Competition and Consumer Commission (No 3)* (2003) 137 FCR 317; [2003] FCA 1525], French J observed (at [348]) that:

> The meaning of "likely" reflecting a "real chance or possibility" does not encompass a mere possibility. The word can offer no quantitative guidance but requires a qualitative judgment about the effects of an acquisition or proposed acquisition. The judgment it requires must not set the bar so high as effectively to expose acquiring corporations to a finding of contravention simply on the basis of possibilities, however plausible they may seem, generated by economic theory alone. On the other hand it must not set the bar so low as effectively to allow all acquisitions to proceed save those with the most obvious, direct and dramatic effects upon competition. By the language it adopts and the function thereby cast upon the Court and the regulator in their consideration of acquisitions s 50 gives effect to a kind of competition risk management policy. The application of that policy, reflected in judgments about the application of the section, must operate in the real world. The assessment of the risk or real chance of a substantial lessening of competition cannot rest upon speculation or theory. To borrow the words of the Tribunal in the Howard Smith case, the Court is concerned with "commercial likelihoods relevant to the proposed merger". The word "likely" has to be applied at a level which is commercially relevant or meaningful as must be the assessment of the substantial lessening of competition under consideration—*Rural Press Ltd v ACCC* (2003) 216 CLR 53; 203 ALR 217; [2003] HCA 75 at [41].

'[246] In the present case, the primary judge followed the authorities referred to above in construing the word "likely" as meaning "real commercial likelihood" (at [1275]), as explained by French J in *AGL (No 3)*. In our view, there is no error in his Honour's interpretation of the statutory language. We also respectfully agree with his Honour's statement of the proper approach to the application of s 50, namely:

(a) the application of s 50 requires a single evaluative judgment (at [1276]);
(b) it is a distraction (and, we would add, wrong) to ask what standards of proof apply to the primary facts which will involve predictions about the future (at [1278]);
(c) however, the degree of likelihood of any particular future fact existing or arising will be relevant to the assessment of the likely effect on competition of the acquisition (at [1279]).'

Australian Competition and Consumer Commission v Pacific National Pty Ltd [2020] FCAFC 77, (2020) 378 ALR 1 at [105], [243]–[246], per Middleton and O'Bryan JJ

LIMITATION LAW

Australia [Civil Aviation (Carriers' Liability) Act 1959 (Cth), s 34: whether a 'limitation law' within the meaning of the Federal Courts (State Jurisdiction) Act 1999 (NSW), s 11(1).] '[66] It was contended that a limitation law, properly understood, was a law which barred the remedy but did not extinguish the underlying right. The observations of the plurality in *Agtrack* [*Agtrack (NT) Pty Ltd (t/a Spring Air) v Hatfield* (2005) 223 CLR 251; 218 ALR 677; [2005] HCA 38] at [59] in relation to s 34 of the Commonwealth Act, which have been extracted at [11] above, were also called in aid by the Applicant in support of its argument that s 34 was not a limitation law. It should be noted, however, that the Court was not there considering whether or not s 34 of the Commonwealth Act was a limitation law within the meaning of that term as defined in s 11(1) of the State Jurisdiction Act. That subsection defines a "limitation law" for the purposes of the State Jurisdiction Act as meaning:

(a) the Limitation Act 1969, or
(b) any other law that provides for the limitation of liability or the barring of a right of action in respect of a claim by reference to the time when a proceeding on, or the arbitration of, the claim is commenced.

'[67] There is a well-recognised distinction between the extinguishment of a right and the barring of an action to enforce a right and obtain a remedy. ...,

...

'[69] At [65] of her decision, the primary judge held that:

"While there is plainly a distinction, established by the authorities referred to above, between laws which bar a right of action and those which are effective to extinguish a right of action, I am not persuaded that this distinction is material to the classification of s 34 as a limitation law. Whether or not s 34 of the Commonwealth Carriers' Act bars a right of action, it limits the liability of the carrier by reference to the time when a proceeding on the claim is commenced. A carrier will, if other matters are established, be liable if the action has been brought within two years of the material date (in this case the death of the plaintiff's daughter). A carrier will not be liable if the action has been brought outside that time. Accordingly, I consider that the definition of limitation law in s 11(1) is apt to include s 34 of the Commonwealth Carriers' Act."

'[70] I respectfully disagree with her Honour's reasoning in this regard as there is a clearly recognised distinction in a wealth of authorities between the barring of a right of action and its extinguishment. Such a distinction was recognised by the plurality in *Agtrack* at [59], which has been extracted at [11] above. Section 34 of the Commonwealth Act is not, in my opinion, a "limitation law" within the meaning of s 11(1) of the State Jurisdiction Act.' *Sydney Seaplanes Pty Ltd (t/a Sydney Seaplanes) v Page* [2021] NSWCA 204, (2021) 393 ALR 485 at [66]–[67], [69]–[70], per Bell P

LIMITATION OF CLAIMS

[For 68 Halsbury's Laws of England (5th Edn) (2016) para 901 see now 68 Halsbury's Laws of England (5th Edn) (2021) para 1001.]

LIQUIDATOR

[For 16 Halsbury's Laws of England (5th Edn) (2011) para 505 see now 16 Halsbury's Laws of England (5th Edn) (2017) para 466.]

LITIGATION FRIEND

[For 10 Halsbury's Laws of England (5th Edn) (2012) paras 1314–1315 see now 10 Halsbury's Laws of England (5th Edn) (2017) paras 1400–1401.]

LOAN RELATIONSHIP

(1) For the purposes of the Corporation Tax Acts a company has a loan relationship if–

(a) the company stands in the position of a creditor or debtor as respects any money debt (whether by reference to a security or otherwise), and

(b) the debt arises from a transaction for the lending of money.

(2) References to a loan relationship and to a company being a party to a loan relationship are to be read accordingly.

…

(5) In this Part [Pt 5] 'creditor relationship', in relation to a company, means any loan relationship of the company where it stands in the position of a creditor as respects the debt in question.

(6) In this Part 'debtor relationship', in relation to a company, means any loan relationship of the company where it stands in the position of a debtor as respects the debt in question.

(Corporation Tax Act 2009, s 302)

LOCKDOWN

'[2] This claim for judicial review arises from the unprecedented circumstances arising from the COVID-19 or coronavirus pandemic, which at the time of the hearing before us had been the cause (or a cause) of the deaths of more than 40,000 people in the UK and many hundreds of thousands of people around the world. In particular it is brought in the interests of those workers whose incomes are seriously affected by stringent social distancing measures imposed by the Government, generally referred to as the "lockdown", which began in March 2020. …

…

'[14] On 23 March 2020 a nationwide "lockdown" was announced. The Prime Minister announced that people would only be permitted to leave their homes to buy food, exercise once a day or go to work if they could not work from home, and that these restrictions would be enforced by fines.' *R (on the application of Adiatu) v HM Treasury* [2020] EWHC 1554 (Admin), [2021] 2 All ER 484 at [2], [14], per Bean LJ and Cavanagh J

LODGING HOUSE

The definition of 'hotel' [in the Hotel Proprietors Act 1956, s 1(3)], which is also the definition of an inn, still excludes those establishments formerly held at common law not to be inns, ie lodging houses …, boarding houses … and public houses which are mere alehouses … . In none of these instances is there an obligation to receive and entertain guests. (68 Halsbury's Laws of England (5th Edn) (2021) para 664 n 6)

LOCK OUT

[For 41 Halsbury's Laws of England (5th Edn) (2014) para 1340 see now 41A Halsbury's Laws of England (5th Edn) (2021) para 1312.]

LOOKED AFTER

[Children Act 1989, s 22(1).] '[34] Section 25(1) makes clear that s 25 [use of accommodation for restricting liberty] applies only to a child who is being looked after by the local authority. Section 22(1) of the Children Act 1989 defines being looked after as being either "in the care of" the local authority or "provided with accommodation" by the local authority. Section 105(1) of the 1989 Act provides that any reference to a child who is "in the care of" any authority means '"a child who is in their care by virtue of a care order". The court cannot make a care order in respect of a child who has reached the age of 17 years old (Children Act 1989 s 31(3)). Section 20 of the Children Act 1989 governs the provision of accommodation for children. Within the context of these proceedings, s 20(7) of the 1989 Act stipulates that a local authority may not provide accommodation under s 20 of the Act for a child if any person who has parental responsibility for that child objects.' *A City Council v LS* [2019] EWHC 1384 (Fam), [2020] 1 All ER 652 at [34], per MacDonald J

LOST MODERN GRANT

[For 87 Halsbury's Laws of England (5th Edn) (2017) para 819 see now 87 Halsbury's Laws of England (5th Edn) (2022) para 814.]

LUGGAGE

Ordinary luggage

[For 7 Halsbury's Laws of England (5th Edn) (2015) paras 53–54 see now 7 Halsbury's Laws of England (5th Edn) (2020) para 27.]

M

MAGISTRATE

[For 71 Halsbury's Laws of England (5th Edn) (2013) para 401 see now 71 Halsbury's Laws of England (5th Edn) (2020) para 401.]

MAINTENANCE (OF INFANT)

[For 98 Halsbury's Laws of England (5th Edn) (2013) para 515 see now 98 Halsbury's Laws of England (5th Edn) (2019) para 488.]

MALICE

[For 32 Halsbury's Laws of England (5th Edn) (2012) para 651 see now 32 Halsbury's Laws of England (5th Edn) (2019) para 647.]

Acting maliciously

[War risks insurance policy; cover provided for inter alia, in cl 1.5 'any terrorist or any person acting maliciously or from a political motive'. Vessel owned by the appellant was used by unknown third parties in an unsuccessful attempt to export drugs from Venezuela and was detained by Venezuelan authorities.] '[13] The present owners' case thus turns on the fact that the Institute War and Strikes Clauses identify as perils insured, not merely detainment etc under cl 1.2, but also loss

or damage to the vessel caused by "any person acting maliciously" under cl 1.5. Once relied on, the specific cover against malicious acts should not, the owners submit, be undermined or cut back by an exception of "detainment … by reason of infringement of customs …regulations" [in cl 4.1.5] which the owners submit is most obviously addressing other situations–or which, on the owners' alternative case, is not even addressing cl 1.5 at all.

'[14] It is in the light of these submissions that the Supreme Court concluded that, despite the common ground between the parties, the necessary starting point is to examine the scope of the concept of "any person acting maliciously" in cl 1.5. This is a phrase which must be seen in context, appearing as it does in the middle of perils insured involving "loss of or damage to the Vessel caused by … [1.5] any terrorist or any person acting maliciously or from a political motive". Its companions in that context are terrorists and persons acting from a political motive, causing loss or damage to the vessel. What the drafters appear to have had in mind are persons whose actions are aimed at causing loss of or damage to the vessel, or, it may well be, other property or persons as a by-product of which the vessel is lost or damaged. Applying a similar rationale to the central phrase "any person acting maliciously", it can be said that the present circumstances involve no such aim. Foreseeable though the risk may be that drugs being smuggled may be detected, their detection and any consequent loss or damage to the vessel were the exact opposite of the unknown smugglers' aim or, presumably, expectation.

…

'[22] In my view, therefore, the concept of "any person acting maliciously" in cl 1.5 would have been understood in 1983 and should now be understood as relating to situations where a person acts in a way which involves an element of spite or ill-will or the like in relation to the property insured or at least to other property or perhaps even a person, and consequential loss of, or damage to, the insured vessel or cargo. It is not designed to cater for situations where the state of mind of spite, ill-will or the like is absent. In the present case, foreseeable though the vessel's seizure and loss were if the smuggling attempt was discovered, the would-be smugglers cannot have had any such state of mind. They were, on the contrary, intent on avoiding detection. …' *Atlasnavios - Navegac¸ão, Lda v Navigators Insurance Co Ltd; The B Atlantic* [2018] UKSC 26, [2018] 4 All ER 589 at [13]–[14], [22], per Lord Mance DP

Malice aforethought

[For 25 Halsbury's Laws of England (5th Edn) (2016) para 102 see now 25 Halsbury's Laws of England (5th Edn) (2020) para 130.]

MANAGED SERVICE COMPANY PROVIDER

'[6] Section 61B(1) of the ITEPA [Income Tax (Earnings and Pensions) Act 2003] defines an MSC in the following terms:

"(1) A company is a 'managed service company' if—
(a) its business consists wholly or mainly of providing (directly or indirectly) the services of an individual to other persons,
(b) payments are made (directly or indirectly) to the individual (or associates of the individual) of an amount equal to the greater part or all of the consideration for the provision of the services,
(c) the way in which those payments are made would result in the individual (or associates) receiving payments of an amount (net of tax and national insurance) exceeding that which would be received (net of tax and national insurance) if every payment in respect of the services were employment income of the individual, and
(d) a person who carries on a business of promoting or facilitating the use of companies to provide the services of individuals ('an MSC provider') is involved with the company."

'[7] For the condition in sub-s (1)(d) to be satisfied the putative MSC provider must be "involved with the company". That concept is defined in s 61B(2) ITEPA ….

'[8] Thus, an MSC is a company which (i) provides the services of an individual to others; (ii) pays that individual all or most of the fees it charges to those others; (iii) pays the individual in a way which increases the net amount received by the individual, as compared with what he would have received net if he had earned the fees as his employment income; and (iv) involves an MSC provider in its business in one of the ways then set out in s 61B(2). An MSC can be a partnership as well as a body corporate: see s 61C(3).

…

'[19] The issue before us is the issue dealt with at paras [64] onwards of the decision. It was contended before us that the definition of an MSC provider as "a person who carries on a business of promoting or facilitating the use of companies to provide the services of individuals" could either mean:

(1) HMRC's construction: that, in order for a company to be an MSC provider, the company's business must be the business of promoting or facilitating the use by individuals of companies through which the individuals will provide their services to clients; the putative MSC provider does not need also to promote or facilitate the services themselves;
(2) The Appellants' construction: that, in order to be an MSC provider, a company must promote or facilitate the services provided by the companies the use of which it has promoted or facilitated.

'[20] It was common ground that Costelloe did not promote or facilitate the services that each of the individual owners provided to the Appellants' end clients. Each Appellant arranged and negotiated its own contracts, including payment rates and terms, with the end clients, sometimes through a recruitment agency but without any control or supervision by Costelloe.

…

'[31] There is nothing either in the wording of Ch 9 ITEPA or in the external material on which the Appellants rely that supports their construction of the definition of an MSC provider in s 61B(1)(d). The business that the Government was trying to catch in the definition is precisely the business that Costelloe runs; its business is in promoting a situation in which the workers provide their services through a company instead of directly to the end client and it thereby promotes the use of companies to provide those services. Costelloe then provides the Gold Business Service to the MSC, thereby facilitating the use of the MSC by that individual in order for him or her to provide services to the end client. There is no doubt that this business is what the legislation is aimed at catching and in my judgment it succeeds in its aim.

…

'[40] I would therefore dismiss the appeal because Costelloe is, in my judgment, undoubtedly an MSC provider and the Appellants are undoubtedly MSCs.' *Christianuyi Ltd v Revenue and Customs Commissioners* [2019] EWCA Civ 474, [2019] 3 All ER 178 at [6]–[8], [19]–[20], [31], [40], per Rose LJ

MANAGEMENT

Of ship

[For 7 Halsbury's Laws of England (5th Edn) (2015) para 389 see now 7 Halsbury's Laws of England (5th Edn) (2020) para 510.]

MANDATE

[For 4 Halsbury's Laws of England (5th Edn) (2011) para 126 see now 4 Halsbury's Laws of England (5th Edn) (2020) para 126.]

MANDATORY ORDER

[For 61 Halsbury's Laws of England (5th Edn) (2010) para 703 et seq see now 61A Halsbury's Laws of England (5th Edn) (2023) para 122 et seq.]

MANDATORY TARIFF

Canada [Copyright Act, RSC 1985, c C-42, s 68.2(1)] '29 Access Copyright argues that s 68.2(1), incorporated by reference in s 70.15(2), means that any person who makes an otherwise unauthorized use of a work captured by an approved tariff is liable to be sued for royalties, regardless of whether the user agrees to be bound by a licence on the approved terms. This is known as the "mandatory tariff" theory. In this case, that means that any use of a work in Access Copyright's repertoire that was not separately licensed or authorized by fair dealing would trigger York's liability to pay the full annual blanket rate of $3.38 per full-time equivalent student (and by extension the substantially higher rates approved under the final tariffs), in addition to the per-page rate applicable to course pack copies. A single unauthorized use would result in liability to pay six figure annual fees under the interim tariff, and over one million dollars per year under the 2011–2014 final tariff.' *York University v Canadian Copyright Licensing Agency (Access Copyright)* [2021] SCJ No 32, 2021 SCC 32 at para 29, per Abella J

MANIFEST ERROR

'[30] The narrowness of the permitted defences of "manifest or mathematical error or fraud" is relevant to the implications of the interpretation that the landlord's certification is conclusive subject only to those defences. "Mathematical error" and "fraud" are self-explanatory terms but the meaning of "manifest error" is less clear. Whilst its precise meaning may depend on the particular contract and context in which it is used, there are a number of authorities which have considered the meaning of these words in conclusive evidence clauses.

'[31] An often cited and applied explanation of the meaning of "manifest error" is that given by Lewison J in *IIG Capital LLC v Van Der Merwe* [2007] EWHC 2631 (Ch), [2008] 1 All ER (Comm) 435 (at para [52]): "A 'manifest error' is one that is obvious or easily demonstrable without extensive investigation." This formulation was approved by the Court of Appeal in the same case [2008] EWCA Civ 542, [2008] 2 All ER (Comm) 1173, [2008] 2 Lloyd's Rep 187 (per Waller LJ at paras [33]–[35]) and more recently in *Amey Birmingham Highways Ltd v Birmingham City Council* [2018] EWCA Civ 264, [2018] BLR 225 (per Jackson LJ at paras [83]–[87]).

'[32] Guidance as to what is meant by being "obvious or easily demonstrable" is provided by the Court of Appeal's decision in *Veba Oil Supply & Trading GmbH v Petrotrade Inc* [2001] EWCA Civ 1832, [2002] 1 All ER 703, [2002] 1 Lloyd's Rep 295 in which it was stated that manifest errors were "*oversights and blunders so obvious and obviously capable of affecting the determination* as to admit of no difference of opinion" (per Simon Brown LJ at para [33], his emphasis). This has been applied in a number of recent first instance decisions ....

'[33] What is meant by being demonstrable "without extensive investigation" may depend on the context. Unless the contract makes it clear that only the certificate can be considered, extrinsic evidence will be admissible – see *Amey Birmingham* at para [87]. Although it may not be necessary to be able to demonstrate the error immediately, in most cases this will need to be done readily – ie by an investigation limited in both time and extent. In so far as the decision of the Court of Appeal in *North Shore Ventures Ltd v Anstead Holdings Inc* [2011] EWCA Civ 230, [2011] 2 All ER (Comm) 1024, [2012] Ch 31 suggests otherwise, I agree with Flaux J's observation in *ABN Amro Commercial Finance plc v McGinn* [2014] EWHC 1674 (Comm), [2014] 2 Lloyd's Rep 333 (at paras [51] to [52]) that it "has to be viewed with some circumspection" and that on any view it cannot depend on "a full blown trial".

'[34] It is therefore clear that the permitted defences of "manifest or mathematical error or fraud" are indeed narrow. An arguable error will not suffice, however well founded the allegation of error may ultimately prove to be.' *Sara & Hossein Asset Holdings Ltd v Blacks Outdoor Retail Ltd* [2023] UKSC 2, [2023] 2 All ER 1063 at [30]–[34], per Lord Hamblen JSC

MANIFESTLY UNFOUNDED

New Zealand [Immigration Act 2009, s 140(3): A refugee and protection officer may refuse to consider a subsequent claim for recognition as a refugee or a protected person if the officer is satisfied that the claim: (a) is manifestly unfounded or clearly abusive; or (b) repeats any claim previously made (including a subsequent claim).] '[53] Mr Pidgeon submitted the test for "manifestly unfounded" in s 140(3)(a) was high. Again, by reference to the principle of non-refoulement, he suggested a number of formulae in amplification of the words used in the section. These included that it must be shown the claim is "bound to fail", or has "no realistic prospect of success", and that a claim can only be found to be manifestly unfounded where there is no reasonable risk of refoulement "whatsoever".

'[54] Mr Pidgeon submitted that guidance could be drawn from the interpretation of s 94 of the United Kingdom's Nationality, Immigration and Asylum Act 2002 which employs the similar wording of "clearly unfounded". A claim which is considered to be "clearly unfounded" will attract a certificate precluding any appeal before an applicant can be expelled to that person's country of origin. The House of Lords has opined in relation to s 94 [*ZT (Kosovo) v Secretary of State for the Home Department* [2009] UKHL 6, [2009] 1 WLR 348 at [23] per Lord Phillips] that "[i]f any reasonable doubt exists as to whether the claim may succeed then it is not clearly unfounded".

'[55] The English Court of Appeal also emphasised the "very high threshold" that was required to be met before a claim could be characterised as "manifestly unfounded" in relation to s 72(2)(a) of the Immigration and Asylum Act 1999 (now repealed) [*R (on the application of Razgar) v Secretary of State for the Home Department* [2003] EWCA Civ 840, [2003] INLR 543 at [111]; affd *R v Secretary of State for the Home Department, ex p Razgar* [2004] UKHL 27, [2004] 2 AC 368]:

> The Secretary of State cannot lawfully issue such a certificate unless the claim is *bound* to fail … It is not sufficient that he considers that the claim is likely to fail on appeal, or even that it is very likely to fail. Moreover, as the House of Lords explained in *Yogathas*, the Court will subject the decision of the Secretary of State to "the most anxious scrutiny".

'[56] Care is required before drawing on the interpretation of the words of a statute from a different jurisdiction. However, we consider a standard whereby an officer must be sure that a claim will fail, which appears to be the approach taken by the English courts, is well within the terms of the statutory test of being "manifestly unfounded". We consider "manifestly unfounded" denotes a high standard, something which is self-evident from the particulars on which the claim relies, and is unfounded or untenable.' *WK v Refugee and Protection Officer* [2018] NZCA 258, [2019] 2 NZLR 223 at [53]–[56], per Mander J

MANOR

[For 32 Halsbury's Laws of England (5th Edn) (2012) para 95 see now 32 Halsbury's Laws of England (5th Edn) (2019) para 95.]

MANSION HOUSE

Principal mansion house

For 91 Halsbury's Laws of England (5th Edn) (2012) paras 690, 692 see now 91 Halsbury's Laws of England (5th Edn) (2019) paras 588–599.]

MANSLAUGHTER

[For 25 Halsbury's Laws of England (5th Edn) (2016) paras 99, 125 see now 25 Halsbury's Laws of England (5th Edn) (2020) paras 125, 132.]

MARKED DEPARTURE

Canada [Criminal Code, RSC 1985, c C-46, s 215.] '27 Section 215 creates a penal negligence offence. It is "aimed at establishing a uniform minimum level of care to be provided for those to whom it applies, and this can only be achieved if those under the duty are held to a societal, rather than a personal, standard of conduct" (*R v Naglik* [1993] 3 SCR 122, at p 141 (emphasis deleted)). Liability is premised on what a reasonable person in the accused's position would have known or foreseen, so "fault lies in the absence of the requisite mental state of care" (*R v Beatty* 2008 SCC 5, [2008] 1 SCR 49, at para 8). The provision punishes conduct that is a marked departure from an objectively reasonable standard of care. More specifically, the *mens rea* requirement for s 215 is established when the Crown proves that the accused's conduct constitutes "a marked departure from the conduct of a reasonably prudent parent in circumstances where it was objectively foreseeable that the failure to provide the necessaries of life would lead to a risk of danger to the life, or a risk of permanent endangerment to the health, of the child" (*Naglik*, at p 143; see also *R v JF* 2008 SCC 60, [2008] 3 SCR 215, at para 8).

...

'56 ... The alleged marked departure in this case relates to whether a reasonable person would have foreseen that failing to provide food or fluids to young children – one of whom ultimately died as a result of brain injury that developed following a cardiac arrest caused by malnutrition and dehydration – would result in a risk of danger to life or of permanent endangerment to health. Given this context, the jury was easily able to assess whether the failure to provide food or fluids to young children constituted a marked departure from the standard of care of a reasonably prudent person in the circumstances.' *R v Goforth* [2021] SCJ No 103, 2022 SCC 25 at paras 27, 56, per Côté J

MARKET

[For 71 Halsbury's Laws of England (5th Edn) (2013) para 801 see now 71 Halsbury's Laws of England (5th Edn) (2020) para 701.]

MARKET OVERT

[For 71 Halsbury's Laws of England (5th Edn) (2013) para 824 see now 71 Halsbury's Laws of England (5th Edn) (2020) para 724.]

MARRIAGE

[For 72 Halsbury's Laws of England (5th Edn) (2015) paras 251, 4 see now 71 Halsbury's Laws of England (5th Edn) (2019) paras 3, 5.]

Void and voidable

[For 72 Halsbury's Laws of England (5th Edn) (2015) paras 375, 382 see now 72 Halsbury's Laws of England (5th Edn) (2019) paras 373, 379; and for 72 Halsbury's Laws of England (5th Edn) (2015) paras 387–391 see now 72 Halsbury's Laws of England (5th Edn) (2019) paras 384–389.]

MATERIAL

[For 76 Halsbury's Laws of England (5th Edn) (2013) para 773 see now 76 Halsbury's Laws of England (5th Edn) (2019) para 767.]

MATERIAL

Material consideration

[Town and Country Planning Act 1990 s 70(2): in dealing with an application for planning permission or permission in principle a local planning authority must have regard to ... '(c) any other material considerations'] '[4] The issue on the appeal is whether the promise to provide a community fund donation qualifies as a "material consideration" for the purposes of s 70(2) of the Town and Country Planning Act 1990 as amended ("the 1990 Act") and s 38(6) of the Planning and Compulsory Purchase Act 2004 ("the 2004 Act"). These are very familiar provisions in planning law. ...

...

'[31] Planning permission is required "for the carrying out of any development of land": s 57(1) of the 1990 Act. So far as is relevant, "development" is defined in s 55(1) to mean "the making of any material change in the use of any buildings or other land". Section 70(2) of the 1990 Act requires a planning authority to have regard to the development plan and certain other matters "so far as material to the application" and to "any other material considerations": that is to say, material to the change of use which is proposed. Similarly, in relation to an application for planning permission, the "material considerations" referred to in s 38(6) of the 2004 Act are considerations material to the change of use which is proposed.

'[32] In *Newbury* [*Newbury District Council v Secretary of State for the Environment*] [1980] 1 All ER 731 at 739–740, [1981] AC 578 at 599–601 Viscount Dilhorne treated the scope of the concept of "material considerations" in s 29(1) of the Town and Country Planning Act

1971 (which corresponds to what is now s 70(2) of the 1990 Act) as the same as the ambit of the power of a local planning authority (in what is now s 70(1)(a) of the 1990 Act) to impose such conditions "as they think fit" on the grant of planning permission. …

…

'[37] It has long been recognised that a consequence of this approach of relying on the *Newbury* criteria to identify 'material considerations' is that planning permission cannot be bought or sold. …

…

'[39] A principled approach to identifying material considerations in line with the *Newbury* criteria is important both as a protection for landowners and as a protection for the public interest. It prevents a planning authority from extracting money or other benefits from a landowner as a condition for granting permission to develop its land, when such payment or the provision of such benefits has no sufficient connection with the proposed use of the land. It also prevents a developer from offering to make payments or provide benefits which have no sufficient connection with the proposed use of the land, as a way of buying a planning permission which it would be contrary to the public interest to grant according to the merits of the development itself.

…

'[44] In the present case, the community benefits promised by Resilient Severndale did not satisfy the *Newbury* criteria and hence did not qualify as a material consideration within the meaning of that term in s 70(2) of the 1990 Act and s 38(6) of the 2004 Act. Dove J and the Court of Appeal were right so to hold. The benefits were not proposed as a means of pursuing any proper planning purpose, but for the ulterior purpose of providing general benefits to the community. Moreover, they did not fairly and reasonably relate to the development for which permission was sought. Resilient Severndale required planning permission for the carrying out of "development" of the land in question, as that term is defined in s 55(1) of the 1990 Act. The community benefits to be provided by Resilient Severndale did not affect the use of the land. Instead, they were proffered as a general inducement to the Council to grant planning permission and constituted a method of seeking to buy the permission sought, in breach of the principle that planning permission cannot be bought or sold. This is so whether the development scheme is regarded as commercial and profit-making in nature, as Hickinbottom LJ thought it was (para [39]), or as a purely community-run scheme to create community benefits.

'[45] For the appellants, Mr Kingston submitted that the planning statutes had to be regarded as "always speaking" so far as concerns what counts as a "material consideration", and that this meant that the meaning of this concept should be updated in line with changing government policy. I do not agree. The meaning of the term "material consideration" in s 70(2) of the 1990 Act and s 38(6) of the 2004 Act is not in doubt and updating the established meaning of the term is neither required nor appropriate. To say that the meaning of the term changes according to what is said by Ministers in policy statements would undermine the position, as explained above, that what qualifies as a "material consideration" is a question of law on which the courts have already provided authoritative rulings. The interpretation given to that statutory term by the courts provides a clear meaning which is principled and stable over time. I note that Parliament has considered it necessary to amend s 70(2) when it wishes to expand the range of factors which may be treated as material for the purposes of that provision, for instance in relation to the Welsh language: sub-para (aa).' *R (on the application of Wright) v Resilient Energy Severndale Ltd* [2019] UKSC 53, [2020] 2 All ER 1 at [4], [31]–[32], [37], [39], [44]–[45], per Lord Sales

MATRIMONIAL HOME

[For 72 Halsbury's Laws of England (5th Edn) (2015) para 269 et seq see now 72 Halsbury's Laws of England (5th Edn) (2019) para 267 et seq.]

MATTERS IN DIFFERENCE

[For 2 Halsbury's Laws of England (5th Edn) (2017) para 515 see now 2 Halsbury's Laws of England (5th Edn) (2023) para 615.]

MAY

Permissive

[For 96 Halsbury's Laws of England (5th Edn) (2012) para 615 see now 96 Halsbury's Laws of England (5th Edn) (2018) para 215.]

[Environmental Protection Act 1990, s 160; methods of service of notices under the Act; notice may be served or given ….] '[40] In our judgment Mr McDermott was right to concede that s 160 is permissive not mandatory. Although this was not in issue, we think it right to set out at a little length our reasons for such a conclusion because it may be relevant to other statutes adopting the same or similar wording. Our reasons are as follows.

'[41] First, that is indicated by the language of the section. Subsections (1), (2) and (3) each use the word "may", rather than "shall", when referring to methods of service. This is permissive language. It is true that, depending on surrounding language and context, the word "may" can sometimes mean "must". Nevertheless, the starting point is that the use of the word "may" connotes something which is permitted but is not mandatory. This is reinforced in this case by the contrast with the mandatory language "shall" in sub-s (4).

'[42] Furthermore, if the word "may" were to be given a mandatory meaning in s 160(2), it would follow that it would also have to be given a mandatory meaning in s 160(3), and vice versa; and conversely if s 160(2) is permissive, so too must be s 160(3), and vice versa. As Mr McDermott recognised in his submissions, if the word "may" were to be interpreted in a mandatory sense in s 160(3), this would cause real difficulties. …

…

'[69] Drawing the strands of these authorities together, they support the conclusion that s 160 is permissive rather than mandatory.' *Allen v Ealing London Borough Council* [2021] EWHC 948 (Admin), [2022] 1 All ER 554 at [40]–[42], [69], per Popplewell LJ

Canada '[48] The meaning of words is often derived from a number of contextual factors, including the purpose of the agreement and the nature of the relationship created by the agreement (see *Moore Realty Inc v Manitoba Motor League*, 2003 MBCA 71, 173 Man R (2d) 300, at para 15, per Hamilton JA; see also *Hall* [Geoff R Hall, *Canadian Contractual Interpretation Law*, 3d edn], at p 22; and *McCamus* [John D McCamus, *The Law of Contracts*, 3d edn], at pp 749–50). As stated by Lord Hoffmann in *Investors Compensation Scheme Ltd v West Bromwich Building Society*, [1998] 1 All ER 98 (HL):

> The meaning which a document (or any other utterance) would convey to a reasonable man is not the same thing as the meaning of its words. The meaning of words is a matter of dictionaries and grammars; the meaning of the document is what the parties using those words against the relevant background would reasonably have been understood to mean.'

Mosten Investments LP v Manufacturers Life Insurance Co (cob Manulife Financial) 2021 SKCA 36, 2021 DTC 5022, CA (Sask), at [48], per Caldwell, Barrington-Foote and Tholl JJA

MEANING

Australia '[112] … In the tort of defamation, the meaning of a statement is not that which other people may actually have attached to it, but that which is derived from an objective assessment of the defamatory meaning that the notional ordinary reasonable reader would attach to it. In the tort of misuse of private information, part of the factual enquiry is as to the effect of publication of the information on the claimant. The question becomes how would others perceive the claimant if the information was published? That enquiry does not require the application of an objective assessment of the defamatory meaning that the notional ordinary reasonable reader would attach to the information.' *ZXC v Bloomberg LP* [2022] UKSC 5, [2022] 3 All ER 1 at [112], per Lord Hamblen and Lord Stephens JJSC

'[86] Regulations are to be construed according to the ordinary principles of statutory construction. The starting point for the ascertainment of the meaning of a provision is its text, while at the same time regard is to be had to its context and purpose. Of course, the statutory context of regulations includes the Act under which the regulations were made and are sustained. Context should be regarded at the first stage and not at some later stage and it should be regarded in its widest sense, including by reference to legislative history and extrinsic material. As Kiefel CJ, Nettle and Gordon JJ explained in [*SZTAL v Minister for Immigration and Border Protection* (2017) 262 CLR 362; 347 ALR 405; [2017] HCA 34 at [14]]

> "This is not to deny the importance of the natural and ordinary meaning of a word … Considerations of context and purpose simply recognise that, understood in its statutory, historical or other context, some

other meaning of a word may be suggested, and so too, if its ordinary meaning is not consistent with the statutory purpose, that meaning must be rejected."

'[87] The context of the words, consideration of the consequences of adopting a provision's literal meaning, the purpose of the statute and principles of construction may lead a court to adopt a construction that departs from the literal meaning of the words of a provision. One such principle is that legislation must be construed on the prima facie basis that its provisions are intended to give effect to harmonious goals. As expressed by Gageler J in *SAS Trustee Corporation v Miles* [(2018) 265 CLR 137; 361 ALR 206; [2018] HCA 55 at [41]], "statutory text must be considered from the outset in context and attribution of meaning to the text in context must be guided so far as possible by statutory purpose on the understanding that a legislature ordinarily intends to pursue its purposes by coherent means". Where conflict appears to arise in construing an Act, "the conflict must be alleviated, so far as possible, by adjusting the meaning of the competing provisions to achieve that result which will best give effect to the purpose and language of those provisions while maintaining the unity of all the statutory provisions", and this "will often require the court 'to determine which is the leading provision and which the subordinate provision, and which must give way to the other'". Ultimately, the task in applying the accepted principles of statutory construction is to discern what Parliament is to be taken to have intended.' *ENT19 v Minister for Home Affairs* [2023] HCA 18, (2023) 410 ALR 1 at [86]–[87], per Gordon, Edelman, Steward and Gleeson JJ

MEASURE (LEGISLATIVE)

[For 96 Halsbury's Laws of England (5th Edn) (2012) para 606, 606n see now 96 Halsbury's Laws of England (5th Edn) (2018) para 206, para 206 n 5.]

MEDICAL DEVICE

'Medical device' means any instrument, apparatus, appliance, software, material or other article, whether used alone or in combination, together with any accessories, including the software intended by its manufacturer to be used specifically for diagnosis or therapeutic purposes or both and necessary for its proper application, which—

(a) is intended by the manufacturer to be used for human beings for the purpose of—
   (i) diagnosis, prevention, monitoring, treatment or alleviation of disease,
   (ii) diagnosis, monitoring, treatment, alleviation of or compensation for an injury or handicap,
   (iii) investigation, replacement or modification of the anatomy or of a physiological process, or
   (iv) control of conception; and
(b) does not achieve its principal intended action in or on the human body by pharmacological, immunological or metabolic means, even if it is assisted in its function by such means,

and includes devices intended to administer a medicinal product or which incorporate as an integral part a substance which, if used separately, would be a medicinal product and which is liable to act upon the body with action ancillary to that of the device. (Medical Devices Regulations 2002, SI 2002/618, reg 2(1) (as amended by SI 2008/2936))

In vitro diagnostic medical device

'In vitro diagnostic medical device' means a medical device which—

(a) is a reagent, reagent product, calibrator, control material, kit, instrument, apparatus, equipment or system, whether used alone or in combination; and
(b) is intended by the manufacturer to be used in vitro for the examination of specimens, including blood and tissue donations, derived from the human body, solely or principally for the purpose of providing information—
   (i) concerning a physiological or pathological state,
   (ii) concerning a congenital abnormality,
   (iii) to determine the safety and compatibility of donations, including blood and tissue donations, with potential recipients, or
   (iv) to monitor therapeutic measures,

and includes a specimen receptacle but not a product for general laboratory use, unless that product, in view of its characteristics, is specifically intended by its manufacturer to be used for in vitro diagnostic examination. (Medical Devices Regulations 2002, SI 2002/618, reg 2(1))

MEDICAL PRACTITIONER

Physician

[For 74 Halsbury's Laws of England (5th Edn) (2011) para 176 see now 74 Halsbury's Laws of England (5th Edn) (2019) para 197.]

MENS REA

[For 25 Halsbury's Laws of England (5th Edn) (2016) para 4 see now 25 Halsbury's Laws of England (5th Edn) (2020) para 5.]

MERCANTILE GENT

[For 1 Halsbury's Laws of England (5th Edn) (2017) para 12 see now 1 Halsbury's Laws of England (5th Edn) (2022) para 12.]

MERGER

[For 87 Halsbury's Laws of England (5th Edn) (2017) paras 267–268 see now 87 Halsbury's Laws of England (5th Edn) (2022) paras 267–268.]

'[1] The issue raised by this second appeal is whether the doctrine of merger, whereby a judgment on a cause of action precludes a new action for further relief on the same cause of action, applies where the judgment is for declaratory relief only. It appears that this is an issue on which there is no decided case either in this country or in any other Commonwealth country. The current edition of a leading textbook, *Spencer Bower and Handley: Res Judicata* (5th edn, 2019), expresses the view that merger does not apply in the case of a purely declaratory judgment, as have all previous editions since the first edition published in 1924.

'[2] The present proceedings were dismissed by an order of Chief Master Marsh dated 23 July 2019, which declared that the court had no jurisdiction to hear the claim. The order was made on the basis that the doc-trine of merger applied in the case of a prior declaratory judgment, so as to preclude a subsequent claim on the same cause of action for payment of a debt.

...

...

'[27] The doctrine of merger is a rule of substantive law that is strictly applied. It does not involve the exercise of any discretion by the court. At a time when the means available to the courts to control abusive litigation were significantly less than they have since become, merger played an important role. As the passage from Lord Sumption's judgment [in *Virgin Atlantic Airways Ltd v Zodiac Seats UK Ltd* [2013] UKSC 46, [2013] 4 All ER 715, [2014] AC 160] quoted above shows, there is now an extensive range of tools available to control the abuse of the court's process. I cannot think of any circumstances in which those tools would not be sufficient to prevent abuse, even if merger ceased to exist. There is, of course, no question of abolishing merger, but there is no good reason for widening its scope beyond its established bounds. ...

'[28] A doctrine that prevents a party bringing a second claim to recover a remedy that has already been the subject of a judgment between the same parties makes obvious sense. A doctrine that would prevent a party from bringing a claim for an enforceable remedy, such as a judgment for debt or damages, because it had earlier obtained a declaration as to its rights and the defendant's obligations serves no obvious purpose, if the circumstances are such that the second action is not an abuse of the court's process.

...

'[31] It is not necessary on the present appeal to decide whether the doctrine of merger applies only to claims for the same relief. What does, however, clearly emerge from the authorities is that merger applies where an obligation under the cause of action is embodied in, and replaced by, a final order of the court.

...

'[37] A declaration is a quite different remedy from judgment for a debt or damages. It makes sense to speak of a merger of a claim for a debt or damages into a judgment for the payment of a specified sum as debt or damages, so creating "an obligation of a higher nature". The lesser right is merged into the higher. The same simply cannot be said of a purely declaratory judgment, which itself imposes no obligation but only confirms the obligation which already exists. As Birss J aptly put it, "I do not see how a declaration which declares to exist the right which the claimant already had before judgment was given, could be said to extinguish that pre-existing right. It does the opposite."

'[38] It has been stated in all editions of *Spencer Bower* that the doctrine of merger does not apply to a declaration: see the current edition at para 20.01 and the first edition at para 304. No authority is cited for that proposition, but none can be when, so far as known, it has never previously been contended that it does apply to a declaration. It is, however, consistent with the underlying rationale of the doctrine. Moreover, it is hard, indeed I would say impossible, to think of a sound reason why a declaration of legal right or obligation should automatically bar a subsequent claim for enforceable relief.

'[39] There is a further consideration as regards declarations. As the authorities demonstrate, merger (or former recovery) is a very longstanding doctrine of the common law. Declaratory relief was an equitable remedy, and declarations as a sole remedy were virtually unknown until the mid-nineteenth century: see *Zamir & Woolf: The Declaratory Judgment* (4th edn, 2011) para 2–01 et seq. It is clear from judgments given in the early years of the nineteenth century that the doctrine of merger was by then fully formed and well understood. In view of the growth in other means to prevent abuse of the court's process, there is no case for expanding the scope of the rigid doctrine of merger or for applying it to a remedy that was never in the contemplation of the judges who developed it.

...

'[41] On one matter, I respectfully disagree with Birss J. While he considered that the application of merger to declarations would depend on the terms of the declaration, it is my view that the basis and development of the doctrine shows that it has no application at all to declarations. Of course, depending on the circumstances of the case, a claimant who first seeks only declaratory relief may be precluded, by the other principles designed to prevent abuse, from bringing further proceedings.' *Zavarco plc v Nasir* [2021] EWCA Civ 121,7 [2022] 2 All ER 388 at [1]–[2], [27]–[28], [31], [37]–[39], [41], per Sir David Richards

MESNE PROFITS

[For 62 Halsbury's Laws of England (5th Edn) (2016) para 279 see now 62 Halsbury's Laws of England (5th Edn) (2022) para 302.]

MINE

[For 76 Halsbury's Laws of England (5th Edn) (2013) para 3 see now 76 Halsbury's Laws of England (5th Edn) (2019) para 3.]

Open mine

[For 76 Halsbury's Laws of England (5th Edn) (2013) para 5 see now 76 Halsbury's Laws of England (5th Edn) (2019) para 5.]

MINERALS

[For 76 Halsbury's Laws of England (5th Edn) (2013) para 10 see now 76 Halsbury's Laws of England (5th Edn) (2019) para 10.]

MISCARRIAGE

[For 49 Halsbury's Laws of England (5th Edn) (2015) para 677 see now 49 Halsbury's Laws of England (5th Edn) (2021) para 640.]

MISCARRIAGE OF JUSTICE

'[19] Section 133 [of the Criminal Justice Act 1988] was then amended, with effect from 13 March 2014, by s 175 of the 2014 Act [Anti-social Behaviour, Crime and Policing Act 2014], so as to confine the term "miscarriage of justice" to category (1) cases. Section 133(1) remained unaltered: it continued to be necessary for the conviction to be reversed "on the ground that a new or newly discovered fact shows beyond reasonable doubt that there has been a miscarriage of justice". However, s 175 of the 2014 Act inserted s 133(1ZA) into the 1988 Act, providing a statutory definition of the term "miscarriage of justice":

> "(1ZA) For the purposes of subsection (1), there has been a miscarriage of justice in relation to a person convicted of a criminal offence in England and Wales or, in a case where subsection (6H) applies, Northern Ireland, if and only if the new or newly discovered fact shows beyond reasonable doubt that the person did not commit the offence (and references in the rest of this Part to a miscarriage of justice are to be construed accordingly)."

The words "did not commit the offence" can be read as synonymous in this context with the words 'is innocent' used by this court in category (1) in *Adams* [*R (on the application of Adams) v Secretary of State for Justice* [2011] UKSC 18, [2011] 3 All ER 261, [2012] 1 AC 48]. The effect of s 133(1ZA) is therefore that there is a miscarriage of justice, for the purposes of s 133(1), only where the new or newly discovered fact shows beyond reasonable doubt that the case falls into category (1) recognised in *Adams*.' *R (on the application of Hallam) v Secretary of State for Justice; R (on the application of Nealon) v Secretary of State for Justice* [2019] UKSC 2, [2019] 2 All ER 841 at [19], per Lord Mance

Australia '[28] There was no issue between the parties as to the test to be applied in order to determine whether fresh evidence requires that a conviction be set aside and a new trial had on the basis that a miscarriage of justice has occurred. It is settled that a miscarriage of justice will be established where fresh evidence, when viewed in combination with the evidence given at trial, shows that there is a "significant possibility that the jury, acting reasonably, would have acquitted the accused" had the fresh evidence been before the jury. Nor was it in dispute that the additional evidence adduced in the Court of Appeal was fresh evidence insofar as it was evidence which was not available to or obtainable by the appellant with the exercise of reasonable diligence. That being so, a miscarriage of justice would be established if there were a significant possibility that the jury acting reasonably might have acquitted the appellant had that evidence been available to it.' *Rodi v State of Western Australia* [2018] HCA 44, (2018) 360 ALR 54 at [28], per Kiefel CJ, Bell, Keane, Nettle and Gordon JJ

MISFEASANCE

In Companies Acts

[For 17 Halsbury's Laws of England (5th Edn) (2011) para 646 see now 17 Halsbury's Laws of England (5th Edn) (2017) para 243.]

MISPRISION

It is an offence at common law, punishable by fine and imprisonment at the discretion of the court, for a person who knows that treason is being planned or committed not to report it as soon as he can to a justice of the peace or other authority. (26 Halsbury's Laws of England (5th Edn) (2020) para 555)

MISREPRESENTATION

[For 76 Halsbury's Laws of England (5th Edn) (2013) paras 740–741 see now 76 Halsbury's Laws of England (5th Edn) (2019) paras 740–741.]

Fraudulent misrepresentation

[For 76 Halsbury's Laws of England (5th Edn) (2013) paras 755–756 see now 76 Halsbury's Laws of England (5th Edn) (2019) paras 755–756.]

Innocent misrepresentation

[For 76 Halsbury's Laws of England (5th Edn) (2013) para 761 see now 76 Halsbury's Laws of England (5th Edn) (2019) para 761.]

MISTAKE

[Limitation Act 1980, s 32(1)(c): limitation period postponed where action is for relief from the consequences of a mistake.] '[243] For these reasons, although there is undeniable force in the argument that s 32(1)(c) should be construed as being confined to mistakes of fact, the balance of the arguments in our view favours giving the language of s 32(1)(c) its ordinary meaning, so that it is applicable also to actions for relief from the consequences of a mistake of law. That approach to the construction of the provision best gives effect to Parliament's intention to relieve claimants from the necessity of complying with a time limit at a time when they cannot reasonably be expected to do so, and does not have unacceptable consequences for the legal certainty which the 1980 Act is primarily designed to protect. That is only so, however, if the court departs from the reasoning in *Deutsche Morgan Grenfell Group plc v IRC* [2006] UKHL 49, [2007] 1 All ER 449, [2007] 1 AC 558, since that reasoning would defeat Parliament's intention. On that basis, we consider that this court should adhere to the decision in *Kleinwort Benson* [*Kleinwort Benson Ltd v Lincoln City Council* [1999] 2 AC 349, [1998] 4 All ER 513, HL], so far as relating to limitation.' *Test Claimants in the Franked Investment Income Group Litigation v Revenue and Customs Commissioners* [2020] UKSC 47, [2021] 1 All ER 1001 at [243], per Lord Reed P and Lord Hodge DP

MOÇAMBIQUE RULE

New Zealand '[69] However, in ruling that an Irish court would be precluded from entertaining Sophie's land claims, the Judge considered himself bound to apply a common law rule known as "the Moçambique rule".

'[70] The rule is derived from a 19th century decision of the House of Lords from which it takes its name [*British South Africa Co v Companhia de Moçambique* [1893] AC 602, HL]. The House of Lords held that English courts have no jurisdiction in proceedings primarily concerned with title to or possession of immovable property situated outside England.

'[71] The land at issue in this case is of course situated in New Zealand, not outside it. However, the Associate Judge found the *Moçambique* rule "applies both ways". By that he meant it applied not only to preclude New Zealand courts from having jurisdiction to hear a proceeding involving land situated overseas, but also to preclude a foreign court (here an Irish court) having jurisdiction over land situated in New Zealand. The Judge said it was established that under New Zealand common law, New Zealand courts "will not recognise a foreign court asserting jurisdiction over land in New Zealand, particularly when questions of title are concerned".

'[72] The *Moçambique* rule is subject to two exceptions, these being the "in personam exception" and "administration of an estate exception" which we go on to discuss at [79]–[109] below, but the Judge held neither of those exceptions applied in this case.

...

'[74] In modern times, the *Moçambique* rule has been widely criticised as an anomalous historic relic. It is said to be out of step with what is now internationally acceptable, as well as being illogical and productive of injustice. There have been calls for it to be abolished in New Zealand and for proceedings relating to foreign land to be dealt with solely under the High Court Rules relating to jurisdiction and forum conveniens.

'[75] The criticisms appear to be well founded. However, we are satisfied this is not the case to decide whether the *Moçambique* rule should still be good law in New Zealand. That is because in our view, the rule has only ever applied to foreign land and not to land situated in New Zealand. To put it another way, it is not a domestic exclusive jurisdiction rule and cannot be the basis for a New Zealand court to hold that an Irish court would have no jurisdiction. None of the cases and texts cited to us by counsel support that approach.' *Christie v Foster* [2019] NZCA 623, [2020] 2 NZLR 238 at [69]–[72], [74]–[75], per French J

MODERN SLAVERY

'[73] The concepts of slavery, servitude and forced labour, together with human trafficking, are now often grouped together under the description of "modern slavery". The Explanatory Notes to the UK Modern Slavery Act 2015, at para 4, describe modern slavery as "a brutal form of organised crime in which people are treated as commodities and exploited for criminal gain". The United Nations also uses this concept, as exemplified by the existence since 2007 of a UN Special Rapporteur on "contemporary forms of slavery". So does the ILO, which has described modern slavery as an "umbrella term" that refers, essentially, to "situations of exploitation that a person cannot refuse or leave because of threats, violence, coercion, deception, and/or abuse of power": ILO "Global Estimates of Modern Slavery: Forced Labour and Forced Marriage" (2017) p 9. Underlying the use of the term "modern slavery" is the point that, in the words of Anti-Slavery International (the world's oldest international human rights organisation):

> "Today slavery is less about people literally owning other people – although that still exists – but more about being exploited and completely controlled by someone else, without being able to leave."

See Anti-Slavery International, "What Is Modern Slavery?", quoted in G Gyulai, "Slavery, Servitude and Forced Labour in International Law: Should the Difference Still Matter?" (2021) 32 King's LJ 228 at 253.

'[74] The practices subsumed within the description "modern slavery" are, however, the subject of separate legal definitions.

...

'[100] In cases of the present kind the forms of modern slavery primarily relevant, in our view, are likely to be forced labour and servitude (which, as noted above, can be seen as an "aggravated" form of forced labour). It is those international law concepts which provide appropriate criteria for distinguishing between, on the one hand, the voluntary employment of a domestic worker which is an ordinary incident of living in the receiving state and, on the other hand, the exploitation of a domestic worker which is properly characterised as a commercial activity for the purpose of art 31(1)(c) of the Diplomatic Convention. The assumed facts of the present case make it a paradigm example of domestic servitude.' *Basfar v Wong* [2022] UKSC 20, [2022] 4 All ER 1 at [73]–[74], [100], per Lord Briggs and Lord Leggatt JJSC

MOLEST

New Zealand [Wildlife Act 1953, s 2: hunting or killing in relation to any wildlife includes pursuing, disturbing, or molesting.] '[67] The verb molest is more elusive of meaning than the others. The *Oxford English Dictionary* gives the following two meanings of molest:

(a) "To cause trouble, grief, or vexation to; to vex, annoy, put to inconvenience".
(b) "To interfere or meddle with (a person) injuriously or with hostile intent. Now almost exclusively in negative contexts".

'[68] In context, we consider that molest means intentionally troubling, distressing or injuring a protected animal.' *Shark Experience Ltd v PauaMAC5 Inc* [2019] NZSC 111, [2019] 1 NZLR 791 at [67]–[68], per Winkelmann CJ

MONEY

General meaning

[For 49 Halsbury's Laws of England (5th Edn) (2015) paras 1–2 see now 49 Halsbury's Laws of England (5th Edn) (2021) paras 1–2.]

In will

[For 102 Halsbury's Laws of England (5th Edn) (2010) para 295 see now 102 Halsbury's Laws of England (5th Edn) (2021) para 295.]

MOORING (OF VESSEL)

Moored in good safety

[For 60 Halsbury's Laws of England (5th Edn) (2011) para 307 see now 60 Halsbury's Laws of England (5th Edn) (2018) para 286.]

MORTGAGE

[For 77 Halsbury's Laws of England (5th Edn) (2016) paras 101–102 see now 77 Halsbury's Laws of England (5th Edn) (2021) paras 101–102; and for 91 Halsbury's Laws of England (5th Edn) (2012) para 2 see now 91 Halsbury's Laws of England (5th Edn) (2019) para 2.]

Equitable mortgage

[For 77 Halsbury's Laws of England (5th Edn) (2016) para 105 see now 77 Halsbury's Laws of England (5th Edn) (2021) para 105.]

Legal mortgage

[For 77 Halsbury's Laws of England (5th Edn) (2016) para 104 see now 77 Halsbury's Laws of England (5th Edn) (2021) para 104.]

Puisne mortgage

[For 77 Halsbury's Laws of England (5th Edn) (2016) para 160 see now 77 Halsbury's Laws of England (5th Edn) (2021) para 160 n 5.]

MOTHER

[Gender Recognition Act 2004, ss 9, 12; European Convention for the Protection of Human Rights and Fundamental Freedoms, arts 8, 14]
'[1] In this case the court is required to define the term "mother" under the law of England and Wales. Down the centuries, no court has previously been required to determine the definition of "mother" under English common law and, it seems, that there have been few comparable decisions made in other courts elsewhere in the Western World. Hitherto, a person who has given birth to a child has always been regarded as that child's mother. The issue arises in modern times where an individual, who was born female, undergoes gender transition and becomes legally recognised as male before going on to conceive, carry and give birth to a child, with the result that the parent who has given birth is legally a man rather than a woman. The question posed to this court is: Is that man the "mother" or the "father" of his child?

...

'[123] The task of discerning the approach in domestic law to the issue in this case is not an easy one. The circumstances of TT, and his role, as a male, in the conception and birth of his son YY, are not expressly provided for in either the legislation governing artificial insemination or that for gender recognition. Even though the HFEA 2008 [Human Fertilisation and Embryology Act 2008] was passed four years after the GRA 2004 [Gender Recognition Act 2004], the HFEA 2008 retains the basic definitions of "mother" and "father" that appeared in the HFEA 1990 and which are expressly tied to either "a woman" or "a man", respectively. The additional concept of a second 'parent' that was introduced by the 2008 Act is, as was accepted in submissions, restricted to a second female parent in the specific circumstances of HFEA 2008, ss 42 and 43 and has no application to the facts of this case.

…

'[269] On the above analysis, the ECHR [European Convention for the Protection of Human Rights and Fundamental Freedoms] aspect of this claim turns on the same point as that which lies at the centre of the case in domestic law, namely whether the term "mother" is exclusively female or whether it is a free-standing term which, in the context of a birth applies to the person who carries a pregnancy and gives birth to a child, irrespective of their legal gender.

'[270] In the context of domestic law my conclusion at para [149] on that central point was that the latter is the case. There is no ground to support a different interpretation of the term "mother" in the context of the evaluation of proportionality under the ECHR.

…

'[279] The principal conclusion at the centre of this extensive judgment can be shortly stated. It is that there is a material difference between a person's gender and their status as a parent. Being a "mother", whilst hitherto always associated with being female, is the status afforded to a person who undergoes the physical and biological process of carrying a pregnancy and giving birth. It is now medically and legally possible for an individual, whose gender is recognised in law as male, to become pregnant and give birth to their child. Whilst that person's gender is "male", their parental status, which derives from their biological role in giving birth, is that of "mother".

'[280] At para [149], I set out my preliminary conclusions with respect to domestic law, these can now be firmly stated as:

(a) At common law a person whose egg is inseminated in their womb and who then becomes pregnant and gives birth to a child is that child's "mother";
(b) The status of being a "mother" arises from the role that a person has undertaken in the biological process of conception, pregnancy and birth;
(c) Being a "mother" or a "father" with respect to the conception, pregnancy and birth of a child is not necessarily gender specific, although until recent decades it invariably was so. It is now possible, and recognised by the law, for a "mother" to have an acquired gender of male, and for a "father" to have an acquired gender of female;
(d) GRA 2004, s 12 is both retrospective and prospective. The status of a person as the father or mother of a child is not affected by the acquisition of gender under the Act, even where the relevant birth has taken place after the issue of a GR certificate.'

R (on the application of McConnell) v Registrar General for England and Wales [2019] EWHC 2384, [2020] 2 All ER 813 at [1], [123], [269]–[270], [279]–[280], per Sir Andrew McFarlane P; affirmed [2020] EWCA Civ 559, [2020] 2 All ER 813

(1) The woman who is carrying or has carried a child as a result of the placing in her of an embryo or of sperm and eggs, and no other woman, is to be treated as the mother of the child.
(2) Subsection (1) does not apply to any child to the extent that the child is treated by virtue of adoption as not being the woman's child.

(Human Fertilisation and Embryology Act 2008, s 33)

MURDER

[For 25 Halsbury's Laws of England (5th Edn) (2016) para 99 see now 25 Halsbury's Laws of England (5th Edn) (2020) para 125.]

N

NAME

[For 80 Halsbury's Laws of England (5th Edn) (2013) para 802 see now 80 Halsbury's Laws of England (5th Edn) (2020) para 802; and for 88 Halsbury's Laws of England (5th Edn) (2012) paras 326–329 see now 88 Halsbury's Laws of England (5th Edn) (2019) paras 329–332.]

Working name

(4) In this Act, any reference to a working name of a charity is a reference to a name that is not the name of the charity but which is used to designate the charity and under which activities of the charity are carried out. (Charities Act 2011, s 42(4) (as substituted by the Charities Act 2022, s 25))

NATIONAL BODY

Australia [Insurance Contracts Act 1984 ss 14, 54. Insurance policy exclusion for loss caused by any communicable disease or threat or fear of communicable disease which leads to the imposition of quarantine or restriction in movement of people or animals by any national or international body or agency; or any travel advisory or warning being issued by a national or international body or agency.] '[66] The applicant submitted that border closures by States were not by a national body. The word "national" in exclusion 6.20 is, however, in juxtaposition to "international". In the context of an attempted co-ordinated national response to a pandemic with a significant degree of co-ordination among all Governments and the existence of a National Cabinet, imposition of restriction in movement of people within the nation by a constituent Government of the nation satisfies the expression "national body or agency", as distinct from "international body or agency". Further, the minutes referred to "restrictions on gatherings, events, travel, and social distancing" which "would also need to be lifted before the event, to enable the delivery of the event." At least some of these involved restriction in movement of people or travel advisories or warnings that were the product of decisions of National Cabinet (a national body). Such can be seen as directly contributing to the operational fear of a drop out rate of 20% of volunteers (all of whom were to come from around Australia) which "would make it impossible to manage the event." Likewise as to provision of food: the decision minute stating "[w]ith tourists being discouraged to travel to the outback" and other events in the outback being cancelled, no food vans were planning "to make the trip as it is not viable for them to travel …". …' *Outback Music Festival Group Pty Ltd (fka Big Run Events Pty Ltd) v Everest Syndicate 2786 at Lloyd's* [2022] FCA 13, (2022) 398 ALR 327 at [66], per Allsop CJ

NATIONAL DEBT

[For 49 Halsbury's Laws of England (5th Edn) (2015) paras 112–114 see now 49 Halsbury's Laws of England (5th Edn) (2021) paras 81–83.]

NATIONALITY

[For 4 Halsbury's Laws of England (5th Edn) (2011) para 401 et seq see now 4 Halsbury's Laws of England (5th Edn) (2020) para 401 et seq.]

NECESSARIES

Of child

[For 9 Halsbury's Laws of England (5th Edn) (2012) paras 18–19 see now 9 Halsbury's Laws of England (5th Edn) (2017) paras 18–19; and for 91 Halsbury's Laws of England (5th Edn) (2012) para 38 see now 91 Halsbury's Laws of England (5th Edn) (2019) para 37.]

Of wife

[For 72 Halsbury's Laws of England (5th Edn) (2015) para 262 see now 72 Halsbury's Laws of England (5th Edn) (2019) para 260.]

NECESSITY

Agency of

[For 1 Halsbury's Laws of England (5th Edn) (2017) para 24 see now 1 Halsbury's Laws of England (5th Edn) (2022) para 24.]

NEGLIGENCE

Criminal negligence

[For 25 Halsbury's Laws of England (5th Edn) (2016) para 18 see now 25 Halsbury's Laws of England (5th Edn) (2020) para 147.]

NEW INFORMATION

Australia [Migration Act 1958 (Cth), s 473DC(1).] '[16] The meaning given to "new information" by s 473DC(1) for the purposes of Pt 7AA is "any documents or information" that satisfy two conditions. The first condition, specified in s 473DC(1)(a), requires that the documents or information not have been before the Minister or delegate at the time of the making of the decision under review. The second condition, specified in s 473DC(1)(b), requires that the Authority consider that the documents or information "may be relevant".

...

'[20] The fundamental difficulty with the notion that the Certificate [that disclosure of information or matter contained in the Identity Assessment Form would be contrary to the public interest] met the definition of "new information" in s 473DC(1) is essentially that captured in the central argument of the Minister in the appeal to this Court that the Certificate was incapable of satisfying the description of "information".

...

'[22] Interpreted in accordance with the authority of *Plaintiff M174/2016 [Plaintiff M174/2016 v Minister for Immigration and Border Protection* (2018) 264 CLR 217; 353 ALR 600; [2018] HCA 16] and *SZMTA [Minister for Immigration and Border Protection v SZMTA* (2019) 264 CLR 421; 363 ALR 599; 163 ALD 1; [2019] HCA 3], the reference to "any documents or information" in the definition of "new information" in s 473DC(1) has no application to a certificate issued or purporting to be issued under s 473GB(5) for the purpose of s 473GB(1)(a), just as the definition has no application to a written notification made or purporting to be made under s 473GB(2)(a). A certificate or notification of that nature is an instrument which, if valid, has statutory consequences under s 473GB(3)(a) and (b). It is not a document which communicates knowledge of facts or circumstances of an evidentiary nature.

'[23] Consistently with the confinement of s 473DC(1)'s reference to "any documents or information" to documentation or information of an evidentiary nature, the word "relevant" in s 473DC(1)(b) can only sensibly be read as having the same meaning that the word "relevant" has in s 473CB(1)(c). Documentation or information of an evidentiary nature that the Authority considers may be "relevant" is documentation or information of an evidentiary nature that the Authority considers "capable directly or indirectly of rationally affecting assessment of the probability of the existence of some fact about which the Authority might be required to make a finding in the conduct of its review of the referred decision".

'[24] The Certificate was therefore not a "document" nor did it contain "information" within the reference to "any documents or information" in the definition of "new information" in s 473DC(1). Moreover, even if the Authority had treated the Certificate as valid to enliven the powers conferred by s 473GB(3)(a) and (b), and even if the Authority had gone on to exercise the power conferred by s 473GB(3)(a) to take the Identity Assessment Form into account in making some finding of fact in the review, the Authority cannot thereby be taken to have considered that the Certificate "may be relevant" within the meaning of s 473DC(1)(b).

...

'[30] In light of the context in which "new information" appears in s 473DB(1)(a), I agree with the joint judgment that these words should not be interpreted to mean all information which is new. The words must mean only new information of an evidentiary nature. This restriction upon the ordinary meaning of "new information" in Pt 7AA can be most directly seen in the "definition" of "new information" in s 473DC(1), which provides that subject to

Pt 7AA the Authority "may, in relation to a fast track decision, get any documents or information (***new information***) that: (a) were not before the Minister when the Minister made the decision under section 65; and (b) the Authority considers may be relevant". The relevance to which s 473DC(1) refers is relevance to the Authority's decision. The documents or information which comprise "new information" must therefore be documents or information that are capable of being considered by the Authority to be relevant to its decision. That class of documents concerns material or documentation of an evidentiary nature.' *Minister for Immigration and Border Protection v CED16* [2020] HCA 24, (2020) 380 ALR 216 at [16], [20], [22]–23], per Gageler, Keane, Nettle and Gordon JJ and at [30], per Edelman J

NEWSPAPER

[Value Added Tax Act 1994, Sch 8, item 2, group 3.] '[1] Supplies of (printed) newspapers are zero-rated for value added tax ("VAT") pursuant to s 30 and Item 2, Group 3 of Sch 8 to the Value Added Tax Act 1994 ("the VAT Act"). The question that arises on this appeal is whether the word used to describe this zero-rated item, "newspapers", can be properly interpreted (applying the relevant canons of construction including the "always speaking" principle) for VAT purposes in the period from September 2010 to December 2016, to apply also to what I have termed "the digital news services" in the form of digital editions of certain newspaper titles (*The Times*, *The Sunday Times* and *The Sun*, including *The Sun on Sunday*), published and supplied by News Corp UK & Ireland Ltd (referred to below as "News UK"). Although the appeal is confined to "newspapers" the logic of the reasoning may also extend to other items in Group 3, and elsewhere – in particular to "books", "journals" and "periodicals".

...

'[67] There can be no doubt that the ordinary meaning of the words in Item 2 as understood at any time between 1972 and 1991 at least, would have been of a printed newspaper, journal or periodical. The digital news services would not naturally have fallen within the ordinary meaning of "newspapers" and were not envisaged at the time of the enactment of this provision (or by 31 December 1975). So the question is whether they nevertheless fall within the scope of Parliament's original intention as reflected in the words used to describe the items that were included.

'[68] I have come to the conclusion that the words used by Parliament do lead to the inference that the clear legislative intent was to include tangible or physical items only and to exclude from Group 3 (and in particular from Item 2) supplies that were not of tangible things.

...

...

'[72] In these circumstances, and given also the need for a strict approach to be taken to the interpretation of zero-rating provisions not permitted to be extended beyond their 1975 and 1991 limits, I do not consider that the word "newspapers" in Item 2 of Group 3 can be read as including intangible digital news services. Although the content and social purpose of a printed newspaper and the digital news services may be the same, and the two are edition based and contain curated news, put shortly, digital news services are not the same, or in the same genus, as the tangible items expressly included within Item 2. It is an intrinsic part of the statutory definition of Item 2 that the items within it are tangible or physical articles. The digital news services are intangible and different in kind and in the dimension of their complexity for determining issues like the place of supply. Although not directly relevant, I note as part of the context that these differences have justified distinct and different treatment in EU law.' *News Corp UK & Ireland Ltd v Revenue and Customs Commissioners* [2021] EWCA Civ 91, [2021] 2 All ER 1276 at [1], [67]–[68], [72], per Simler LJ

NEXT

Australia [Migration Act 1958 (Cth), s 494AA(4): ineligibility period means the period from the time of the offshore entry until the time when the person next ceases to be an unlawful non-citizen.] '[95] The function of the word "next" in the definition of "ineligibility period" appears curious, until it is recalled that an individual may move in and out of the status of an unlawful non-citizen, depending on whether an individual holds a visa or not. The function of the word "next" is, in my opinion, to indicate that the period which is defined as the "ineligibility period" runs from the time a person enters Australia until that person is granted a visa *for the first time* after the unauthorised entry. The word "next" relates back to the time of unauthorised entry and is used to signify the end point of the ineligibility period. That is, it is not a recurring period of time, it is a fixed period of time which will expire when an individual is first granted a visa after her or his unauthorised entry.

'[96] Therefore, hypothetically, if an individual who is an unauthorised maritime arrival is granted a visa, this visa is then cancelled, and the person becomes an unlawful non-citizen again, the "ineligibility period" will not apply to that person again. That period has expired for that particular individual. Indeed, consistently with my observation above, it may be that it is also no longer correct to assign to such a person the status of an unauthorised maritime arrival.' *DBE17 (by his litigation guardian Arthur) v Commonwealth* [2018] FCA 1307, (2018) 361 ALR 423 at [95]–[96], per Mortimer J

NEXT OF KIN

[For 102 Halsbury's Laws of England (5th Edn) (2010) paras 344–345 see now 102 Halsbury's Laws of England (5th Edn) (2021) paras 345–346.]

NON-BINARY

'[5] "Non-binary" people are those who identify their gender outside the male-female binary. Either included within or sitting alongside this category (which may be a matter of legitimate differences of opinion) are "non-gendered" people who, like the Appellant, identify as having no gender or describe their gender as neutral.' *R (on the application of Elan-Cane) v Secretary of State for the Home Department (Human Rights Watch intervening)* [2020] EWCA Civ 363, [2021] 1 All ER 25 at [5], per King LJ

NON EST FACTUM

[For 32 Halsbury's Laws of England (5th Edn) (2012) para 269 see now 32 Halsbury's Laws of England (5th Edn) (2019) para 269.]

NON-NEG

'[58] … The respondent at its casinos provides to selected customers "Non-Negs", that is, non-negotiable vouchers for gaming conferring the right to place free bets in order to induce those customers to visit its casinos and engage in gaming. The vouchers can only be used for that purpose and they are non-negotiable in that they cannot be exchanged for cash or used to pay for goods or services such as food and drink, but, if the customer using Non-Negs wins, he receives redeemable cash chips and is given back his Non-Negs. Non-Negs are not subject to any restriction on transfer. They bear a face value amount which is the amount for which they can be wagered.' *London Clubs Management Ltd v Revenue and Customs Commissioners)* [2020] UKSC 49, [2021] 2 All ER 333 at [58], per Lady Arden JSC

NOTARY (PUBLIC)

[For 66 Halsbury's Laws of England (5th Edn) (2015) para 992 see now 66 Halsbury's Laws of England (5th Edn) (2020) para 942.]

NOTICE

Of intended prosecution

[For 90 Halsbury's Laws of England (5th Edn) (2011) para 785 see now 90A Halsbury's Laws of England (5th Edn) (2022) para 783.]

NOTORIETY

[For 22 Halsbury's Laws of England (5th Edn) (2012) para 598 see now 22 Halsbury's Laws of England (5th Edn) (2019) para 389; and for 95 Halsbury's Laws of England (5th Edn) (2017) para 588 see now 95 Halsbury's Laws of England (5th Edn) (2023) para 788.]

NOVATION

[For 22 Halsbury's Laws of England (5th Edn) (2012) para 598 see now 22 Halsbury's Laws of England (5th Edn) (2019) para 389.]

NUISANCE

To highway

[For 55 Halsbury's Laws of England (5th Edn) (2012) para 325 see now 55 Halsbury's Laws of England (5th Edn) (2019) para 354.]

NULLITY

[For 72 Halsbury's Laws of England (5th Edn) (2015) paras 375–376 see now 72 Halsbury's Laws of England (5th Edn) (2019) paras 373–374.]

NUPTIAL AGREEMENT

[For 22 Halsbury's Laws of England (5th Edn) (2012) para 441 see now 22 Halsbury's Laws of England (5th Edn) (2019) para 232.]

NURSERY GROUNDS

[For 1 Halsbury's Laws of England (5th Edn) (2017) para 324 see now 1 Halsbury's Laws of England (5th Edn) (2022) para 324; and for 1A Halsbury's Laws of England (5th Edn) (2017) para 10 see now 1A Halsbury's Laws of England (5th Edn) (2023) para 32.]

O

OATH

[For 12 Halsbury's Laws of England (5th Edn) (2015) paras 824, 826–827 see now 12 Halsbury's Laws of England (5th Edn) (2020) paras 816, 818–819.]

OBJECT RESTRICTION

[Treaty on the Functioning of the European Union, art 101; s 2(1) Competition Act 1998, s 2(1): prohibition on restriction of competition 'by object'.] '[91] On this point, I consider that there is now a body of case law and decisional practice that shows that, for the purposes of art 101, the imposition by a supplier of a prohibition on internet sales by authorised dealers in a selective distribution network does, at this first stage of the analysis, reveal a sufficient degree of harm to competition and is a restriction by object.

…

'[97] The case law I have cited establishes that one must examine the economic and legal context of the operation of the clause before deciding whether it is an object restriction or not. …

…

'[107] The CAT [Competition Appeal Tribunal] was right to conclude that there was nothing in the economic or legal context in which the ISP [Internet Sales Policy] operated that negated the conclusion that the ISP revealed a sufficient degree of harm to justify being regarded as an object restriction.

…

'[132] Moreover, I do not think that the growing popularity of the internet as a sales medium can be minimised. It may be that, when the CMA [Competition and Markets Authority] reached its decision, relatively few customers actually bought their golf clubs online. But the speed of the internet is increasing and we are living in an age of technological innovation. It would, I think, be inappropriate in this context for us to accept that the ISP did not reveal a sufficient degree of harm to competition to be considered a restriction of competition by object within the meaning of art 101(1) of the Treaty on the Functioning of the European Union. Applying para 47 of the CJEU's decision in *Pierre Fabre* (Case C-439/09) EU:C:2011:649, [2013] All ER (EC) 281, [2011] ECR I-9419, art 101(1) must, in my view, be interpreted as meaning that, in the context of this selective distribution system, a contractual clause requiring sales of golf clubs after a dynamic custom fitting effectively in physical premises, and banning any type of internet sales of such clubs, amounts to a restriction by object. I reach that conclusion having paid full regard to the content and objective of the ISP and the legal and economic context in which it is set. Put simply, having regard to all the properties of golf clubs, the ISP is not, as the CMA decided and the CAT held, objectively justified.' *Ping Europe Ltd v Competition and Markets Authority* [2020] EWCA Civ 13, [2020] 4 All ER 276 at [91], [97], [101], per Rose LJ and at [132], per Sir Geoffrey Vos C

OBLIGATION

[For 32 Halsbury's Laws of England (5th Edn) (2012) para 291 see now 32 Halsbury's Laws of England (5th Edn) (2019) para 291.]

OBLIGEE—OBLIGOR

[For 32 Halsbury's Laws of England (5th Edn) (2012) para 289 see now 32 Halsbury's Laws of England (5th Edn) (2019) para 289.]

OBLITERATION

[For 103 Halsbury's Laws of England (5th Edn) (2010) para 735 see now 103 Halsbury's Laws of England (5th Edn) (2021) para 738.]

OBSTRUCT

In Malicious Damage Act

[For 25 Halsbury's Laws of England (5th Edn) (2016) para 402 see now 86 Halsbury's Laws of England (5th Edn) (2023) para 372.]

OCCUPANCY

[For 80 Halsbury's Laws of England (5th Edn) (2013) para 821 see now 80 Halsbury's Laws of England (5th Edn) (2020) para 821.]

OCCUPATION (OF PROPERTY)

Australia [Native Title Act 1993 (Cth), ss 47A, 47B.] '[418] The primary judge stated that whether activity amounted to occupation is a question of fact and degree to be determined on the evidence before the Court in each case (at [270]–[272]). His Honour referred to a series of general propositions drawn from [215] of *Moses* [*Moses v Western Australia* (2007) 160 FCR 148; 241 ALR 268; [2007] FCAFC 78]:

> It is largely a matter of common sense, but is founded upon the words of ss 47A and 47B in their context and as considered in the authorities:
>
> (1) to "occupy" an area for the purposes of ss 47A and 47B of the NTA involves the exercise of some physical activity or activities in relation to the area;
> (2) to "occupy" an area does not require the performance of an activity or activities on every part of the land;
> (3) to "occupy" an area does not necessarily involve consistently or repeatedly performing the activity or activities over part of the area;
> (4) to "occupy" an area does not require constant performance of the activity or activities over parts of the area; it is possible to conclude that an area is occupied where there are spasmodic or occasional physical activities carried on over the area;
> (5) to occupy an area at a particular time does not necessarily require contemporaneous activity on that area at the particular time; it is possible to conclude that an area of land is occupied in circumstances where at the time the application is made there is no immediately contemporaneous activity being carried on in the area;
> (6) the fact of occupation does not necessarily entail a frequent physical presence in the area; for example, the storage of sacred objects on the area or the holding, from time to time, of traditional ceremonies on the area may constitute occupation for the purposes of the NTA: see, eg *Rubibi Community v Western Australia* (2001) 112 FCR 409; [2001] FCA 607 at [182];
> (7) evidence to establish occupation need not necessarily be confined to evidence of activities occurring on the particular area; it may be possible to establish that a particular area is occupied by reference to occupation of a wider area which includes the particular area: *Risk (on behalf of the Larrakia Peoples) v Northern Territory* [2006] FCA 404 at [890];
> (8) occupation need not be "traditional": Rubibi Community v Western Australia (No 7) [2006] FCA 459 at [84];
> (9) whether occupation has been made out in a particular case is always a question of fact and degree.

'[419] The primary judge said that at common law a person may be in occupation of a large expanse of land without physically exercising their rights over every part of it (at [271]). He referred to the well-known example of a person residing in a homestead as nevertheless being in occupation of an entire farm or pastoral station despite the fact that he or she may not have physically exercised their rights over every part of it.

...

'[442] The authorities make clear that the question of "occupy" in s 47B(1)(c) is distinct from the question of connection to country under s 223(1)(c): *Moses* at [210]; *Risk (on behalf of the Larrakia Peoples) v Northern Territory* [2006] FCA 404 (*Risk*) at [890]–[891]; *Rubibi (No 7)* [83]; *Sebastian* at [288]; *Narrier v Western Australia* [2016] FCA 1519 at [1223] (*Narrier (No 1)*). Although the contrary view in *Daniel* at [938] had been referred to without adverse comment in *Alyawarr* at [194], *Moses* cleared away any remaining ambiguity.

...

'[462] It is clear that "occupy" is a term of long ancestry within the common law and that it describes a particular relationship to land and that "occupy" in s 47B(1)(c) means "actual occupation" or "occupation in fact". However, contrary to FMG's position, this does not mean that it is appropriate to derive from *Wagga*

Wagga Motor Registry Claim [*Daruk; Minister Administering Crown Lands Act v New South Wales Aboriginal Land Council* (2008) 237 CLR 285; 249 ALR 602; [2008] HCA 48] and *Berrima Gaol* [*New South Wales Aboriginal Land Council v Minister Administering the Crown Lands Act* (2016) 260 CLR 232; 339 ALR 367; [2016] HCA 50] a specific standard or threshold that "requires a particular nature and degree of presence on the land" or is limited to what FMG described as "indigenous presence on the land … in a concrete real world sense, not simply in the sense of spiritual beliefs in respect of that land". Similarly, we do not see these authorities as requiring a particular type of physical presence or intensity of use before there can be a conclusion of occupation in fact. While intensity of use may be one way of establishing that one or more persons treat the land as their own, it is not the only way to establish occupation.

'[463] In our view, to derive and impose a requirement by transplanting statements and conclusions made in the context of s 36(1)(b) of the ALR Act [Aboriginal Land Rights Act 1983 (NSW)] into the different context of s 47B(1)(c) of the Native Title Act would be to commit the very error repeatedly warned against. Whereas the enquiry under the ALR Act is concerned with determining whether the State is in occupation of the land, the enquiry under the Native Title Act is concerned with determining whether one or members of the claim group occupy the relevant area over which native title would otherwise be extinguished.

'[464] The proper approach, and the one outlined in *Alyawarr* [*Northern Territory v Alyawarr, Kaytetye, Warumungu, Wakaya Native Title Claim Group* (2005) 145 FCR 442; 220 ALR 431; [2005] FCAFC 135], *Moses and Banjima* [*Tucker (on behalf of the Banjima People) v Western Australia* (2015) 231 FCR 456; 322 ALR 199; [2015] FCAFC 84]], to which we now turn, is one that is sensitive to the traditions of Aboriginal people and their unique relationship with their country. In that context, it is important that taxonomical categories of relationship, right or interest developed in an Anglo-Australian context (eg possession, use and occupation) are applied in a manner sensitive to the full complexity of the relationship between Indigenous peoples and their land. This does not mean they are devoid of content, only that the application of these concepts will necessarily be different in the context of the Native Title Act.

…

'[473] In our view, there is nothing unsound in the primary judge's analysis as a question of principle. FMG's complaints are in substance challenges to the primary judge's findings of fact. To the extent FMG submits that evidence of a spiritual, cultural or social kind can **never** be relevant to an enquiry into occupation, or contribute to a factual finding of occupation, we reject that contention.' *Fortescue Metals Group Ltd v Warrie (on behalf of the Yindjibarndi People)* [2019] FCAFC 177, (2019) 374 ALR 448 at [418]–[419], [442], [462]–[464], [473], per Robertson and Griffiths JJ

Australia '[73] Whether a person does or does not occupy or inhabit premises are not necessarily straightforward questions. "Occupation" is a word with different meanings in different contexts. In ordinary usage, a person would not be described as "occupying" a holiday property that they own but are not inhabiting. A furnished apartment rented to tourists but intermittently empty would not be described as "occupied". But, in law, "occupation" is a term of art used to mean the exercise of "physical control over land". Even then, the legal relevance of occupation, or "physical possession", has only been as an element which, combined with an intention, can establish a legal right to possession. …

…

'[75] The facts of "occupation" or "habitation" may be difficult to determine in the context of domestic or family violence, especially where one spouse or family member leaves or is ejected from or locked out of the family home. That person may be either a perpetrator or a victim of domestic or family violence who may seek to return to the family home in a multiplicity of circumstances. Cases of shared households may raise similar problems about whether or not a member or former member of the household is in occupation or habitation, and who has the right to exclude them. …' *BA v R* [2023] HCA 14, (2023) 409 ALR 41 at [73], [75], per Gordon, Edelman, Steward and Gleeson JJ

Occupier

[Communications Act 2003, Sch 3A (Electronic Communications Code), para 9: a code right in respect of land may only be conferred on an operator by an agreement between the occupier of the land and the operator.] '[100] The decisions of the Upper Tribunal and the Court of Appeal focus on the meaning of the word "occupier" in para 9 in the new Code. The issue before this Court is whether, as Mr Pymont QC argues on behalf of AP Wireless, the word "occupier" includes an operator who is presently on the site as a result of having installed and operated ECA (electronic communications apparatus) there or whether as Mr McGhee QC (appearing for Cornerstone) and Mr Seitler QC (appearing for On Tower) argue, you must ignore the presence of an operator on the site when deciding who is capable of conferring code rights for the purposes of para 9.

...

'[102] I start from the proposition that the word "occupier" when it appears in different statutory provisions has no fixed meaning but must take its content from the context in which it appears and the purpose of the provisions in which it is used.

...

'[159] The textual indicators therefore confirm my view that an operator which has ECA installed on a site is not to be regarded as the occupier of that site for the purposes of para 9 of the new Code. Thus, it can agree new code rights with the occupier of the site, identified in accordance with para 105. Such an operator can also give notice under para 20 requesting a relevant person to confer a new code right on it and may apply to the Upper Tribunal under para 20 for an order imposing an agreement conferring those rights on it.' *Cornerstone Telecommunications Infrastructure Ltd v Compton Beauchamp Estates Ltd* [2022] UKSC 18, [2022] 4 All ER 967 at [100], [102], [159], per Lady Rose JSC

OFFENCE

Motoring offence

[For 90 Halsbury's Laws of England (5th Edn) (2011) para 815 see now 90 Halsbury's Laws of England (5th Edn) (2022) para 712 et seq.]

OFFER

[For 22 Halsbury's Laws of England (5th Edn) (2012) para 234 see now 22 Halsbury's Laws of England (5th Edn) (2019) para 34.]

OFFICE (EMPLOYMENT)

Public office

[For 20 Halsbury's Laws of England (5th Edn) (2014) para 606 see now 20 Halsbury's Laws of England (5th Edn) (2023) para 519.]

OFFICIAL RECEIVER

[For 5 Halsbury's Laws of England (5th Edn) (2013) para 35 see now 5 Halsbury's Laws of England (5th Edn) (2020) para 34.]

OFFSPRING

[For 102 Halsbury's Laws of England (5th Edn) (2010) para 336 see now 102 Halsbury's Laws of England (5th Edn) (2021) para 337.]

ON THE FAITH OF

New Zealand [Securities Act 1978, s 56(1).] '[93] The liability imposed on issuers, directors and promoters under s 56(1) is a liability to compensate investors who invested "on the faith of [the prospectus]" for any loss or damage they may have sustained "by reason of such untrue statement". The positions of the parties as to the interpretation of s 56(1) were starkly contrasting. Mr Houghton's position was that all he needed to prove was that there had been an untrue statement in the prospectus, upon which he would be entitled to compensation equal to the total amount of his investment. On this view, no element of materiality is required. The respondents argued in the High Court that an investor had to prove they had read the untrue statement in the prospectus and had relied on it explicitly, in the same way as for a claim for negligent misstatement. They argued that, if the investor could prove such reliance, their loss would be the difference between the price they paid for their Feltex shares and the fair value of the shares had accurate disclosure been made.

...

'[121] The phrase "on the faith of" has a long statutory pedigree, beginning with the Directors Liability Act 1890 (UK). In New Zealand, it has appeared in provisions relating to prospectuses since 1891. In all instances, it has been used in the context of a provision referring to a prospectus that constitutes the offer document for the securities being offered for subscription and the subscription is made on the terms of the prospectus. In that context, the phrase can be seen as broadly synonymous with "in reliance on", as the Court of Appeal noted.

'[122] There are also other statutory references to "on the faith of" in different contexts that indicate it is intended to be broadly synonymous with "in reliance on".

...

'[127] We consider that "on the faith of" means in reliance on the truth of the publicly registered document, which informs the market, but does not require that investors have seen or read the prospectus. Investors rely on the accuracy of the prospectus in the sense that they assume it contains no untrue statements and that the advice they receive or the market commentary they observe is founded on accurate and complete disclosure of the information included in the prospectus. So, to adapt the approach taken by Lord Halsbury in *Arnison v Smith* [(1889) 41 ChD 365] to which the Court of Appeal referred to when discussing the present statutory context, it can be inferred that if a prospectus contained a misleading statement, the investor who subscribed for shares invested on the faith of the prospectus assuming the statement was true. This inference would be displaced if the investor knew the truth and invested anyway. We leave open whether there may be other circumstances where the inference may be displaced.

'[128] We recognise that this means that the "on the faith of" aspect of s 56(1) will not be difficult for an investor to satisfy in the event that a prospectus contains an untrue statement. We see that as consistent with the investor protection objective of the Securities Act. …' *Houghton v Saunders* [2018] NZSC 74, [2019] 1 NZLR 1 at [93], [121]–[122], [127]–[128], per Elias CJ, Glazebrook, O'Regan, Arnold and Kós JJ

ONE VOICE

'[93] A statement by HMG [Her Majesty's Government] that it recognises a state, ruler or government is conclusive. This is the "one voice" principle, which takes its name from (but was already well established by the time of) Lord Atkin's observation in *The Arantzazu Mendi* [[1939] 1 All ER 719] that:

> "Our state cannot speak with two voices on such a matter, the judiciary saying one thing, the executive another."

'[94] Equally, a statement by HMG that it does not recognise a state, ruler or government is conclusive. …' *'Maduro Board' of the Central Bank of Venezuela v 'Guaidó Board' of the Central Bank of Venezuela; Banco Central de Venezuela v Governor and Co of the Bank of England; Deutsche Bank AG, London Branch v Central Bank of Venezuela* [2020] EWCA Civ 1249, [2021] 1 All ER 719 at [93]–[94], per Males LJ

ONLINE SPACE

Canada

'43 While sustained by a vast physical infrastructure, the Internet, at least as most users experience it, is first and foremost a network of information and a means of connecting with others. That information is stored on servers but is accessible from an increasing array of devices in many physical locations. To say that individuals gather in online "spaces" means only that people have accessed shared information, wherever they happen to be geographically – which, today, may be from nearly anywhere.

'44 Freed of geographical constraints, online spaces permit unique experiences. They are permeable, allowing users to seamlessly traverse from one space to another. They are often interactive, facilitating that movement and encouraging users to express themselves and engage with content. They can also be coded to enable varying levels of supervision, regulation or control. The Internet can be manipulated in ways that physical spaces cannot.

'45 And its information comes in all types. Functionally, the Internet encompasses the most public and the most private human behaviour. It is the largest megaphone or billboard ever conceived, allowing publishers to connect with audiences far vaster than could ever physically congregate. Yet many millions also conduct private activities online, confident that their information – whether touching their work, social or personal lives – will remain as secure from general circulation as if they had transacted in person.

…

'49 Online spaces, in short, differ from physical spaces in at least three ways: the Internet, being informational rather than geographical, sheds many of the physical world's limitations in terms of scale and functions; people behave differently when online; and virtual spaces raise unique rights concerns. As *Ahmad* [*R v Ahmad* 2020 SCC 11] stated, online spaces are *qualitatively* different.' *R v Ramelson* [2022] SCJ No 44, 2022 SCC 44 at paras 43–45, 49, per Karakatsanis J

ONLY IF

[Town and Country Planning Act 1990, s 61N: legal challenges in relation to neighbourhood development orders allowed 'only if' certain critwria are met.] '[48] The express recognition in s 61N that there may be public law challenges to acts or omissions during stages 5, 6 and 7 of the process does not amount to the fresh creation of those rights. The only purpose ascertainable from s 61N is to subject those particular existing rights of challenge to the twin conditions in each of the subsections, namely that they be brought by way of judicial review and commenced within a rigid, non-extendable six week time-limit. That is the plain meaning of "only if" in each subsection. Section 61N is therefore entirely restrictive, not permissive, in its effect.

'[49] In the Court of Appeal, Lindblom LJ said (para [33]) that the three subsections in s 61N "are not expressed in merely permissive terms, but both permissively and restrictively". With respect, reading the subsections against the background of the general law and in the context of the section as a whole, we do not think that is right. The words at the start of each subsection ("[a] court may entertain proceedings … only if") are not permissive in effect. Rather, they recognise that general public law means that legal proceedings are capable of being brought if there is unlawfulness at any stage and they introduce a series of limitations.' *R (on the application of Fylde Coast Farms Ltd (formerly Oyston Estates Ltd)) v Fylde Borough Council* [2021] UKSC 18, [2021] 4 All ER 381 at [48]–[49], per Lord Briggs and Lord Sales JJSC

OPENNESS

'[1] The short point in this appeal is whether the appellant county council, as local planning authority, correctly understood the meaning of the word "openness" in the national planning policies applying to mineral working in the Green Belt, as expressed in the National Planning Policy Framework ("NPPF"). …

'[22] The concept of "openness" in para 90 of the NPPF seems to me a good example of such a broad policy concept. It is naturally read as referring back to the underlying aim of Green Belt policy, stated at the beginning of this section "to prevent urban sprawl by keeping land permanently open". Openness is the counterpart of urban sprawl and is also linked to the purposes to be served by the Green Belt. As PPG2 [Planning Policy Guidance 2: Green Belts] made clear, it is not necessarily a statement about the visual qualities of the land, though in some cases this may be an aspect of the planning judgement involved in applying this broad policy concept. Nor does it imply freedom from any form of development. Paragraph 90 shows that some forms of development, including mineral extraction, may in principle be appropriate, and compatible with the concept of openness. A large quarry may not be visually attractive while it lasts, but the minerals can only be extracted where they are found, and the impact is temporary and subject to restoration. Further, as a barrier to urban sprawl a quarry may be regarded in Green Belt policy terms as no less effective than a stretch of agricultural land.' *R (on the application of Samuel Smith Old Brewery (Tadcaster)) v North Yorkshire County Council* [2020] UKSC 3, [2020] 3 All ER 527 at [1], [22], per Lord Carnwath

OPTION

[For 22 Halsbury's Laws of England (5th Edn) (2012) para 241 see now 22 Halsbury's Laws of England (5th Edn) (2019) para 41.]

ORDER IN COUNCIL

[For 96 Halsbury's Laws of England (5th Edn) (2012) para 1031 see now 96 Halsbury's Laws of England (5th Edn) (2018) para 638.]

ORDER OF COUNCIL

[For 96 Halsbury's Laws of England (5th Edn) (2012) para 1031 see now 96 Halsbury's Laws of England (5th Edn) (2018) para 638.]

ORGANISATION

[Ministry of Housing and Local Government Provisional Order Confirmation (Greater London Parks and Open Spaces) Act 1967, Sch 1, art 7(1)(a)(vi): power for local authority in any open space to provide and maintain 'centres and other facilities (whether indoor or open air) for use of clubs, societies or organisations whose objects or activities are wholly or mainly of a recreational, social or educational character'; whether this included a day nursery for pre-school children.] '[29] I am prepared to assume in Mr Giffin's favour, without deciding, that para (vi) does not impose a hard-edged requirement that the organisation be not-for-profit. Nevertheless I consider that the interested party is not the type of "club, society or organisation" with which sub-para (vi) is concerned.

'[30] It is common ground that the interested party is not a club or society. The term "organisation" in sub-para (vi) is, in my judgment, there to sweep up organisations which are not strictly or properly described as clubs or societies, but which nevertheless share their principal characteristic of being run for the benefit of members sharing a common interest. The interested party does not operate on this basis, but is a limited company providing services for clients or customers. If Wandsworth's construction were correct, it is difficult to see why the words "clubs" and "societies" were used in sub-para (vi) when the words "any organisation" would have had the effect for which they contend.' *R (on the application of Muir) v Wandsworth Borough Council (Smart Pre-Schools Ltd, interested party)* [2018] EWCA Civ 1035, [2018] 4 All ER 422 at [29]–[30], per Floyd LJ

OTHER STATUS

[European Convention for the Protection of Human Rights and Fundamental Freedoms 1950, art 14, as set out in the Human Rights Act 1998, Sch 1, Pt I, art 14: prohibition of discrimination. 'The enjoyment of the rights and freedoms set forth in this Convention shall be secured without any discrimination on any ground such as sex, race, colour, language, religion, political or other opinion, national or social origin, association with a national minority, property, birth or other status.'] '[173] It is accepted that art 14 does not create a freestanding right. To found a claim it must be associated with another Convention right (per Mostyn J in *K* [*R (K) v Secretary of State for the Home Dept* [2018] EWHC 2951 (Admin), [2019] 4 WLR 92]). But in this case I have no difficulty in holding that it is associated with the rights in art 8. The family unit is being broken up. That affects the art 8 rights of all the Claimants. I agree with Mr Buttler that this is sufficient to place the Second to Seventh Claimants in the "other status" category within art 14.' *R (on the application of Mahabir) v Secretary of State for the Home Department* [2021] EWHC 1177 (Admin), [2022] 1 All ER 895 at [173], per Tim Smith

OTHER SUITABLE PERSON

[Children Act 1989, Sch 2, para 19(4): where the court is satisfied that a child does not have sufficient understanding to give or withhold his consent to living in a country other than England and Wales, it may disregard the requirement for consent and give approval if the child is to live in the country concerned with a parent, guardian, special guardian, or 'other suitable person'.] '[40] On the first issue, (i), para 19(4) applies only if the child is "to live … with a parent, guardian, special guardian or other suitable person". As Floyd LJ observed during the hearing it is not easy to see how a child could live with a company or an unincorporated "body of persons". For example, while a child can live in a residential home which might be owned by a company it would be difficult to argue that, as a result, the child was living with a person. Further, when this is added to the fact that the words "other suitable person" follow a list comprising natural persons, I do not consider it is possible to interpret this provision as meaning other than that it is confined, as decided by Sir James Munby P, to natural persons. Whilst I recognise that there might well be a practical need, as submitted by Mr Howling, this cannot counter the factors referred to above and such a need alone would not provide a legitimate basis for the proposed statutory interpretation.

'[41] The result of this conclusion is that, when a child does not consent, and regardless of whether they do or do not have sufficient understanding, the court is not permitted to approve their placement in Scotland other than with a natural person. The consequence is that a local authority cannot "arrange for, or assist in arranging for, any child in their care", who does not consent, to live in a residential home in Scotland (or, indeed, anywhere else outside England and Wales).

'[42] Given the limited submissions we heard on the history which might lie behind this particular provision and on the broader potential ramifications, I do not propose to address Ms Irving's additional submission as to whether the term "other suitable person" might be further confined. All I would say is that a court would clearly need to establish who would have parental responsibility or, in broader terms, legal responsibility, for a child before that child could be placed outside England and Wales. …' *Re C (a child)* [2019] EWCA Civ 1714, [2020] 3 All ER 634 at [40]–[42], per Moylan LJ

OUT-OF-DATE

[2012 National Planning Policy Framework ('NPPF'), para 14 (later reflected in the 2018 NPPF, para 11d): presumption in favour of sustainable development where relevant policies were 'out-of-date'.] '[65] There is nothing in para 11d of the 2018 NPPF, or its predecessor para 14 of the 2012 Framework, to suggest that the expiry of the period of the plan automatically renders the policies in the plan out-of-date. I agree with Sir Duncan Ouseley's observations in *Paul Newman New Homes* [*Paul Newman New Homes Ltd v Secretary of State for Housing, Communities and Local Government* [2019] EWHC 2367 (Admin), [2020] 1 P & CR 212, [2020] PTSR 434] that a policy is not out-of-date simply because it is in a time-expired plan and that, if the Framework had intended to treat as out-of-date all saved but time-expired policies, it would not have used the phrase "out-of-date" but rather the language of time-expired policies or policies in a time-expired plan. As a matter of construction of the terms of the NPPF, the appellant's argument on ground one is unsustainable.

'[66] I endorse and adopt the careful and precise analysis of para 14 of the 2012 NPPF carried out by Lindblom J in *Bloor Homes* [*Bloor Homes East Midlands Ltd v Secretary of State for Communities and Local Government* [2014] EWHC 754 (Admin), [2017] PTSR 1283]. His analysis plainly applies to the revised terms of the presumption in favour of sustainable development in para 11d of the 2018 Framework. If the policies which are most important for determining the planning application have been overtaken by things that have happened since the plan was adopted, either on the ground or through a change in national policy, or for some other reason, so that they are now out-of-date, the decision-makers must apply the tilted balance expressed in the presumption in favour of sustainable development.' *Peel Investments (North) Ltd v Secretary of State for Housing, Communities and Local Government* [2020] EWCA Civ 1175, [2021] 2 All ER 581 at [65]–[66], per Baker LJ

OUTRAGE

[For 26 Halsbury's Laws of England (5th Edn) (2016) para 826 see now 25 Halsbury's Laws of England (5th Edn) (2021) para 518.]

OUTSTANDING BENEFIT

[Patents Act 1977, s 40: employee entitled to compensation where he has made an invention belonging to the employer for which a patent has been granted and the patent is (having regard among other things to the size and nature of the employer's undertaking) of outstanding benefit to the employer.] '[30] An employee who makes an invention which belongs to his employer from the outset and for which a patent has been granted is therefore entitled to compensation if he or she establishes: first, that the patent is, having regard among other things to the size and nature of the employer's undertaking, of outstanding benefit to the employer; and secondly, that, by reason of these matters, it is just that he or she be awarded compensation.

...

'[39] In my view these cases are all helpful to a point as illustrations of circumstances which were found to fall each side of the line. But at the end of the day they provide no substitute for the statutory test which requires the benefit to be outstanding. This is an ordinary English word meaning exceptional or such as to stand out and it refers here to the benefit (in terms of money or money's worth) of the patent to the employer rather than the degree of inventiveness of the employee. It is, however, both a relative and qualitative term and so I must now consider the context in which the question is to be asked and answered. Put another way, in relation to what must the benefit from the patent be outstanding? Which factors may be taken into account in making that assessment?

'[40] Here the 1977 Act provides some guidance. It says that the court must have regard among other things to the size and nature of the employer's undertaking. But this gives rise to two further questions which were the subject of a good deal of argument before us. What is the employer's undertaking for this purpose? And what is the relevance of that undertaking's size and nature?

...

'[52] In some cases it may be possible to see that a patent has been of outstanding benefit to an employer by looking at the size and profitability of the whole business. In the *Kelly* case [*Kelly v GE Healthcare Ltd* [2009] EWHC 181 (Pat), [2009] IP & T 927, [2009] RPC 363] ..., for example, the benefits of patent protection went far beyond anything which one would normally expect to arise from the sort of work the employees were doing. The patents protected Amersham's business from generic competition and allowed it to make major deals; and sales of the patented product accounted for a large proportion of its profits. In short, the patents transformed its business. Similarly, as Patten LJ explained at para [28], a straightforward comparison of profitability may be sufficient, in the case of a smaller company, to show an outstanding benefit without recourse to wider considerations of the scope of an employee's duties or the expectations the employer may have had about the anticipated level of return.

'[53] I also recognise that a large undertaking may be able to exert greater leverage than a smaller undertaking when negotiating licence fees. This was a matter to which the hearing officer referred in para [207] of his judgment. There he explained and I agree that a particular sum might represent an excellent return for a small undertaking but might not be so regarded by a large undertaking which was in a position to spend substantial sums on litigation to enforce its rights. Much the same might apply to sales of a patented product. A large undertaking might be able to harness its goodwill and sales force in a way that a smaller undertaking could not do. These would be appropriate matters to take into account.

'[54] On the other hand, I think a tribunal should be very cautious before accepting a submission that a patent has not been of outstanding benefit to an employer simply because it has had no significant impact on its overall profitability or the value of all of its sales. Those profits and sales may have been generated by a range of different products which have nothing to do with the technology the subject of the patent; the parts of the business responsible for them may not have contributed to any commercial success of the patented invention; and they may be a very poor guide to whether the benefit the employer has derived from the patent is out of the ordinary. Indeed, I find it very hard to see how a failure materially to affect the aggregated sales value or overall profitability of the business could, in and of itself, justify a finding that the benefit of a patent has not been outstanding.' *Shanks v Unilever plc* [2019] UKSC 45, [2020] 2 All ER 733 at [30], [39]–[40], [52]–[54], per Lord Kitchin

OVERLOOKING

[Whether 'overlooking' from a public gallery could amount to nuisance.] '[90] It is important to be clear about what "overlooking" means. In ordinary speech the word refers to a spatial relationship between two places such that one affords a view, from a greater height, of the other – as in a statement such as "your flat overlooks my back garden". I agree with the Court of Appeal that the fact that a building or other structure erected on someone's land overlooks neighbouring land cannot give rise to liability in nuisance. …

'[91] As well as using the word "overlooking" in its ordinary sense, the Court of Appeal in their judgment also use the term to mean looking at what is happening on land from a building which overlooks it. In this (I think unconventional) sense, the word "overlooking" refers to an action done by a person rather than a spatial relationship between two places. For example, the Court of Appeal's judgment refers (at para [51]) to "a deliberate act of overlooking" and (at para [53]) to "overlooking by a neighbour". If I say that I am overlooked by my neighbour, I would normally be understood to mean that my property is capable of being seen from my neighbour's property – not that my neighbour is engaged in an act of looking at me. Adopting the Court of Appeal's unconventional meaning of the term, however, I think that they are again right that in the ordinary course merely looking at what is happening on neighbouring land is not an actionable nuisance. It is hard to see how such an "act of overlooking" could by itself reasonably be regarded as anything more than a minor annoyance of a kind that neighbouring occupiers have to put up with under the rule of give and take, live and let live.' *Fearn v Board of Trustees of the Tate Gallery* [2023] UKSC 4, [2023] 2 All ER 1 at [90]–[91], per Lord Leggatt JSC

OVERRIDING INTEREST

[For 87 Halsbury's Laws of England (5th Edn) (2017) para 386 see now 87 Halsbury's Laws of England (5th Edn) (2022) para 384.]

OWNER

[For 80 Halsbury's Laws of England (5th Edn) (2013) paras 812–813 see now 80 Halsbury's Laws of England (5th Edn) (2020) paras 812–813.]

P

PARENT

Australia

[Australian Citizenship Act 2007 (Cth), s 12.] '[6] At the hearing of the appeal, the Court had requested the parties deal with some matters it considered arose on the appeal as a result of the Full Court's decision in *H v Minister for Immigration and Citizenship* (2010) 188 FCR 393; 272 ALR 605; 117 ALD 293; [2010] FCAFC 119 (*H*). Senior counsel for the Minister informed the Court that the Minister accepted the word "parent" in s 12 of the Act was to be construed in the same way as the Full Court construed the word in s 16 of the Act in *H*.

'[7] In other words, quoting from *H* at [128] and [129]:

> The word "parent" is an everyday word in the English language, expressive both of status and relationship to another. …
>
> Being a parent within the ordinary meaning of the word may depend on various factors, including social, legal and biological.

'[8] That concession was properly made. Just as the Full Court held in relation to s 16 of the Act, there is no justification for construing s 12 of the Act as meaning that "a person can only be a 'parent' within the meaning of [s 12] where it can be established that he or she has a relevant genetic link to the applicant": *H* at [131].' *Minister for Immigration, Citizenship and Multicultural Affairs v Lieu, by her Litigation Representative Nguyen* [2023] FCAFC 57, (2023) 409 ALR 719 at [6] [8], per Mortimer CJ

PARENTAL RESPONSIBILITY

[Children Act 1989, s 3.] '[9] In *Re AC* [*Re AC (A Child: Parental Responsibility)* [2020] EWFC 90, [2021] 1 FLR 1297] I said as follows:

> '[17] Section 3 of the CA 1989 provides as follows (omitting sub-paras (4) and (5) which are of no relevance to this application):
>
> (1) In this Act "parental responsibility" means all the rights, duties, powers, responsibilities and authority which by law a parent of a child has in relation to the child and his property.
> (2) It also includes the rights, powers and duties which a guardian of the child's estate (appointed, before the commencement of section 5, to act generally) would have had in relation to the child and his property.
> (3) The rights referred to in subsection (2) include, in particular, the right of the guardian to receive or recover in his own name, for the benefit of the child, property of whatever description and wherever situated which the child is entitled to receive or recover.
>
> [18] Sub paragraph (1) is very widely drafted. I do not read into it any restriction to its applicability. It is all encompassing and should be construed purposively. Of particular note in this case is the emphasis on responsibilities as well as rights. Thus, M has a clear responsibility under (1) to act in AC's interests in relation to property to which he is entitled. By (2) and (3) M has not only rights and powers, but also duties to take steps to receive or recover property for the benefit of the child. The wording of (2) and (3) plainly embraces the Property in this case, being a house in Italy in which AC has an entitlement. And in my judgment a purposive reading of subss (1)–(3) also includes the responsibility and duty of the person with responsibility to take steps which enable the child to receive or recover property in the child's own name, and not merely enabling the person with pa-rental responsibility to receive or recover property in his or her own name for the benefit of the child. The former is apt for a situation like the one

before me, the latter might be apt where the child has a beneficial interest in property by virtue of trust or otherwise as understood at English law.

...

'[10] Applying the same reasoning, I am satisfied that it is appropriate to authorise the applicant to accept succession to the French estate on B's behalf, and I therefore accede to the first limb of the application.

...

'[12] In this case, the second limb arises directly as the applicant specifically seeks authorisation to enter into a contract for sale of the French property. Counsel for the applicant submits that I am entitled to, and should, so authorise. I acknowledge that I have received no submissions to the contrary, albeit I have previously noted the differing view of Master Matthews (as he then was) in *Hays v Hays* [2015] EWHC 3825 (Ch). Having now considered this aspect in fuller detail, and received very helpful and able written and oral submissions, I am satisfied that I do indeed have the power to authorise the applicant to enter into a contract for sale ....' *Re B (a child)* [2022] EWFC 7, [2022] 3 All ER 1036 at [9]–[10], [12], per Peel J

PARLIAMENTARY PRIVILEGE

Canada '19. Parliamentary privilege is defined as "the sum of the privileges, immunities and powers enjoyed by the Senate, the House of Commons and provincial legislative assemblies, and by each member individually, without which they could not discharge their functions" (*Vaid* [*Canada (House of Commons) v Vaid* 2005 SCC 30, [2005] 1 SCR 667], at para 29(2)). These privileges, immunities, and powers exceed those afforded to the general population (*Erskine May's Treatise on The Law, Privileges, Proceedings and Usage of Parliament* (24th ed 2011), by M Jack, at p 203). Therefore, parliamentary privilege "is an exemption from some duty, burden, attendance or liability to which others are subject" (Maingot [Maingot, J P Joseph: *Parliamentary Immunity in Canada*, Toronto: LexisNexis, 2016], at p 13). Decisions falling within the scope of parliamentary privilege cannot be reviewed by an external body, including a court (*Stockdale v Hansard* (1839) 9 Ad & E 1, 112 ER 1112 (QB), at p 1168; *New Brunswick Broadcasting* [*New Brunswick Broadcasting Co v Nova Scotia (Speaker of the House of Assembly)* [1993] 1 SCR 319], at pp 350 and 382–384; *Vaid*, at para 29(9)).' *Chagnon v Syndicat de la fonction publique et parapublique du Québec* [2018] 2 SCR 687, [2018] SCJ No 39, at para 19, per Karakatsanis J

PARTICULAR

Canada [Tobacco Damages and Health Care Costs Recovery Act, SBC 2000, c 30, s 2(5).] '2. ... This appeal requires the Court to interpret one of those procedural provisions—specifically, s 2(5)(b), which governs the compellability of health care documents where the Province has sued to recover the cost of health care benefits "on an aggregate basis" (that is, for a population of insured persons, as opposed to for particular individual insured persons). Section 2(5)(b) provides, generally, that "the health care records and documents of particular individual insured persons or the documents relating to the provision of health care benefits for particular individual insured persons are not compellable".

...

'31. The ordinary meaning of the word "particular" is *distinct* or *specific*. This is consistent with the *Oxford English Dictionary* (online) which defines "particular" as meaning "one among a number ... single; distinct, individual, specific" (emphasis added). This definition supports the view that the databases—even once anonymized—fall within s 2(5)(b)'s scope as comprising the "health care records and documents of", and the "documents relating to the provision of health care benefits for", each *distinct* and *specific* individual in British Columbia.

...

'36. It follows from the foregoing that I agree with the Province that the databases constitute "health care records and documents of particular individual insured persons or ... documents relating to the provision of health care benefits for particular individual insured persons". As such, by operation of s 2(5)(b) the databases are not compellable. To be clear, the databases will be compellable once "relied on by an expert witness": s 2(5)(b). A "statistically meaningful sample" of the databases, once anonymized, may also be compelled on a successful application under ss 2(5)(d) and 2(5)(e).' *British Columbia v Philip Morris International Inc* [2018] SCJ No 36, [2018] 2 SCR 595 at paras 2, 31, 36, per Brown J

PARTITION

[For 87 Halsbury's Laws of England (5th Edn) (2017) para 222 see now 87 Halsbury's Laws of England (5th Edn) (2022) para 222.]

PARTNERSHIP

[For 79 Halsbury's Laws of England (5th Edn) (2014) para 4 see now 79 Halsbury's Laws of England (5th Edn) (2020) para 4.]

PARTY-WALL

[For 4 Halsbury's Laws of England (5th Edn) (2011) para 365 see now 4 Halsbury's Laws of England (5th Edn) (2020) para 364.]

PATENT

[For 79 Halsbury's Laws of England (5th Edn) (2014) para 303 see now 79 Halsbury's Laws of England (5th Edn) (2020) para 304.]

PATENT BARGAIN

'[2] The starting point is the "patent bargain" which promotes innovation and justifies the monopoly which a patent gives an inventor. The patent bargain is this: an inventor receives the reward of a time-limited monopoly of the industrial use of its invention in return for disclosing the invention and dedicating it to the public for use after the monopoly has expired. See for example *Actavis Group PTC EHF v ICOS Corp* [2019] UKSC 15, [2020] 1 All ER 213, [2019] Bus LR 1318 (at [53]). The patents conferring such monopoly rights are national in scope and are usually conferred by national governments. Legal questions as to their validity and their infringement are determined by the national courts of the state which has conferred the patent right or, in the case of a European patent, in a designated state. An inventor has to protect its invention by applying for patents to the national authorities of each of those states in which it seeks to obtain a monopoly (unless it obtains a patent from the European Patent Office under the European Patent Convention which creates a nationally enforceable patent within each designated state). It is not unusual for a national patent for an invention to be upheld by the courts of one state and another national patent for what in substance is the same invention to be invalidated by the courts of another state. Within Europe, the same European patent can on occasion be upheld by the courts in one signatory state but be invalidated in another. Much may depend on the differing evidence led and arguments advanced in national legal proceedings.' *Unwired Planet International Ltd v Huawei Technologies (UK) Co Ltd; Conversant Wireless Licensing SÀRL v Huawei Technologies Co Ltd; Conversant Wireless Licensing SÀRL v ZTE Corp* [2020] UKSC 37, [2021] 1 All ER 1141 at [2], per Lord Reed P, Lord Hodge DP, Lady Black, Lord Briggs and Lord Sales JJSC

PAWN

[For 4 Halsbury's Laws of England (5th Edn) (2011) paras 189–190 see now 4 Halsbury's Laws of England (5th Edn) (2020) paras 188–189.]

PAWNBROKER

[For 4 Halsbury's Laws of England (5th Edn) (2011) para 189 see now 4 Halsbury's Laws of England (5th Edn) (2020) para 188.]

PAYMENT

[Finance Act 2004, s 160: unauthorised payments made from registered pension scheme.]

'[36] Mr Clark's first ground of appeal states the issue with commendable brevity. It alleges that:

> "The UT erred in law in concluding that a transfer of funds or assets which did not transfer the beneficial title to those funds or assets, and in particular the Suffolk Life Transfer, was a '*payment*' for the purposes of s. 160(2) FA 2004."

It is convenient to adopt the expression "the Suffolk Life Transfer" to refer to the initial transfer of the £2.115m made from the Suffolk Life SIPP to the LML Pension on 21 April 2009.

'[37] Unknown to the parties at the time, the Suffolk Life Transfer gave rise to a resulting trust in favour of the Suffolk Life SIPP because the trusts of the LML Pension were void for uncertainty. The LML Pension had been registered by HMRC on 2 March 2009, and a registration certificate had been issued on that date: see the First FTT Decision at [29]. Accordingly, the transfer, viewed in isolation, was intended to be a straightforward transfer from one registered pension scheme to another, and (as such) a "recognised transfer" within s 169(1) of the 2004 Act, and therefore an authorised member payment within s 164(1)(c). It is agreed, however, that the effect of the failure of the trusts of the LML Pension is that the transfer conveyed only bare legal title to the money, because an immediate resulting trust arose by operation of law.

…

'[39] As a preliminary comment, I have to say that in such a context it strikes me as deeply unrealistic to approach the question whether the Suffolk Life Transfer was a "payment" for the purposes of s 160(2) on the basis that the failure of the trusts of the LML Pension should, without more, prevent the subsection from applying. As a matter of practical reality, the money left the Suffolk Life SIPP and was credited by means of a CHAPS transfer to an LML Pension bank account with National Westminster Bank in Bristol: see the First FTT Decision at [31]. The money therefore passed from the direct control of Suffolk Life, and as we have seen it was then used to implement (with some variations) the subsequent stages of the scheme devised for Mr Clark by Aston Court. Meanwhile, the Suffolk Life SIPP must have been closed, because there were no longer any assets in Mr Clark's account. There is no express finding to this effect, but it is the natural inference to draw from the documents in the bundle relating to the Suffolk Life Transfer, including in particular a summary of the plan details supplied by Suffolk Life to Aston Court IOM on 22 April 2009 which concluded with a signed declaration "that the transfer value represents the whole of the applicant's accrued rights to benefits under the transferring scheme/arrangements".

'[40] In those circumstances, the natural reaction of anybody to the question whether there had been a payment of the £2.115m by Suffolk Life to the LML Pension would surely be that of course there had. The money was intended to pass from the control and supervision of one registered pension scheme to another, the Suffolk Life SIPP was thereby left apparently defunct, and legal title (at least) to the money had passed from Suffolk Life to the LML Pension. From a practical and commonsense perspective, why should it make any difference to this analysis if it later transpired that, unknown to everybody at the time, the transfer was in fact defective and gave rise to a resulting trust? In the context of the carefully designed scheme of the 2004 Act, one would not expect the meaning of an everyday word like "payment" to depend on legal niceties of that kind.

…

'[53] For these reasons, I conclude that the linguistic indications relied on by Mr Jones carry little, if any, weight. Nor do I accept his submission that there are no indicators the other way which support HMRC's construction. On the contrary, the legislative scheme as a whole seems to me to point strongly towards the conclusion that the Suffolk Life Transfer was indeed an unauthorised member payment within the meaning of s 160(2). …

…

'[64] … The "reality" of the payment is, I agree, an important aspect of the statutory purpose, but I would not for my part contrast it with "a fiction". The question is, rather, what kind of reality a transfer of money or other assets must possess in order to qualify as a "payment" within the meaning of s 160(2). As I have already indicated, I think that, in the context of unauthorised member payments, it is the practical or business reality of the transaction which counts, rather than a legal analysis of whether beneficial title passed to the recipient.

…

'[82] … In my view, the clear purpose of Pt 4 of FA 2004 is to impose a charge to tax at a high rate (40% or 55%, depending on the amount of the fund used up) in respect of unauthorised payments as defined, whether the payment in question is an unauthorised member payment or an unauthorised employer payment, and whether or not a breach of the scheme rules or a breach of trust is involved. In most cases, there probably will be such a breach, but that is not an essential feature of the charge. Rather, it is the responsibility of scheme trustees and administrators, as well as of scheme members and sponsoring employers, to ensure that payments which are made out of the fund to or in respect of members or employers fall within one of the authorised categories. If they do, no tax will be chargeable, but if they do not, tax will be chargeable under ss 207 to 209. The question whether a "payment" is made for these purposes should be answered by looking at the practical, business reality of the transaction, including any composite transaction of which the payment forms part. If the intended purpose and effect of the transactions is that money leaves the scheme and is placed at the free disposal of the member, the mere fact that the money may be subject to an equitable obligation to restore it to the scheme will not prevent it from being a "payment" in the ordinary sense of that word. To conclude otherwise would deprive the charge to tax of effect in many of the most egregious cases where it is most needed.' *Clark v Revenue and Customs Commissioners* [2020] EWCA Civ 204, [2020] 4 All ER 652 at [36]–[37], [39]–[40], [53], [64], [82], per Henderson LJ

PEDIGREE

[For 12 Halsbury's Laws of England (5th Edn) (2015) para 882 see now 12 Halsbury's Laws of England (5th Edn) (2020) para 873.]

PEDLAR

[For 71 Halsbury's Laws of England (5th Edn) (2013) para 907 et seq see now 71 Halsbury's Laws of England (5th Edn) (2020) para 809 et seq.]

PEERAGE

[For 79 Halsbury's Laws of England (5th Edn) (2014) paras 803–806 see now 79 Halsbury's Laws of England (5th Edn) (2020) paras 803–806.]

PENALTY

New Zealand '[51] With the assistance of the foregoing, I consider that the following factors are relevant to whether a measure may qualify as a penalty:

(a) The measure is imposed following a conviction.
(b) The measure forms part of an arsenal of sanctions imposed in furtherance of sentencing purposes and principles and/or has a significant impact on the liberty of the person.
(c) The measure forms part of an arsenal of sanctions imposed in furtherance of sentencing purposes and principles and/or has a significant impact on the liberty of the person.
(d) The process used to impose the measure is a criminal process.
(e) The measure is given effect to in a prison or a prison-like institution or may result in imprisonment.
(f) The measure is non-therapeutic or not implemented in a therapeutic way.
(g) The severity of the conditions of the measure.

…

'[160] I answer the questions as follows:

(c) Is an ESO [extended supervision order] a penalty?
For present purposes, there are two types of ESO, a retrospective ESO and a prospective ESO. A retrospective ESO is an ESO imposed on an offender who committed their qualifying offending before the ESO regime came into force in respect of that offending. A prospective ESO is an ESO imposed on an offender who committed their qualifying offending after the ESO regime came into force in respect of that offending. Both types of ESO are penalties….
(e) Is a PPO [public protection order] a penalty?
No, but elements of the PPO regime appear to be punitive, and a PPO may be imposed with punitive effect. …'

[The ESO regime is set out in the Parole Act 2002 at ss 107A–107Z. The PPO regime is set out in the Public Safety (Public Protection Orders) Act 2014.] *Chief Executive of the Department of Corrections v Chisnall* [2019] NZHC 3126, [2020] 2 NZLR 110 at [51], [160], per Whata J

PER STIRPES

[For 50 Halsbury's Laws of England (4th Edn) (2005 reissue) para 682 see now 102 Halsbury's Laws of England (5th Edn) (2021) para 398.]

PERAMBULATION

[For 32 Halsbury's Laws of England (5th Edn) (2012) para 40 see now 32 Halsbury's Laws of England (5th Edn) (2019) para 40.]

PERIOD OF OWNERSHIP

[Taxation of Chargeable Gains Act 1992, ss 222, 223.] '[13] The FTT [First-tier Tribunal]

concluded that principal private residence relief relieved Mr Higgins from any liability to CGT on his sale of the Apartment. In the FTT's view (see para [6](10) of its decision):

> "The period of ownership for the purpose of ss 222 and 223 began when Mr Higgins owned the legal and equitable interest in the lease of the Apartment and owned the legal right to occupy the Apartment. That was the date of legal completion of the purchase of the lease on 5 January 2010. The period of ownership ended on 5 January 2012 when the contract for sale (entered into on 15 December 2011) was completed."

…

'[15] The central question on this appeal is as to the meaning of the words "period of ownership" in s 223 of the TCGA. If in Mr Higgins' case that period did not begin until 5 January 2010, then the Apartment was his main residence "throughout the period of ownership" and no CGT can be payable. If, on the other hand, Mr Higgins' "period of ownership" began when contracts for the purchase were exchanged, s 223(2) will be in point and he will enjoy relief from CGT as to only part of the gain he made on the Apartment.

…

'[21] HMRC's case also, as it seems to me, runs counter to the ordinary meaning of the words 'period of ownership'. The expression would not naturally, I think, be taken to extend to the interval between contract and completion. A purchaser would, as a matter of ordinary language, be described as 'owner' only once the purchase had been completed. … The mere fact that someone has contracted to buy a property will not give him "ownership" such as could allow him to possess, occupy or even use the property, let alone to make it his "only or main residence".

'[22] It would anyway be hard to see how Mr Higgins' "period of ownership" of the Apartment could have begun before late 2009. When contracts were exchanged in 2006, the Apartment was just a "space in the tower". The present case is thus distinguishable from one in which someone contracts to buy a plot of land on which a house is to be built. The plot of land will, of course, already exist. In contrast, the Apartment did not come into existence until November/December 2009.

…

'[29] In all the circumstances, I agree with Miss Shaw QC that the FTT was right about how the legislation should be interpreted and, hence, that Mr Higgins' "period of ownership" of the Apartment for the purpose of s 223 of the TCGA did not begin until his purchase was completed.' *Higgins v Revenue and Customs Commissioners* [2019] EWCA Civ 1860, [2020] 2 All ER 451 at [13], [15], [21]–[22], [29], per Newey LJ

PERILS OF THE SEAS

[For 60 Halsbury's Laws of England (5th Edn) (2011) para 323 see now 60 Halsbury's Laws of England (5th Edn) (2018) para 302.]

[For 7 Halsbury's Laws of England (5th Edn) (2015) para 272 see now 7 Halsbury's Laws of England (5th Edn) (2020) para 315.]

PERJURY

[For 26 Halsbury's Laws of England (5th Edn) (2016) para 778 et seq see now 26 Halsbury's Laws of England (5th Edn) (2020) para 974 et seq.]

PERMANENT

[Employment contract containing term that retained pay would remain a 'permanent' feature of an individual's contractual eligibility subject to principles including that it could only be changed by mutual consent and that on promotion it would cease.] '[19] On the argument about the proper construction of the express term as to Retained Pay, the judge said: …

> "[39] In the *Oxford English Dictionary*, the word 'permanent' is defined to mean '*continuing or designed to continue or last indefinitely without change; abiding, enduring, lasting; persistent. Opposed to temporary*.' It is a word in common usage. In the contracts with which I am concerned, its use in relation to Retained Pay might, devoid of context, be considered to confer an entitlement which is permanent for as long as the particular contract endures, other than in specified circumstances with which I am not concerned. So construed, it would not be in conflict with the Defendant's express unfettered right to terminate the contract on notice. …"

…

'[32] Before considering the effect of the pre-contractual documents the starting point should be to consider on ordinary principles of construction what the contract itself means. The important phrases in the collective agreement are that Retained Pay "will remain a permanent feature of an individual's contractual eligibility"; that it "can only be changed by mutual consent"; and that on "promotion to a new role" it will cease. This wording seems to me at least consistent with that contained in the original contracts of employment: in that of Mr Singh dated 26 September 2007 it is stated that Retained Pay "can only be altered in agreement with yourself and ceases when you agree to a promotion".

'[33] If the matter rested there the Claimants' case would be unsustainable. There is nothing in the wording of the Retained Pay provisions themselves, whether in the 2007 version in the individual contracts or the 2010 version in the collective agreement, which could prevent the employer from giving notice to terminate the contract in the usual way.

...

'[36] Whether one focuses on the phrase "guaranteed for life" or the word "permanent" I cannot accept that it has been shown that it was the mutual intention of the parties to the collective agreement, or the parties to the individual contracts of employment into which the 2010 Retained Pay clauses were incorporated, that the contracts would continue for life, or until normal retirement age, or until the closure of the site concerned. Nor can I accept that it was the mutual intention of the parties to limit the circumstances in which Tesco could bring the contracts to an end. There is no evidence that anyone addressed their mind to the possibility that in the future the company might seek to "fire and rehire". Furthermore, it does not seem to me to make any sense to say that if, having given notice of termination, the company makes no offer of a new job it has no liability for breach of contract; if it then offers the employee a new job in a different role there is no continuing entitlement to Retained Pay; but that if it makes an offer to re-engage the employee in the same role as before it can only be on the original terms.

'[37] It is true that the Retained Pay provisions incorporated into the contracts specified no time limit, nor what Parliamentary draftsmen would call a sunset clause. But that is not sufficient to get round the lack of clarity in the Claimants' case as to what *both* parties to the contract meant by "permanent".

...

'[40] I therefore conclude that the express terms of the contracts should be interpreted in accordance with what the judge rightly found to be their natural and ordinary meaning, namely that Tesco would have the right to give notice in the ordinary way, and that the entitlement to Retained Pay would only last as long as the particular contract.' *Union of Shop, Distributive and Allied Workers v Tesco Stores Ltd* [2022] EWCA Civ 978, [2023] 1 All ER 326 at [19], [32]–[33], [36]–[37], [40], per Bean LJ

PERSON ACTING IN AN OFFICIAL CAPACITY

[Criminal Justice Act 1988, s 134: offence of torture committed by a 'public official or person acting in an official capacity'.] '[23] Section 134 CJA was intended to give effect to UNCAT [the United Nations Convention against Torture and Other Cruel, Inhuman or Degrading Treatment or Punishment 1984] in domestic law. As a result, the words "person acting in an official capacity" must bear the same meaning in s 134 as in art 1, UNCAT. (See *R v Bow Street Metropolitan Stipendiary Magistrate, ex p Pinochet Ugarte (Amnesty International intervening) (No 3)* [1999] 2 All ER 97 at 109, [2000] 1 AC 147 at 200 per Lord Browne-Wilkinson.) ...

...

'[76] First, I am persuaded that the prosecution is correct in its interpretation of art 1 UNCAT and s 134 CJA. I consider that the words of those provisions in their ordinary meaning support this reading. They are sufficiently wide to include conduct by a person acting in an official capacity on behalf of an entity exercising governmental control over a civilian population in a territory over which it exercises de facto control. In particular, I can see no justification for imposing the limitation on those words for which the appellant contends, which would require the conduct to be on behalf of the government of the State concerned. On the contrary, the words in their ordinary meaning are apt to include conduct on behalf of a de facto authority which seeks to overthrow the government of the State. This reading also conforms with the object and purpose of the provisions. Here I attach particular significance to the purpose of the Convention in seeking to establish a regime for the international regulation of "official" torture as opposed to private acts of individuals. Torture perpetrated on behalf of a de facto governmental authority is clearly a matter of proper concern to the international community and within the rationale of the scheme. In addition, some support for this conclusion can be found in the decisions of the CAT under art 22(7), UNCAT and it is favoured by the preponderant weight of academic comment. I would express the principle in the following terms.

> " 'A person acting in an official capacity' in section 134(1) of the Criminal Justice Act 1988 includes a person who acts or purports to act, otherwise than in a private and individual capacity, for or on behalf of an organisation or body which exercises, in the territory controlled by that organisation or body and in which the relevant conduct occurs, functions normally exer-cised by governments over their civilian populations. Furthermore, it covers any such person whether acting in peace time or in a situation of armed conflict."

R v Reeves Taylor [2019] UKSC 51, [2020] 3 All ER 177 at [23], [76], per Lord Lloyd-Jones

PERSON AGGRIEVED

In Patents Act or Trade Marks Act

[For 97A Halsbury's Laws of England (5th Edn) (2014) para 107 see now 97A Halsbury's Laws of England (5th Edn) (2021) para 512.]

PERSON IMPOSING THE REQUIREMENT

[Financial Services and Markets Act 2000, s 177(1).] '[12] Section 177(1) provides:

> "If a person other than the investigator ('the defaulter') fails to comply with a requirement imposed on him under this Part the person imposing the requirement may certify that fact in writing to the court."

'[13] The principal point raised by Neville relies on the phrase in s 177(1): "the person imposing the requirement". Neville's argument is that the person imposing the requirement of 18 October 2018 was Mr Cawser and so the subsection required Mr Cawser to certify the fact that Neville had not complied with the requirement. The same point would arise in relation to the requirement of 18 April 2018 where the investigator was Mr Craddock. …

'[14] Although the FCA [Financial Conduct Authority] has not put its case in these terms, it would seem that it proceeds on the basis that it was the FCA which imposed the requirement of 18 October 2018 and therefore it was open to the FCA to certify non-compliance for the purposes of s 177(1).

…

'[27] Having regard to the material and the considerations set out above, I hold that it was open to the FCA to certify for the purposes of s 177(1) that Neville had failed to comply with a requirement imposed on it. For this purpose, the FCA can say that it was "the person imposing the requirement" when the requirement was imposed by an investigator acting "on its behalf".' *Financial Conduct Authority v Neville Registrars Ltd* [2019] EWHC 1611 (Ch), [2020] 1 All ER 78 at [12]–[14], [27], per Morgan J

PERSON … INTERESTED

[Companies Act 2006, s 1029: restoration to the register on application by a person interested in the restoration.] [22] Overall, whilst there is guidance in existing case law, highlighting various factors considered relevant to the issue of standing, in my judgment it would be wrong to treat the reported cases as providing a comprehensive checklist of factors which must be present to establish standing. What may be a sufficient factor for the purposes of establishing standing in one case should not be treated as a necessary factor in another. The court should be slow to attempt to legislate on the scope of a provision which Parliament has deliberately left open. The issue of who may or may not qualify as a "person … interested" must always depend on consideration of the actual circumstances of each case.

'[23] From existing case law, however, what is clear is that the Claimants must identify some interest in the "matter" of restoration beyond idle (or officious) curiosity: *Re Roehampton Swimming Pool Ltd* [1968] 3 All ER 661, [1968] 1 WLR 1693. As put by Hoffmann J, albeit in a different statutory context: "Not everyone who volunteers himself as interested … will be a person 'interested'…": *Bradshaw v University College of Wales, Aberystwyth* [1987] 3 All ER 200 at 202, [1988] 1 WLR 190 at 193.' *Re BCB Environmental Management Ltd (in liquidation); Hellard v Registrar of Companies* [2020] EWHC 1561 (Ch), [2021] 1 All ER 1221 at [22]–[23], per ICC Judge Barber

PERSONAL PROPERTY

[For 80 Halsbury's Laws of England (5th Edn) (2013) paras 801, 805 see now 80 Halsbury's Laws of England (5th Edn) (2020) paras 801, 805.]

PERSONAL REPRESENTATIVE

[For 103 Halsbury's Laws of England (5th Edn) (2010) para 608 see now 103 Halsbury's Laws of England (5th Edn) (2021) para 610.]

PICKETING

[For 41 Halsbury's Laws of England (5th Edn) (2014) paras 1369, 1384 see now 41A Halsbury's Laws of England (5th Edn) (2021) paras 1341, 1357.]

PIG'S EYE TEST

Canada

'**12** Courts rely on the "pig's eye test" to determine whether a barrelled weapon is capable of causing serious bodily injury or death and thus meets the definition of a "firearm" in the *Criminal Code* (*Dunn* [*R v Dunn* 2013 ONCA 539, 117 OR (3d) 171; aff'd 2014 SCC 69, [2014] 3 SCR 490] at paras 8 and 40). The test asks whether a projectile fired from the device can rupture a pig's eye, which is physiologically similar to a human eye (para 8). Since a ruptured eye is a "serious bodily injury", a "firearm" is any barrelled, projectile-firing device capable of putting someone's eye out (paras 8 and 40). As the expert evidence on this appeal establishes, some air-powered devices, like BB guns, airsoft guns, and paintball guns, are capable of firing projectiles with enough velocity to rupture a pig's eye. As a result, they can be classified as firearms under the *Criminal Code.*' *R v Hills* [2023] SCJ No 2, 2023 SCC 2 at para 12, per Martin J

PIN MONEY

[For 91 Halsbury's Laws of England (5th Edn) (2012) para 625 see now 91 Halsbury's Laws of England (5th Edn) (2019) para 523.]

PIRACY

[For 61 Halsbury's Laws of England (5th Edn) (2010) para 156 see now 61 Halsbury's Laws of England (5th Edn) (2018) para 168.]

[For 60 Halsbury's Laws of England (5th Edn) (2011) para 331 see now 60 Halsbury's Laws of England (5th Edn) (2018) para 310.]

PIT

[For 76 Halsbury's Laws of England (5th Edn) (2013) para 16 see now 76 Halsbury's Laws of England (5th Edn) (2019) para 16.]

PLACE OF ABODE

Australia [Income Tax Assessment Act 1936 (Cth), s 6(i): a 'resident of Australia' includes a person whose domicile is in Australia, unless the commissioner is satisfied that the person's permanent place of abode is outside Australia.] '[40] In the context of the legislative history, in our view, the phrase "place of abode" is not a reference, as one might have thought, only to a person's specific house or flat or other dwelling. If that had been Parliament's intention it would have used the phrase "permanent abode" rather than "permanent place of abode". The word "place" in the context of the phrase "outside Australia" in subpara (i) invites a consideration of the town or country in which a person is physically residing "permanently". So long as the taxpayer has "definitely abandoned" his or her residence in Australia, it does not serve the function or purpose of the exception to subpara (i) to require that the taxpayer be permanently located at a particular house or flat in a particular town within a foreign country. Nor, indeed, does it serve the functional purpose of the exception to require the person to live in one particular town, suburb or village within a given country. In our view, drawing a distinction between someone who buys a singular flat in a foreign country as against someone who lives in a series of temporary flats in that same country does not promote the rationale of the exception in subpara (i). That rationale is that a person domiciled in Australia is not to be made subject to federal income tax when they have abandoned in a permanent way their Australian residence. For the promotion of that rationale, it is unnecessary for the taxpayer to live outside of Australia in any particular way. It follows that the word "place" should accordingly be read as including a reference to a country or state. Having said that, we do not favour the proposition that it does not matter if the taxpayer is not permanently in one country, but moves between foreign countries. In our view, the words "permanent place" require the identification of a country in which the taxpayer is living permanently. We shall return to the concept of permanence.' *Harding v Commissioner of Taxation* [2019] FCAFC 29, (2019) 365 ALR 286 at [40], per Davies and Steward JJ

PLAIN VIEW

Canada

'**37** … Key to my reasoning is the application of the plain view doctrine to the files disclosing evidence of sexual assault. This common law doctrine defeats the presumption that seizures must be judicially authorized. Our Court's jurisprudence teaches that two requirements must be satisfied for the plain view doctrine to apply: (1) the police officers must have a legitimate "prior justification for the intrusion into the place where the 'plain view' seizure occurred" (*R v Buhay* 2003 SCC 30, [2003] 1 SCR 631, at para 37); and (2) the incriminating evidence must be in plain view in that it is "immediately obvious" and "discovered inadvertently" by the police (*R v Law* 2002 SCC 10, [2002] 1 SCR 227, at para 27; see also *Buhay*, at para 37). Concerns have been expressed about the plain view doctrine in relation to electronic seizures (eg, L Jrgensen, "In Plain View?: *R v Jones* and the Challenge of Protecting Privacy Rights in an Era of Computer Search" (2013), 46 UBC L Rev 791). In light of the way this case was argued, I feel it is unnecessary to express a settled opinion on the limits of the doctrine. However, I am satisfied that it does apply in some form to electronic devices (*R v Jones* 2011 ONCA 632, 107 OR (3d) 241). In the case at bar, there can be no doubt that the doctrine applies.

'**38** A warrant usually provides a legitimate prior justification for the intrusion, thereby satisfying the first requirement of the plain view doctrine. This is not the case, however, where police officers carry out a search unreasonably. In the context of digital searches, the prior justification extends only to the types of files that are "reasonably necessary" for the proper execution of such a search (*Vu* [*R v Vu* 2013 SCC 60, [2013] 3 SCR 657], at para 22). In other words, there must be a reasonable nexus between the files examined and the purposes of the warrant for a search to satisfy the first requirement of the plain view doctrine.

'**39** Even where police officers are initially justified in examining a digital file, the unanticipated evidence contained therein is not necessarily in plain view. This Court's reasoning in *Law* offers a useful illustration of the second requirement of the plain view doctrine. In that case, a police officer conducted a cursory examination of the documents in question and found "nothing facially wrong with [them]" (para 27). The officer failed to "detec[t] anything incriminating through the unaided use of his senses", as the incriminating nature of the evidence "came to light only after he examined, translated and photocopied several documents" (para 27; see also *Buhay*, at para 37; *R v Gill* 2019 BCCA 260, at para 59 (CanLII)). Consequently, this Court rejected the argument that the documents were in plain view, since they "were neither discovered inadvertently nor immediately evident" (*Law*, at para 10).' *R v McGregor* [2023] SCJ No 4, 2023 SCC 4 at paras 37–39, per Côté J

PLAINLY WRONG

'[30] Thus, it is a long settled principle, stated and restated in domestic and wider common law jurisprudence, that an appellate court should not interfere with the trial judge's conclusions on primary facts unless it is satisfied that he was plainly wrong: *McGraddie v McGraddie* [2013] UKSC 58, [2013] 1 WLR 2477, 2013 SLT 1212. What does "plainly wrong" mean? The Supreme Court explained in *Henderson v Foxworth Investments Ltd* [2014] UKSC 41, 2014 SC (UKSC) 203, [2014] 1 WLR 2600 (at [62]):

> "Given that the Extra Division correctly identified that an appellate court can interfere where it is satisfied that the trial judge has gone 'plainly wrong', and considered that that criterion was met in the present case, there may be some value in considering the meaning of that phrase. There is a risk that it may be misunderstood. The adverb 'plainly' does not refer to the degree of confidence felt by the appellate court that it would not have reached the same conclusion as the trial judge. It does not matter, with whatever degree of certainty, that the appellate court considers that it would have reached a different conclusion. What matters

is whether the decision under appeal is one that no reasonable judge could have reached."

'[31] The mere fact that a trial judge has not expressly mentioned some piece of evidence does not lead to the conclusion that he overlooked it. That point, too, was made in *Henderson* at [48]:

"An appellate court is bound, unless there is compelling reason to the contrary, to assume that the trial judge has taken the whole of the evidence into his consideration …"

'[32] At [57] Lord Reed added:

"I would add that, in any event, the validity of the findings of fact made by a trial judge is not aptly tested by considering whether the judgment presents a balanced account of the evidence. The trial judge must of course consider all the material evidence (although, as I have explained, it need not all be discussed in his judgment). The weight which he gives to it is however pre-eminently a matter for him, subject only to the requirement, as I shall shortly explain, that his findings be such as might reasonably be made. An appellate court could therefore set aside a judgment on the basis that the judge failed to give the evidence a balanced consideration *only if the judge's conclusion was rationally insupportable*." (Emphasis added.)'

ACLBDD Holdings Ltd v Staechelin; Note [2019] EWCA Civ 817, [2019] 3 All ER 429 at [30]–[32], per Lewison LJ

PLY FOR HIRE

[Whether a driver soliciting passengers by means of the Free Now app (which was in all material respects identical to the Uber app) was 'plying for hire' within the meaning of the Metropolitan Public Carriage Act 1869.] '[39] The concept of "plying for hire" goes back to the era of the horse and carriage when not only the internet and smartphones, but even the motorcar, could not have been imagined. The earliest legislation to which we were referred in which this concept was used was s 35 of the London Hackney Carriage Act 1831. The current law is contained in the 1869 Act, s 4 of which contains definitions as follows:

"In this Act 'stage carriage' shall mean any carriage for the conveyance of passengers which plies for hire in any public street, road, or place within the limits of this Act, and in which the passengers or any of them are charged to pay separate and distinct or at the rate of separate and distinct fares for their respective places or seats therein.

'Hackney carriage' shall mean any carriage for the conveyance of passengers which plies for hire within the limits of this Act, and is neither a stage carriage nor a tramcar."

'[40] There was, however, no definition of "plying for hire". Parliament must have considered that no definition was needed.

…

'[45] Thus plying for hire consists of soliciting or waiting for passengers without any previous contract with them. In the case of a black cab, which is hailed in the street, there is no such prior contract or arrangement.

'[46] Second, in *Cogley v Sherwood* [1959] 2 All ER 313, [1959] 2 QB 311 it was held that there must be some "exhibition" of the vehicle to the public in order for the vehicle to be plying for hire. …

'[47] Lord Parker recognised, however, that there were cases where a vehicle had been held to be plying for hire without being on view. Donovan J agreed that the term connotes "some exhibition of the vehicle to potential hirers as a vehicle which may be hired", although this does not necessarily require that the vehicle must be on view. Salmon J also said that "a vehicle plies for hire if the person in control of the vehicle exhibits the vehicle and makes a present open offer to the public, an offer which can be accepted, for example, by the member of the public stepping into the vehicle".

'[48] The question is how the concept of plying for hire, including the requirements of soliciting, exhibiting and the absence of a prior contract, should be applied to the process of booking a private hire vehicle for an almost immediate journey by means of a smartphone app – in effect, how to apply concepts developed in an analogue world to digital technology. That was the question addressed in the third case which we refer to here, *Reading BC v Ali* [2019] EWHC 200 (Admin), [2019] 1 WLR 2635, [2019] LLR 389, which concerned an Uber driver. The Council prosecuted the driver for an offence under the Act as it maintained he was "plying for hire". This failed, and the Council appealed by way of case stated to the Divisional Court. The facts found by the Chief Magistrate included the following:

(1) The vehicle in question had no markings indicating that it was for hire; it did not advertise any telephone number to contact in order to hire the car.
(2) The vehicle was parked lawfully, not waiting in a taxi stand or next to a bus stop.
(3) The vehicle was not available to a person hailing it on the street, but could only be booked by means of the Uber app.
(4) The vehicle was one of a number shown on the Uber app, where it was visible to any Uber customer; it was depicted by an icon showing the outline of a car.
(5) The app did not show any features which might identify a particular driver or a particular car.

'[49] On these facts the Divisional Court, agreeing with the Chief Magistrate, held that there was no plying for hire. …

…

'[54] … Since the question whether a vehicle is plying for hire necessarily focuses on what it is doing before any contract is concluded, it can make no difference whether any contract of hire which may result is made with the operator or the driver.

'[55] It is therefore our duty to follow *Reading v Ali*. We conclude, therefore, that Free Now does not facilitate or encourage its drivers to ply for hire and that this ground of challenge to TfL's decision to grant it an operator's licence must fail.' *Uber London Ltd v Transport for London (Transopco (UK) Ltd (trading as Free Now) intervening)* [2021] EWHC 3290 (Admin), [2022] 2 All ER 797 at [39]–[40], [45]–[49], [54]–[55], per Males LJ and Fraser J

'[42] The Appellants argue that as a matter of ordinary language a vehicle plies for hire if it "drives around or parks in a public place waiting for someone to hire it". That cannot possibly be enough. Such a test would criminalise almost the entire PHV industry, except perhaps one-person operators working from home; and would mean that the careful provision made by Parliament for regulation of PHVs in London (under the 1998 Act) was contradicted by a phrase in the 1869 statute dealing with hackney carriages. The Appellants have to go further and show that the tests of exhibition and solicitation laid down in 1959 in *Cogley v Sherwood* [[1959] 2 All ER 313] are made out.

…

'[44] Lord Parker's conclusion that "there is no decided case where a hackney carriage was held to be plying for hire where it was not exhibited so as to be visible to would-be customers" is in my view correct. The two-stage test of exhibition of the vehicle and solicitation of passengers is clear and intelligible and has stood the test of time. If it is still necessary for *Cogley v Sherwood* to be approved in this court, I would approve it.

'[45] I agree with the Divisional Court in *Reading BC v Ali* [[2019] EWHC 200 (Admin), [2019] LLR 389, [2019] 1 WLR 2635] that plying for hire requires a vehicle to be not just exhibited or on view but, while exhibited, to be soliciting custom in the sense of inviting members of the public to hire it without a prior contract. I do not consider that drivers of PHVs using the FREE NOW app can be said to be plying for hire. Neither the "exhibition" nor the "solicitation" element of the test is satisfied.

'[46] As to the element of exhibiting the vehicle, I do not consider that the depiction of the vehicle and others as rectangular blobs on the passenger's smartphone screen amounts to exhibiting. The passenger is not being given any details that would identify a vehicle and no means of finding it or contacting it directly. The individual vehicles depicted on the screen are neither "visible" nor "on view" in any real sense. I agree with Mr Matthias that the case would be the same if, instead of being shown a map of the area with a number of blobs representing cars, the customer was simply told by an on-screen message "there are five cars currently available within five minutes of where you are waiting". But that would not be exhibition either. Like Flaux LJ in the *Reading* case, I accept that the case is no different from that of the traditional minicab firm which takes phone calls from prospective customers and where the operator tells them "we have five cars within five minutes of you". All that the FREE NOW app does is to speed up that process.' *R (on the application of United Trade Action Group Ltd) v Transport for London (Transopco (UK) Ltd (trading as FREE NOW), interested party)* [2022] EWCA Civ 1026, [2023] 2 All ER 98 at [42], [44]–[46], per Bean LJ

POLICY

'[1] This appeal is concerned with the standards to be applied by a court when it is asked to conduct a judicial review of the contents of a policy document or statement of practice issued by the Government. We will refer to these as "policies".

…

'[3] Policies are different from law. They do not create legal rights as such. In the case of policies in relation to the exercise of statutory discretionary powers, it is unlawful for a public authority to fetter the discretion conferred on it by statute by applying a policy rigidly and without being willing to consider whether it should not be followed in the particular case. However, in an important development in public law in the last decades, the courts have given policies greater legal effect. In certain circumstances a policy may give rise to a legitimate expectation that a public authority will follow a particular procedure before taking a decision and it may give rise to a legitimate expectation that the authority will confer a particular substantive benefit when it does decide how to exercise its discretion. In these cases, the courts will give effect to the legitimate expectation unless the authority can show that departure from its policy is justified as a proportionate way of promoting some countervailing public interest. If the policy is not made public, and an affected individual is unaware of its relevance to his case and in that sense has no actual expectation arising from it, the authority may still be required to comply with it unless able to justify departing from it: *Mandalia v Secretary of State for the Home Dept* [2015] UKSC 59, [2016] 4 All ER 189, [2015] 1 WLR 4546. Under some conditions the holder of a discretionary power may be required to formulate a policy and to publish it: *R (on the application of Lumba) v Secretary of State for the Home Dept, R (on the application of Mighty) v Secretary of State for the Home Dept* [2011] UKSC 12, [2011] 4 All ER 1, [2012] AC 245. Thus, policies have moved increasingly centre stage in public law.' *R (on the application of A) v Secretary of State for the Home Department* [2021] UKSC 37, [2022] 1 All ER 177 at [1], [3], per Lord Sales and Lord Burnett CJ

Canada [Whether city's snow clearance policy was core policy decision immune from negligence liability.] '1 Under Canadian tort law, there is no doubt that governments may sometimes be held liable for damage caused by their negligence in the same way as private defendants. At the same time, the law of negligence must account for the unique role of public authorities in governing society in the public interest. Public bodies set priorities and balance competing interests with finite resources. They make difficult public policy choices that impact people differently and sometimes cause harm to private parties. This is an inevitable aspect of the business of governing. Accountability for that harm is found in the ballot box, not the courts. Courts are not institutionally designed to review polycentric government decisions, and public bodies must be shielded to some extent from the chilling effect of the threat of private lawsuits.

'2 Accordingly, courts have recognized that a sphere of government decision-making should remain free from judicial supervision based on the standard of care in negligence. Defining the scope of this immunity has challenged courts for decades. In *R v Imperial Tobacco Canada Ltd* 2011 SCC 42, [2011] 3 SCR 45, this Court explained that "core policy" government decisions – defined as "decisions as to a course or principle of action that are based on public policy considerations, such as economic, social and political factors" – must be shielded from liability in negligence (para 90). In ascertaining whether a decision is one of core policy, the key focus is always on the nature of the decision.

'3 In the decade since *Imperial Tobacco*, there has been continued confusion on when core policy immunity applies. This appeal requires the Court to clarify how to distinguish immune policy decisions from government activities that attract liability for negligence. We conclude that the rationale for core policy immunity serves as an overarching guiding principle. Core policy decisions are immune from negligence liability because each branch of government has a core institutional role and competency that must be protected from interference by the other branches. We identify four factors from this Court's jurisprudence that help in assessing the nature of a government's decision: (1) the level and responsibilities of the decision-maker; (2) the process by which the decision was made; (3) the nature and extent of budgetary considerations; and (4) the extent to which the decision was based on objective criteria. The separation of powers rationale animating the immunity guides how the factors weigh in the analysis.

...

'59 The second clarification is that the word "policy" has a wide range of meaning, from broad directions to a set of ideas or a specific plan (see, eg, *Cambridge Dictionary* (online): "policy" means "a set of ideas or a plan of what to do in particular situations that has been agreed to officially by a group of people, a business organization, a government, or a political party"; *Merriam-Webster's Collegiate Dictionary* (11th ed 2003), at p 960: "policy" means "a definite course or method of action selected from among alternatives and in light of given conditions to guide and determine present and future decisions" or "a high-level overall plan embracing the general goals and acceptable procedures especially of a governmental body"). This is why our jurisprudence has so often qualified the word policy to focus on "true" or "core" policy, pointing towards the type of policy question that requires immunity. Accordingly, the fact that the word "policy" is found in a written document, or that a plan is labelled as "policy" may be misleading and is certainly not determinative of the question. Similarly, that a certain course of conduct is mandated by written government documents is of limited assistance. While core policy might be expected to be reduced to writing, this may depend on the public authority and the circumstances; implementation procedures may also be documented. The focus must remain on the nature of the decision itself rather than the format or the government's label for the decision.' *Nelson (City) v Marchi* [2021] SCJ No 41, 2021 SCC 41 at paras 1–3, 59, per Karakatsanis and Martin JJ

POLICY OF INSURANCE

[For 60 Halsbury's Laws of England (5th Edn) (2011) paras 96–97 see now 60 Halsbury's Laws of England (5th Edn) (2018) paras 73–74.]

POLITICALLY EXPOSED PERSON

In subsection (4)(a), 'politically exposed person' means a person who is—

(a) an individual who is, or has been, entrusted with prominent public functions by an international organisation or by a State other than the United Kingdom or another EEA State,
(b) a family member of a person within paragraph (a),
(c) known to be a close associate of a person within that paragraph, or
(d) otherwise connected with a person within that paragraph.

(Proceeds of Crime Act 2002, ss 326B(7), 396B(7) (inserted by the Criminal Finances Act 2017, ss 1, 4))

PORT

[For 60 Halsbury's Laws of England (5th Edn) (2011) para 305 see now 60 Halsbury's Laws of England (5th Edn) (2018) para 284.]

[For 85 Halsbury's Laws of England (5th Edn) (2013) para 8 see now 85 Halsbury's Laws of England (5th Edn) (2020) para 8.]

Dockyard port

[For 85 Halsbury's Laws of England (5th Edn) (2013) para 11 see now 85 Halsbury's Laws of England (5th Edn) (2020) para 11.]

Franchise port

[For 85 Halsbury's Laws of England (5th Edn) (2013) para 5 see now 85 Halsbury's Laws of England (5th Edn) (2020) para 5.]

PORTION

[For 91 Halsbury's Laws of England (5th Edn) (2012) para 628 see now 91 Halsbury's Laws of England (5th Edn) (2019) para 528.]

POST OBIT

[For 32 Halsbury's Laws of England (5th Edn) (2012) para 297 see now 32 Halsbury's Laws of England (5th Edn) (2019) para 297.]

POSSESSION

[For 80 Halsbury's Laws of England (5th Edn) (2013) paras 834–837 see now 80 Halsbury's Laws of England (5th Edn) (2020) paras 834–837.]

Of land

[For 87 Halsbury's Laws of England (5th Edn) (2017) para 161 see now 87 Halsbury's Laws of England (5th Edn) (2022) para 161.]

Writ of possession

[For 12A Halsbury's Laws of England (5th Edn) (2015) para 1382 see now 12A Halsbury's Laws of England (5th Edn) (2020) para 1356.]

POUND BREACH

[Delete the entry for 26 Halsbury's Laws of England (5th Edn) (2016) para 811; for 2 Halsbury's Laws of England (5th Edn) (2017) para 62 see now 2 Halsbury's Laws of England (5th Edn) (2023) para 67; and for 62 Halsbury's Laws of England (5th Edn) (2016) para 282 see now 62 Halsbury's Laws of England (5th Edn) (2022) para 305.]

POWER

[For 98 Halsbury's Laws of England (5th Edn) (2013) para 43 see now 98 Halsbury's Laws of England (5th Edn) (2019) paras 1, 39–43.]

PRACTICAL INJUSTICE

Australia [Migration Act 1958 (Cth), s 438: if the Secretary of the Department of Immigration and Border Protection gives to the Administrative Appeals Tribunal a document or information to which s 438 applies, the Secretary must notify the Tribunal in writing that s 438 applies in relation to the document or information.] '[38] Because procedural fairness requires disclosure of the fact of notification, non-disclosure of the fact of notification constitutes, without more, a breach of the Tribunal's implied obligation of procedural fairness. For such a breach to constitute jurisdictional error on the part of the Tribunal, however, the breach must give rise to a "practical injustice": the breach must result in a denial of an opportunity to make submissions and that denial must be material to the Tribunal's decision.' *Minister for Immigration and Border Protection v SZMTA (Matter No S36 of 2018)* [2019] HCA 3, (2019) 363 ALR 599 at [38], per Bell, Gageler and Keane JJ

PREAMBLE

[For 96 Halsbury's Laws of England (5th Edn) (2012) para 671 see now 96 Halsbury's Laws of England (5th Edn) (2018) para 272.]

PRECARIOUS

[Nationality, Immigration and Asylum Act 2002, s 117B(5).] '[1] The Home Secretary determines to exercise his power to remove a foreign national from the UK. The foreign national contends that the determination is unlawful on the ground that her removal would violate her right to respect for her private life under art 8 of the European Convention on Human Rights and s 6(1) of the Human Rights Act 1998 ("the 1998 Act"). Section 117B(5) of the Nationality, Immigration and Asylum Act 2002 ("the 2002 Act") provides that little weight should be given to a private life which she established at a time when her immigration status was "precarious". What does the word "precarious" mean in this context? This is the primary question posed by the present appeal.

…

'[42] The provisional view of Sales LJ, set out in para [25] above, was that leave to remain short of indefinite leave might sometimes confer on a person a status not properly to be described as precarious; and that the concept of precariousness might fall to be applied having regard to the person's overall circumstances. The view of Sales LJ is entitled to great respect. In para [36] above I have recognised the need for a degree, no doubt limited, of flexibility in the application of Pt 5A of the 2002 Act. But I will shortly explain how, elsewhere, the statute does permit a limited degree of it. I do not consider that the ordinary meaning of the word "precarious" requires, or that in its context Parliament must have intended the word to require, that its application to the facts of a case should depend upon a subtle evaluation of the overall circumstances such as Sales LJ had in mind.

'[43] The bright-line interpretation of the word "precarious" in s 117B(5), commended by the specialist tribunal with the maximum weight of its authority, is linguistically and teleologically legitimate; and, for that matter, it is consistent with the way in which the ECtHR expressed itself in the *Jeunesse* case [*Jeunesse v Netherlands* (App no 12738/10) (2014) 60 EHRR 789, [2014] ECHR 12738/10] (see para [34] above) and in which this court expressed itself in the *Agyarko* case [*R (on the application of Agyarko) v Secretary of State for the Home Dept, R (on the application of Ikuga) v Secretary of State for the Home Dept* [2017] UKSC 11, [2017] 4 All ER 575, [2017] 1 WLR 823] (see para [35] above).

'[44] The answer to the primary question posed by the present appeal is therefore that everyone who, not being a UK citizen, is present in the UK and who has leave to reside here other than to do so indefinitely has a precarious immigration status for the purposes of s 117B(5).' *Rhuppiah v Secretary of State for the Home Department* [2018] UKSC 58, [2019] 1 All ER 1007 at [1], [42]–[44], per Lord Wilson JSC

PREMIUM

Insurance

[For 60 Halsbury's Laws of England (5th Edn) (2011) para 150 see now 60 Halsbury's Laws of England (5th Edn) (2018) para 128.]

Rent

[For 63 Halsbury's Laws of England (5th Edn) (2016) para 752 see now 63 Halsbury's Laws of England (5th Edn) (2022) para 805.]

PREROGATIVE

[For 20 Halsbury's Laws of England (5th Edn) (2014) paras 166, 168 see now 20 Halsbury's Laws of England (5th Edn) (2023) paras 164, 166.]

PRESCRIPTION

[For 87 Halsbury's Laws of England (5th Edn) (2017) paras 803–804, 810 see now 87 Halsbury's Laws of England (5th Edn) (2022) paras 797–798, 804.]

PRESENTED TO THE COURT

[Matrimonial Causes Act 1973, s 3(1).] [28] In the light of *Butler v Butler (Queen's Proctor Intervening)* [1990] 1 FLR 114, [1990] FCR 336, the case admits of no possible argument. District Judge Simmonds was correct to treat the petition as having been "presented to the court" within the meaning of s 3(1) on the day when it was received by the court, namely on 22 June 2015. The petition was therefore presented in breach of s 3(1), with the inevitable consequences spelt out by Sir Stephen Brown P. …' *Baron v Baron* [2019] EWFC 26, [2020] 1 All ER 272 at [28], per Sir James Munby

PRESUMPTION

[For 28 Halsbury's Laws of England (5th Edn) (2015) paras 454–457 see now 28 Halsbury's Laws of England (5th Edn) (2021) paras 462–465.]

Of fact

[For 12 Halsbury's Laws of England (5th Edn) (2015) para 755 see now 12 Halsbury's Laws of England (5th Edn) (2020) para 748.]

Of law

[For 12 Halsbury's Laws of England (5th Edn) (2015) para 756 see now 12 Halsbury's Laws of England (5th Edn) (2020) para 749.]

PREVIOUS REPRESENTATION

Australia [Evidence Act 1995 (Cth), s 59(1): evidence of a previous representation made by a person is not admissible to prove the existence of a fact that it can reasonably be supposed that the person intended to assert by the representation.] '[33] The dictionary to the Evidence Act defines a "previous representation" as:

> *previous representation* means a representation *made otherwise than in the course of giving evidence in the proceeding* in which evidence of the representation is sought to be adduced.

…

'[35] Both the operation of the hearsay rule and the definition of an "admission" are predicated on the existence of a "previous representation". If a representation is made "in the course of giving evidence in the proceeding in which evidence of the representation is sought to be adduced", then that representation is not a previous representation. It therefore cannot be an admission as that term is defined in the Evidence Act. However, the contents of an affidavit is not evidence adduced in the Court until such time as it has been formally read. That is, the "giving" of the evidence occurs not at the time of swearing or affirming the affidavit, but at the time of being "read" at the hearing of the proceeding, being in this case the hearing of the final relief and not any previous interlocutory stage. Until that time, it remains a previous representation subject both to the hearsay rule and the exception to that rule in the case of admissions.

'[36] Having now revisited this issue and considered it again with the benefit of the additional authorities cited by the Commissioner, I am of the view that an affidavit filed but not read in the same proceeding in which its tender is sought is still a "previous representation" such that the hearsay rule, and the exception to that rule in the case of admissions applies.' *Commissioner of Taxation v Bosanac (No 7)* [2021] FCA 249, (2021) 390 ALR 74, BC202101954 at [33], [35]–[36], per McKerracher J

PRIVATE LIFE

[European Convention for the Protection of Human Rights and Fundamental Freedoms 1950 (as set out in the Human Rights Act 1998,

Sch 1), art 8: the right to respect for private life.] '[46] Moreover, in my judgment it is obvious and indeed beyond argument that the facts of this case concern the Appellant's private life and engage art 8. There can be little more central to a citizen's private life than gender, whatever that gender may or may not be. No-one has suggested (nor could they) that the Appellant has no right to live as a non-binary, or more particularly as a non-gendered, person. Indeed, a gender identity chosen as it has been here, achieved or realised through successive episodes of major surgery and lived through decades of scepticism, indifference and sometimes hostility must be taken to be absolutely central to the person's private life. It is the distinguishing feature of this Appellant's private life.

'[47] It must be remembered that art 8 protects the citizen's private (or family) life; gender is relevant as one of the most important aspects of private life. In the absence of any prohibition (and there is none), the Appellant's gender identification undoubtedly engages art 8. The question then becomes: what, if any, positive obligation is placed on the state to protect that aspect of the Appellant's private life? That provides the jumping-off point for the main points in this case.

...

'[123] I agree with King LJ and with her reasoning. I too would dismiss the appeal. In particular, I would wish to underscore her remarks in paras [46] to [48], and [56]. It is a completely untenable proposition that gender identification does not engage art 8, because the identification concerned is non-binary, or non-gendered. There can be little that is more central to private life than the gender of an individual, and few circumstances where gender is more important than in relation to people who have altered their gender identification, in whatever direction or to whatever destination. That must be obviously so where the process has involved extensive surgery. Article 8 is concerned with private life, not any particular sex or gender. If and insofar as this argument has affected the thinking of the government, it is to be hoped that this analysis may lead to a reconsideration of their approach.' *R (on the application of Elan-Cane) v Secretary of State for the Home Department (Human Rights Watch intervening)* [2020] EWCA Civ 363, [2021] 1 All ER 25 at [45]–[47], per King LJ and at [123], per Orwin LJ

PRIVILEGE

Australia [Native Title Act 1993 (Cth), s 253.] '[55] In ascertaining the meaning of the word "privilege" in s 253 of the Native Title Act, it is also necessary to bear steadily in mind that the task is one of statutory construction, not Hohfeldian claim right analysis. The nature of the right, interest, obligation or liberty described by the word is not "disposed of by nomenclature" and it is by no means unprecedented to find the terms "right" and "privilege" used in the "wider and laxer sense" in legislation. "Privilege", being a protean term, takes its meaning from its context.

'[56] If the definition of "interest" in s 253 of the Native Title Act stood alone, it might be that "privilege" would be taken to mean some advantage in relation to land that is peculiar to an individual or group of individuals as opposed to members of the public generally. But s 253 of the Native Title Act does not stand alone, and it is not to be construed as if it did. Although a definitional provision, it is part of the Native Title Act, and, like all other provisions of an Act, it is to be construed in the context of the Act as a whole. Just as the definition of "interest" and, therefore, the meaning of "privilege" in s 253 informs the meaning of the other provisions of the Native Title Act that refer to "interest" or "interests", such other provisions, bearing in mind their purpose and the mischief to which they are directed, inform the meaning of "interest" and, therefore, the meaning of "privilege" in s 253. As McHugh J noticed in *Kelly v R* [(2004) 218 CLR 216; 205 ALR 274; [2004] HCA 12], "[n]othing is more likely to defeat the intention of the legislature than to give a definition a narrow, literal meaning and then use that meaning to negate the evident policy or purpose of a substantive enactment".

'[57] If "privilege" in the definition of "interest" in s 253 were confined to a privilege in the sense of some right, advantage or immunity enjoyed by some beyond the usual rights or advantages of others, it would exclude the ability of the public to access and enjoy the foreshore which exists as a result of the lack of legal prohibition from entering upon unallocated Crown land, validly confirmed by s 14 of the Titles Validation Act in accordance with s 212(2) of the Native Title Act.65 In that event, the confirmed ability would not be within the description of "any other interests" in s 225(c), and so would not be recorded in the native title determinations to which it relates despite impairing the relevant native title rights. That this is so provides a strong indication that "other interests" in s 225(c) is a sufficiently broad concept to include the confirmed ability of the public to access and enjoy the foreshore. And in turn, that provides a strong indication that the confirmed ability is within the notion of a "privilege" in the definition of "interest" in s 253.

'[58] Given, then, that it is the duty of the Court to avoid, so far as the text of the Act permits, a construction inconsistent with the purpose of a provision and instead "look to see whether any other meaning produces a more reasonable result",66 and, as has been seen, that one available, and not inapposite, meaning of "privilege" is of a liberty that the law tolerates but does not support by imposing a duty on anyone else, it should be concluded that "privilege" in the definition of "interest" in s 253 includes the confirmed ability of the public to access and enjoy the foreshore which exists as a result of the lack of legal prohibition on entering upon unallocated Crown land.' *Western Australia v Manado (on behalf of the Bindunbur Native Title Claim Group)* [2020] HCA 9, (2020) 376 ALR 427 at [55]–[58], per Nettle J

Absolute privilege

[For 32 Halsbury's Laws of England (5th Edn) (2012) paras 595–596 see now 32 Halsbury's Laws of England (5th Edn) (2019) paras 594–595.]

Qualified privilege

[For 32 Halsbury's Laws of England (5th Edn) (2012) paras 595, 609 see now 32 Halsbury's Laws of England (5th Edn) (2019) paras 594, 607.]

PRIVITY

[For 12A Halsbury's Laws of England (5th Edn) (2015) para 1634 see now 12A Halsbury's Laws of England (5th Edn) (2020) para 1599.]

PRIZE

Admiralty

[For 85 Halsbury's Laws of England (5th Edn) (2012) paras 601–603 see now 85 Halsbury's Laws of England (5th Edn) (2020) paras 701–703.]

PRO-MUTUUM

[For 4 Halsbury's Laws of England (5th Edn) (2011) para 142 see now 4 Halsbury's Laws of England (5th Edn) (2020) para 142.]

PROCEEDINGS

[Application for third party disclosure. CPR 31.17 – CPR PD 6B, para 3.1(20), which provides for service out of the jurisdiction with permission where a claim is made under an enactment which allows proceedings to be brought and those proceedings are not covered by any of the other grounds referred to in para 3.1.] '[31] Mr O'Leary's submission was that the word "claim" in para 3.1 of Practice Direction 6B refers to a claim to enforce a substantive as distinct from a procedural right; and that the term "proceedings" in gateway (20) refers to "claims or similar matters which are essentially freestanding", as distinct from applications (such as an application for third party disclosure) within such proceedings. He acknowledged that an application for pre-action disclosure would be a claim, but submitted that an application for pre-action disclosure was significantly different from an application for third party disclosure.

...

'[35] Jacobs J considered the question whether an application for third party disclosure constitutes "proceedings" at [65] to [86] of his judgment. ...

'[36] Once again, I respectfully agree with the conclusion of Jacobs J on this issue. An application for third party disclosure constitutes "proceedings" for the purpose of gateway (20). That gives the term "proceedings", in my view, a neutral and common sense meaning.' *Gorbachev v Guriev* [2022] EWCA Civ 1270, [2023] 2 All ER 809 at [31], [35]–[36], per Males LJ

Proceedings for an offence

[Criminal Justice (Northern Ireland) Order 1996, SI 1996/3160, art 33: in deciding what sentence to pass on an offender who had pleaded guilty, the court should take into account the stage in the proceedings for the offence at which the offender indicated his intention to plead guilty.] '[37] The interpretation section of the 1996 Order does not include a definition of when criminal proceedings are instituted. The term 'proceedings for the offence' in art 33 contemplates an offence in respect of which proceedings have been issued. The police investigation by way of questioning is concerned with confirming or dispelling a suspicion that an offence has been committed. The offence which is the subject of proceedings only crystallises at the moment of charge, summons or, unusually, presentation of an indictment, in other words after the police interview.

...

'[52] In summary, the meaning of "proceedings" in art 33 of the Criminal Justice (Northern Ireland) Order 1996 does not include the investigative process leading up to charge or the issue of a summons. Article 33 does not, however, prevent the development by the Court of Appeal of guidelines in respect of the reduction in sentence for a guilty plea based on administrative resources, inconvenience to witnesses and vindication and relief to victims. There was no error of law arising from the consideration of those guidelines by the Crown Court or the Court of Appeal.' *R v Maughan (Northern Ireland)* [2022] UKSC 13, [2022] 4 All ER 873 at [37], [52], per Sir Declan Morgan

Proceedings in a criminal cause or matter

[Justice and Security Act 2013, s 6: whether judicial review proceedings were 'proceedings in a criminal cause or matter'.] '[4] The issue on this appeal is whether on the hearing of the application for judicial review, it would be open to the Court to receive closed material disclosed only to the court and a special advocate but not to the Appellants. As will appear, this depends on whether the judicial review proceedings are "proceedings in a criminal cause or matter".

...

'[15] In my opinion, the Appellants are entitled to succeed on this appeal because in its ordinary and natural meaning "proceedings in a criminal cause or matter" include proceedings by way of judicial review of a decision made in a criminal cause, and nothing in the context or purpose of the legislation suggests a different meaning.' *R (on the application of Belhaj) v Director of Public Prosecutions* [2018] UKSC 33, [2018] 4 All ER 561 at [4], [15], per Lord Sumption

Proceedings in Parliament

[Bill of Rights (1688), art 9. Report of Inquiry by panel appointed by Foreign and Commonwealth Office into allegations of child sex abuse on St Helena.] '[2] The principal issue in this appeal is whether the report of an inquiry ordered to be published by the House of Commons following a Motion for an Unopposed Return is protected by Parliamentary privilege.

...

...

'[10] The FCO served its defence to both claims in June 2017. It denied the substance of the claims but also pleaded that the Report amounts to "proceedings in Parliament" for the purposes of art 9 of the Bill of Rights 1689. This means, according to the defence, that "pursuant to the fundamental principle of parliamentary privilege, this claim seeking to impeach the findings contained in the report and/or the procedure pursuant to which those findings were reached must fail".

...

'[12] Three issues were dealt with at the hearing and determined in Master McCloud's judgment handed down on 15 June 2018 ([2018] EWHC 1461 (QB)) ("the Main Judgment"). The first was whether and to what extent the claims were defeated by the defence of Parliamentary privilege. On this issue the Master held that the expression "proceedings in Parliament" did include the Unopposed Return procedure with the result that art 9 of the Bill of Rights barred the claims to the extent that they sought to challenge the accuracy of content of the Report: see para [110] of the Main Judgment. However, Parliamentary privilege did not extend to claims relating to matters which occurred outside Parliament, such as the FCO's initial decision to undertake the Inquiry and the procedures adopted by the Panel in conducting the Inquiry, including the steps taken in the drafting of the Report: para [113].

...

'[44] *Erskine May* [Erskine May *Parliamentary Practice* (25th edn, 2019)] says at para 13.12 that the term "proceedings in Parliament" has received judicial attention but comprehensive lines of decision have not emerged and "indeed it has been concluded that an exhaustive definition could not be achieved" ....

...

'[60] Despite [the warning of Lord Rodger in *R v Chaytor* [2010] UKSC 52, [2011] 1 All ER 805 at [101]], we have no doubt that the Unopposed Return is a proceeding in Parliament for the purposes of art 9 of the Bill of Rights 1689 and does confer on the content of the Report the protection of Parliamentary privilege. ...

...

'[70] We therefore conclude that the Report constitutes proceedings in Parliament for the purposes of art 9 of the Bill of Rights. It enjoys the protection of Parliamentary privilege and of the Parliamentary Papers Act 1840.' *Warsama v Foreign and Commonwealth Office (Speaker of the House of Commons, interested party)* [2020] EWCA Civ 142, [2020] 4 All ER 486 at [2], [10], [12], [44], [60], [70], per Lord Burnett CJ, Coulson and Rose LJJ

PROFILING

[In Part 2.] 'Profiling' means any form of automated processing of personal data consisting of the use of personal data to evaluate certain personal aspects relating to an individual, in particular to analyse or predict aspects concerning that individual's performance at work, economic situation, health, personal preferences, interests, reliability, behaviour, location or movements. (Data Protection Act 2018, s 33(4))

PROFIT

[Income Tax (Earnings and Pensions) Act 2003, s 62(2)(b).] '[1] This appeal concerns the meaning of the term "profit" as it is used in s 62(2)(b) of the Income Tax (Earnings and Pensions) Act 2003 ("ITEPA") which defines "earnings" for the purpose of the employment income parts of that Act.

...

'[50] One of the definitions of the word "profit" in the *Oxford English Dictionary* is "a material benefit derived from a property, position, etc; income, revenue. Frequently in plural". In my judgment that is the sense in which the word is being used in the definition of "earnings" in s 62(2)(b) of ITEPA. Once the "from" [employment] test is satisfied, then the only deductions that are permissible are those which are stipulated in Ch 5 of ITEPA.' *Murphy v Revenue and Customs Commissioners* [2022] EWCA Civ 1112, [2023] 1 All ER 504 at [1], [50], per Andrews LJ

PROFIT À PRENDRE

[For 87 Halsbury's Laws of England (5th Edn) (2017) paras 773, 974 see now 87 Halsbury's Laws of England (5th Edn) (2022) paras 767, 968.]

[For 76 Halsbury's Laws of England (5th Edn) (2013) para 21 see now 76 Halsbury's Laws of England (5th Edn) (2019) para 21.]

Appendant

[For 87 Halsbury's Laws of England (5th Edn) (2017) para 980 see now 87 Halsbury's Laws of England (5th Edn) (2022) para 974.]

Appurtenant

[For 87 Halsbury's Laws of England (5th Edn) (2017) para 981 see now 87 Halsbury's Laws of England (5th Edn) (2022) para 975.]

In gross

[For 87 Halsbury's Laws of England (5th Edn) (2017) para 982 see now 87 Halsbury's Laws of England (5th Edn) (2022) para 976.]

PROHIBITING ORDER

[For 61 Halsbury's Laws of England (5th Edn) (2010) para 689 see now 61A Halsbury's Laws of England (5th Edn) (2023) para 111.]

PROPERTY OF THE COMMONWEALTH

Australia [Archives Act 1983 (Cth), ss 3(1), 70, Pt V; whether archived correspondence between former Governor-General and HM the Queen was property of the Commonwealth.] '[6] We would allow Professor Hocking's appeal from the judgment of the Full Court, declare the deposited correspondence to be Commonwealth records within the meaning of the Archives Act and order that a writ of mandamus issue to compel the Director-General to reconsider Professor Hocking's request for access. ...

...

'[40] The critical expression "Commonwealth record" is in relevant part defined [in the Archives Act 1983, s 3(1)(a)] to mean "a record that is the property of the Commonwealth or of a Commonwealth institution" other than a record of that description which is "exempt material" because it is included in a collection maintained by another custodial institution, such as the National Library of Australia. The cognate expression "current Commonwealth record" is defined to mean "a Commonwealth record that is required to be readily available for the purposes of a Commonwealth institution".

. . .

'[89] Property is not "a monolithic notion of standard content and invariable intensity"; it is not "a term of art with one specific and precise meaning". It is "a term that can be, and is, applied to many different kinds of relationship with a subject matter". The relationship with a subject matter is in some contexts best understood in terms of a "bundle of rights". In other contexts, it is best understood in terms of a "legally endorsed concentration of power".

. . .

'[92] The question, however, is not as to the content of the common law concepts of "possession" or "possessory title" but as to the meaning of "property" within the context of the Archives Act. The two are not the same.

'[93] Within the definition of "Commonwealth record", "property" obviously connotes a relationship between a record — a tangible thing — on the one hand and either the Commonwealth as a body politic or a Commonwealth institution as a functional unit of government on the other hand. The nature and intensity of the requisite relationship is a question of statutory construction the resolution of which is informed by the statutory context.

. . .

'[95] Purposively construed in the context of the Archives Act, the relationship between a record and either the Commonwealth as a body politic or a Commonwealth institution as a functional unit of government connoted by "property" is best understood as a legally endorsed concentration of power to control the physical custody of the record. The power might arise from a capacity to exercise a common law or statutory right arising from ownership or possession. But it need not so arise. The power might be exclusive. But it need not be.' *Hocking v Director-General of the National Archives of Australia* [2020] HCA 19, (2020) 379 ALR 395 at [6], [40], [89], [92]–[93], per Kiefel CJ, Bell, Gageler, Keane JJ

PROPERTY OF THE COMPANY

Australia [Corporations Act 2001 (Cth), s 433: whether the insolvent corporate trustee's right of indemnity is 'property of the company' within the meaning of s 433.] '[269] The primary judge's conclusion that the corporate trustee's right of indemnity by way of exoneration was not "property of the company" cannot be sustained in the light of relevant High Court authority.

'[270] The primary judge emphasised from the outset of his analysis that the character of the relevant assets would never change. Money used by a trustee in exercise of the right of exoneration "remained trust money", in the primary judge's view. The assets "remain trust assets". The right of indemnity was "property held in trust", rather than "the corporate trustee's own beneficial 'personal property".

'[271] It is inconsistent, in our opinion, with High Court authority to hold that the right of indemnity is not property of the corporate trustee because the assets are trust assets. In *Octavo* [*Octavo Investments Pty Ltd v Knight* (1979) 144 CLR 360; 27 ALR 129; 4 ACLR 575] the High Court held the trustee's interest "amounts to a proprietary interest". In *Buckle* [*Chief Commissioner of Stamp Duties (NSW) v Buckle* (1998) 192 CLR 226; 151 ALR 1; [1998] HCA 4] the High Court held that once a right of indemnity (including for exoneration) arose "there exist the respective proprietary rights, in order of priority, of the trustee and the beneficiaries". In both *Buckle* and *CPT* [*CPT Custodian Pty Ltd v Commissioner of State Revenue* (2005) 224 CLR 98; 221 ALR 196; [2005] HCA 53] the High Court said that it was not possible to identify the trust fund until account was taken of the right of exoneration. In *Bruton* [*Bruton Holdings Pty Ltd (in liq) v Commissioner of Taxation* (2009) 239 CLR 346; 258 ALR 612; 73 ACSR 241; [2009] HCA 32] the High Court reiterated that the trustee's right "amounted to a proprietary interest".' *Commonwealth v Byrnes (in their capacity as joint and several Recs and Mgrs of Amerind Pty Ltd (recs and mgrs apptd) (in liq))* [2018] VSCA 41, (2018) 354 ALR 789 at [269]–[271], per Ferguson CJ, Whelan, Kyrou, McLeish and Dodds-Streeton JJA

PROROGATION

'[2] Parliamentary sittings are normally divided into sessions, usually lasting for about a year, but sometimes less and sometimes, as with the current session, much longer. Prorogation of Parliament brings the current session to an end. The next session begins, usually a short time later, with the Queen's Speech. While Parliament is prorogued, neither House can meet, debate and pass legislation. Neither House can debate Government policy. Nor may members of either House ask written or oral questions of Ministers. They may not meet and take evidence in committees. In general, Bills which have not yet completed all their stages are lost and will have to start again from scratch in the next session of Parliament. In certain circumstances, individual Bills may be "carried over" into the next session and pick up where they left off. The Government remains in office and can exercise its powers to make delegated legislation and bring it into force. It may also exercise all the other powers which the law permits. It cannot procure the passing of Acts of Parliament or obtain Parliamentary approval for further spending.

'[3] Parliament does not decide when it should be prorogued. This is a prerogative power exercised by the Crown on the advice of the Privy Council. In practice, as noted in the House of Commons Library Briefing Paper (No 8589, 11 June 2019), "this process has been a formality in the UK for more than a century: the Government of the day advises the Crown to prorogue and that request is acquiesced to". In theory the monarch could attend Parliament and make the proclamation proroguing it in person, but the last monarch to do this was Queen Victoria in 1854. Under current practice, a proclamation is made by Order in Council a few days before the actual prorogation, specifying a range of days within which Parliament may be prorogued and the date on which the prorogation would end. The Lord Chancellor prepares a commission under the great seal instructing the Commissioners accordingly. On the day chosen for the prorogation, the Commissioners enter the House of Lords; the House of Commons is summoned; the command of the monarch appointing the Commission is read; and Parliament is formally prorogued.

'[4] Prorogation must be distinguished from the dissolution of Parliament. The dissolution of Parliament brings the current Parliament to an end. Members of the House of Commons cease to be Members of Parliament. A general election is then held to elect a new House of Commons. The Government remains in office but there are conventional constraints on what it can do during that period. These days, dissolution is usually preceded by a short period of prorogation.

'[5] Dissolution used also to be a prerogative power of the Crown but is now governed by the Fixed-term Parliaments Act 2011. This provides for general elections to be held every five years and for an earlier election to be held in only two circumstances: either the House of Commons votes, by a majority of at least two-thirds of the number of seats (including vacant seats) in the House, to hold an early election; or the House of Commons votes that it has no confidence in Her Majesty's Government and no-one is able to form a Government in which the House does have confidence within 14 days. Parliament is dissolved 25 days before polling day and cannot otherwise be dissolved. The Act expressly provides that it does not affect Her Majesty's power to prorogue Parliament (s 6(1)).

'[6] Prorogation must also be distinguished from the House adjourning or going into recess. This is decided, not by the Crown acting on the advice of the Prime Minister, but by each House passing a motion to that effect. The Houses might go into recess at different times from one another. In the House of Commons, the motion is moved by the Prime Minister. In the House of Lords, it is moved by the Lord Speaker. During a recess, the House does not sit but Parliamentary business can otherwise continue as usual. Committees may meet, written Parliamentary questions can be asked and must be answered.' *R (on the application of Miller) v Prime Minister; Cherry v Advocate General for Scotland* [2019] UKSC 41, [2019] 4 All ER 299 at [2]–[6], per Lady Hale P and Lord Reed DP

PROTECTED NEW ZEALAND OBJECT

New Zealand [Protected Objects Act 1975, s 2(1)(a).] '[89] The purpose of the Protected Objects Act is to protect certain objects of particular national value to New Zealand. The focus is therefore on individual items that, as individual items, have significance for one or more of the reasons set out in s 2(1)(a). The Act is not designed, as the Courts below held, to protect natural materials such as swamp kauri in bulk. It is true that protected New Zealand object is defined to include a collection or assemblage of objects but these terms imply that the collection or assemblage is in one place or in the hands of one owner. That does not apply to swamp kauri.

'[90] Further, to require all pieces of a bulk natural material, such as swamp kauri, to be subject to an application process before export would create a major administrative burden, both on the Ministry and the public. This cannot have been the intention of the Act. It is true that an exemption could be granted if there are sufficient examples of swamp kauri in public ownership but, if swamp kauri generally had been intended to be covered by the Act, this then raises the question, given the finite nature of the resource, as to what would be a sufficient amount in public ownership in order for it to satisfy the criteria for an exemption.' *Northland Environmental Protection Society Inc v Chief Executive of the Ministry for Primary Industries* [2018] NZSC 105, [2019] 1 NZLR 257 at [89]–[90], per Glazebrook J

PROTEST

Ship's protest

[For 66 Halsbury's Laws of England (5th Edn) (2015) para 1038 see now 66 Halsbury's Laws of England (5th Edn) (2020) para 986.]

PROXIMATE CAUSE

[For 60 Halsbury's Laws of England (5th Edn) (2011) para 347 see now 60 Halsbury's Laws of England (5th Edn) (2018) para 326.]

PUBLIC AUTHORITY

[For 20 Halsbury's Laws of England (5th Edn) (2014) para 601n see now 20 Halsbury's Laws of England (5th Edn) (2023) para 514, note 4.]

[Human Rights Act 1998, s 6(3). Panel appointed by Foreign and Commonwealth Office to conduct inquiry into allegations of child sex abuse on St Helena.] '[101] Ms Wass was one of the panel members conducting an inquiry on behalf of the Government. The question is whether the Inquiry, a collective description of the panel members, was a "public authority" for the purpose of the HRA, and thus obliged to act compatibly with the ECHR rights of those affected by its actions. …

'[102] Mr Payne QC, for Ms Wass, accepts that if the Inquiry had been established under the Inquiries Act 2005 its members would have been a public authority for the purposes of the HRA. They would have been performing "functions of a public nature". He submits, however, that a combination of features points away from the conclusion that she (and her colleagues) were a public authority when conducting the Inquiry because its functions were not of a public nature. First, and in contradistinction to a statutory inquiry, she had no statutory powers. Secondly, she was paid her day rate as a barrister and undertook other professional work whilst conducting the Inquiry. Thirdly, she was not taking the place of government nor providing a public service. Fourthly, the Inquiry did not carry out its functions in public.

…

'[109] We have set out the circumstances in which the Inquiry came to be established in para [4], above. Its function was to investigate on behalf of Her Majesty's Government a matter of public concern about the safeguarding of children in the context of allegations of serious impropriety by public servants. It might have been established under the Inquiries Act 2005 but, as has been the case with other inquiries, was not clothed with statutory powers (another example of a non-statutory inquiry into matters of serious public concern was that established to investigate the convictions of the Guildford Four and the Maguire Family chaired by Sir John May (1990 Cmd 556 and 1994 Cmd 449)). The announcement of the Inquiry included an assurance from the Minister that all relevant papers would be made available to the Inquiry. Ms Wass's inquiry was funded by the FCO and was provided with a secretariat (solicitor and administrative support). Its establishment was announced in Parliament and its very detailed terms of reference were made available in the library of the House of Commons. Those terms of reference explained that the Panel would produce a public report of its findings. Its progress was marked by statements by Ministers in Parliament.

'[110] Whilst it is true that the concerns that led to this Inquiry being established could have been left to the police, at least in so far as they raised the spectre of criminal conduct, their broad nature was such that only government could initiate a comprehensive inquiry. That was a core governmental function. Ms Wass and her team were performing a function on behalf of the Government in the public interest to establish the truth about worrying allegations and make a public report. Given the nature of the inquiry and the likelihood that its report would include criticism of individuals, publication through Parliament would always have been the most likely option.

'[111] All of these factors point inexorably, in our view, to the conclusion that the Inquiry was performing a public and not private function and that Ms Wass and her colleagues were a "public authority" for the purposes of s 6 of the HRA. Whilst the Strasbourg Court has not had occasion to consider an argument that an independent inquiry established by the government of a State party to investigate a matter of public concern is not subject to the ECHR, we consider that such an argument is unsustainable.' *Warsama v Foreign and Commonwealth Office (Speaker of the House of Commons, interested party)* [2020] EWCA Civ 142, [2020] 4 All ER 486 at [101]–[102], [109]–[111], per Lord Burnett CJ, Coulson and Rose LJJ

Australia [Civil Liability Act 2003 (Qld), s 36.] '[116] While some degree of broad guidance may be obtained from the authorities, the relevant criteria will need to be determined in the context of the specific authority under consideration. For present purposes there are two statutes in question, namely the Restructuring Act (from which the institutional nature of Seqwater is to be derived) and the Civil Liability Act (providing a degree of protection from suits in tort). Whether Seqwater constituted a public authority depends on an analysis of its constituting legislation, namely the Restructuring Act. As has been noted, its title "The Queensland Bulk Water Supply Authority" appears to engage the term "authority" as found in the Civil Liability Act. As an entity which can sue and be sued, it has legal personality and, as found by the primary judge, it owed a duty of care to the plaintiff.

'[117] It is aptly described as a "public authority" because it is established under statute, has the functions and powers conferred by the statute, has no corporators or individuals who would benefit from the exercise of its powers as members of a corporate body, is responsible for the supply of water and other services relating to the water industry and is run by a board appointed by the responsible Ministers. Although the characterisation of Seqwater is required for the purposes of the Civil Liability Act, the language of that Act in s 34(c), referring to "any public authority constituted under an Act", cannot be read down so as to exclude a body having the characteristics of Seqwater.

...

'[121] The term "public authority", as used in s 36, is not defined. Accordingly, it should be understood in the context of the regulation of water supply and flood control set out above. These considerations demonstrate that Seqwater was a public authority within the meaning of that term in s 34, and therefore in s 36 of the Civil Liability Act.' *Queensland Bulk Water Supply Authority (t/a Seqwater) v Rodriguez & Sons Pty Ltd* [2021] NSWCA 206, (2021) 393 ALR 162 at [116]–[117], [121], per Basten, Meagher and Leeming JJA

PUBLIC BODY

New Zealand [Subsidies and Countervailing Measures Agreement ('SCM Agreement') annexed to the World Trade Organisation ('WTO') Agreement. Whether the Ministry of Business, Innovation and Employment ('MBIE') interpreted the "public body" test correctly before advising the Minister that state-owned commercial banks in China ('SOCB's) and state-invested enterprises ('SIE's) were not public bodies.] '[82] Article 1.1(a) of the SCM Agreement deems subsidies to exist where financial contributions of certain kinds (as set out in (i) to (iv)) are made by a "government or any public body". Consistent with this, the DCD Act [Dumping and Countervailing Duties Act 1988] defines "subsidy" as including a financial contribution provided by a "foreign Government" and, also consistently, "foreign Government" is defined as including "a person, agency, or institution acting for, or on behalf of, a Government".

'[83] The proper test to be applied for determining whether an entity is a "public body" is relevant to two of the alleged subsidy programmes: (1) whether Chinese producers of the subject goods received benefits by way of policy loans from SOCBs; and (2) whether Chinese producers of the subject goods received benefits because SIEs provided inputs to them at LTAR ['less than adequate remuneration']. MBIE's Final Report rejected these claims on the basis it was not established that SOCBs and the SIEs were public bodies.

'[118] In my view the quoted paragraphs are not entirely clear on this point. MBIE is correct that the test for whether an entity is a public body is not whether it is meaningfully controlled by government. The test is whether an entity possesses, exercises or is vested with government authority. In DS436 the WTO Appellate Body held that formal indicia of control (the ability to appoint shareholders and directors) were not sufficient to determine if an entity possessed, exercised or was vested with government functions. The WTO Appellate Body also held that the entity did not need to have the power to regulate, control, or supervise individuals or otherwise restrain their conduct.

[119] It is not clear in the above quoted paragraphs that MBIE appreciated that ADRP 2013 (Gal) had concluded that the "material did not show that the control amounted to meaningful control in the sense intended by the WTO Appellate Body [in DS379]" on an erroneous

basis: namely, that there was no material to demonstrate there had been "a delegation of governmental authority to SIEs to impose state-mandated policies on participants in the iron and steel industry". The correct position, as clarified in DS436, is that SIEs could potentially possess, exercise or be vested with government authority even if they did not have a power of control over third parties.' *New Zealand Steel Ltd v Minister of Commerce and Consumer Affairs* [2018] NZHC 2454, [2019] 2 NZLR 525 at [82]–[83], [118]–[119], per Malton J

PUBLIC HOUSE

[For 68 Halsbury's Laws of England (5th Edn) (2016) para 648n see now 68 Halsbury's Laws of England (5th Edn) (2021) para 664 n 6.]

PUBLIC INTEREST

Contrary to the public interest

'[1] This is the first time the highest court (whether the House of Lords or Supreme Court) has been required to decide an appeal on s 84 of the Law of Property Act 1925. That section confers on the Upper Tribunal a power, in specified circumstances, to discharge or modify restrictive covenants affecting land.

...

'[41] The essential elements of s 84 in relation to the "contrary to public interest" jurisdictional ground are ss 84(1)(aa) and (1A)(b). ... Reduced to their core, they read as follows:

"(1) [The Upper Tribunal shall have the power to discharge or modify a restrictive covenant on being satisfied]—

(aa) that (in a case falling within subsection (1A) below) the continued existence [of the restriction under the covenant] would impede some reasonable user of the land ...

(1A) Subsection (1)(aa) above authorises the discharge or modification of a restriction by reference to its impeding some reasonable user of land in any case in which the Upper Tribunal is satisfied that the restriction, in impeding that user, either

...

...

(b) is contrary to the public interest;

and that money will be an adequate compensation for the loss or disadvantage (if any) which any ... person will suffer from the discharge or modification."

'[42] Mr Hutchings submitted that the statute requires a narrow interpretation of what is meant by "contrary to the public interest". I agree. It is clear from the statutory words that one must ask whether the impeding of the reasonable user of the land by the continuation of the restrictive covenant is contrary to the public interest. If one is satisfied that the proposed use of the land is reasonable (and it was common ground that that was satisfied in this case) one must ask whether the impediment of that use by the continuation of the restrictive covenant is contrary to the public interest. It is of central importance that the question that has to be asked is not the wider one of whether in all the circumstances of the case it would be contrary to the public interest to maintain the restrictive covenant. Rather the wording requires one to focus more narrowly on the impeding of the reasonable user of the land and to ask whether that impediment, by continuation of the restrictive covenant, is contrary to the public interest.

'[43] On the facts of this case, therefore, that narrow wording required the Upper Tribunal to determine whether it was contrary to the public interest for the 13 housing units not to be able to be used. The waste involved would be a very strong factor indicating that that would indeed be contrary to the public interest. To be weighed against that would be the public interest in the hospice providing a sanctuary for children dying of cancer which would be protected by the continuation of the restrictive covenant. Two competing uses of the land are therefore pitted against each other. It is the resolution of a land-use conflict that we are here dealing with. That was the approach taken by the Upper Tribunal and there was no error of law in its deciding that the "contrary to public interest" jurisdictional ground was made out on these facts.

'[44] Once one appreciates that the relevant wording requires a narrow enquiry and does not involve asking the wide question of whether in all the circumstances it is contrary to the public interest to maintain the restrictive covenant, it is clear that the good or bad conduct of the applicant is irrelevant at this jurisdictional stage. The manner of the breach of the restrictive covenant (ie whether the breach was cynical or not) is irrelevant because that tells us nothing about the merits of what the burdened land is being used for or will be used for. This, of course, is not to deny that the manner of breach – the cynical breach by the applicant – is a highly relevant consideration when it comes to the discretionary stage of the decision. But it is irrelevant at the jurisdictional stage.' *Alexander Devine Children's Cancer Trust v Housing Solutions Ltd* [2020] UKSC 45, [2021] 2 All ER 871 at [1], [41]–[44], per Lord Burrows JSC

PUBLIC POLICY

[For 22 Halsbury's Laws of England (5th Edn) (2012) paras 429–431 see now 22 Halsbury's Laws of England (5th Edn) (2019) paras 220–222.]

PUBLICATION—PUBLISH

Defamation

[For 32 Halsbury's Laws of England (5th Edn) (2012) paras 562, 579 see now 32 Halsbury's Laws of England (5th Edn) (2019) paras 562, 579.]

PUFFING

[For 76 Halsbury's Laws of England (5th Edn) (2013) paras 713–714 see now 76 Halsbury's Laws of England (5th Edn) (2019) paras 713–714.]

PUNISHMENT

[For 25 Halsbury's Laws of England (5th Edn) (2016) para 3 see now 25 Halsbury's Laws of England (5th Edn) (2020) para 4.]

PURSUE

New Zealand [Wildlife Act 1953, s 2: hunting or killing in relation to any wildlife includes pursuing, disturbing, or molesting.] '[63] The dictionary meaning of the word "pursue" includes to follow with intent to overtake for some purpose — usually capturing in some way. It is implicit in the act of "pursuing" that the defendant intends to chase the animal. Travelling the same path through water as a marine species as a matter of chance is not pursuing it if there is no intention to follow. In the context of this Act, we are satisfied that "pursuing" is to be construed as to mean intentionally chasing. We use the word "chase" because we do not consider the term was intended to capture merely following an animal at a safe distance.

'[64] The Court of Appeal has given "pursue" a broader meaning than intentionally chasing to include, as a prohibited action, luring a protected animal. On its analysis, the use of baits and berley to attract sharks amounts to pursuit. Shark Experience argues that the Court of Appeal erred in this as "pursue" does not naturally bear this meaning. It argues that if such activity was intended to be prohibited, the language of luring or attracting would have been used.

'[65] We agree that the meaning the Court of Appeal gave to the word "pursue" is neither consistent with the natural and ordinary meaning of the word pursue, nor with the statutory purpose. Pursuing something normally entails following it or chasing it. Luring an animal with the use of attractants is not normally spoken of as pursuing it, although if the purpose for which attractants are used is catching or killing the animal, it is likely to be prohibited as the act of hunting.

'[66] The purpose of the Act is to protect wildlife. Pursuing an animal in the sense of chasing it for whatever reason can be stressful for the animal, and so prohibiting pursuit of an animal is consistent with that purpose. But attracting an animal to food, or to scent, thereby allowing the animal to be observed is not necessarily, on its own, obviously harmful. We accept Shark Experience's submission that adopting the broader interpretation of "pursue" favoured by the Court of Appeal would over criminalise conduct. The Court of Appeal attempted to manage this risk by adding the "risk of harm" gloss to both this and the prohibited act of disturbing protected wildlife. On our interpretation of "pursue", the addition of that gloss is not necessary.

...

'[93] ... In the s 2(1) definition of "hunt or kill": "pursuing" means to intentionally chase but does not include luring or attracting or merely following the animal at a safe distance.' *Shark Experience Ltd v PauaMAC5 Inc* [2019] NZSC 111, [2019] 1 NZLR 791 at [63]–[66], [93], per Winkelmann CJ

PYX (TRIAL OF THE)

[For 49 Halsbury's Laws of England (5th Edn) (2015) para 12, 12n see now 49 Halsbury's Laws of England (5th Edn) (2021) para 12, 12 n 1.]

Q

QUANTUM MERUIT

[For 88 Halsbury's Laws of England (5th Edn) (2012) para 408 see now 88 Halsbury's Laws of England (5th Edn) (2019) para 408.]

QUARRY

[For 76 Halsbury's Laws of England (5th Edn) (2013) para 4 see now 76 Halsbury's Laws of England (5th Edn) (2019) para 4.]

QUASHING ORDER

[For 61 Halsbury's Laws of England (5th Edn) (2010) para 689 see now 61A Halsbury's Laws of England (5th Edn) (2023) para 106.]

QUASI CONTRACT

[For 88 Halsbury's Laws of England (5th Edn) (2012) para 401 see now 88 Halsbury's Laws of England (5th Edn) (2019) para 401.]

QUASI EASEMENT

[For 32 Halsbury's Laws of England (5th Edn) (2012) para 29 see now 32 Halsbury's Laws of England (5th Edn) (2019) para 29.]

QUAY

[For 52 Halsbury's Laws of England (5th Edn) (2014) para 673 see now 52 Halsbury's Laws of England (5th Edn) (2020) para 706.]

QUIET ENJOYMENT

[For 62 Halsbury's Laws of England (5th Edn) (2016) paras 404–405 see now 62 Halsbury's Laws of England (5th Edn) (2022) paras 438–439.]

QUO WARRANTO

[For 20 Halsbury's Laws of England (5th Edn) (2014) para 660 see now 20 Halsbury's Laws of England (5th Edn) (2023) para 573.]

R

RATE

Or any other rate

[Pension plan; annual rate of increase to be the percentage increase in the retail prices index during the year ending the previous 31 May but subject to a maximum of 5 per cent (or any other rate decided by the Principal Employer).]
'[1] The main issue in this appeal is beguilingly simple. It is whether the words "or any other rate decided by the Principal Employer" in a pension increases provision in the Rules of an occupational pension scheme mean "any higher rate" or "any other rate, whether higher or lower" decided by that employer. …

…

'[26] Plainly the judge was right to say that the words "any other rate" qualified the "rate of increase". The question, however, is whether he was right to say that the words "any other rate" meant "any higher rate". Shorn of complexity, I can completely understand why the judge thought, as Mr Bryant had submitted, that it would have been better in a number of different ways if the drafter of rule C.10(2) had given the employer only the power to select a rate of increase higher than capped RPI. Allowing the employer a discretion limited to increasing the rate is more consistent with the admissible factual matrix and the legislative background, just as the judge said.

…

'[30] Accordingly, in this case, considerable weight must be accorded to the fact that the drafter has used the unambiguous words "or any other rate", which do not naturally mean "or any higher rate". It is true that the words are not "or any other rate whatsoever", but this is not a case where an eiusdem generis interpretation is possible as it was, at least, in *The Laconian Confidence* [*Andre & Cie SA v Orient Shipping (Rotterdam) BV, The Laconian Confidence* [1997] 1 Lloyd's Rep 139]. The scope for importing a limitation on the words of rule C.10(2) in this case are, therefore, rather limited, despite the obvious advantages of doing so.

…

'[35] … I am satisfied that, on a proper application of the principles expressed in the recent Supreme Court authorities, the objective meaning of the language which the parties chose to include in rule C.10(2) is what it actually says. The employer's discretion expressed in brackets in rule C.10(2) allows it to decide that the rate of increase shall be at "any other rate", whether higher or lower, not just a higher rate of increase.' *Britvic plc v Britvic Pensions Ltd* [2021] EWCA Civ 867, [2022] 2 All ER 457 at [1], [26], [30], [35], per Sir Geoffrey Vos MR

RATIFICATION

[For 1 Halsbury's Laws of England (5th Edn) (2017) para 58 see now 1 Halsbury's Laws of England (5th Edn) (2022) para 58.]

RATIO DECIDENDI

[For 11 Halsbury's Laws of England (5th Edn) (2015) para 25 see now 11 Halsbury's Laws of England (5th Edn) (2020) para 25.]

READ BETWEEN THE LINES

Canada '15 Contrary to what the appellants argue in their factum, I do not think that the expression "read between the lines" reflects any error by the Court of Appeal. A careful reading of the passage shows that this figurative expression was used simply to caution against being overly literal in analyzing a motion for authorization to institute a class action, and not to signal a change in the law. When the Court of Appeal's reasons are read as a whole and the justifications it gave for intervening are considered in context, one plainly understands that "read between the lines" is not an invitation to search in a vacuum – on the blank page – for allegations that are missing from the motion.

…

'**18** In using the expression "read between the lines", the Court of Appeal also intended to denounce the rigidity and literalism that, in its view, were reflected in the motion judge's decision. …

…

'**20** In short, contrary to what the appellants suggest, the Court of Appeal did not invent wording or a cause of action by using this expression. To "read between the lines" is to take the wording as a starting point from which to discover the full message it conveys, including the necessarily implied message. Paradoxically, the appellants take the expression literally by insisting that "read between the lines" means to read into the blank spaces something not written there. They seem to forget the meaning of the metaphor chosen by the Court of Appeal, lapsing into precisely the same literalism that the expression is intended to denounce.

'**21** Indeed, the appellants have not cited any decision in which the expression "read between the lines" has caused confusion or has been interpreted as an invitation to rewrite a cause of action. …' *Desjardins Financial Services Firm Inc v Asselin* [2020] SCJ No 30, 2020 SCC 30 at paras 15, 18, 20, 21, per Kasirer J

REAL PROPERTY

[For 87 Halsbury's Laws of England (5th Edn) (2017) para 1 see now 87 Halsbury's Laws of England (5th Edn) (2022) para 1.]

REALISABLE PROPERTY

[Criminal Justice Act 1988, s 80: confiscation order; provision for a receiver to be appointed in respect of 'realisable property'.] '[7] This appeal relates to an order made by Jay J on 29 June 2017. The order provided, among other things, for the schedule to the receivership order of 13 January 2016 to be amended to include certain pension policies in Mr Ahmed's name.

'[8] Mr Ahmed challenges that part of Jay J's order. His case is that the pension policies have as yet no realisable value and that they will continue to have none for a number of years. That being so, he said, they cannot represent "realisable property". In contrast, Mr Jonathan Kinnear QC, who appeared for the CPS with Mr Michael Newbold, submitted that the policies are "realisable property" within the meaning of the 1988 Act and, hence, that Jay J was right to include them in the schedule to the receivership order.

'[9] Mitting J was empowered to appoint a receiver by s 80 of the 1988 Act. That provided for a receiver to be appointed "in respect of realisable property" (s 80(2)) and to be granted power "to realise any realisable property in such manner as the court may direct" (s 80(5)). The term "realisable property" was defined in s 74 of the Act to include "any property held by the defendant", and s 102 explained that "Property is held by any person if he holds any interest in it" (s 102(7)) and that " 'interest', in relation to property, includes right" (s 102(1)).

'[10] Mr Ahmed does not dispute that he has an interest in each of the pension policies that Jay J decided should be added to the schedule to the receivership order. It inevitably follows, having regard to the provisions of the 1988 Act quoted in the previous paragraph, that the policies are "realisable property" within the meaning of the Act. Equally, they must form part of the "realisable property of the Defendants" of which Mr Long was appointed receiver. That being so, there can, as I see it, be no valid objection to the policies being included in the schedule to the receivership order.' *Ahmed v Crown Prosecution Service* [2018] EWCA Civ 2543, [2019] 1 All ER 1003 at [7]–[10], per Newey LJ

REASONABLE

[Data Protection Act 1988, s 7(4)(b): data controller not required to comply with a request for personal data where it would entail disclosing information relating to another individual who can be identified from that information, unless it is reasonable in all the circumstances to comply with the request without the consent of the other individual.] '[105] It is therefore in my judgment significant that Parliament has used the word "reasonable" and not some other word such as "appropriate". The word "reasonable" conveys that there may be one or more courses open to the data controller and that his choice, if within sub-s (4), will prevail. In that sense, I agree with Sales LJ that the court should defer to the data controller and not substitute the court's own opinion.' *DB v General Medical Council* [2018] EWCA Civ 1497, [2019] 2 All ER 219 at [105], per Arden LJ

REBUILD

[For 91 Halsbury's Laws of England (5th Edn) (2012) para 716 et seq see now 91 Halsbury's Laws of England (5th Edn) (2019) para 613 et seq.]

RECEIVER

[For 88 Halsbury's Laws of England (5th Edn) (2012) para 1 see now 88 Halsbury's Laws of England (5th Edn) (2019) para 1.]

RECORDS OF THE COURT

[CPR 5.4C: copies from court records for a person not a party to proceedings.] '[22] The Master considered that the "records of the court" comprised all documents filed with the court and that this included trial bundles and documents, such as skeleton arguments and transcripts, held with them.

'[23] CIH [Cape Intermediate Holdings Ltd] contended that none of these documents, other than statements of case, are properly to be regarded as being part of the "records of the court" and that the Master had no jurisdiction to make the order she did.

…

'[36] The critical issue in relation to the court's jurisdiction under CPR 5.4C(2) is the meaning of the "records of the court". This is not a defined term under the CPR.

…

'[40] In my judgment CIH's core submission is correct. The "records of the court" are essentially documents kept by the court office as a record of the proceedings, many of which will be of a formal nature. The principal documents which are likely to fall within that description are those set out in para 4.2A of CPR 5APD.4, together with "communication between the court and a party or another person", as CPR 5.4C(2) makes clear. In some cases there will be documents held by the court office additional to those listed in para 4.2A of CPR 5APD.4, but they will only be "records of the court" if they are of an analogous nature.

'[41] This will include a list of documents, but not the disclosed documents themselves. It may include witness statements and exhibits filed in relation to an application notice or Pt 8 proceedings (see CPR 8.5), but not usually witness statements or expert reports exchanged by the parties in relation to a trial. Such statements and reports are not generally required to be filed with the court and they will typically be provided to the court only as part of the trial bundles.

'[42] The receipt document for the trial bundles may be a record of the court, but not the trial bundles themselves. …

…

'[49] The Master's finding that the trial bundles were "records of the court" was the essential basis upon which she ordered copying of the documents listed in the Order. The Order in fact went further and also treated skeleton arguments and trial transcripts as being part of the "records of the court".

…

'[54] The Order made in this case was of unprecedented scope and went far beyond the relatively narrow confines of CPR 5.4C(2). For the avoidance of doubt, I consider that it should be made clear that the "records of the court" for the purpose of that rule do not generally include:

(1) The trial bundles.
(2) The trial witness statements.
(3) The trial expert reports.
(4) The trial skeleton arguments or opening or closing notes or submissions.
(5) The trial transcripts.'

Dring (on behalf of the Asbestos Victims Support Groups Forum UK) v Cape Intermediate Holdings Ltd [2018] EWCA Civ 1795, [2019] 1 All ER 804 at [22]–[23], [36], [40]–[42], [49], [54], per Hamblen LJ

REFERENDUM EXPENSES

[Political Parties, Elections and Referendums Act 2000, s 111(2): offence if total 'referendum expenses' incurred by or on behalf of any individual or body during the referendum period exceeded £10,000, unless the individual was a 'permitted participant'.] '[1] The issue in this case is whether the Electoral Commission (the statutory body responsible for overseeing elections and referendums in the UK) has correctly interpreted the law which limited spending by participants in connection with the referendum held in June 2016 on whether or not the UK should remain a member of the European Union. More particularly, the issue is whether the Electoral Commission was correct to conclude that, on the proper interpretation of the legislation, certain payments made by Vote Leave Ltd were not "referendum expenses" incurred by Vote Leave but only donations made by Vote Leave to meet expenses incurred by another campaigner for a "leave" outcome of the referendum called Mr Darren Grimes.

...

'[94] For the reasons given, we conclude that the Electoral Commission has misinterpreted the definition of" 'referendum expenses" in s 111(2) of PPERA. The source of its error is a mistaken assumption that an individual or body which makes a donation to a permitted participant cannot thereby incur referendum expenses. As a result of this error, the Electoral Commission has interpreted the definition in a way that is inconsistent with both the language and the purpose of the legislation.

'[95] The email communications which we summarised at paras [13]–[20] above show that Vote Leave made each of the AIQ Payments (totalling £620,000) at the request of Mr Grimes for the agreed purpose of paying for advertising which Mr Grimes ordered from AIQ [AggregateIQ Data Services Ltd]. We see no reason to doubt that the payments were, as they were said to be, donations made by Vote Leave to Mr Grimes to meet referendum expenses which he incurred by purchasing advertising services from AIQ. But it is also clear that, on the proper interpretation of the statutory provisions as we have analysed them, Vote Leave "incurred expenses" by making the payments, that those expenses were incurred "in respect of" advertising (one of the matters listed in Pt I of Sch 13 to PPERA) and that the expenses were incurred "for referendum purposes" within the meaning of s 111(3) of PPERA. They were therefore "referendum expenses" as defined in s 111(2) of PPERA irrespective of whether they were also "common plan expenses" within the meaning of para 22 of Sch 1 to EURA, as the Electoral Commission has now found.

'[96] It was suggested on behalf of the Electoral Commission that this is not a rational conclusion because Vote Leave could equally well have sent the money to Mr Grimes to enable him to pay AIQ instead of paying AIQ itself directly and that, even on the claimant's case, Vote Leave would then have avoided the regulatory control on referendum expenses because the expenses would not then have been qualifying expenses falling within Pt I of Sch 13 to PPERA. It was suggested that it is not reasonable to adopt an interpretation which leads to such an arbitrary difference in result.

'[97] However, if Vote Leave had sent the money to Mr Grimes on the agreed basis that he would use it to pay for services ordered from AIQ, the result would not have been different. In that case too, as we interpret the statutory test, the payments would also have been referendum expenses incurred by Vote Leave.' *R (on the application of the Good Law Project) v Electoral Commission (Vote Leave Ltd and another, interested parties)* [2018] EWHC 2414 (Admin), [2019] 1 All ER 365 at [1], [94]–[97], per Leggatt LJ

RELATING TO

Australia [Australian Security Intelligence Organisation Act 1979 (Cth), s 17(1)(c); function of organisation to advise Ministers and authorities of the Commonwealth in respect of matters relating to security.] '[56] The phrase "relating to" in s 17(1)(c) is broad. It is well settled that the phrase "relating to" is "one of wide import" and that the degree of connection required between two subject matters joined by that phrase "is ordinarily to be determined by reference to the text, context, legislative purpose and history of the provision and, of course, the facts of the case" (*Minister for Home Affairs v DMA18 (as litigation guardian for DLZ18)* (2020) 385 ALR 16; 95 ALJR 14; [2020] HCA 43 at [43]).

'[57] In construing s 17(1)(a) of the ASIO Act, which provides that one of ASIO's functions is "to obtain, correlate and evaluate intelligence relevant to security", Mason J made the following relevant observations in *Church of Scientology Inc v Woodward* (1982) 154 CLR 25 at 60–1; 43 ALR 587 at 602:

> ... Intelligence is relevant to security if it establishes or tends to establish that a person suspected of being a security risk is, or is not such a risk. Moreover, it may well be that intelligence is relevant to security, so long as it is obtained for the purpose of determining whether a person alleged or thought to be a security risk, is such a risk. ... Intelligence is relevant to security if it can reasonably be considered to have a real connexion with that topic, judged in the light of what is known to ASIO at the relevant time.

Section 17(1)(c) should be construed consistently with those observations. That is, a "matter" will be one "relating to" security if it establishes or tends to establish that a person suspected of being a security risk is, or is not, such a risk.' *CCU21 v Minister for Home Affairs* [2022] FCA 28, (2022) 398 ALR 535 at [56]–[57], per Griffiths J

RELATIONS

[For 102 Halsbury's Laws of England (5th Edn) (2010) para 350 see now 102 Halsbury's Laws of England (5th Edn) (2021) para 351.]

RELEVANT

Relevant criminal activity

Australia [Australian Crime Commission Act 2002 (Cth), s 7C: power of the board of the ACC to authorise, in writing, the ACC to undertake intelligence operations or to investigate matters relating to federally relevant criminal activity.] '[100] The defined phrase "relevant criminal activity" indicates that the subject matter of an investigation need not concern or respond to a particular allegation that a relevant offence has been committed, is being committed or may be committed by a person or class of persons. The concept is wider than that. It includes any *circumstances implying that* (for present purposes) serious and organised crime may have been, may be being, or may in future be, committed against a law of the Commonwealth, of a State or of a Territory. Where circumstances imply that serious and organised crime is being committed, it may be that the Board will not, at the time of an authorisation or determination, have in its possession information identifying or tending to identify the persons responsible for engaging in or organising the criminal activity, the particular offences that might sanction the activity, the scale of the activity, the place of its commission or other particulars. The discovery of as yet unknown particular information of that kind may permissibly form a part of the investigatory purpose.' *CXXXVIII v Commonwealth of Australia* [2019] FCAFC 54, (2019) 366 ALR 436 at [100], per Charlesworth J

Relevant order

Australia [Federal Courts (State Jurisdiction) Act 1999 (NSW), s 11.] '[16] … Section 11(2) of the Federal Courts (State Jurisdiction) Act 1999 (NSW) (State Jurisdiction Act) provides that:

> "A person who was a party to a proceeding in which a relevant order is made may apply to the Supreme Court for an order that the proceeding be treated as a proceeding in the Supreme Court, and the Supreme Court may make such an order."

'[17] "Relevant order" is defined as meaning "an order of a federal court, whether made before or after the commencement of this section, dismissing, striking out or staying a proceeding relating to a State matter for want of jurisdiction": s 11(1) of the State Jurisdiction Act.

…

'[53] When one has regard to the context and purpose of the Act, both as explicitly stated and as is evident from a consideration of its terms as a whole including its long title, the specific context in which it was passed, namely the immediate aftermath of the decision in *Re Wakim* [*Re Wakim; Ex parte McNally* (1999) 198 CLR 511; 163 ALR 270; 31 ACSR 99; [1999] HCA 27], and the mischief which it was intended to address, all reinforced by the explanatory memorandum and the second reading speech, it seems to me to be unavoidable that, where the defined term "relevant order" refers to a decision of the Federal Court "dismissing, striking out or staying a proceeding relating to a State matter for want of jurisdiction", the want of jurisdiction being referred to is not any general want of jurisdiction but rather a want of jurisdiction by reason of a constitutionally invalid conferral of jurisdiction of the kind addressed in *Re Wakim*.

'[54] In the present case, the Federal Court never had jurisdiction to entertain a case involving a claim for damages in relation to an intra-state air carriage of the kind brought by the Respondent. The State Jurisdiction Act was not directed to a situation where a party simply invoked the jurisdiction of the Federal Court by mistake.' *Sydney Seaplanes Pty Ltd (t/a Sydney Seaplanes) v Page* [2021] NSWCA 204, (2021) 393 ALR 485 at [16]–[17], [53]–[54], per Bell P

RELIGIOUS PURPOSES

[For 8 Halsbury's Laws of England (5th Edn) (2015) para 27 et seq see now 8 Halsbury's Laws of England (5th Edn) (2019) para 28 et seq.]

RENT

Generally

[For 62 Halsbury's Laws of England (5th Edn) (2016) para 236 see now 62 Halsbury's Laws of England (5th Edn) (2022) para 254; and for 87 Halsbury's Laws of England (5th Edn) (2017)

para 28 see now 87 Halsbury's Laws of England (5th Edn) (2022) para 28.]

RENTCHARGE

[For 87 Halsbury's Laws of England (5th Edn) (2017) para 1033 see now 87 Halsbury's Laws of England (5th Edn) (2022) para 1028.]

REPLEVIN

[For 62 Halsbury's Laws of England (5th Edn) (2016) para 282 see now 62 Halsbury's Laws of England (5th Edn) (2022) para 305.]

REPRESENTATION

[Delete the reference to 60 Halsbury's Laws of England (5th Edn) (2011) para 36.]

[For 76 Halsbury's Laws of England (5th Edn) (2013) paras 702, 715–716 see now 76 Halsbury's Laws of England (5th Edn) (2019) paras 702, 715–716.]

REPRESENTATIVES

In will

[For 102 Halsbury's Laws of England (5th Edn) (2010) para 365 see now 102 Halsbury's Laws of England (5th Edn) (2021) para 366.]

RES GESTAE

[For 12 Halsbury's Laws of England (5th Edn) (2015) para 692 see now 12 Halsbury's Laws of England (5th Edn) (2020) para 687.]

RES JUDICATA

[For 12A Halsbury's Laws of England (5th Edn) (2015) para 1603 see now 12A Halsbury's Laws of England (5th Edn) (2020) para 1568.]

RESCUE

[For 26 Halsbury's Laws of England (5th Edn) (2016) para 807 see now 26 Halsbury's Laws of England (5th Edn) (2020) para 1010; and for 62 Halsbury's Laws of England (5th Edn) (2016) para 282 see now 62 Halsbury's Laws of England (5th Edn) (2022) para 305.]

RESERVATION

[For 32 Halsbury's Laws of England (5th Edn) (2012) para 440 see now 32 Halsbury's Laws of England (5th Edn) (2019) para 440; and for 62 Halsbury's Laws of England (5th Edn) (2016) para 162 see now 62 Halsbury's Laws of England (5th Edn) (2022) para 180.]

RESERVED LEGAL ACTIVITY

(1) In this Act 'reserved legal activity' means—
- (a) the exercise of a right of audience;
- (b) the conduct of litigation;
- (c) reserved instrument activities;
- (d) probate activities;
- (e) notarial activities;
- (f) the administration of oaths.

(2) Schedule 2 makes provision about what constitutes each of those activities.

(Legal Services Act 2007, s 12)

[Legal Services Act 2007, s 12.] '[176] Sections 12 and 13 of the 2007 Act make clear that there is a category of legal activity which does not amount to reserved legal activity. Section 13(2)(b) defines legal activity to encompass activity, not being reserved legal activity, which consists of the provision of legal advice and assistance in connection with any form of legal disputes and the provision of representation in connection with any matter concerning any form of the resolution of legal disputes. It follows that it cannot be the case that all types of provision of legal advice, assistance, or representation in relation to any form of legal dispute will amount to the reserved legal activity consisting of the conduct of litigation.' *Baxter v Doble* [2023] EWHC 486 (KB), [2023] 3 All ER 395 at [176], per Cavanagh J

RESIDE—RESIDENCE

'[46] I accept entirely that there is a difference between residence and habitual residence. Unlike with habitual residence, a person can be resident in two countries at the same time (see *Marinos* [*Marinos v Marinos* [2007] EWHC 2047 (Fam), [2007] 2 FLR 1018] at para [48] and *V v V* [*V v V (Divorce: Jurisdiction)* [2011] EWHC 1190 (Fam), [2011] 2 FLR 778] at paras [50] and [51]). The obvious example would be the wife in *Marinos* who had homes in Greece (where her husband and children lived) and in England (where she worked and lived with her parents). In that case, she divided her time roughly equally between the two, but I accept Mr Howard's submission that it does not have to be equal. He postulated the case of a barrister who lives and works in London from Monday to Friday and goes home to his/her family in Dorset (per Mr Howard) or France every weekend.

'[47] Mr Marks is, however, correct that residence has to be something more than just a place where you or your spouse own a property. It has to be somewhere where you reside as opposed to where you visit. The most obvious example would be a holiday home which would not amount to residence, but another example might be the super-rich who own numerous homes all around the world. They visit these homes. They do not reside in each and every one of them.' *Pierburg v Pierburg* [2019] EWFC 24, [2019] 3 All ER 551 at [46]–[47], per Moor J

[European Parliament and Council Directive 2004/38/EC ('the Citizens Directive'), art 17(1)(a); Immigration (European Economic Area) Regulations 2006, SI 2006/1003, reg 5(2): entitlement to state pension credit conditional on having a right of residence in the UK.] '[81] … The reference in Recital (19) to the Citizens Directive to rights of permanent residence acquired under Regulation 1251/70 is a strong indication that the EU legislature intended the concept of continuous residence as used in art 17(1)(a) of the Directive to reflect the concept of continuous residence as used in art 2(1)(a) of the Regulation. Accordingly, both in its text, which contrasts with the text of recital (17), and by reason of its reference back to rights acquired under Regulation 1251/70, Recital (19) indicates that the concept of residence as referred to in art 17(1)(a) is factual residence, as the respondent contends.

'[82] We consider that recital (3) to the Citizens Directive reinforces this interpretation of art 17(1)(a). It explains that the EU legislature intended to codify and review the existing EU instruments dealing with workers and others "in order to simplify and strengthen the right of free movement and residence of all Union citizens". Thus, it was part of the purpose of the Directive to enhance existing rights of free movement and residence, such as those which had arisen under Regulation 1251/70, and not to subject them to new restrictive conditions. The same point emerges from recital (1) to Regulation 635/2006, which repealed Regulation 1251/70, as follows:

"[The Citizens Directive] consolidated in a single text the legislation on the free movement of citizens of the Union. Article 17 thereof includes the main elements of [Regulation 1251/70] and amends them by granting beneficiaries of the right to remain a more privileged status, namely that of the right of permanent residence."

…

'[88] In the *Alarape* case [*Alarape v Secretary of State for the Home Dept (AIRE Centre intervening)* (Case C-529/11) EU:C:2013:290, [2014] All ER (EC) 470, [2013] 1 WLR 2883, ECJ] the CJEU addressed the question whether periods of residence completed pursuant to art 12 of Regulation 1612/68, which provides a right for the child of a worker to be admitted to educational courses in the host member state, could count towards the five years of "legal residence" required for acquisition of a right of permanent residence under art 16(1) of the Citizens Directive. The CJEU applied its ruling in the *Ziolkowski* judgment [*Ziolkowski v Land Berlin* (Joined cases C-424/10 and C-425/10) [2014] All ER (EC) 314, [2013] 3 CMLR 1013, ECJ] regarding the meaning of "legal residence" in art 16(1) and held that residence pursuant to art 12 of Regulation 1612/68, but which did not comply with art 7 of the Citizens Directive, did not count for the purposes of art 16(1). In our view, this does not support Mr Chamberlain's interpretation of art 17(1) of the Citizens Directive. If anything, it tends to support Judge Ward's interpretation of that provision. That is because, following the guidance in the judgments in *Ziolkowski* and *Alarape*, residence in a host member state pursuant to rights under Regulation 1251/70 and Directive 75/34/EEC likewise would not count as "legal residence" for the purpose of art 16(1) of the Citizens Directive; but it is rights acquired by residence pursuant to Regulation 1251/70 and Directive 75/34/EEC which are intended to be respected and protected by art 17 of the Citizens Directive: see recital (19) to that Directive.

…

'[92] For the reasons set out above, in our judgment the Court of Appeal erred in its interpretation of art 17(1). Judge Ward arrived at a correct interpretation of that provision, in holding that residence in art 17(1) refers to factual residence rather than "legal residence" as required under art 16(1), as interpreted by the CJEU in the *Ziolkowski* judgment.' *Gubeladze v Secretary of State for Work and Pen-*

sions [2019] UKSC 31, [2019] 4 All ER 389 at [81]–[82], [88], [92], per Lord Lloyd-Jones and Lord Sales

Habitual residence

[Council Regulation 2201/2003/EC, art 3: jurisdiction in relation to divorce.] '[43] There is no dispute that, for these purposes, you can only have one habitual residence. Habitual residence is defined as the place where the person has established, on a fixed basis, his or her permanent or habitual centre of interests. All relevant facts will be taken into account in determining that. There is no specific timeframe for having established habitual residence. In some cases, it can be done very quickly. In others, it will take longer. If there is a planned, purposeful and permanent relocation to another country, habitual residence can be acquired contemporaneously (or virtually contemporaneously) with the loss of a previous habitual residence. For example, in *Z v Z (Divorce: Jurisdiction*) [2009] EWHC 2626 (Fam), [2010] 1 FLR 694, Ryder J found that a wife had established habitual residence in England "at or shortly after" the family moved to London.

'[44] There was some debate as to whether a person could ever be without a habitual residence. It seems that you can be for a brief period but only whilst you establish your new centre of interests. The example given by Munby J in *Marinos* [*Marinos v Marinos* [2007] EWHC 2047 (Fam), [2007] 2 FLR 1018] is that of a wife who lost her habitual residence in Greece as the aircraft on which she and the children were travelling to London took off. She then acquired a new habitual residence in this country as the aircraft touched down at Heathrow.

'[45] The test is qualitative not quantitative. In other words, it is not simply a head-count of days and nights, although time spent in a particular location will be a relevant factor in most cases.' *Pierburg v Pierburg* [2019] EWFC 24, [2019] 3 All ER 551 at [43]–[45], per Moor J

Canada [Convention on the Civil Aspects of International Child Abduction ('Hague Convention'), art 3.] '5. For the reasons that follow, I conclude that this Court should adopt the hybrid approach to determining habitual residence under Article 3 of the *Hague Convention*, and a non-technical approach to considering a child's objection to removal under Article 13(2).

...

'43. On the hybrid approach to habitual residence, the application judge determines the focal point of the child's life – "the family and social environment in which its life has developed" – immediately prior to the removal or retention: Pérez-Vera, at p 428; see also *Jackson v Graczyk* (2006) 45 RFL (6th) 43 (Ont SCJ), at para 33. The judge considers all relevant links and circumstances – the child's links to and circumstances in country A; the circumstances of the child's move from country A to country B; and the child's links to and circumstances in country B.

...

'47. The hybrid approach is "fact-bound, practical, and unencumbered with rigid rules, formulas, or presumptions": *Redmond v Redmond*, 724 F 3d 729 (7th Cir 2013), at p 746. It requires the application judge to look to the entirety of the child's situation. While courts allude to factors or considerations that tend to recur, there is no legal test for habitual residence and the list of potentially relevant factors is not closed. The temptation "to overlay the factual concept of habitual residence with legal constructs" must be resisted: *A v A* [*A v A (Children: Habitual Residence)* [2013] UKSC 60, [2014] AC 1] at paras 37–39.' *Office of the Children's Lawyer v Balev* [2018] SCJ No 16, [2018] 1 SCR 398 at paras 5, 43, 47, per McLachlin CJ

RESTITUTIO IN INTEGRUM

[For 29 Halsbury's Laws of England (5th Edn) (2014) para 440 see now 29 Halsbury's Laws of England (5th Edn) (2019) para 440.]

RESTRAINT OF PRINCES

[For 60 Halsbury's Laws of England (5th Edn) (2011) para 323 see now 7 Halsbury's Laws of England (5th Edn) (2020) para 314.]

RETAINED DIRECT EU LEGISLATION

'Retained direct EU legislation' means any direct EU legislation which forms part of domestic law by virtue of section 3 (as modified by or under this Act or by other domestic law from time to time, and including any instruments made under it on or after IP completion day). (European Union (Withdrawal) Act 2018, s 20(1) (definition amended by the European

Union (Withdrawal Agreement) Act 2020, s 41(4), Sch 5, Pt 2, paras 38, 44(1), (2)(f))

RETAINER

[For 66 Halsbury's Laws of England (5th Edn) (2015) para 561 see now 66 Halsbury's Laws of England (5th Edn) (2020) para 515.]

RETROSPECTIVE

[For 96 Halsbury's Laws of England (5th Edn) (2012) paras 1185–1186 see now 96 Halsbury's Laws of England (5th Edn) (2018) paras 801–802.]

REVERSE DOMAIN NAME HIJACKING

[12] At para 14, Mr Morgan stated that various of Mr Gleissner's companies had been accused of involvement in "reverse domain name hijacking" which involves filing trade mark applications in respect of well-known third-party trade marks whilst simultaneously attempting to cancel earlier registrations which could be used to oppose the application. Once registered, the new trade mark is used as the basis for a domain name complaint ("a UDRP complaint") against the domain name corresponding to the revoked trade mark. Once the domain name is transferred to the owner of the new trade mark, it can be sold at a profit or retained whilst it appreciates in value.' *Trump International Ltd v DTTM Operations llc (Comptroller General of Patents, Design and Trade Marks intervening)* [2019] EWHC 769 (Ch), [2019] Bus LR 2048 at [12], per Henry Carr J

RIDE HAILING APP

'[10] While there continue to be many minicab offices where a customer can make a booking either in person or by telephone, either for an immediate journey or for a future time, the introduction of smart phones and app-based services has significantly changed the way many private hire vehicle services are delivered, both in and outside London. In London there are a number of private hire vehicle operators, including Uber and Free Now, which only accept bookings by means of an app, generally known as a "ride hailing app".' *Uber London Ltd v Transport for London (Transopco (UK) Ltd (trading as Free Now) intervening)* [2021] EWHC 3290 (Admin), [2022] 2 All ER 797 at [10], per Males LJ and Fraser J

RIGHT

Enjoyment as of right

[For 32 Halsbury's Laws of England (5th Edn) (2012) para 23 see now 32 Halsbury's Laws of England (5th Edn) (2019) para 23.]

RIGHT OF WAY

[For 32 Halsbury's Laws of England (5th Edn) (2012) para 36 see now 32 Halsbury's Laws of England (5th Edn) (2019) para 36; and for 87 Halsbury's Laws of England (5th Edn) (2017) paras 876–877 see now 87 Halsbury's Laws of England (5th Edn) (2022) paras 870–871.]

Way of necessity

[For 87 Halsbury's Laws of England (5th Edn) (2017) para 885 see now 87 Halsbury's Laws of England (5th Edn) (2022) para 879.]

RIGHT TO BEAR ARMS

New Zealand '[13] Underpinning almost all aspects of the Kiwi Party's case is the claim that New Zealand citizens have a constitutional right to bear arms and in particular, weapons, magazines and gun parts that have been prohibited by the Amendment Act [the Arms (Prohibited Firearms, Magazines, and Parts) Amendment Act 2019].

'[14] This so-called constitutional right is said to be derived from ancient custom, which evolved into a common law right and was affirmed by Magna Carta, the Bill of Rights 1688 and the Treaty of Waitangi. In his supplementary submissions filed on 20 March Mr Minchin, counsel for the Kiwi Party, maintained "the right to bear arms is the practical application of the legal principles that 'no power is unfettered' and is the mark of a free society".

...

'[17] An examination of the constitutional instruments relied upon by Mr Minchin quickly exposes the fallacy of his argument that New Zealanders have a constitutional right to bear arms.

...

'[26] It is striking that the so-called right to bear arms is not referred to in any international human rights instrument, such as the International Covenant on Civil and Political Rights or the European Convention on Human Rights. Of the 190 countries that have a written constitution, only the constitutions of Guatemala, Mexico and the United States refer to a right to bear arms. The relevant parts of the constitutions of Guatemala and Mexico are modelled on the Second Amendment of the United States Constitution but expressly provide for limits according to law. Thus, it can be fairly said that the right to bear arms is an example of American constitutional exceptionalism. Even in the United States, the ability of a citizen to possess and use firearms may be subject to legislative control. Thus, assault weapons have been banned by seven State legislatures, including those in California and New York.

'[27] Our examination of the arguments advanced by Mr Minchin leads to the following conclusions:

(a) The so-called right to bear arms is not supported by any constitutional instruments that apply in New Zealand.
(b) In this country, as in almost all countries, a citizen's ability to possess, own and use firearms is regulated by legislation.
(c) There are only three countries which have some form of constitutional right to bear arms.
(d) There is no constitutional right to bear arms in New Zealand let alone the arms that are prohibited by the Amendment Act.'

Kiwi Party Inc v Attorney-General [2020] NZCA 80, [2020] 2 NZLR 224 at [13]–[14], [17], [26]–[27], per Collins J

RIOT

[For 26 Halsbury's Laws of England (5th Edn) (2016) para 550 see now 26 Halsbury's Laws of England (5th Edn) (2020) para 688.]

ROLE

Person's role in the incident

Canada [Criminal Code, RSC 1985, c C-46, s 34(2)(c).] '3 In March 2013, Parliament's redesigned Criminal Code provisions on self-defence came into force. These changes not only expanded the offences and situations to which self-defence could apply, but also afforded an unprecedented degree of flexibility to the trier of fact. This flexibility is most obviously expressed by the requirement to assess the reasonableness of the accused's response by reference to a non-exhaustive list of factors, one of which is "the person's role in the incident". The interpretation and breadth of this new phrase is at the heart of this appeal.

'4 Is this factor, as argued by Mr Khill, restricted to cases of unlawful conduct, morally blameworthy behaviour or provocation as previously defined in the repealed provisions? Or does it include any relevant conduct by the accused throughout the incident that colours the reasonableness of the ultimate act that is the subject matter of the charge? I conclude that it is the latter. While the ultimate question is whether the act that constitutes the criminal charge was reasonable in the circumstances, the jury must take into account the extent to which the accused played a role in bringing about the conflict to answer that question. It needs to consider whether the accused's conduct throughout the incident sheds light on the nature and extent of the accused's responsibility for the final confrontation that culminated in the act giving rise to the charge.' *R v Khill* [2021] SCJ No 37, 74 CR (7th) 223 at paras 3–4, per Martin J

ROYAL ASSENT

[For 96 Halsb'ry's Laws of England (5th Edn) (2012) paras 871–873 see now 96 Halsb'ry's Laws of England (5th Edn) (2018) paras 488–490.]

ROYALTY

[For 76 Halsb'ry's Laws of England (5th Edn) (2013) para 334 see now 76 Halsb'ry's Laws of England (5th Edn) (2019) para 331.]

RULE OF LAW

Australia

'[87] It also reflects that the Constitution "is framed upon the assumption of the rule of law". While the precise meaning of the rule of law is often contested, the irreducible meaning of the rule of law, about which there cannot be any debate, is "that Government should be under law, that the law should apply to and be observed by Government and its agencies, those given power in the community, just as it applies to the ordinary citizen" [*MZAPC v Minister for Immigration and Border Protection* (2021) 273 CLR 506; 95 ALJR 441; 390 ALR 590; [2021] HCA 17 at [91], quoting Stephen "The Rule of Law" (2003) 22(2) Dialogue 8 at 8.]. The "agreed beginning" for debates about the rule of law is "that State power must be exercised in accordance with promulgated, non-retrospective law made according to established procedures". Public power is not to be exercised in a way that is contrary to law, and, of no less significance, the Executive cannot itself authorise a breach of the law.' *Davis v Minister for Immigration, Citizenship, Migrant Services and Multicultural Affairs* [2023] HCA 10, (2023) 408 ALR 381 at [87], per Kiefel CJ, Gageler and Gleeson JJ (footnotes omitted)

S

SAFE PORT

[For 7 Halsbury's Laws of England (5th Edn) (2015) para 519 see now 7 Halsbury's Laws of England (5th Edn) (2020) para 201.]

SALE OF GOODS

[For 91 Halsbury's Laws of England (5th Edn) (2012) para 1 see now 91 Halsbury's Laws of England (5th Edn) (2019) para 1.]

By description

[For 91 Halsbury's Laws of England (5th Edn) (2012) para 73 see now 91 Halsbury's Laws of England (5th Edn) (2019) para 75.]

By sample

[For 91 Halsbury's Laws of England (5th Edn) (2012) para 94 see now 91 Halsbury's Laws of England (5th Edn) (2019) para 96.]

SALIENT FEATURES

Australia '[210] The recognition of duties of care despite such problems [tending to hinder the recognition, or qualify the scope, of duties of care] has come to depend on the presence of "salient features" in the relationship between the alleged tortfeasor and victim, such as the former's control, assumption of responsibility or knowledge and the latter's vulnerability or reliance: *Caltex Oil (Australia) Pty Ltd v The Dredge "Willemstad"* (1976) 136 CLR 529 at 576–577, 11 ALR 227 at 261–262 (Stephen J); *Perre* [*Perre v Apand Pty Ltd* (1999) 198 CLR 180, 164 ALR 606, [1999] HCA 36] at [198]–[201] (Gummow J); *Caltex v Stavar* [*Caltex Refineries (Qld) Pty Ltd v Stavar* (2009) 259 ALR 616, 75 NSWLR 649, [2009] NSWCA 258] at [102]–[104] (Allsop P). Those expressions have, however, acquired restricted meanings from the cases in which they are applied: see, for example, the authorities collected in *Ku-ring-gai Council v Chan* (2017) 224 LGERA 330, [2017] NSWCA 226 at [69], [71], [81] as to "vulnerability" and "reliance". Such restrictions prevent each salient feature from becoming, like "proximity", a statement of conclusion without practical content, and they ensure that consideration of salient features is undertaken to facilitate, not supplant, analogical reasoning: see *Brookfield* [*Brookfield Multiplex v Owners—Corporation Strata Plan 61288* (2014) 254 CLR 185, [2014] HCA 36] at [20]–[25] (French CJ).' *Ibrahimi v Commonwealth of Australia* [2018] NSWCA 321, (2018) 366 ALR 341 at [210], per Payne JA

SALVAGE

Salvage charges

[For 60 Halsbury's Laws of England (5th Edn) (2011) para 400 see now 60 Halsbury's Laws of England (5th Edn) (2018) para 378.]

SAME

Same interest

[CPR 19.6(1).] '[83] The procedural rule is clear: a representative action may only be started, and the court may only order that a claim be continued as a representative action, if the representative party and those whom that party represents, have "the same interest in" the claim. …

…

'[85] … Mr Tomlinson makes four central submissions:

(1) Persons have the "same interest" if they have a common interest and a common grievance.
(2) Persons may have the same interest in a claim even if there are disagreements between them and even if the quantum of damages that they have suffered is different.

(3) A representative claimant may represent a class, even if the members of that class have been affected by the defendant's actions in different ways.
(4) There is no limit to the number of persons that can be within the class to be represented.

'[86] The first three of these propositions give rise to dispute. Google submits that the existence of a common grievance against the same defendant is not enough to satisfy the "same interest" condition. In particular, where the defendant is alleged to have damaged individual rights and interests, the representative action will be unavailable unless every member of the class has suffered the same damage (or their share of a readily ascertainable aggregate amount is clear). Further, and in any event, the procedure will be unavailable where different potential defences are available in respect of claims by different members of the class. I accept Google's submissions, and in my judgment these principles apply to the facts of this case, so as to disqualify this claim.' *Lloyd v Google LLC* [2018] EWHC 2599 (QB), [2019] 1 All ER 740 at [83], [85], per Warby J

[CPR 19.6: representative actions where more than one person has the 'same interest' in a claim. Claim by iPhone users for data protection breach.] '[69] In its current form in CPR 19.6 the rule imposes no limit (either as a minimum or maximum) on the number of people who may be represented. Only one condition must be satisfied before a representative claim may be begun or allowed to continue: that is, that the representative has "the same interest" in the claim as the person(s) represented.

'[70] The phrase "the same interest" is capable of bearing a range of meanings and requires interpretation. …

'[71] The phrase "the same interest", as it is used in the representative rule, needs to be interpreted purposively in light of the overriding objective of the civil procedure rules and the rationale for the representative procedure. The premise for a representative action is that claims are capable of being brought by (or against) a number of people which raise a common issue (or issues): hence the potential and motivation for a judgment which binds them all. The purpose of requiring the representative to have "the same interest" in the claim as the persons represented is to ensure that the representative can be relied on to conduct the litigation in a way which will effectively promote and protect the interests of all the members of the represented class. That plainly is not possible where there is a conflict of interest between class members, in that an argument which would advance the cause of some would prejudice the position of others. …

'[72] As Professor Adrian Zuckerman has observed in his valuable book on civil procedure, however, a distinction needs to be drawn between cases where there are conflicting interests between class members and cases where there are merely divergent interests, in that an issue arises or may well arise in relation to the claims of (or against) some class members but not others. So long as advancing the case of class members affected by the issue would not prejudice the position of others, there is no reason in principle why all should not be represented by the same person: see *Zuckerman on Civil Procedure: Principles of Practice* (4th edn, 2021), para 13.49. …

…

'[74] Even if it were considered inconsistent with the 'same interest' requirement, or otherwise inappropriate, for a single person to represent two groups of people in relation to whom different issues arise although there is no conflict of interest between them, any procedural objection could be overcome by bringing two (or more) representative claims, each with a separate representative claimant or defendant, and combining them in the same action.

…

'[84] In the present case I could see no legitimate objection to a representative claim brought to establish whether Google was in breach of the [Data Protection Act] 1998 and, if so, seeking a declaration that any member of the represented class who has suffered damage by reason of the breach is entitled to be paid compensation. The individual claims that could theoretically have been brought by each iPhone user who was affected by the Safari workaround clearly raise common issues; and it is not suggested that there is any conflict of interest among the members of the represented class. For the purpose of CPR 19.6(1), all would therefore have the same interest in such a claim as the representative claimant. …' *Lloyd v Google LLC* [2021] UKSC 50, [2022] 2 All ER 209 at [69]–[72], [74], [84], per Lord Leggatt JSC

SCHOOL

County school

[For 35 Halsbury's Laws of England (5th Edn) (2015) para 106n see now 35 Halsbury's Laws of England (5th Edn) (2020) para 99 n 12.]

Maintained school

[For 35 Halsbury's Laws of England (5th Edn) (2015) para 106 see now 35 Halsbury's Laws of England (5th Edn) (2020) para 99.]

Public school

[For 35 Halsbury's Laws of England (5th Edn) (2015) para 370 see now 35 Halsbury's Laws of England (5th Edn) (2020) para 315.]

Voluntary school

[For 35 Halsbury's Laws of England (5th Edn) (2015) para 106n see now 35 Halsbury's Laws of England (5th Edn) (2020) para 99 n 12.]

[For 35 Halsbury's Laws of England (5th Edn) (2015) para 106 et seq see now 35 Halsbury's Laws of England (5th Edn) (2020) para 99 et seq.]

SCIRE FACIAS

For 20 Halsbury's Laws of England (5th Edn) (2014) para 661 see now 20 Halsbury's Laws of England (5th Edn) (2023) para 574.]

SCOPE

[Coroners and Justice Act 2009, s 5: scope of inquest.] '[20] In two important paragraphs 18 and 19 of the ruling, the Coroner said:

> "18. The word 'scope' has no special meaning of its own. By 'scope' all that is generally meant is a list of the topics upon which the coroner, in the coroner's discretion, will call relevant evidence so as to be able to answer the four key statutory questions: Who died? How, when and where did they come by their death?
>
> "19. These questions and the answers to them, known as the determination, are provided by statute in Sections 5 and 10 of the Coroners and Justice Act 2009. They are the four central questions in every inquest. When decided the answers to them are recorded by the coroner or the jury, if there is one, in the statutory Record of Inquest."

…

'[57] In our judgment the Coroner's statement of "the meaning of scope", in paras 18 and following of his ruling (see [20] above) was correct. Moreover, however the test is formulated, his decision in the present case to exclude the Perpetrator Issue from the scope of this inquest was not, in our view, unlawful in the public law sense.' *R (on the application of Hambleton and others) v Coroner for the Birmingham Inquests (1974)* [2018] EWCA Civ 2081, [2019] 2 All ER 251 at [20], [57], per Lord Burnett CJ, Hallett VP and McCombe LJ

SEAWORTHY

[For 60 Halsbury's Laws of England (5th Edn) (2011) paras 257–258 see now 60 Halsbury's Laws of England (5th Edn) (2018) paras 236–237.]

[For 7 Halsbury's Laws of England (5th Edn) (2015) para 419 et seq see now 7 Halsbury's Laws of England (5th Edn) (2020) para 223 et seq.]

SECURE ACCOMMODATION

[Children Act 1989, s 25.] '[46] The phrase "secure accommodation" is defined in s 25(1) as meaning "accommodation … provided for the purpose of restricting liberty". The same definition appears in [the Children (Secure Accommodation) Regulations 1991, SI 1991/1505,] reg 2 ("accommodation which is provided for the purpose of restricting the liberty of children to whom section 25 … applies"). At first sight, this looks like a relatively straightforward definition, although, as will become clear, it is by no means necessarily easy to apply.

'[47] The ALC [Association of Lawyers for Children] argues that the effect of s 25(7)(d) and reg 3 of the 1991 Regulations is to incorporate into the definition of "secure accommodation" for the purposes of s 25 the qualification that, if the accommodation is a children's home, it must be approved by the Secretary of State for that use. But there is nothing in s 25 itself to suggest that the meaning of the words "secure accommodation" is qualified by reference to s 25(7)(d) or reg 3. A close examination of the words of the section and the Regulation demonstrates that this is not so. Section 25(7)(d) provides that "the Secretary of State may by regulations provide that … a child may only be placed in secure accommodation that is of a description specified in the regulations …". Adopting a straightforward construction of s 25(7)(d), the phrase "secure accommodation that is of a description specified in the regulations" describes a subset, not a prerequisite, of "secure accommodation". Similarly, a straightforward construction of reg 3(1) ("accommodation in a children's home shall not be used as secure accommodation unless … approved by the Secretary of State for that use") is that it excludes certain accommodation from being used as secure accommodation, but does not alter the definition of "secure accommodation" itself. Although reg 3(1) (as reg 3 in the original form of the Regulations made pursuant to powers granted in the original Sch 2 to the 1989 Act) has been in force since the early days of the Children Act 1989, s 25(7)(d) was only inserted by amendment introduced in the Children and Social Work Act 2017. Thus, if the ALC's submission is correct, the definition of "secure accommodation" was changed by this amendment. If it had been Parliament's intention to change the meaning of "secure accommodation", it would surely have done so in much clearer terms.

'[48] A straightforward construction of the words of s 25 therefore leads to the conclusion that "secure accommodation" means nothing more or less than accommodation provided for the purpose of restricting liberty.' *Re B (a child) (Association of Lawyers for Children intervening)* [2019] EWCA Civ 2025, [2020] 3 All ER 375 at [46]–[48], per Baker LJ

SECURED CREDITOR

[For 5 Halsbury's Laws of England (5th Edn) (2013) para 574 see now 5 Halsbury's Laws of England (5th Edn) (2020) para 555.]

SECURITIES

In will

[For 102 Halsbury's Laws of England (5th Edn) (2010) para 296 see now 102 Halsbury's Laws of England (5th Edn) (2021) para 296.]

SEDITION

[Note that 11(1) Halsbury's Laws (4th Edn 2006 Reissue) para 371 is not reproduced in 25 and 26 Halsbury's Laws of England (5th Edn) (2020).]

SEISED

[European Parliament and Council Regulation 1215/2012/EU, art 29: where proceedings involving the same cause of action and between the same parties are brought in the courts of different member states, any court other than the court first seised must of its own motion stay its proceedings until such time as the jurisdiction of the court first seised is established.] '[17] I will take first the issue whether the Cypriot court is now seised of the Cypriot proceedings. The immediate effect of the order made on 22 May 2018 was that there were no longer any proceedings pending before the Cypriot court. But, at that time, the appellants had the right to file an appeal against that order, which they did within the time permitted for doing so. The effect of filing an appeal did not stay or suspend the effect of the order but, I assume (although the court does not have evidence on the point), a successful appeal will set aside the order with effect from the time it was made. It was not suggested to us that the effect would be different from this but Ms Wickenden, on behalf of the respondent, submitted that the correct position currently was that the Cypriot court had ceased to be seised on 22 May 2018 and that the Supreme Court of Cyprus became seised on the filing of the appeal, but it was for the purposes of art 29 the court second seised. I am unable to accept this analysis. The Supreme Court is seised only of an appeal. The choice, as it seems to me, must be between the Cypriot court not being currently seised as a result of the order of 22 May 2018 (and only becoming seised again if an appeal succeeds, at which time it will be the court second seised) and the Cypriot court still being seised by reason of filing the appeal and remaining so at least until the appeal is determined.

…

'[20] … I would hold … that the Cypriot court remains seised of the Cypriot proceedings until the appeal against the order of 22 May 2018 is determined. It is true that, because of the particular circumstances prevailing in the Supreme Court of Cyprus, it will probably be a long time until the appeal is finally disposed of, but the autonomous meaning of "seised" in art 29 cannot depend on factors of this sort which will vary greatly among member states.' *Easy Rent a Car Ltd v Easygroup Ltd* [2019] EWCA Civ 477, [2019] 4 All ER 1087 at [17], [20], per David Richards LJ

SEIZURE

Of ship

[For 60 Halsbury's Laws of England (5th Edn) (2011) para 328 see now 60 Halsbury's Laws of England (5th Edn) (2018) para 307.]

SEND

Sent to the parties

[Employment Appeal Tribunal Rules 1993, SI 1993/2854, r 3(3): an appeal must be brought within '42 days from the date on which the written reasons were sent to the parties'.]

'[24] The issue is whether a judgment is "sent to the parties" where in the case of one of the parties it is sent to a person other than that party or his or her representative. I should make two points by way of preliminary.

'[25] First, it was common ground before us, and is plainly right, that it is irrelevant for the purpose of r 3(3) when or whether the judgment is *received* by any party: what matters is when they were *sent*. …

'[26] Secondly, although what happened in this case was that the judgment was sent to a former representative, that is not the only kind of error that could occur. It will be important to test any proposed answer as it would apply to other kinds of "mis-sending". …

…

'[35] The starting-point must be the words of the rule itself. I see the force of Mr Margo's submission that as a matter of ordinary English it is hard to describe a document as having been "sent to the parties" when in the case of one of them it has been sent neither to the party himself or herself nor to their nominated representative. I also agree with him that the reasoning at para 52 of Judge Hand's judgment in *Carroll* [*Carroll v Mayor's Office for Policing and Crime* [2015] ICR 835, [2015] All ER (D) 209 (Feb)] (see para [27](4) above) is unconvincing: to say that a document is "sent to the parties" even where it is sent to someone who is not a party only asserts what it is necessary to prove, and Mr Margo's submission does not require any words to be read in (at least as regards "category (1) cases"). However, I also see force in Mr Moretto's point that the language of the rule refers to a single date, which is difficult to reconcile with a construction under which different dates would apply in the event of the mis-sending of the judgment to one of the parties. That being so, a strictly literal approach may not be appropriate: the phrase "sent to the parties" could reasonably be read as connoting the act of promulgation—perhaps equivalent to "sent out" or "published"—rather than the mechanics of despatch to each of the parties. I am not to be taking as saying that, as a matter of language, Mr Moretto's construction is to be preferred to Mr Margo's—only that both are reasonably possible. But once that point is reached it is necessary to consider which produces the more sensible result in practice.

'[36] As to that, I prefer Mr Moretto's contention. In my view there is an obvious practical advantage in having a single, contemporaneously recorded, date from which time for appealing runs for both parties, so that everyone knows where they stand from the moment that the judgment is promulgated; and I think it very likely that that is what the rule-maker intended. Even though there appears to be no formal obligation on the tribunal to include the standard-form endorsement recording the date at which the judgment is sent to the parties, the EAT Practice Direction clearly shows that that was the practice at the time that the Rules were made, and it can safely be assumed that the rule-maker was aware of it (and even if he was not he would certainly have assumed that the date of sending would appear in the covering letter).

'[37] Of course justice requires that where the judgment is mis-sent the party affected should not be unfairly prejudiced by the tribunal's mistake; but construing the rule so that time will not run until whatever date the mistake is corrected is a rigid solution which goes further than is necessary to correct the problem.

…

'[38] In my view a just outcome in mis-sending cases can be achieved more flexibly and sensibly, as Judge Hand held in *Carroll*, by the appropriate use of the EAT's discretion to extend time under r 37. I do not agree with Mr Margo that having to rely on the discretion causes any substantial prejudice to the party in question, at least if the principles governing its exercise are clear. …

…

'[92] For the reasons given by Underhill LJ at paras [35]–[36] of his judgment I agree that it is possible to construe "sent to the parties" as meaning "promulgated" (even if the tribunal then fails to send the document to one party at the correct address). I agree that this construction of r 3(3), when coupled with the discretion to extend time conferred by r 37, produces the more sensible result in practice; and therefore it seems to me that it was the result which the draftsman was seeking to achieve. I also agree with all that Underhill LJ says about the way in which the r 37 discretion should be exercised in cases of this kind where the tribunal has made an error.' *Rana v Ealing London Borough Council; Bonnie v Department for Work and Pensions* [2018] EWCA Civ 2074, [2019] 1 All ER 1078 at [24]–[26], [35]–[38], per Underhill VP and at [92], per Bean LJ

SEQUESTRATION

Writ of sequestration

[For 22 Halsbury's Laws of England (5th Edn) (2012) para 97 see now 24 Halsbury's Laws of England (5th Edn) (2019) para 95.]

SERIES OF DEDUCTIONS

[Employment Rights Act 1996, s 23(3)(a).] '[92] As I indicated earlier, a claim for unpaid leave can be brought as a claim for unlawful deduction from wages under s 23 ERA. In general such a claim must be presented before the end of the period of three months beginning with the date of payment of the wages from which the deduction is made. However, where a complaint is made about "a series of deductions", the three-month period runs from the last deduction in the series: see s 23(3). …

…

'[100] It seems to me that s 23(3) means what it says: the period within which a claim can be brought is three months from the date when the last deduction was made. There is nothing to suggest that the three-month time limit was intended to restrict or qualify the meaning of a "series of deductions".

'[101] Further, I agree with the EAT in *Bear Scotland* [*Bear Scotland Ltd v Fulton* (2014) UKEATS/47/13, UKEAT/160/14 UKEAT/161/14, [2015] IRLR 15, [2015] ICR 221] at [79], the word "series" is an ordinary English word connoting a number of things of a similar or related kind coming one after another. It is a question of fact and degree, based on the evidence, whether deductions are sufficiently similar or related over time to constitute a "series". The identification of a sufficient factual and temporal link between deductions will answer the question whether there is a "series" without the need to imply or infer a limit on the gaps between particular deductions relied on as making up the series.' *Pimlico Plumbers Ltd v Smith (No 2)* [2022] EWCA Civ 70, [2022] 4 All ER 563 at [92], [100]–[101], per Simler LJ

SERVANT

Household servant

[For 102 Halsbury's Laws of England (5th Edn) (2010) para 367 see now 102 Halsbury's Laws of England (5th Edn) (2021) para 368.]

SERVICES

Canada [Canadian Human Rights Act, RSC 1985, c H-6, s 5.] '92. This case is about the scope of s 5 of the *CHRA*, which reads as follows:

5 It is a discriminatory practice in the provision of goods, services, facilities or accommodation customarily available to the general public:

(a) to deny, or to deny access to, any such good, service, facility or accommodation to any individual, or

(b) to differentiate adversely in relation to any individual,

on a prohibited ground of discrimination.

'93. Do the present complaints allege a discriminatory practice in the provision of a service customarily available to the general public? Before the Tribunal, the complainants sought to challenge the registration provisions of the *Indian Act* as making discriminatory distinctions on the basis of race, national or ethnic origin, sex and family status …. They did not challenge the actions of the Registrar in processing their applications. At their core, these complaints are about Parliament's decision not to extend "Indian" status to persons in similar circumstances. This was properly characterized by the Tribunal as a bare challenge to legislation.

…

'95. What, then, is encompassed in s 5? The wording of this section focuses on the *provision* of services. The French version of the *CHRA* says that it is a discriminatory practice for the *service provider* ("*le fournisseur … de services*") to deny or differentiate adversely in relation to an individual. The use of this language suggests that s 5 is geared towards discrimination perpetrated by service providers.

'96. In our view, Parliament is not a service provider, and was not providing a service when it enacted the registration provisions of the *Indian Act*. Moreover, law-making is unlike any of the other terms listed in s 5; it does not resemble a good, facility or accommodation (see *Forward* [*Forward v Canada (Citizenship and Immigration)* 2008 CHRT 5], at para 42 (CanLII)). As observed by the Tribunal in *Andrews*, the legislative process is unique ….

'97. Parliament can be distinguished from the administrative decision makers that operate under legislative authority. These individuals and statutory bodies, which include the Registrar, may be "service providers", or entities that "provi[de] … services … customarily available to the general public". If they use their statutory discretion in a manner that effectively denies access to a service or makes an adverse differentiation on the basis of a prohibited ground, s 5 will be engaged. But, when their job is simply to apply legislated criteria, the challenge is not to the provision of services, but to the legislation itself (*Murphy* [*Public Service Alliance of Canada v Canada Revenue Agency*, 2012 FCA 7, 428 NR 240], at para 6).

'98. Furthermore, the relevant jurisprudence suggests that the enactment of legislation is not a service. This Court has defined a service as (1) something of benefit (2) that is held out or offered to the public (*Gould* [*Gould v Yukon Order of Pioneers* [1996] 1 SCR 571]; see also *Watkin* [*Canada (Attorney General) v Watkin* 2008 FCA 170, 378 NR 268], at para 31). In *Gould*, La Forest J (concurring) said, at para 55:

> There is a transitive connotation from the language employed by the various provisions; it is not until the service, accommodation, facility, etc, passes from the service provider and has been held out to the public that it attracts the anti-discrimination prohibition.

Again, La Forest J's definition in *Gould* focuses on the service provider. When Parliament crafts statutory eligibility criteria, there is no "transitive connotation". Nothing is being held out by Parliament to the public. It is only when the service provider itself discriminates that s 5 is engaged.

…

'104. In sum, we agree with the Tribunal and the courts below that bare challenges to legislation cannot be brought under s 5 of the *CHRA*. The act of legislating is not a service. …' *Canada (Canadian Human Rights Commission) v Canada (Attorney General)* [2018] SCJ No 31, [2018] 2 SCR 230 at paras 92–93, 95–98, 104, per Côté and Rowe JJ

SERVITUDE

For 87 Halsbury's Laws of England (5th Edn) (2017) para 733 see now 87 Halsbury's Laws of England (5th Edn) (2022) para 727.]

SERVITUDE (LABOUR)

'[79] Unlike slavery and forced labour, the concept of servitude is not defined in an international convention, though it is used in a number of international instruments including the Universal Declaration of Human Rights adopted by the United Nations General Assembly in 1948, which states in art 4 that "No one shall be held in slavery or servitude". The term "servitude" is generally understood to refer to a form of exploitation which lies on a scale of gravity or severity between slavery and forced labour and involves coercion. Thus, the US Supreme Court has interpreted the phrase "involuntary servitude", prohibited by the Thirteenth Amendment to the Constitution, to mean "compulsion of services through the use or threatened use of physical or legal coercion": see *US v Kozminski* (1988) 487 US 931 at 945. The European Court of Human Rights has held that, in art 4 of the ECHR, "servitude" means an obligation to provide one's services that is imposed by the use of coercion: *Siliadin v France* (App no 73316/01) (2005) 20 BHRC 654, (2006) 43 EHRR 287 (para 124). The Court has further described servitude as "aggravated" forced or compulsory labour, distinguished by the fact or perception that it is impossible for the individual concerned to change her situation: *CN v France* (App no 67724/09) (judgment, 11 October 2012) (paras 90–91); *Chowdury v Greece* (App no 21884/15) (judgment, 30 March 2017) (para 99).

'[80] To similar effect, a definition of "servitude" included in the seventh revised draft of the Palermo Protocol, though not in the final text, defined it as—

> "the condition of a person who is unlawfully compelled or coerced by another to render any service to the same person or to others

and who has no reasonable alternative but to perform the service, and shall include domestic servitude and debt bondage".'

Basfar v Wong [2022] UKSC 20, [2022] 4 All ER 1 at [79]–[80], per Lord Briggs and Lord Leggatt JJSC

SET-OFF

[For 11 Halsbury's Laws of England (5th Edn) (2015) para 382 see now 11 Halsbury's Laws of England (5th Edn) (2020) para 380.]

SETTLEMENT

[For 91 Halsbury's Laws of England (5th Edn) (2012) para 501 see now 91 Halsbury's Laws of England (5th Edn) (2019) para 401.]

Compound settlement

[For 91 Halsbury's Laws of England (5th Edn) (2012) para 501 see now 91 Halsbury's Laws of England (5th Edn) (2019) para 401.]

Marriage settlement

[For 91 Halsbury's Laws of England (5th Edn) (2012) para 503 see now 91 Halsbury's Laws of England (5th Edn) (2019) para 403.]

Post-nuptial settlement

[For 91 Halsbury's Laws of England (5th Edn) (2012) para 504 see now 91 Halsbury's Laws of England (5th Edn) (2019) para 404.]

Protective settlement

[For 91 Halsbury's Laws of England (5th Edn) (2012) para 507 see now 91 Halsbury's Laws of England (5th Edn) (2019) para 407.]

Strict settlement

[For 91 Halsbury's Laws of England (5th Edn) (2012) para 506 see now 91 Halsbury's Laws of England (5th Edn) (2019) para 406.]

SEWER

[For 46 Halsbury's Laws of England (5th Edn) (2010) para 998 see now 46 Halsbury's Laws of England (5th Edn) (2019) para 636.]

SEXUAL ASSAULT

[Sexual Offences Act 2003, s 3: offence of sexual assault.] '[10] Section 78 SOA provides:

"'Sexual'

For the purposes of this Part (except sections 15A and 71), penetration, touching or any other activity is sexual if a reasonable person would consider that—

(a) whatever its circumstances or any person's purpose in relation to it, it is because of its nature sexual, or

(b) because of its nature it may be sexual and because of its circumstances or the purpose of any person in relation to it (or both) it is sexual."

...

'[47] Notwithstanding Ms Heeley's cautionary submission that this is an offence that carries serious consequences on a conviction, we are confident that the answer to the question posed by the Attorney General is that it is not necessary for the prosecution to prove, as an element of the offence of sexual assault, that the offender not only intentionally touched another person without their consent and without reasonable belief in their consent, and that the touching was sexual, but also that the offender additionally intended his touching of that person to be sexual.

'[48] Instead, under s 78(b) the accused's purpose in relation to the activity may be relevant if a reasonable person would consider that, given the nature of the activity, it may be sexual and, because of the accused's purpose, it was sexual.' *Attorney General's Reference (No 1 of 2020)* [2020] EWCA Crim 1665, [2021] 3 All ER 890 at [10], [47]–[48], per Fulford VP

SHIPMENT

[For 91 Halsbury's Laws of England (5th Edn) (2012) para 341 see now 7 Halsbury's Laws of England (5th Edn) (2020) para 394.]

SHIPPED

New Zealand [Performance payments under agreement due when coal 'shipped' from the permit areas.] '[31] As noted above, the first issue between the parties is whether the first performance payment obligation has been triggered. This issue concerns the meaning of the expression "shipped from the Permit Areas", which appears in cl 3.4 of the Agreement. It is L&M's case that the obligation to make the first performance payment was triggered by Bathurst's extraction and shipment off-site of 25,000 tonnes of non-coking coal, which it sold into the New Zealand market.

'[32] Bathurst's case is that the first performance payment is only triggered when the first 25,000 tonnes of coal is extracted and exported by ship—it argues that "shipped" in cl 3.4 is to be given its ordinary literal meaning, being carriage by ship. This is, it says, a necessary construction, because the commercial purpose of the Agreement was always to extract coking coal from Escarpment for sale into overseas markets. Coal that is exported is always transported by ship in this way.

...

'[134] We begin with the words of the Agreement. Whatever the etymology of "shipped" (which no doubt originates from transportation of a thing on a ship), it is a word which has come to be used in a variety of contexts to describe all means of transport of goods from one place to another. Anyone who has ever purchased goods online knows that. Bathurst accepts that this is an available meaning, but submits that it is not the right one to best do justice given the context and purpose of the Agreement. In our view, when we zoom out from the word to the phrase in which it appears, this broader meaning of the word "shipped" is reinforced. The action "to ship" is linked in the sentence to moving goods away from the permit areas. But the permit areas are inland—it is impossible to transport coal directly from the permit areas on a ship.

...

'[158] The text of the Agreement strongly supports interpreting the expression "shipped from the Permit Areas" as meaning "transported" from the permit areas. The word "shipped" is now commonly used, following a sale, to mean transported. The language and structure of the clause and the broader Agreement is supportive of this meaning, and is not consistent with the meaning argued for by Bathurst. As to the extrinsic evidence relied upon by the parties, to the extent that such evidence is admissible, it provides little assistance as to the interpretation of the term, and does not support the meaning contended for by Bathurst.' *Bathurst Resources Ltd v L & M Coal Holdings Ltd* [2021] NZSC 85, [2021] NZCCLR 17, [2021] 1 NZLR 696, SC, at [31]–[32], [134], [158], per Winkelmann CJ, Glazebrook, O'Regan, Ellen France and Williams JJ

SHOP

[For 52 Halsbury's Laws of England (5th Edn) (2014) para 337 see now 52 Halsbury's Laws of England (5th Edn) (2020) para 338.]

SKINNY LABEL

'[2] The essence of the problem is fairly simply stated, although the details are more complicated. The patentee markets a prescription-only drug for three different indications under a single registered trade mark. Patent protection for the drug itself has now expired, but the patentee still has a second medical use patent for one of the three indications. A supplier of generic pharmaceuticals wishes to enter the market for the drug for the two non-patented indications, as it is lawfully entitled to do. To that end, the generic supplier obtains a marketing authorisation for a generic version of the drug limited to those two indications (a so-called "skinny label"), and it only identifies those indications in its summary of product characteristics ("SmPC") and patient information leaflet ("PIL").' *Warner-Lambert Co LLC v Actavis Group PTC EHF* [2015] EWHC 72 (Pat) at [2], per Arnold J

'[9] Actavis' product is marketed under the trade mark Lecaent. Actavis have now obtained a marketing authorisation for Lecaent on the basis that Lecaent and Lyrica are bioequivalent. So there can be no doubt that Lecaent is in fact suitable for treating neuropathic pain. However, the summary of product characteristics ("SmPC") and patient information leaflet ("PIL") for Lecaent only identify the medicine as suitable for epilepsy and GAD, ie the non-patented indications. It is important to understand that neither the SmPC nor the PIL contains any warning or injunction against using the medicine for other indications or indeed for the patented indication. The same is true of the packaging of the product. A marketing authorisation which is restricted in this way is described in the industry as a "skinny label" to reflect the narrowness of the indications compared with another authorisation with a wider range of indications. Another expression which is used is that the patented indication has been "carved out".' *Warner Lambert Co LLC v Acta-*

vis Group PTC EHF [2015] EWCA Civ 556, [2015] IP & T 875 at [9], per Floyd LJ

'[8] Lecaent is marketed under a "skinny label", ie for the treatment of some indications only. The Summary of Product Characteristics prepared for the purpose of obtaining marketing authorisation and the Patient Information Leaflet included in the packet state that the conditions for which Lecaent is indicated are epilepsy and GAD, for which patent protection has expired.

...

'[66] Because doctors commonly prescribe generically and the pharmacist generally does not usually know what indication is being treated, the use of "skinny labels" specifying the purpose of the generic product cannot reliably prevent the pharmacist from dispensing the generic product for a patent-protected use. Dispensing pharmacists know that Lyrica and Lecaent are identical, and the same dosage regime can be used for all indications for which pregabalin has received marketing authorisation.' *Warner-Lambert Co LLC v Generics (UK) Ltd (t/a Mylan) (Secretary of State for Health and others intervening)* [2018] UKSC 56, [2019] 3 All ER 95 at [8], [66], per Lord Sumption

SLANDER

[For 32 Halsbury's Laws of England (5th Edn) (2012) para 512 see now 32 Halsbury's Laws of England (5th Edn) (2019) para 511.]

Slander of goods or title

[For 32 Halsbury's Laws of England (5th Edn) (2012) para 778 see now 32 Halsbury's Laws of England (5th Edn) (2019) para 776.]

SLAVERY

'[75] The Convention to Suppress the Slave Trade and Slavery 1926 (the "1926 Slavery Convention") defines slavery, in art 1(1), as "the status or condition of a person over whom any or all of the powers attaching to the right of ownership are exercised". This represents the classic definition of slavery in international law and is reproduced, in substance, in both the Supplementary Convention on the Abolition of Slavery, the Slave Trade, and Institutions and Practices Similar to Slavery 1956 (art 7), and the definition of "enslavement" in art 7(2)(c) of the Statute of the International Criminal Court 1998.

'[76] The powers attaching to a right of ownership include the power to sell or otherwise transfer ownership and to use what is owned as a possession, like livestock or furniture. Such "chattel slavery" of human beings is nowadays rare, but the language of the definition, with its reference to 'any' of the powers attaching to the right of ownership, permits a more expansive interpretation. Thus, according to a report commissioned by the United Nations:

> "In the modern context, the circumstances of the enslaved person are crucial to identifying what practices constitute slavery, including: (i) the degree of restriction of the individual's inherent right to freedom of movement; (ii) the degree of control of the individual's personal belongings; and (iii) the existence of informed consent and a full understanding of the nature of the relationship between the parties."

See *Abolishing Slavery and its Contemporary Forms*, Office of the United Nations High Commissioner for Human Rights (2002), para 21.' *Basfar v Wong* [2022] UKSC 20, [2022] 4 All ER 1 at [75]–[76], per Lord Briggs and Lord Leggatt JJSC

SLIP RULE

The court may at any time correct an accidental slip or omission in a judgment or order. (CPR 40.12(1))

The court may at any time correct an accidental slip or omission in a judgment or order (the 'slip rule'). Where good practice has not been followed and, as a result the court has been misled, it is appropriate to correct or vary the order. However, the slip rule is limited to accidental slips or omissions and the court should be very cautious before going behind an apparent agreement between counsel. The slip rule cannot be used to enable the court to have second thoughts or to add to its original order but it can be used to amend an order to give effect to the court's intentions at the relevant time. (12A Halsbury's Laws of England (5th Edn) (2015) para 1226)

[Tribunal Procedure (Upper Tribunal) Rules 2008, SI 2008/2698, r 42: tribunal may 'at any time correct any clerical mistake or other accidental slip or omission in a decision or record of a decision'.] '[18] ... It was common ground before us that that rule, in common with slip rules applying to other jurisdictions, applies only to what I have above called "errors of expression". If the error was substantial the rule has no application. …

…

'[29] I accept, nevertheless, that there is a conceptual difference between the formal decision and the reasons for that decision, even if it is not always reflected in the form of the decision. The real question is whether Parliament in enacting the provision empowering the TPC [Tribunal Procedure Committee], or the TPC in making the rule, intended that the Upper Tribunal (and, in the case of the statute, the First-tier Tribunal) should only have the power to correct slips in its formal decision and not the reasons. I start with the language itself, ignoring at this stage any consideration of the scope of the slip rule in the CPR. As to that, the language is not explicit, and I think there are two possible approaches to the formula "a decision or record of a decision"; but on neither approach do I think that there can be detected a clear intention to limit the power of correction to the formal decision. I take the two approaches in turn.

'[30] A strict approach would be that it was necessary to give some different content to the two different elements—"decision" and "record of a decision". That can be done by treating the former as referring to the reasons and the latter as referring to the formal decision. I accept that if that were the intention the language is not very apt; but it is not impossible, and I am unable to see any other way of differentiating between them.

'[31] The alternative approach, which I would favour, is that the strict approach attributes to the draftsman a greater degree of precision than was intended, and that the two elements in the phrase can be taken as a composite. On that approach it seems to me more in accordance with ordinary legal usage to read the reference to a "decision" as being to the totality of the decision, comprising both the formal decision and the reasons. It is true that that would render the reference to the "record of the decision" redundant, but if we are not taking a strict approach it would be enough to recognise that that sometimes happens.

'[32] My reading, on either approach, of the effect of the language used is reinforced by considering the purpose of a slip rule of this kind. It is not only in the case of a formal decision that it may be desirable for a court or tribunal to be able to correct accidental errors. Most obviously, such an error in its reasons might lead to further error, or in any event difficulty, on an appeal or in further proceedings in the same litigation, or in other cases where the decision was followed. The present case would, if the Tribunal's figure could be established to be an accidental error, be a good example of that; and clearly the applicant in *Hazeltine* thought that the missing "not" might create difficulties in understanding Whitford J's reasoning on the pending appeal. There may be other circumstances in which the impossibility of correcting an error could lead to other kinds of injustice or undesirable consequences. I can see no sufficient reason why the draftsman should have intended to frame a slip rule in terms that allowed correction in the one situation but not the other.

'[33] I note in this connection that r 31 of the Tribunal Procedure (First-tier Tribunal) (Immigration and Asylum Chamber) Rules 2014, SI 2014/2604 permits the correction of "any … accidental slip or omission in a decision, direction *or any document produced by it*" (emphasis added). Whatever "decision" might cover if it stood alone, the italicised words appear to put it beyond doubt that the power extends to the written reasons for any decision. The TPC thus regarded it as desirable in that context that the slip rule should not be limited to formal decisions. It would be odd, to put it no higher, if we were to give r 42 a construction which produced a different result in the Upper Tribunal.

'[34] Of course adopting such a construction means that r 42 would be wider in its scope than r 40.12(1) of the Civil Procedure Rules, as construed in *A (a child)* [*Re A (a child) (appeal: jurisdiction)* [2014] EWCA Civ 871, [2014] 1 WLR 4453]. That may be untidy, but I do not regard it as unacceptable. The reasoning in *A (a Child)* depended on the established meaning of the phrase "judgment or order" and not on any view taken by the Court that a wider construction would be undesirable on grounds of policy or principle. Nor is there any reason to suppose that the drafters of the CPR themselves made a deliberate choice in favour of a narrow construction. It appears that they simply adopted the familiar formulation used in the RSC. Indeed if *Hazeltine* [*Hazeltine Corp v International Computers Ltd* [1980] FSR 521, Pat Ct] is correctly decided, any inconveniences caused by a narrow construction of the slip rule in the CPR itself are removed by the fact that there is an inherent jurisdiction to correct the reasons for a judgment or order.

'[35] I would for those reasons hold that the Upper Tribunal has power under r 42 to correct clerical mistakes and other accidental slips or omissions not only in its formal decisions but in its reasons for those decisions.

...

'[39] ... The purpose of the slip rule is to allow the court or tribunal to correct errors of expression so as to express what it actually meant to say. Only it can say whether a particular error is indeed an error of expression and, if so, how it should be corrected. It follows that there would normally be no role for this Court. ...' *AS (Afghanistan) v Secretary of State for the Home Department* [2019] EWCA Civ 208, [2019] 3 All ER 36 at [18], [29]–[35], [39], per Underhill VP

Australia [Uniform Civil Procedure Rules 2005, r 36.17.] '[255] On the slip rule ground, Al Maha submitted that the power under the slip rule is contingent on there being "a clerical mistake, or an error arising from an accidental slip or omission, in a judgment or order" and the exercise of the power under the slip rule is to "correct the mistake or error". Al Maha contended that the amendments made by the Commissioner to the conditions of consent and to approve an amended plan did not correct a "clerical mistake" or "an error arising from an accidental slip or omission", but rather were substantive amendments to the conditions of consent and the approved plans.

'[256] Al Maha submitted that the power to correct an error arising from accidental slip or omission directs attention to what the Court whose record is to be corrected did or intended to do, however "[i]t does not permit reconsideration, let alone alteration, of the substance of the result that was reached and recorded" (*Burrell v R* (2008) 238 CLR 218; 248 ALR 428; [2008] HCA 34 at [21]; *Achurch v R* (2015) 253 CLR 141; 306 ALR 566; 143 ALD 1; [2014] HCA 10 at [18]). Al Maha submitted that the application of the slip rule to correct an error would only be appropriate if the solution to the error does not involve controversy or depend on evaluative or discretionary judgment (*Newmont Yandal Operations Pty Ltd v J Aron Corporation* (2007) 70 NSWLR 411; [2007] NSWCA 195 (*Newmont Yandal*) at [129], citing *Storey & Keers Pty Ltd v Johnstone* (1987) 9 NSWLR 446 at 453). The slip rule cannot be used to "cloak the court with jurisdiction" which it otherwise would not have, or for the purpose of expanding the court's jurisdiction (*Tonab Investments Pty Ltd v Optima Developments Pty Ltd* (2015) 90 NSWLR 268; [2015] NSWCA 287 (*Tonab Investments*) at [61], [67] and [113]).

...

'[266] The slip rule decision was outside the power of the slip rule. The slip rule decision purported to amend order 3 made on 26 February 2018 to grant development consent to the development application on the conditions in Annexure A to the orders. As I have found earlier, the development for which consent was sought in the further amended development application and to which consent was granted included construction of the driveway connection to Hilts Road on Al Maha's land. The slip rule decision purported to modify the development consent so as to no longer authorise the carrying out of this development on Al Maha's land. It sought to achieve this modification of the consent by amending certain conditions of consent and substituting an amended plan. None of these modifications, however, could be described as corrections of "a clerical mistake" or "an error arising from an accidental slip or omission" in order 3 of the Commissioner's orders or in the annexed conditions of consent. The order and the annexed conditions of consent did not contain any mistake or error in granting consent to the construction of the driveway connection to Hilts Road.

'[267] The power under the slip rule could be exercised to correct mistakes or errors in the decision or orders of the Commissioner in order to carry into effect the intention of the Commissioner making the order: *Newmont Yandal* at [116]. The relevant intention of the Commissioner is the objective intention, not the subjective intention, of the Commissioner at the time the decision and orders were made: *Newmont Yandal* at [91], [102] and see *Tonab Investments* at [65]. The Commissioner's ex post facto observation in making the slip rule amendments, that "these amendments confirm that the consent and approved plans do not authorise the carrying out of any development on 36 Leicester Avenue, Strathfield", is at best "no more than evidentiary and may not even be admissible over objection": *Newmont Yandal* at [95].

'[268] Where the order sought to be amended under the slip rule is an order of the Court granting development consent, the intention of the Commissioner (or Judge) who made the order is to be discerned from the reasons for judgment (if there are reasons) and a construction of the development consent granted by the Commissioner (or Judge). ...' *Al Maha Pty Ltd v Huajun Investments Pty Ltd* [2018] NSWCA 245, (2018) 365 ALR 86 at [255]–[256], [266]–[268], per Preston CJ of LEC

SOLICITOR

[For 65 Halsbury's Laws of England (5th Edn) (2015) para 435 et seq see now 65 Halsbury's Laws of England (5th Edn) (2020) para 397 et seq.]

SOLICITOR'S EQUITABLE LIEN

'[78] I do not think it is possible to rationalise, so as to produce coherence, all the situations in which non-contractual liens are imposed by law (whether at common law or in equity or by statute). Equitable liens have been described as "something of a themeless rag-bag" (by Donovan Waters, "Where is Equity Going? Remedying Unconscionable Conduct" (1988) 18 University of Western Australia Law Review 3, at p 24: see also John Phillips, "Equitable Liens – A Search for Unifying Principle" in Norman Palmer and Ewan McKendrick (eds) *Interests in Goods* (1993) p 635, at p 637, reprinted in 2nd edn (1998) p 975, at p 977). But it is clear from long-established authority that a solicitor is entitled to an equitable lien over the fruits of litigation in order to give the solicitor security for the recovery of the costs (ie the fees) legally owed to the solicitor by his or her client. This is the solicitor's litigation equitable lien.

...

'[80] In *Gavin Edmondson [Gavin Edmondson Solicitors Ltd v Haven Insurance Co Ltd* [2018] UKSC 21, [2018] 3 All ER 273] the Supreme Court examined the role of the solicitor's equitable lien in the context of modern litigation, in particular in a climate where access to justice is a central underlying goal and out of court settlements and alternative dispute resolution are encouraged. On the facts of the case, the solicitor had entered the relevant claim on an online portal in line with the pre-action protocol for low value personal injury claims. The Supreme Court decided that the solicitor was entitled to an equitable lien over the settlement fund because the work had made a significant contribution to the settlement of the client's personal injury claim.

...

'[84] It has not been suggested by Brian Kennelly QC, counsel for Ryanair, that we should depart from the decision in *Gavin Edmondson*. In any event, I would not have wanted to do so because, in my view, it recognises in an important way the realities of modern litigation and dispute resolution. In other words, it updates the role of the solicitor's equitable lien in recognition of the modern approach to litigation and dispute resolution (using the latter as a term of art that can include instances where there is no real dispute as in *Gavin Edmondson*).

'[85] It follows that we are required in this case to apply *Gavin Edmondson*. The fact that *Gavin Edmondson* means that, in a wider range of situations than before, a solicitor is entitled to an equitable lien when others doing similar work are not so entitled is largely irrelevant. Similarly, it is largely irrelevant that solicitors doing transactional work, and not work that can be classed as "litigation or dispute resolution" work, are not entitled to an equitable lien. They are largely irrelevant factors because the historical position we are required to apply takes the fact that solicitors are entitled to an equitable lien in respect of litigation work as a starting point even if others doing the same or very similar work have no such lien. It would not be appropriate in this case – and neither counsel is suggesting that it is – to try to rationalise why solicitors in relation to litigation work may be regarded as enjoying a favoured position over others doing similar work or over solicitors doing different work that also results in a fund over which a lien could be enforced.

...

'[88] Therefore, assuming that the solicitor is acting for a potential claimant rather than a potential defendant, the appropriate test for a solicitor's equitable lien is whether a solicitor provides services (within the scope of the retainer with its client) in relation to the making of a client's claim (with or without legal proceedings) which significantly contribute to the successful recovery of a fund by the client. That seems to me to be the best interpretation of what *Gavin Edmondson* laid down. It is a clear and simple test to apply. Solicitors (and potential defendants) will know exactly where they stand. Although, given the context, further elaboration of the test seems unnecessary, one might add, lest there be any doubt, that by "claim" one is referring to a claim asserting a legal entitlement or, as one can also describe it, a legal claim.

...

'[96] It is true that the test I have adopted rests on the assumption that, as in this case and *Gavin Edmondson*, the solicitors are concerned with the making of a claim (or, one can add, a counterclaim) rather than the putting forward of a defence. We heard no submissions on the circumstances in which solicitors representing defendants are entitled to an equitable lien over a relevant fund and I therefore prefer to say nothing about that situation. However, it is very important to stress that this judgment, and the test put forward, is in no sense intended to cut back on the traditional ambit of the equitable lien where proceedings have been issued (whether in court or in arbitration).

...

'[104] The solicitor's equitable lien has been developed over time to meet new circumstances. It is at least 200 years old. It began as a principle to enable the court to intervene if a solicitor obtained a judgment for his client, and that led to a recovery for the client. It was extended to a case where the parties decided to refer their dispute to arbitration and most recently where the claimant uses a protocol or scheme for presenting a claim that enables him or her to receive a settlement offer without having to issue court proceedings. The equitable lien is therefore a dynamic legal concept, not one which is hard-edged, circumscribed by immutable rules and incapable of further development. Courts have developed the law to meet changing times and on the basis that they were satisfied that it was appropriate to do so. Parliamentary approval to the equitable lien can be seen in the creation of the parallel scheme for charging orders described by Lord Leggatt and Lady Rose at para [23] above. But that is a parallel stream of development limited to litigation that does not affect the equitable lien. But, although the concept is capable of development, in my judgment it should be developed only if there is a coherent principle which justifies that development.' *Bott & Co Solicitors Ltd v Ryanair DAC* [2022] UKSC 8, [2022] 4 All ER 255 at [78], [80], [84]–[85], [88], [96], per Lord Burrows JSC, and at [104], per Lady Arden JSC

SOLIDARITY

Canada [Civil Code of Québec, art 1526.] '1. This appeal illustrates the apparent conflict that sometimes exists between two core principles of extracontractual liability in Quebec civil law. The first of these principles is that of full compensation for injury. The second is the principle that, unless an exception applies, a person is liable for reparation only of injuries caused by his or her own fault.

'2. The *Civil Code of Québec* ("*CCQ*" or "*Code*") establishes a scheme that strikes a balance between these principles. Article 1457 of the *Code* provides for full compensation for injury caused by a fault. Article 1525 para 1 provides that solidarity between debtors is not presumed. Articles 1480 and 1526 set out the circumstances in which there is a solidary obligation to make reparation for injury caused by an extracontractual fault. The *Code* thus lays down the general principle that a person is liable only for damage he or she causes, but qualifies this principle to favour full compensation of a victim who suffers a single injury as a result of extracontractual faults committed by two or more persons. However, because solidarity represents a deviation from the general principle, it must be applied strictly (see D Lluelles and B Moore, *Droit des obligations* (2nd ed 2012), at No 2581).

...

'74. Article 1526 *CCQ* provides for solidarity in the case of persons who have, by committing a common fault or contributory faults, caused one and the same injury to another person (Baudouin, Deslauriers and Moore, at Nos 1–720 to 1–722; *Code civil du Québec: Annotations—Commentaires 2017–2018*, at p 1287; Lluelles and Moore, at No 2578). It is of the very essence of extracontractual solidarity that the debtors be obligated to the creditor for "the same thing" (art 1523 *CCQ*; Lluelles and Moore, at No 2577; see also M Tancelin, *Des obligations en droit mixte du Québec* (7th ed 2009), at No 1388). The injury contemplated in art 1526 *CCQ* is therefore subject to the requirement that there be a single injury.' *Montréal (Ville) v Lonardi* [2018] SCJ No 29, [2018] 1 SCR 104 at paras 1, 2, 74, per Gascon J

SOVEREIGN

[State Immunity Act 1978, s 20.] '[56] I reject the Defendant's contention that, notwithstanding his abdication, his constitutional position in Spain means that he nevertheless remains a "sovereign" and entitled to the personal immunity afforded under s 20(1)(a).

'[57] Following his abdication, the Defendant has enjoyed certain status and privileges provided by Royal Decree 470/2014 and he remains part of the Spanish Royal Family. Prior to his retirement from public duties, the Defendant has also represented the King and the Spanish State at several events ([22](xiv) above). Whilst it is, therefore, clear that the Defendant retains a special, and unprecedented, status of "King Emeritus" under the law and Constitution of Spain, it is equally clear that there is only one King of Spain and head of state of Spain and, since 19 June 2014, that has been his son, King Felipe VI.

'[58] I reject that, having regard to his special status, the Defendant should be regarded as falling within the definition of "sovereign" in s 20(1)(a). The subsection cannot be interpreted to sustain that construction. I accept Mr Lewis QC's submissions. Section 20, as the title to the section demonstrates, confers immunity on the head of state (and associated personnel). It does not, by s 20(1)(a) confer, and extend, that personal immunity to a former head of state, however much s/he may retain a special and respected position within the relevant state. As a matter of statutory construction, if the words "sovereign" and "head of state" in s 20(1)(a) were read disjunctively, then the word "other" would be redundant. The plain reading of the subsection indicates that, for those countries where this applies, the sovereign will be the head of state. Whatever his special constitutional position following abdication, the Defendant is neither the sovereign nor the head of state of Spain. Since abdication, he is not entitled to personal immunity under s 20(1)(a) SIA.

'[59] More generally, and in support of my construction of s 20(1)(a) as not including the Defendant, the personal immunity of a head of state is "only narrowly available" and confined to serving heads of state. It is justified because of his/her special status as the holder of the relevant state's highest office: "It would be an affront to the dignity and sovereignty of the state which he personifies and a denial of the equality of sovereign states to subject him to the jurisdiction of the municipal courts of another state, whether in respect of his public acts or private affairs": *Pinochet (No 3) [R v Bow Street Metropolitan Stipendiary Magistrate, ex p Pinochet Ugarte (No 3)]* per Lord Millett [1999] 2 All ER 97 at 170, [2000] 1 AC 147 at 268–269.' *Zu Sayn-Wittgenstein-Sayn v HM Juan Carlos de Borbón y Borbón* [2022] EWHC 668 (QB), [2023] 2 All ER 156 at [56]–[59], per Nicklin J

SPACECRAFT

In this Act … 'spacecraft' means a space object, or a craft to which section 1(5) applies, that is used or (as the case may be) is to be used for the purpose of spaceflight activities. (Space Industry Act 2018, s 2(6))

This subsection applies to—

(a) a rocket or other craft that is capable of operating above the stratosphere;
(b) a balloon that is capable of reaching the stratosphere carrying crew or passengers.

(Space Industry Act 2018, s 1(5))

Space activities and sub-orbital activities are referred to in this Act as 'spaceflight activities'. (Space Industry Act 2018, s 1(6))

'Space activity' means—

(a) launching or procuring the launch or the return to earth of a space object or of an aircraft carrying a space object,
(b) operating a space object, or
(c) any activity in outer space;

'sub-orbital activity' means launching, procuring the launch of, operating or procuring the return to earth of—

(a) a craft to which subsection (5) applies, or
(b) an aircraft carrying such a craft,

but does not include space activity.

(Space Industry Act 2018, s 1(4))

SPACEPORT

(2) In this Act … 'spaceport' means—
 (a) a site from which spacecraft or carrier aircraft are launched or (as the case may be) are to be launched, or
 (b) a site at which controlled and planned landings of spacecraft take place or (as the case may be) are to take place.
(3) In subsection (2), the reference to a site in paragraph (b) of the definition of 'spaceport' does not include an installation at sea that can be moved from place to place without major dismantling or modification.

(Space Industry Act 2018, s 3(2), (3))

SPECIFIC PERFORMANCE

For 95 Halsbury's Laws of England (5th Edn) (2017) para 501 see now 95 Halsbury's Laws of England (5th Edn) (2023) para 501.]

SPOUSE

[Social Security Contributions and Benefits Act 1992, ss 36, 39A; Social Security and Family

Allowances (Polygamous Marriages) Regulations 1975, SI 1975/561.] '[200] However, the issue in the present case is the meaning of the word "spouse" in the SSCBA 1992 and whether it can be interpreted as including a party to a marriage which is void under English law.

...

'[202] The word "spouse" is not defined in the primary legislation. In the absence of any alternative definition, it is clear to me that the word "spouse" cannot be interpreted as meaning a party to a marriage which is void under English law. However, although I put it this way for the purposes of this case, I would also agree with Ms Leventhal's submission that, because of the developments referred to in para [125] (para 3.10 of the 1985 Report) and as explained in para [199] above, "spouse" should be interpreted as meaning a party to a marriage recognised as valid under English law. As a result, I agree with the [Upper Tribunal Judge] when he said, at [101]: "In the absence of any other definition of 'spouse' in the SSCBA 1992, one must fall back on the understanding supplied by matrimonial legislation".

'[203] Accordingly, in my view, the word "spouse" cannot mean a party to a marriage which is void under English law, for the simple reason that a party to a void marriage is not a spouse. There would have to be some express, or possibly implied, provision which makes it clear that the conventional construction does not apply. There is nothing in the primary legislation which would support this conclusion. In particular, there is nothing to suggest that the introduction of the term spouse (in place of widow) was intended to include a party to a void marriage. Further, as Ms Leventhal submitted, this conclusion is supported by the contrast drawn in ss 36 and 39A of the SSCBA 1992 between a spouse or civil partner and a person living together with another person, to whom they are not married or in a civil partnership, "as a married couple": s 39A(5)(b).

'[204] That this is the effect of the primary legislation in this case was not significantly disputed. The focus of Ms Rooney's submissions was on the meaning of the 1975 Regulations and the question of whether they had broadened the scope of the benefits provisions so as to include those who would otherwise be excluded; in particular, whether they applied to a party to a religious marriage which was polygamous.

'[205] I would first note that, as with the primary legislation, the 1975 Regulations do not contain any definition of the word "spouse". Accordingly, absent some alternative necessary implication, in my view, it must mean a party to a marriage which is, at least, not void under English law.' *Akhtar v Secretary of State for Work and Pensions* [2021] EWCA Civ 1353, [2022] 2 All ER 937 at [200], [202]–[205], per Moylan LJ

STAKE (GAMBLING)

'[76] ...A "stake" is an ordinary English word meaning:

> "That which is placed at hazard; esp a sum of money or other valuable commodity deposited or guaranteed, to be taken by the winner of a game, race, contest, etc." (*Oxford English Dictionary* (2nd edn, 1989)).'

London Clubs Management Ltd v Revenue and Customs Commissioners [2020] UKSC 49, [2021] 2 All ER 333 at [76], per Lady Arden JSC

STALLAGE

[For 71 Halsbury's Laws of England (5th Edn) (2013) para 834 see now 71 Halsbury's Laws of England (5th Edn) (2020) para 737.]

STATUTE

[For 96 Halsbury's Laws of England (5th Edn) (2012) paras 606, 619–624, 625–633 see now 96 Halsbury's Laws of England (5th Edn) (2018) paras 206, 219–224, 225–233.]

Codifying statute

[For 96 Halsbury's Laws of England (5th Edn) (2012) para 639 see now 96 Halsbury's Laws of England (5th Edn) (2018) para 239.]

Consolidating statute

[For 96 Halsbury's Laws of England (5th Edn) (2012) para 638 see now 96 Halsbury's Laws of England (5th Edn) (2018) para 238.]

Penal statute

[For 96 Halsbury's Laws of England (5th Edn) (2012) para 617 see now 96 Halsbury's Laws of England (5th Edn) (2018) para 217.]

Statutory interpretation

Canada '28 The issue in this case is one of statutory interpretation, which, as this Court has repeatedly said, is an exercise in discerning legislative intent by looking at the grammatical and ordinary meaning of the text in the context of the statute's scheme and objectives.' *York University v Canadian Copyright Licensing Agency (Access Copyright)* [2021] SCJ No 32, 2021 SCC 32 at para 28, per Abella J

STATUTORY INSTRUMENT

[For 96 Halsbury's Laws of England (5th Edn) (2012) para 1045 see now 96 Halsbury's Laws of England (5th Edn) (2018) para 656.]

[See also the Statutory Instruments Act 1946, s 1(1A) (inserted by the Government of Wales Act 1998, s 125, Sch 12 para 2; and substituted by the Government of Wales Act 2006, s 160(1), Sch 10 paras 1, 2); and the Deregulation Act 2015, s 105.]

STEP

In proceedings

[For 2 Halsbury's Laws of England (5th Edn) (2017) para 521 see now 2 Halsbury's Laws of England (5th Edn) (2023) para 621.]

STRANDING

[For 60 Halsbury's Laws of England (5th Edn) (2011) para 340 see now 60 Halsbury's Laws of England (5th Edn) (2018) para 319.]

STREET

[For 55 Halsbury's Laws of England (5th Edn) (2012) para 9 see now 55 Halsbury's Laws of England (5th Edn) (2019) para 9.]

Private street

[For 55 Halsbury's Laws of England (5th Edn) (2012) para 10 see now 55 Halsbury's Laws of England (5th Edn) (2019) para 10.]

STRIKE (STOPPAGE OF WORK)

For 41A Halsbury's Laws of England (5th Edn) (2014) para 1340 see now 41A Halsbury's Laws of England (5th Edn) (2021) para 1312.]

STRUCTURED PROPORTIONALITY

Australia '[143] To be clear, my concern is with *structured* proportionality ("Verhältnismäßigkeit"), of the kind translated and presented in tabular form in *McCloy* [*McCloy v New South Wales* (2015) 257 CLR 178; 325 ALR 15; [2015] HCA 34], and of the kind which the Second Senate of the German Federal Constitutional Court recently castigated the European Court of Justice for failing to understand [in Bundesverfassungsgericht [German Federal Constitutional Court], Judgment of the Second Senate of 5 May 2020, 2 BvR 859/15, 2 BvR 1651/15, 2 BvR 2006/15, 2 BvR 980/16]. Structured proportionality commands the undertaking of consecutive inquiries into "suitability" ("Geeignetheit"), "necessity" ("Erforderlichkeit"), and "adequacy of balance" ("Zumutbarkeit") or "appropriateness" ("Angemessenheit"). Structured proportionality exhaustively defines, and in so doing confines, each of those standardised inquiries. Relevant considerations not captured within "suitability", as strictly defined, or "necessity", as strictly defined, are pushed down to be swept up in the residual inquiry into "adequacy of balance" or "appropriateness".' *Palmer v State of Western Australia* [2021] HCA 5, (2021) 388 ALR 180, BC202101051 at [143], per Gageler J

SUBJECT TO TERMINATION

[Housing Act 1985 s 82(1)(b): a secure tenancy which is a tenancy for a term certain but subject to termination by the landlord, cannot be brought to an end by the landlord except as mentioned in s 82(1A).] '[44] The key to this analysis is an understanding, contrary to the assumption inherent in the parties' submissions, that a tenancy for a term certain is not "subject to termination by the landlord" under s 82(1)(b) merely because the tenancy agreement contains a provision of some kind for early termination. It only becomes subject to (early) termination when a provision to that effect in the tenancy agreement becomes exercisable. Thus a landlord's break clause becomes exercisable only when the conditions for its exercise are first satisfied. A forfeiture clause becomes exercisable only when there has been a qualifying breach of the terms of the tenancy and (if the breach is not rent arrears or the tenant's bankruptcy) the landlord has served a s 146 notice. By the same token the early termination right may cease to be exercisable. A break clause may require the landlord to exercise it on a particular date, or within a defined period. A forfeiture may be waived by acceptance of rent after the occurrence of a non-continuing breach. In such a case the tenancy ceases to be subject to early termination by the landlord under s 82(1)(b), so that, at the relevant time when it wishes to recover possession, the landlord has none of the termination options set out in s 82(1A).

...

'[47] I would therefore answer the question posed by the first issue as follows:

a. The 1980 and 1985 Acts do not detract from the security of tenure enjoyed by a secure tenant under the terms of a fixed-term tenancy agreement.
b. Nonetheless the obtaining of a termination order in lieu of forfeiture is not the only way in which a landlord can bring about the termination of a fixed-term secure tenancy. If a means of early termination other than forfeiture has become available to the landlord under the tenancy agreement, so that the tenancy has become "subject to termination" within the meaning of s 82(1)(b) of the 1985 Act, then the landlord may obtain possession on the statutory grounds. An unexpired fixed term is not subject to termination by the landlord under s 82(1)(b) unless the landlord has an existing right to terminate early under the terms of the tenancy, such as a break clause, which has become exercisable and (if exercise requires procedural steps to be taken, such as a period of notice or needs to be exercised within a specified period) any requisite steps have been taken.
c. But if the only terms of the tenancy agreement which would, on the relevant facts, enable the landlord to obtain early termination are forfeiture provisions, then the landlord will need to seek an order for termination in lieu of forfeiture under s 82(3) before, or at the same time as, seeking possession on the statutory grounds.'

Croydon London Borough Council v Kalonga [2022] UKSC 7, [2022] 3 All ER 885 at [44], [47], per Lord Briggs JSC

SUBORDINATE LEGISLATION

[For 96 Halsbury's Laws of England (5th Edn) (2012) paras 1030–1031 see now 96 Halsbury's Laws of England (5th Edn) (2012) paras 637–638.]

SUBROGATION

[For 60 Halsbury's Laws of England (5th Edn) (2011) para 216 see now 60 Halsbury's Laws of England (5th Edn) (2018) para 195.]

SUDDEN

Sudden provocation

Australia [Criminal code (Qld), s 304: defence of sudden provocation.] '[13] The elements of the defence are in subs (1), which is expressed largely in the somewhat antiquated language of the Code at the date of its enactment. It is settled that subs (1) can only be understood by reference to the common law: the provocation must involve conduct of the deceased and that conduct must have the capacity to provoke an ordinary person in the position of the accused to so far lose self-control as to form and act upon the intention to kill or to do grievous bodily harm. This is so notwithstanding that neither requirement is, in terms, found in subs (1). It is also accepted that the "sudden provocation" of which subs (1) speaks is concerned with the accused's temporary loss of self-control excited by the provocative conduct of the deceased albeit that there may be an interval between the conduct and the emotional response to it.' *Peniamina v R* (2020) 385 ALR 367, [2020] HCA 47, BC202012190 at [13], per Bell, Gageler and Gordon JJ

SUFFICIENT

Sufficiently influenced

Australia [Income Tax Assessment Act 1936 (Cth), s 318(2), (6).] '[48] The central issue in this appeal from a decision of the Administrative Appeals Tribunal is the correct construction of s 318(2) and (6) of the Income Tax Assessment Act 1936 (Cth) (ITAA 1936). These provisions are found in Pt X of the ITAA 1936. Section 318(6) describes the meaning of "sufficiently influenced" which, relevantly for present purposes, is a phrase used in s 318(2) to identify the "associates" of a company.

...

'[80] Section 318(6) gives content to the test in s 318(2)(d)(i) and (e)(i) to be applied to identify whether an entity is to be regarded as an "associate" of another as either a "controlling entity" or "controlled company". The terms of s 318(2)(d) and (e) indicate that, whatever else "sufficiently influenced" means, it is more than legal control through majority voting power:

(1) An entity can be a "controlling entity" under s 318(2)(d) without having legal control through a majority voting interest, where the connection between the acts of "the company, or its directors" and the "directions, instructions or wishes" of the "controlling entity" are such that there the "primary entity" is "sufficiently influenced" by the "controlling entity", within the meaning of s 318(6)(b).
(2) An entity can be a "controlled entity" under s 318(2)(e) without the "primary entity" having legal control through a majority voting interest, where the connection between the acts of the "controlled entity" or its directors and the directions, instructions or wishes of the "primary entity" are such that the "controlled entity" is "sufficiently influenced" by the "primary entity", within the meaning of s 318(6)(b).

'[81] Whilst "sufficiently influenced" means something more than legal control through majority voting power, the concept of "control" is relevant to s 318(2)(d) and (e). Unlike paras (a)–(c), paras (d) and (e) are not describing relationships in which an entity might be expected to benefit, absent any consideration of "control". This is perhaps indicated by the use of the terms "controlling entity" and "controlled entity", and is certainly indicated by the text of the provisions, which look to legal control (in the sense of a majority voting interest) or something which is not legal control but attracts the description "sufficiently influenced" in the sense of acting "in accordance with" the "directions, instructions or wishes" of another. The s 318(6)(b) description of "sufficiently influenced" may be seen to describe a species of control or influence, or expected control or influence, which falls short of legal control. The critical issue in the proceedings is how far short it falls.

'[82] A number of observations should also be made concerning the description supplied by s 318(6)(b) of when "a company is sufficiently influenced" for the purposes of s 318(2).

'[83] First, the paragraph directs attention to the position of the company *and* the position of its directors: it is sufficient if either "the company, or its directors" are caught by the terms of the paragraph. The respondent submitted that the reference to "the company" in the phrase "the company, or its directors" was not a reference to the company in general meeting but merely recognised that a company acts through natural persons. This submission is rejected for the reasons given at paragraphs [131]–[134] below.

'[84] Secondly, s 318(6)(b) turns on whether either the company or its directors are:

(1) accustomed;
(2) under an obligation (whether formal or informal); or
(3) might reasonably be expected, to act in accordance with the directions, instructions of wishes of the entity or entities.

[85] These three matters are not a composite phrase denoting a single test (cf: *Sea Shepherd Australia Ltd v Commissioner of Taxation* (2013) 212 FCR 252; [2013] FCAFC 68 at [34] (Gordon J)); whilst each matter must be interpreted having regard to all of the words in s 318(6)(b) and in the context of the whole statute, the three matters comprise different considerations, each of which is independently sufficient to attract the conclusion that a company or its directors are "sufficiently influenced":

(1) The first matter—whether a company or its directors are "accustomed" to act in accordance with another's instructions or wishes—depends upon past facts.
(2) The second matter—whether there is an "obligation" to act in accordance with another's directions, instructions or wishes—depends upon a presently existing (or existing at the time the question is relevantly asked) formal or informal obligation.
(3) The third matter—whether a company or its directors "might reasonably be expected" to act in accordance with another's directions, instructions or wishes—requires a prediction as to future events and a consideration as to the objective likelihood of those future events occurring.

'[86] Thirdly, the terms of s 318(6)(b) do not require that there be a legal ability to require the company (or its directors) to act in accordance with the directions, instructions or wishes conveyed. It is enough if, as a matter of past or present fact or future expectation, the company or its directors are accustomed, or under a formal or informal obligation, or might reasonably be expected, to act in accordance with the directions, instructions or wishes of the primary entity.

'[87] Fourthly, s 318(6)(b) is satisfied only where the act is "in accordance with" the relevant directions, instructions or wishes. This is not established by the mere coincidence that the relevant act accorded with the relevant directions, instructions or wishes. There must be something more. This is because s 318(6)(b) is concerned with when "a company is sufficiently influenced", indicating that something more is required than mere coincidence between: (a) an action by the company or its directors; and (b) the directions, instructions or wishes of another. The parties were agreed that "in accordance with" imports considerations of causation. The level of causation required by the words "in accordance with" when used in a statute is informed by the statutory context in which the words are used.

'[88] Fifthly, there is nothing in s 318(6)(b) which expressly specifies how many, or what types of, acts must be "in accordance with" the directions, instructions or wishes of another.' *Commissioner of Taxation v BHP Billiton Ltd* [2019] FCAFC 4, (2019) 366 ALR 206 at [48], [80]–[88], per Thawley J

SUITABLE ACCOMMODATION

[Housing Act 1996, s 193: duty of local authority to house homeless persons.] '[17] Section 210 of the 1996 Act provides that local housing authorities must have regard to the provisions dealing with slum clearance and overcrowding in the 1985 Act, and those dealing with housing standards and houses in multiple occupation in Pts 1 to 4 of the Housing Act 2004, in determining whether accommodation is suitable. A local housing authority must, so far as reasonably practicable, secure that accommodation is available for occupation within its district: see s 208 of the 1996 Act.

'[18] Section 182 of the 1996 Act provides that local housing authorities must have regard to guidance given by the Secretary of State in exercising their functions relating to homelessness. The Secretary of State has issued a Homelessness Code of Guidance for Local Authorities ("the Code of Guidance"). That provides that consideration of whether accommodation is suitable requires an assessment of the accommodation in the light of relevant needs, requirements and circumstances of the homeless person and his household. Space and arrangement are said to be key factors and location is said always to be a relevant factor. Local authorities are told that they will need to consider carefully the suitability of accommodation for households with particular medical or physical needs. Paragraphs 17.7 and 17.8 of the Code of Guidance provide that:

"17.7 Accommodation that is suitable for a short period, for example accommodation used to discharge an interim duty pending inquiries under section 188, may not necessarily be suitable for a longer period, for example to discharge a duty under section 193(2).

17.8 Housing authorities have a continuing obligation to keep the suitability of accommodation under review, and to respond to any relevant change in circumstances which may affect suitability, until such time as the accommodation duty is brought to an end."

...

'[81] For those reasons, I consider that the Judge was correct to hold that s 193(2) of the 1996 Act imposed an immediate, non-deferrable and unqualified duty and to make a declaration to that effect. It is, however, important to bear in mind that that decision deals with the time when the duty arises and its nature. The duty itself is a duty to secure that accommodation is available for occupation and, by virtue of s 206, that accommodation must be suitable. The duty will continue until it comes to an end in the circumstances prescribed by s 193. Whilst the duty is owed, it is to be performed by securing that suitable accommodation is available. Suitability is, as the Judge said, a flexible concept. It will include factors such as the nature of the accommodation, the length of time that the homeless person has been in the accommodation and his and his family's needs. The lack of alternative accommodation may also be a factor affecting what is suitable in the short or medium term as may the fact that the housing authority has limited resources available to secure accommodation. There may be other factors which are relevant either generally or in a particular case. This judgment is not intended to suggest any exhaustive list of factors capable of being relevant to the question of suitability.

'[82] In other words, the duty to secure that suitable accommodation is available does not mean that permanent accommodation suitable for long term occupation must be provided immediately once the duty is owed. Different accommodation may be provided at different times to ensure that the duty is being performed. There may be stages on the way to the offer of secure accommodation under Pt VI, or an assured tenancy in the private sector. What is suitable may, therefore, evolve or change over time depending on all the circumstances.

...

'[108] The duty under s 193(2) is a duty to secure that suitable accommodation is available. That duty arises once the criteria in s 193(1) are met. The duty is an immediate, non-deferrable, unqualified duty to secure that suitable accommodation is available. What is "suitable" will depend upon a number of factors. Furthermore, accommodation may be suitable in the short term even if that particular accommodation would not be suitable in the medium or long term. If the duty is owed, and particular accommodation ceases to be suitable, the local housing authority is under a duty to secure that other suitable accommodation is available (whether or not that is also only suitable in the short term) until the duty in s 193(2) comes to an end. ...' *R (on the application of Elkundi) v Birmingham City Council* [2022] EWCA Civ 601, [2022] 4 All ER 302 at [17]–[18], [81]–[82], [108], per Lewis LJ

SUPERSEDE

Supersedes any right

[Civil Liability (Contribution) Act 1978, s 7(3).] '[46] Section 7(3) provides that the right to recover contribution under s 1 "supersedes any right ... to recover contribution ... otherwise than under this Act in corresponding circumstances" subject to certain exceptions. In the Court of Appeal both Irwin LJ and Phillips LJ considered that this provision supported the implication of overriding effect. Irwin LJ considered (at paras [60], [67], [68]) that the reference to "any right" must include rights of contribution existing under a foreign law. Phillips LJ considered (at para [74]) that the rights of contribution superseded by virtue of s 7(3) must be taken, in the context of provisions which fully recognise the likely relevance of private international law, to include rights of contribution under the otherwise applicable foreign law. In his view, the creation of a statutory right of contribution as between persons notwithstanding that the liability of one or more of them arises under foreign law and the exclusion of other rights of contribution (save for express contractual rights) can and should be read together as giving rise to the plain implication that the 1978 Act has "extraterritorial" effect. David Richards LJ, however, considered (at para [95]) that s 7(3) does not give rise to any such implication. In his view, if on analysis of the remaining features of the 1978 Act it were found that it did not have overreaching effect, s 7(3) could not produce a different conclusion because it is consistent with either conclusion.

'[47] The reference in s 7(3) to superseding "any right" is most obviously a reference to previous common law and equitable rights of contribution in English law which were replaced by the 1978 Act, such as contribution between trustees for a common liability for breach of trust or between company directors under a common liability for breach of an equitable duty owed to the company. (See C Mitchell *The Law of Contribution and Reimbursement* (2003) para 4.25, at p 81.) (In this regard I also note that the promoter in the House of Commons of the Civil Liability (Contribution) Bill stated that the clause which became s 7(3) of the Act was to make "fresh provision on the relationship between the Bill and existing common law rights to contribution" (Mr Geoffrey Pattie MP, Standing Committee C, 14 June 1978, col 55).) More fundamentally, however, as Mr Dougherty puts it in his written case, s 7(3) cannot found an argument that the 1978 Act has overriding effect because, like s 1(6), it begs the question in issue. Whether or not the statute has overriding effect, s 7(3) makes sense. If it does have overriding effect, it makes sense in that it supersedes any rights of contribution in domestic law or otherwise under a foreign law. If it does not have overriding effect, it makes sense in that it supersedes any rights of contribution in domestic law. I agree with David Richards LJ that s 7(3) provides no assistance either way.

'[48] In my view, therefore, the provisions of the 1978 Act relied upon by the defendants are equivocal in this regard. They do not indicate that the statute is intended to have overriding effect nor is their efficacy dependent upon overriding effect. They are equally consistent with a statutory right of contribution arising only where conventional choice of law rules indicate English law as the law with which the contribution claim is most closely connected.

...

'[80] The ordinary and natural meaning of the provisions of the 1978 Act and the scheme of the legislation provide little assistance on the issue as to whether it is intended to have overriding effect. The Act contains no express provision that it applies regardless of the law otherwise applicable to the contribution claim. Furthermore, the provisions are neutral as to whether overriding effect is to be implied. They are equally consistent with the 1978 Act applying only where the applicable law of the contribution claim is English law. They cast no light on the prior question whether the 1978 Act has any application at all. Furthermore, I have been able to find no assistance on this point in the legislative history of the Act.

'[81] Nevertheless, I am persuaded that the 1978 Act was not intended to have overriding effect so as to displace conventional choice of law rules. ...' *Roberts v Soldiers, Sailors, Airmen and Families Association – Forces Help (Allgemeines Krankenhaus Viersen GmbH, Part 20 defendant)* [2022] UKSC 29, [2023] 1 All ER 1 at [46]–[48], [80]–[81], per Lord Lloyd-Jones JSC

SUPPORT

Easement of

[For 76 Halsbury's Laws of England (5th Edn) (2013) paras 117, 119 see now 76 Halsbury's Laws of England (5th Edn) (2019) paras 114, 116; and for 87 Halsbury's Laws of England (5th Edn) (2017) paras 900, 906 see now 87 Halsbury's Laws of England (5th Edn) (2022) paras 894, 900.]

SURRENDER

For 62 Halsbury's Laws of England (5th Edn) (2016) para 521 see now 62 Halsbury's Laws of England (5th Edn) (2022) para 555.]

SURETY

[For 49 Halsbury's Laws of England (5th Edn) (2015) para 643 see now 49 Halsbury's Laws of England (5th Edn) (2020) para 606.]

SURFACE

[For 76 Halsbury's Laws of England (5th Edn) (2013) para 17 see now 76 Halsbury's Laws of England (5th Edn) (2019) para 17.]

SURVEYOR

The term 'surveyor' usually describes a person whose business it is to inspect and examine land, houses or other property and to calculate and report upon its actual or prospective value or productiveness for certain purposes, although surveyors also perform other functions. (6 Halsbury's Laws of England (5th Edn) (2023) para 588)

SURVIVE–SURVIVOR

[For 102 Halsbury's Laws of England (5th Edn) (2010) paras 317–318 see now 102 Halsbury's Laws of England (5th Edn) (2021) paras 317–318.]

SUSPECT (VERB)

Has reasonable cause to suspect

[Terrorism Act 2000, s 17: offence of making money or property available to another when the donor knows or 'has reasonable cause to suspect' that it will or may be used for the purposes of terrorism.] '[4] The question which arises on this appeal concerns the correct meaning of the expression "has reasonable cause to suspect" in s 17(b). Does it mean that the accused must actually suspect, and for reasonable cause, that the money may be used for the purposes of terrorism? Or is it sufficient that on the information known to him there exists, assessed objectively, reasonable cause to suspect that that may be the use to which it is put?

...

'[6] ... Both the trial judge and the Court of Appeal (Criminal Division) concluded that the correct answer was that the words used in the statute plainly mean that it is sufficient that on the information known to the accused, there exists, assessed objectively, reasonable cause to suspect that the money may be used for the purposes of terrorism.

...

'[24] In the present case it would be an error to suppose that the form of offence-creating words adopted by Parliament result in an offence of strict liability. It is certainly true that because objectively assessed reasonable cause for suspicion is sufficient, an accused can commit this offence without knowledge or actual suspicion that the money might be used for terrorist purposes. But the accused's state of mind is not, as it is in offences which are truly of strict liability, irrelevant. The requirement that there exist objectively assessed cause for suspicion focuses attention on what information the accused had. As the Crown agreed before this court, that requirement is satisfied when, on the information available to the accused, a reasonable person would (not might or could) suspect that the money might be used for terrorism. The state of mind of such a person is, whilst clearly less culpable than that of a person who knows that the money may be used for that purpose, not accurately described as in no way blameworthy. It was for Parliament to decide whether the gravity of the threat of terrorism justified attaching criminal responsibility to such a person, but it was clearly entitled to conclude that it did. It is normal, not unusual, for a single offence to be committed by persons exhibiting different levels of culpability. The difference in culpability can, absent other aggravating features of the case, be expected to be reflected in any sentence imposed if conviction results.

'[25] For these reasons it is clear that the conclusions arrived at by the trial judge and the Court of Appeal were correct. …' *R v Lane* [2018] UKSC 36, [2019] 1 All ER 299 at [4], [6], [24]–[25], per Lord Hughes

SUSPENSION

Grounds of suspension … of limitation periods

[Athens Convention relating to the Carriage of Passengers and their Luggage by Sea 1974, art 16(3): the law of the court seised of the case governs the 'grounds of suspension and interruption of limitation periods'.] '[30] In my view, the words in art 16(3) of the Athens Convention, 'the grounds of suspension … of limitation periods' are sufficiently wide to cover domestic rules which postpone the start of a limitation period as well as those which stop the clock after the limitation period has begun. I therefore agree with Lord Glennie in the judgment of the Inner House (para [17]): 'The word "suspension" … is also apt to include the deferment or suspension of something which has not yet started.

…

'[33] … Hirst LJ observed (obiter) [in *Higham v Stena Sealink Ltd* [1996] 3 All ER 660, [1996] 1 WLR 1107] that there were other sections in the Limitation Act 1980, such as s 32, which postpones the limitation period in the case of fraud, concealment or mistake, which might at first sight be eligible to qualify under art 16(3) of the Convention. But he went on to express the tentative view that the fact that in each case the section postponed the periods of limitation "prescribed by this Act" or words to that effect might disqualify them ([1996] 3 All ER 660 at 664, [1996] 1 WLR 1107at 1111). If in expressing that view he meant that the grounds of suspension in the lex fori were to apply under art 16(3) of the Convention only if they were framed to extend beyond the scope of the domestic limitation regime of the lex fori so as to cover limitation periods in conventions such as the Athens Convention, I must respectfully disagree. In my view, where art 16(3) speaks of the law of the court seised governing "the grounds of suspension … of limitation *periods*" (in the plural) it was applying the grounds—such as minority or mental incapacity—which the lex fori would apply to domestic claims for personal injury, or death or loss or damage to property. Thus, the existence of a ground in a domestic limitation statute which suspended the limitation periods set out in that statute, such as s 32 of the Limitation Act 1980 (fraud, concealment or mistake) or in this appeal s 18 of the [Prescription and Limitation (Scotland) Act 1973] (legal disability by reason of non-age or unsoundness of mind) is sufficient to bring art 16(3) into operation and extend the art 16 time bar by one year.' *Warner v Scapa Flow Charters* [2018] UKSC 52, [2019] 2 All ER 1042 at [30], [33], per Lord Hodge

SWAMP KAURI

New Zealand '[1] This appeal concerns the export of swamp kauri and products made from swamp kauri. Swamp kauri is kauri that has been buried and preserved in swamps for anywhere between 800 and 60,000 years. It is found largely in Northland in areas that were, but usually are no longer, wetlands. It is extracted almost exclusively from privately owned scrub or farm land and is of high commercial value, given its age and the size of the timber pieces that can be milled. Exports of swamp kauri increased significantly from 2010 to 2015.'

Northland Environmental Protection Society Inc v Chief Executive of the Ministry for Primary Industries [2018] NZSC 105, [2019] 1 NZLR 257 at [1], per Glazebrook J

SYSTEMIC MĀORI DEPRIVATION

New Zealand '[40] The effects of colonisation on Māori communities are well documented. Loss of land and other tribal resources together with the destruction of traditional social structures, tikanga, culture and language preceded widescale migration from tribal rohe to urban areas. For every generation since, Māori have been disproportionately represented among the poorest, most illiterate and most criminalised in New Zealand. The entrenched asymmetry of Māori in prisons is only one of many indicators of the systemic nature of this social disadvantage. For ease of reference I will refer to this pervasive and persistent social disadvantage affecting Māori as systemic Māori deprivation.

...

'[43] Relevantly, the normative basis for recognition of systemic Māori deprivation as a mitigating sentencing factor is not dependent on racial or ethnic classification. Rather, it is the presence of systemic deprivation in the lives of Māori offenders and their whānau that may trigger the potential for a differential sentencing response. ...' *Solicitor-General v Heta* [2018] NZHC 2453, [2019] 2 NZLR 241 at [40], [43], per Whata J

T

TAKING CONTROL OF GOODS

Provision is made under the Tribunals, Courts and Enforcement Act 2007 that applies where an enactment, writ or warrant confers power to use the statutory taking control of goods procedure ('the TCG procedure'). The power conferred by a writ or warrant of control to recover a sum of money, and any power conferred by a writ or warrant of possession or delivery to take control of goods and sell them to recover a sum of money, is exercisable only by using the TCG procedure. A power to use the TCG procedure to recover a particular sum is called an 'enforcement power'. Only an enforcement agent may take control of goods and sell them under an enforcement power. (12A Halsbury's Laws of England (5th Edn) (2020) para 1308)

TENANCY

[For 62 Halsbury's Laws of England (5th Edn) (2016) paras 1–2 see now 62 Halsbury's Laws of England (5th Edn) (2022) paras 1–2.]

Periodic tenancy

[For 62 Halsbury's Laws of England (5th Edn) (2016) para 227 see now 62 Halsbury's Laws of England (5th Edn) (2022) para 245.]

Tenancy at sufferance

[For 62 Halsbury's Laws of England (5th Edn) (2016) para 200 see now 62 Halsbury's Laws of England (5th Edn) (2022) para 218.]

Tenancy at will

[For 62 Halsbury's Laws of England (5th Edn) (2016) para 192 see now 62 Halsbury's Laws of England (5th Edn) (2022) para 210.]

Tenancy from year to year

[For 62 Halsbury's Laws of England (5th Edn) (2016) para 202 see now 62 Halsbury's Laws of England (5th Edn) (2022) para 220.]

TENANT-RIGHT

[For 1 Halsbury's Laws of England (5th Edn) (2017) para 461 see now 1 Halsbury's Laws of England (5th Edn) (2022) para 361.]

TENEMENT

[For 62 Halsbury's Laws of England (5th Edn) (2016) para 154 see now 62 Halsbury's Laws of England (5th Edn) (2022) para 171; and for 87 Halsbury's Laws of England (5th Edn) (2017) paras 8, 9 see now 87 Halsbury's Laws of England (5th Edn) (2022) paras 8, 9.]

TENURE

[For 87 Halsbury's Laws of England (5th Edn) (2017) para 4 see now 87 Halsbury's Laws of England (5th Edn) (2022) para 4.]

TERM CERTAIN

[Housing Act 1988, s 21(1A)(a).] '[53] Given the foregoing discussion, it is not strictly necessary for us to decide whether Mr Grundy is right that a fixed term tenancy with a break clause allowing it to be terminated during the first year is not a tenancy for a "term certain" within the meaning of s 21(1A)(a). But, having heard argument on the point, I propose to set out my views.

'[54] The words "term certain" are not defined in either HA [Housing Act] 1985 or HA 1988 but they were used as part of the definition of a secure tenancy in HA 1985 prior to the introduction of the provisions dealing with flexible tenancies. Given that a flexible tenancy is a species of secure tenancy (see s 107A(1)), it seems reasonable to suppose that the draftsman of the amendments introduced by the Localism Act adopted that definition for the purposes of the changes made to both HA 1985 and HA 1988.

…

'[56] My reading of [the HA 1985 s 82(1)–(3)] is that a secure tenancy which is not a periodic tenancy is treated as granted for a term certain even if it can be terminated by the landlord during the term. This is made clear by the opening words of s 82(3).

'[57] Such a conclusion would accord with principle. "Term certain" is not, of course, terminology exclusive to the Housing Acts. The requirement that a tenancy should be granted for a term certain has been part of the common law for centuries. …

…

'[59] A tenancy granted for a fixed term of, say, two years is limited by grant to a term certain of that duration notwithstanding that it may be brought to an end sooner by forfeiture or by the operation of a break clause. The word "certain" does not mean certain to last for the duration of the term. It means that the lease was granted for a term expressed to expire on a certain as opposed to an uncertain date. A lease granted for two years but with a break clause is nonetheless granted for a term certain of two years. It will end with certainty on that date regardless of any other circumstances.

…

'[65] I do not therefore accept Mr Grundy's submission that the words "term certain" are otiose in the context of s 21(1A) HA 1988. Certainty of term is a condition of every valid tenancy and the reference to a "tenancy for a term certain" in s 82(1)(a) HA 1985 was no more than the use of well-established nomenclature to describe a tenancy granted for a term of years. In formulating the provisions of s 107A(2)(a) HA 1985 and s 21(1A)(a) HA 1988 the draftsman has merely added the requirement for a two year minimum period to that definition.' *Livewest Homes Ltd v Bamber* [2019] EWCA Civ 1174, [2020] 2 All ER 181 at [53]–[54], [56]–[57], [59], [65], per Patten LJ

TERM OF YEARS

[For 62 Halsbury's Laws of England (5th Edn) (2016) para 229 see now 62 Halsbury's Laws of England (5th Edn) (2022) para 247.]

TESTAMENT

[For 102 Halsbury's Laws of England (5th Edn) (2010) para 1 see now 102 Halsbury's Laws of England (5th Edn) (2021) para 1.]

TESTAMENTARY

Testamentary expenses

[For 103 Halsbury's Laws of England (5th Edn) (2010) paras 1012–1013 see now 103 Halsbury's Laws of England (5th Edn) (2021) paras 1016–1017.]

'*THLIMMENOS*' DISCRIMINATION

[European Convention for the Protection of Human Rights and Fundamental Freedoms 1950, art 14, as set out in the Human Rights Act 1998, Sch 1, Pt I, art 14.] '[57] … Article 14 – prohibition of discrimination. It suffices for the purposes of this summary to note that the art 14 ground is argued on the basis of both direct discrimination and indirect discrimination (otherwise known as "*Thlimmenos*" discrimination after a case of the same name [*Thlimmenos v Greece* (App no 34369/97) (2000) 9 BHRC 12, (2000) 31 EHRR 411, ECtHR]).' *R (on the application of Mahabir) v Secretary of State for the Home Department* [2021] EWHC 1177 (Admin), [2022] 1 All ER 895 at [57], per Tim Smith

THOSE IN THE LOCALITY

[Anti-social Behaviour, Crime and Policing Act 2014, s 59: public spaces protection order ('PSPO').] '[41] It is clear from the terms of the 2014 Act itself that Parliament deliberately decided not to limit, by way of a statutory definition or statutory guidance, the expression "those in the locality". The looseness of that expression is to be contrasted with the express limitation of an "interested person" who may apply under s 66 of the 2014 Act to the High Court to challenge the validity of PSPO or its variation. "Interested person" is defined in s 66(1) as "an individual who lives in the restricted area or who regularly works in or visits that area". Similarly, the obligation on a local authority under s 72 of the 2014 Act to consult before making, extending the duration of, varying or discharging a PSPO, is limited to certain persons representing the police and the community and (under s 72(4)(c)) to "the owner or occupier of land within the restricted area". Parliament plainly decided not to limit s 59(2)(a) in either of those ways.

'[42] Accordingly, while we agree with May J in *Summers* [*Summers v Richmond upon Thames London Borough Council* [2018]

EWHC 782 (Admin), [2018] 1 WLR 4729, [2018] LLR 624] that the expression "those in the locality" in s 59 includes those who regularly visit or work in the locality, in addition to residents, it will depend on the precise local circumstances whether or not it extends to others.

…

'[47] We agree with May J in *Summers* at [25] that the 2014 Act gives local authorities a wide discretion to decide what behaviours are troublesome and require to be addressed within their local area. Equally, in deciding who is "in the locality" for the purpose of protection from such activities by way of a PSPO a local authority will (applying the words of May J to that issue) use its local knowledge, taking into account local conditions on the ground.

'[48] We do not consider there is any scope for narrowing the proper interpretation of the expression "those in the locality" in s 59(2)(a) on the ground that it is a criminal offence to breach a PSPO or because s 72(1) requires a local authority, in deciding whether to make, extend or vary a PSPO, to have particular regard to rights of freedom of expression and freedom of assembly in arts 10 and 11 ECHR [European Convention on Human Rights]. Any general presumption in relation to statutory provisions which criminalise conduct or activity (which was not explored in any detail before us) must be subject to the particular statutory provisions and framework in question. As regards s 72(1), its provisions are neutral on the issue of the proper interpretation of s 59(2)(a) as they pre-suppose that it is indeed lawful, where the statutory conditions for a PSPO are satisfied, for the PSPO to interfere with rights under arts 10 and 11 ECHR.

'[49] We conclude that Ealing was correct to interpret the expression "those in the locality" in s 52(2)(a) as capable of embracing occasional visitors, and were entitled to decide on the facts that the women, their family members and supporters visiting the Centre, in addition to staff and local residents, fell within that section.' *Dulgheriu v Ealing London Borough Council (National Council for Civil Liberties (trading as Liberty) intervening)* [2019] EWCA Civ 1490, [2020] 3 All ER 545 at [41]–[42], [47]–[49], per Sir Terence Etherton MR, King and Nicola Davies LJJ

THREAT

Of legal proceedings

[For 79 Halsbury's Laws of England (5th Edn) (2014) para 557 see now 79 Halsbury's Laws of England (5th Edn) (2020) para 577.]

TILLAGE

[For 1 Halsbury's Laws of England (5th Edn) (2017) para 462 see now 1 Halsbury's Laws of England (5th Edn) (2022) para 362.]

TIMBER

[For 52 Halsbury's Laws of England (5th Edn) (2014) para 55 see now 52 Halsbury's Laws of England (5th Edn) (2020) para 56.]

TOLL

Market toll

[For 71 Halsbury's Laws of England (5th Edn) (2013) paras 826–827 see now 71 Halsbury's Laws of England (5th Edn) (2020) paras 730–731.]

Toll thorough

[55 Halsbury's Laws of England (5th Edn) (2012) para 213 see now 55 Halsbury's Laws of England (5th Edn) (2019) para 241.]

Toll traverse

[55 Halsbury's Laws of England (5th Edn) (2012) para 213 see now 55 Halsbury's Laws of England (5th Edn) (2019) para 241.]

TIME IMMEMORIAL

[For 32 Halsbury's Laws of England (5th Edn) (2012) para 7 see now 32 Halsbury's Laws of England (5th Edn) (2019) para 7.]

TOTAL LOSS (MARINE INSURANCE)

[For 60 Halsbury's Laws of England (5th Edn) (2011) para 424 see now 60 Halsbury's Laws of England (5th Edn) (2018) para 402.]

TRADE EFFLUENT

[Water Industry Act 1991, s 141(1)] '[9] As the judge correctly said, the question on this issue is whether a liquid which contains a mixture of the product of trade or industry and surface water constitutes trade effluent within the meaning of the statutory definition. At [53] the judge set out the approach he would adopt to the interpretation of the statute. Mr Davies-Jones QC, on behalf of Boots, did not criticise anything that the judge had said in that respect; although he showed additional materials which would support the judge's distillation of principle. Since it is common ground that the judge was correct in setting out the principles, it is not necessary to do more than to repeat the relevant parts of his summary:

> "(1) In construing the definition, the Court must strive to give it a '*fully informed construction*'. (2) That requires the Court to have regard to the '*context*' of the statutory provision as well as to its terms. (3) The '*context*' of a statutory provision includes its legislative history, its statutory purpose and other Acts *in pari materia*. (4) The Court must also have regard to the consequences of rival constructions. (5) The Court should presume that the legislator did not intend a construction which would operate unjustly or anomalously and did intend one which promotes consistency in the law."

...

'[13] The consequences of the judge's interpretation, [counsel for Boots] submitted, were unjust. Boots had been charged both for the drainage of surface water by reference to the area of the site; and again for part of that surface water at trade effluent rates in so far as it formed part of the mixed liquid discharged into the foul sewer.

'[14] In my judgment this involves a misreading of the definition. First, the definition in s 141 does not expressly exclude surface or storm water, whereas it does expressly exclude domestic sewage. So the threefold classification [domestic sewage, surface water and trade effluent] is not reproduced in the definition. Second, s 106 refers to at least three (and possibly four) different types of sewer. Three are expressly mentioned: a foul water sewer, a surface water sewer and a storm-water overflow sewer. The fourth is a combined sewer which is implicit in the provision in s 106(2)(b) which applies "where separate public sewers are provided for foul water and surface water". If there are no separate sewers, then necessarily there must be a combined sewer. So that classification does not replicate the threefold division. Third, the definition expressly includes liquid partly produced in the course of trade. That part of the definition which contemplates a liquid partly produced in the course of trade thus contemplates a mixture. Moreover, the definition also contemplates a different kind of mixture, viz a mixture of liquid and suspended particles of matter.' *Boots UK Ltd v Severn Trent Water Ltd* [2018] EWCA Civ 2795, [2019] 3 All ER 371 at [9], [13]–[14], per Lewison LJ

TRADE UNION

[For 41 Halsbury's Laws of England (5th Edn) (2014) para 891 et seq see now 41 Halsbury's Laws of England (5th Edn) (2021) para 884 et seq.]

TRADITIONAL LAW OR CUSTOM

Australia [Native Title Act 1993 (Cth), s 223.] '[143] A traditional law or custom "is one which has been passed from generation to generation of a society, usually by word of mouth and common practice" (see *Yorta Yorta HC* [*Members of the Yorta Yorta Aboriginal Community v Victoria* (2002) 214 CLR 422; 194 ALR 538; [2002] HCA 58] at [46]). Thus, the pivotal role of Aboriginal evidence in native title proceedings of the present kind. Additionally, there are, under the NTA, two further important elements. First, the word "traditional" conveys "an understanding of the age of the traditions: the origins of the content of the law or custom concerned are to be found in the normative rules of the Aboriginal and Torres Strait Islander societies that existed before the assertion of sovereignty by the British Crown. It is only those normative rules that are 'traditional' laws and customs" (see *Yorta Yorta HC* at [46] and [79]).

'[144] Secondly, the normative system of laws and customs under which the rights and interests are possessed must have a "continuous existence and vitality since sovereignty". That is so because:

> If that normative system has not existed throughout that period, the rights and interests which owe their existence to that system will have ceased to exist. And any later attempt to revive adherence to the tenets of

that former system cannot and will not reconstitute the traditional laws and customs out of which rights and interests must spring if they are to fall within the definition of native title.

(*Yorta Yorta HC* at [47])'

Malone (on behalf of the Clermont-Belyando Area Native Title Claim) v Queensland (No 5) [2021] FCA 1639, (2021) 397 ALR 397 at [143]–[144], per Reeves J

TRANSGENDER

'[4] For the purposes of this judgment, "transgender people" or "trans-people" refer to people who identify as the opposite gender from that to which they were assigned at birth. Such people may or may not have "transitioned" (that is to say, aligned their body with their gender identity by hormone treatment and/or surgery).' *R (on the application of Elan-Cane) v Secretary of State for the Home Department (Human Rights Watch intervening)* [2020] EWCA Civ 363, [2021] 1 All ER 25 at [4], per King LJ

TRANSIT

[For 91 Halsbury's Laws of England (5th Edn) (2012) para 257 see now 91 Halsbury's Laws of England (5th Edn) (2019) para 258.]

TREASON

[For 26 Halsbury's Laws of England (5th Edn) (2016) para 419 see now 26 Halsbury's Laws of England (5th Edn) (2020) para 553.]

Treason felony

[For 26 Halsbury's Laws of England (5th Edn) (2016) para 423 see now 26 Halsbury's Laws of England (5th Edn) (2020) para 557.]

TREASURE TROVE

[For 29 Halsbury's Laws of England (5th Edn) (2014) para 297 see now 29 Halsbury's Laws of England (5th Edn) (2019) para 292.]

TREASURY BILL

[For 49 Halsbury's Laws of England (5th Edn) (2015) para 395 see now 49 Halsbury's Laws of England (5th Edn) (2021) para 359.]

TRESPASS

Australia '[69] Trespass occurs when a person enters the premises of another without lawful authority, including when a person enters by licence or permission but with a purpose contrary to the exclusive purpose of the licence or in a manner contrary to the terms of the licence. There is a basic divide at common law between a lease and a licence. An essential element of a lease, in contrast with a licence, is that it confers a right against others to exclusive possession of land as distinct from a mere licence or permission to enter land and use it for some stipulated purpose or purposes. A tenant's right of exclusive possession entitles the tenant (or, if held jointly, co-tenants) to bring an action for ejectment or, after entry, for trespass against all others apart from limited exceptions at common law, such as a landlord exercising a limited right of entry for confined purposes or "using only such force as is necessary" to remove a tenant who remains in possession after the expiry of the tenancy. The right of exclusive possession held by a tenant means, by definition, that others whom the tenant can exclude cannot bring an action for trespass against the tenant. A tenant may be liable to compensate a landlord for damage to premises. But the duty of a tenant to maintain the premises is a separate duty from, and not a condition upon, the tenant's right of exclusive possession.

...

'[72] These legal rules concerning trespass have been developed and refined over hundreds of years based upon the concept of possession. Possession is a different legal concept from occupation or habitation.' *BA v R* [2023] HCA 14, (2023) 409 ALR 41 at [69], [72], per Gordon, Edelman, Steward and Gleeson JJ

TRIBUNAL

The word 'tribunal' is … used in a wide variety of circumstances. The term 'tribunal' originally meant the raised platform provided for a magistrate's seat, from the Latin 'tribunus' or head of a tribe. The term developed to mean a body established to settle certain types of dispute or a court of justice. (24A Halsbury's Laws of England (5th Edn) (2019) para 6)

TRUST

[For 98 Halsbury's Laws of England (5th Edn) (2013) paras 1, 5, 24 see now 98 Halsbury's Laws of England (5th Edn) (2019) paras 1, 5, 24.]

Constructive trust

[For 98 Halsbury's Laws of England (5th Edn) (2013) para 124 see now 98 Halsbury's Laws of England (5th Edn) (2019) para 114.]

Discretionary trust

[For 98 Halsbury's Laws of England (5th Edn) (2013) para 94 see now 98 Halsbury's Laws of England (5th Edn) (2019) para 94.]

Executed or executory trust

[For 98 Halsbury's Laws of England (5th Edn) (2013) para 33 see now 98 Halsbury's Laws of England (5th Edn) (2019) para 33.]

Precatory trust

[For 98 Halsbury's Laws of England (5th Edn) (2013) para 34 see now 98 Halsbury's Laws of England (5th Edn) (2019) para 34.]

Private trust

[For 98 Halsbury's Laws of England (5th Edn) (2013) para 38 see now 98 Halsbury's Laws of England (5th Edn) (2019) para 38.]

Public trust

[For 98 Halsbury's Laws of England (5th Edn) (2013) para 37 see now 98 Halsbury's Laws of England (5th Edn) (2019) para 37.]

Resulting trust

[For 98 Halsbury's Laws of England (5th Edn) (2013) para 132 see now 98 Halsbury's Laws of England (5th Edn) (2019) para 131.]

Secret trust

[For 98 Halsbury's Laws of England (5th Edn) (2013) paras 35, 87 see now 98 Halsbury's Laws of England (5th Edn) (2019) paras 35, 87.]

Voluntary trust

[For 98 Halsbury's Laws of England (5th Edn) (2013) para 36 see now 98 Halsbury's Laws of England (5th Edn) (2019) para 36.]

TRUSTEE

Bare trustee

[For 98 Halsbury's Laws of England (5th Edn) (2013) para 195 see now 98 Halsbury's Laws of England (5th Edn) (2019) para 194.]

U

UNABLE

Unable to admit or deny

[CPR 16.5(1): in his defence, the defendant must state—(b) which allegations he is unable to admit or deny, but which he requires the claimant to prove.] '[49] In my judgment, a number of factors point towards the conclusion that a defendant is "unable to admit or deny" an allegation within the meaning of r 16.5(1)(b) where the truth or falsity of the allegation is neither within his actual knowledge (including attributed knowledge in the case of a corporate defendant) nor capable of rapid ascertainment from documents or other sources of information at his ready disposal. In particular, there is no general obligation to make reasonable enquiries of third parties at this very early stage of the litigation. Instead, the purpose of the defence is to define and narrow the issues between the parties in general terms, on the basis of knowledge and information which the defendant has readily available to him during the short period afforded by the rules for filing his defence.' *SPI North Ltd v Swiss Post International (UK) Ltd* [2019] EWCA Civ 7, [2019] 2 All ER 512 at [49], per Henderson LJ

UNABLE–UNWILLING

Canada [Refugee status was available to certain persons who inter alia were unable or unwilling to seek the protection of their home state.] 'I would agree with the court below that "unable" and "unwilling" have different meanings, which are fairly apparent on their face. One can say that "unable" means physically or literally unable, and that "unwilling" simply means that protection from the state is not wanted for some reason, though not impossible. This would, at first sight, seem to be a clear distinction, but as we shall see it has become somewhat blurred… .

'With respect to "unable", it would appear that physical or literal impossibility is *one* means of triggering the definition, but it is not the *only* way. Thus ineffective state protection is encompassed within the concept of "unable" and "unwilling", and I am left with the conclusion that the appellant here could have pursued his claim under either category.' *Canada (A-G) v Ward* [1993] 2 SCR 689 at 717, 718, 719, per La Forest J

UNAVOIDABLE CAUSE

[For 35 Halsbury's Laws of England (5th Edn) (2015) para 447 see now 35 Halsbury's Laws of England (5th Edn) (2020) para 385.]

UNCONSCIONABLE BARGAIN

[For 22 Halsbury's Laws of England (5th Edn) (2012) para 298 see now 22 Halsbury's Laws of England (5th Edn) (2019) para 98.]

[For 76 Halsbury's Laws of England (5th Edn) (2013) para 850 see now 22 Halsbury's Laws of England (5th Edn) (2012) para 298; 88 Halsbury's Laws of England (5th Edn) (2019) para 457.]

UNCONSCIONABLE CONDUCT

Australia '[1] This appeal raises an important issue as to the meaning and application of statutory provisions that call for a standard of business conduct in Australia that is not, in all the circumstances, unconscionable, in this case s 21 of the Australian Consumer Law being Sch 2 to the Competition and Consumer Act 2010 (Cth) (the ACL and the CC Act, respectively).

'[2] The issue is whether, for conduct to be unconscionable, there is required to be present vulnerability or disadvantage in the person or persons to whom the conduct can be seen as directed and that such was exploited or taken advantage of. That vulnerability or disadvantage was expressed in argument in two alternative ways, although in both the vulnerability or disadvantage was necessarily something more than an attribute or feature of the relationship, whether contractual or commercial. At its highest, the vulnerability or disadvantage had to be a special disadvantage as would be required in the equitable doctrine of unconscionability in setting aside a transaction: see generally *Commercial Bank of Australia Ltd v Amadio* (1983) 151 CLR 447; 46 ALR 402 (*Amadio*); *Kakavas v Crown Melbourne Ltd* (2013) 250 CLR 392; 298 ALR 35; [2013] HCA 25 (*Kakavas*); and *Thorne v Kennedy* (2017) 263 CLR 85; 350 ALR 1; 56 Fam LR 559; [2017] HCA 49. Alternatively, if the equitable requirement of the taking advantage of a special disadvantage was not required to be shown, at least the taking advantage or exploitation of some vulnerability, disability or disadvantage of the person or persons was a necessary aspect of the character or structure of the conduct apt to attract a conclusion of unconscionability.

'[3] As is discussed below, contrary to the primary complaint of the appellant, the Australian Competition and Consumer Commission (the **ACCC**), the primary judge did not approach the matter by reference to a requirement of special disadvantage in the sense of the equitable doctrine. His Honour did, however, approach the matter on the basis of the alternative argument expressed above. ...

'[4] For the reasons that follow, we respectfully consider that this approach is erroneous. Whilst some form of exploitation of or predation upon some vulnerability or disadvantage of people will often be a feature of conduct which satisfies the characterisation of unconscionable conduct under s 21, such is not a necessary feature of the conception or a necessary essence in the embodied meaning of the statutory phrase. The circumstances of this case reveal why this must be so. Here the facts that were agreed for the penalty hearing are such as to permit the conclusions (substantially drawn by the primary judge) that the respondents engaged in deliberate systematic conduct of misusing their superior bargaining position by dishonestly misleading commercial counterparties (referred to as the **investors** of no proven particular vulnerability other than from their place in the relevant commercial circumstances) and pressuring the investors by imposing entirely unjustified and unnecessary requirements upon the investors as their contractual counterparties, thereby clearly exhibiting a dishonest lack of good faith, all in order to extract for at least one of them financial benefits which were surreptitious and undisclosed to the investors.

...

'[83] The legislature has expressly stated that s 21 is not limited by the unwritten law: s 21(4)(a). That alone is sufficient to deny the proposition that a special disability or vulnerability as recognised in equity of which advantage is taken with sufficient knowledge or predatory state of mind (if that be required in equity) is an essential requirement of statutory unconscionability.

...

'[87] The word, "unconscionable", was, however, chosen by Parliament. As the Full Court said in *National Exchange [Australian Securities and Investments Commission v National Exchange Pty Ltd* (2005) 148 FCR 132; 56 ACSR 131; [2005] FCAFC 226] at [33], unconscionable conduct "on its ordinary and natural interpretation, means doing what should not be done in good conscience". The words "unconscionable" and "conscionable" may not be frequently used in everyday parlance, but they have an ordinary meaning, derived from the inner human sense of doing right. At least some of the human values that inform an Australian *business* conscience were set out in *Paciocco* [*Paciocco v Australia and New Zealand Banking Group Ltd* (2015) 236 FCR 199; 321 ALR 584; [2015] FCAFC 50] at [296]. Some of these, and not limited to protection of the vulnerable from victimisation or predation, were adopted by Kiefel CJ and Bell J in *Kobelt* [*Australian Securities and Investments Commission v Kobelt* (2019) 267 CLR 1; 368 ALR 1; [2019] HCA 18] at [14].

...

'[91] Predation on vulnerability, taking advantage of disability or disadvantage and victimisation may be found in business, as in other fields of human life. Such behaviour does not, however, exhaust the meaning of against conscience. The kinds of consideration in s 22 and the kinds of circumstance to which the Chief Justice referred in *Paciocco* at [296]–[298] are apt to inform evaluations about business standards that the courts are required by Parliament to make. They may be contestable judgments; they may be by reference to a standard that is not definable; but they are evaluative judgments that Parliament commands be made. That they are the subject of a civil penalty requires that the boundary of impugned conduct be reasonably known to the subject. This last factor reinforces the proposition that it is no light matter, indeed it is a serious matter, to have one's conduct impugned as against or as offending conscience. Business people understand such things, as do ordinary people. They need no definition to assist them. "Unconscionable" is the language of business morality and unconscionable conduct is referable to considerations expressed and recognised by the statute. The word is not limited to one kind of conduct that is against or offends conscience. Surely to predate on vulnerable consumers or small business people is unconscionable. But why is it not also unconscionable to act in a way that is systematically dishonest, entirely in bad faith in undermining a bargain, involving misrepresentation, commercial bullying or pressure and sharp practice, using a superior bargaining position, behaving contrary to an industry code, using significant market power in a way to extract an undisclosed benefit that will harm others who are commercially related to the counterparty? The proposition that such conduct (not all of which might be seen to be present here) is not unconscionable by an Australian statutory business standard of conscience because the counterparty to the business transaction suffered from no relevant pre-existing disadvantage, disability or vulnerability (other than, perhaps, having a decent degree of trust and faith in its business counterparty's honesty and good faith) is difficult to accept, unless one posits a narrow defined meaning of "unconscionable" that remains hinged in some way to the structural form of the equitable doctrine as expressed in cases such as *Kakavas* at [161]. The history, text and structure of the Act is contrary to such a conclusion. It is not to be derived from the meaning of the word "unconscionable".' *Australian Competition and Consumer Commission v Quantum Housing Group Pty Ltd* [2021] FCAFC 40, (2021) 388 ALR 577, BC202101878 at [1]–[4], [83], [87], [91], per Allsop CJ, Besanko and McKerracher JJ

UNDERTAKING

[Patents Act 1977, s 40(1): employee entitled to compensation where he has made an invention belonging to the employer for which a patent has been granted and the patent is (having regard among other things to the size and nature of the employer's undertaking) of outstanding benefit to the employer.] '[41] In this context I understand the word "undertaking" to mean simply a unit or entity which carries on a business activity, and here the undertaking of interest is that of the company or other entity which employs the inventor. In many cases the identification of that undertaking will be comparatively straightforward. It will be the whole or, if it is divided into economic units, the relevant unit of the employer's business. So, as Aldous J observed in *Memco-Med Ltd's Patent* [1992] RPC 403 at 414 and I agree, the undertaking may be the whole or a division of the employer's business.' *Shanks v Unilever plc* [2019] UKSC 45, [2020] 2 All ER 733 at [41], per Lord Kitchin

UNDUE INFLUENCE

[For 102 Halsbury's Laws of England (5th Edn) (2010) para 56 see now 102 Halsbury's Laws of England (5th Edn) (2021) para 56.]

UNDULY HARSH

[Nationality, Immigration and Asylum Act 2002, s 117C(5); Immigration Rules, para 399. Deportation of foreign criminals; exception where effect of deportation of a parent on a child would be 'unduly harsh'.] '[23] On the other hand the expression "unduly harsh" seems clearly intended to introduce a higher hurdle than that of "reasonableness" under s 117B(6), taking account of the public interest in the deportation of foreign criminals. Further the word "unduly" implies an element of comparison. It assumes that there is a "due" level of "harshness", that is a level which may be acceptable or justifiable in the relevant context. "Unduly" implies something going beyond that level. The relevant context is that set by s 117C(1), that is the public interest in the deportation of foreign criminals. One is looking for a degree of harshness going beyond what would necessarily be involved for any child faced with the deportation of a parent. What it does not require in my view (and subject to the discussion of the cases in the next section) is a balancing of relative levels of severity of the parent's offence, other than is inherent in the distinction drawn by the section itself by reference to length of sentence. Nor (contrary to the view of the Court of Appeal in *IT (Jamaica) v Secretary of State for the Home Dept* [2016] EWCA Civ 932, [2017] 1 WLR 240 (paras [55], [64])) can it be equated with a requirement to show "very compelling reasons". That would be in effect to replicate the additional test applied by s 117C(6) with respect to sentences of four years or more.

...

'[27] Authoritative guidance as to the meaning of "unduly harsh" in this context was given by the Upper Tribunal (McCloskey J President and Upper Tribunal Judge Perkins) in *MK (Sierra Leone) v Secretary of State for the Home Dept, MK (section 55 – tribunal options) Sierra Leone* [2015] UKUT 223 (IAC), [2015] INLR 563 (para [46]), a decision given on 15 April 2015. They referred to the "evaluative assessment" required of the tribunal:

> "By way of self-direction, we are mindful that 'unduly harsh' does not equate with uncomfortable, inconvenient, undesirable or merely difficult. Rather, it poses a considerably more elevated threshold. 'Harsh' in this context, denotes something severe, or bleak. It is the antithesis of pleasant or comfortable. Furthermore, the addition of the adverb 'unduly' raises an already elevated standard still higher."

...

'[33] However, when one comes to the actual decision of Judge Southern in *KO*, it is not clear that his approach was materially different from that of the President in *MK* or indeed the tribunal in *MAB* [*MAB (para 399; 'unduly harsh')* [2015] UKUT 435 (IAC)]. He adopted with one qualification the guidance in *MAB* as to the meaning of [the] "unduly harsh" test:

> "The consequences for an individual will be 'harsh' if they are 'severe' or 'bleak' and they will be 'unduly' so if they are 'inordinately' or 'excessively' harsh taking into account all of the circumstances of the individual. Although I would add, of course, that 'all of the circumstances' includes the criminal history of the person facing deportation." (para [26])'

KO (Nigeria) v Secretary of State for the Home Department (Equality and Human Rights Commission intervening) [2018] UKSC 53, [2019] 1 All ER 675 at [23], [27], [33], per Lord Carnwath

UNITED KINGDOM

[Will dealing with UK assets.] '[11] Jersey (and the other Channel Islands) are the last vestiges of the ancient Duchy of Normandy which, following the Norman Conquest of 1066, was united with the English Crown. Although King John lost the mainland part of the Duchy, the islands remained in the hands of the English Crown. It has its own legislature, its own courts and its own legal system. The monarch continues to exercise jurisdiction over the islands as if she were Duke of Normandy.

'[12] Jersey is not, however, an independent state in international law. The UK government is responsible for its international relations and its defence. Nor was Jersey a member of the EU. This is explained more fully in *R (on the application of Barclay) v Secretary of State for Justice and Lord Chancellor* [2014] UKSC 54, [2015] 1 All ER 429, [2015] AC 276.

'[13] For the purposes of domestic legislation it is not part of the United Kingdom as defined by s 5 of and Sch 1 to the Interpretation Act 1978 (which defines the United Kingdom as "Great Britain and Northern Ireland"); but it is one of the "British Islands" as there defined. Some provisions of that Act are applied to deeds and other instruments (see s 23(3)); but s 5 is not one of them.

...

'[25] In the light of the restricted effect of s 23(3) of the Interpretation Act 1978, I agree that no assistance can be gained from the statutory definition. I do not regard any of these cases as laying down the proposition that "the United Kingdom" as used in a private instrument can never include the Channel Islands; and there are two cases which held that, in the context of the particular instrument under consideration, it did.

...

'[41] The phrase "the United Kingdom" is capable of including the Channel Islands, as shown by *Stoneham* [*Stoneham v Ocean, Railway, and General Accident Insurance Co* (1887) 19 QBD 237, DC] and *Royal Society* [*Royal Society v Robinson* [2015] EWHC 3442 (Ch), [2017] WTLR 299]. Whether it does is a question of interpretation of the particular instrument in question. Since both an inclusive interpretation and an exclusive interpretation are possible (and it is unlikely that the testator intended to die partially intestate), the will is in my judgment ambiguous in the light of surrounding circumstances (excluding evidence of the testator's intention). Nugee J reached the same conclusion, for much the same reasons, in *Royal Society* at [28]. The will is ambiguous in that sense both at the date of execution of the will and also at the date of the testator's death.

'[42] It follows that direct evidence of the testator's intention is admissible.'

'[43] Mr Rossiter's intention is beyond doubt. In the draft that he himself prepared he said on the one hand that it was only to deal with his UK property but, on the other hand, he intended to make specific legacies of his Jersey assets. The two are only rationally reconcilable on the basis that Mr Rossiter intended "the UK" to include Jersey.' *Re Rossiter (deceased); Partington v Rossiter* [2021] EWCA Civ 1564, [2022] 4 All ER 1021 at [11]–[13], [25], [41]–[43], per Lewison LJ

UNLAWFUL ACT MANSLAUGHTER

Canada [Criminal Code, RSC 1985, c C-46, s 222.] '**25** The *actus reus* of unlawful act manslaughter under s 222(5)(a) requires the Crown to prove that the accused committed an unlawful act and that the unlawful act caused death (*R v Creighton* [1993] 3 SCR 3, at pp 42–43; *R v DeSousa* [1992] 2 SCR 944, at pp 959 and 961–962). The underlying unlawful act is described as the "predicate" offence (*DeSousa*, at p 956; *Creighton*, at p 42). The predicate offence in Ms Javanmardi's case is administering the intravenous injection contrary to s 31 of Quebec's Medical Act, a strict liability offence.

'**26** There has been some uncertainty around whether the Crown must prove that the predicate offence was "objectively dangerous" (see Larry C. Wilson, "Too Many Manslaughters" (2007), 52 Crim LQ 433, at p 459 citing Isabel Grant, Dorothy Chunn and Christine Boyle, *The Law of Homicide* (1994), at pp 4-15, 4-16 and 4-20; Stanley Yeo, "The Fault Elements for Involuntary Manslaughter: Some Lessons From Downunder" (2000), 43 Crim LQ 291, at p 293). In my view, the "objective dangerousness" requirement adds nothing to the analysis that is not captured within the fault element of unlawful act manslaughter — objective foreseeability of the risk of bodily harm that is neither trivial nor transitory (*Creighton*, at pp 44–45). An unlawful act, accompanied by objective foreseeability of the risk of bodily harm that is neither trivial nor transitory, is an objectively dangerous act.

...

'**30** As a result, the *actus reus* of unlawful act manslaughter is satisfied by proof beyond a reasonable doubt that the accused committed an unlawful act that caused death. There is no independent requirement of objective dangerousness.' *R v Javanmardi* [2019] SCJ No 54, 2019 SCC 54 at paras 25–26, 30, per Abella J

UNSEAWORTHY

[For 7 Halsbury's Laws of England (5th Edn) (2015) para 420 et seq see now 7 Halsbury's Laws of England (5th Edn) (2020) para 224 et seq.]

UNTRUE STATEMENT

New Zealand [Securities Act 1978, s 56(1): Compensation for loss or damage sustained by reason of an untrue statement. Section 55(a): a statement included in an advertisement or registered prospectus is deemed to be untrue if (i) it is misleading in the form and context in which it is included; or (ii) it is misleading by reason of the omission of a particular which is material to the statement in the form and context in which it is included.] '[77] The definition of "untrue" in s 55(a) is very broad. It is clear that at least s 55(a)(ii) extends the meaning of the term "untrue statement". The term "misleading" is used in both (i) and (ii) of s 55(a). The breadth of the term "misleading" is illustrated by reference to s 37A(1)(b), which refers to a prospectus being false or misleading "by reason of failing to refer, or give proper emphasis, to adverse circumstances". Although those words do not appear in s 55(a), we consider a broad interpretation of the term "misleading" is appropriate. Because of the breadth of the definition in s 55(a), we do not consider that it makes any difference (at least for the purposes of the present appeal) whether it is seen as an exhaustive definition or not. We will therefore treat the definition as exhaustive for the purposes of this judgment.

'[78] We do note, however, that the term "untrue statement" and the definition in s 55(a) must be interpreted in the context of the Act and its investor protection purpose. This means that, to be an untrue statement in terms of s 56(1), any statement must be on a topic that may be relevant (either on its own or in combination with other considerations) to a decision to invest. Statements (even if incorrect) that are incapable of being relevant to an investment decision will not be untrue statements for the purpose of s 56(1). For example, trivial errors, such as an error in the middle name or address of a director or a clear typographical error, are unlikely to be capable of being relevant to an investment decision.

...

'[80] ... A claim that a prospectus is, in its entirety, an untrue statement will be able to be substantiated only if it can be shown that statements in (or omissions from) the prospectus have a cumulative effect, making the overall document misleading. While such an argument may be broadly described as an argument that the prospectus itself is an untrue statement, the reality is that it is unlikely to be successful unless it is supported by identified misleading statements or omissions.

'[81] The High Court found that the failure to achieve the FY04 revenue forecast was not material and, at least implicitly, that it was not therefore an untrue statement. The Court of Appeal accepted that a statement could be an untrue statement under s 55(a)(i) whether or not it was material. The respondents submit that the High Court was correct and that a statement is not an untrue statement if it is not materially untrue.

'[82] There is nothing in the wording of s 55(a) that requires that a statement be misleading to a material extent. Section 55(a)(i) uses the term "misleading" without any reference to materiality. It is true that s 55(a)(ii) refers to a statement that is misleading by reason of the omission of a particular which is material to the statement. That does introduce the word "material", but not as a qualifier of the word "misleading". Rather, it is a qualifier of "a particular". The effect of para (ii) is that a statement that is otherwise true can become an untrue statement for the purposes of s 56(1) if a particular is omitted and the particular that is omitted is such that its omission makes the otherwise true statement misleading. There is nothing in s 55(a)(ii) that supports the proposition that a misleading statement will not breach s 55(a)(i) unless it is misleading to a material extent.

'[83] In the present case, Mr Houghton argues that the FY04 revenue forecast was an untrue statement. To the extent that Mr Houghton relies on s 55(a)(i), we, like the Court of Appeal, do not think there is any requirement that an untrue statement be misleading to a material extent. All that is required is that the statement is misleading in the form and context in which it is included in the prospectus.' *Houghton v Saunders* [2018] NZSC 74, [2019] 1 NZLR 1 at [77]–[78], [80]–[83], per Elias CJ, Glazebrook, O'Regan, Arnold and Kós JJ

URBAN ALE

Australia [Alleged infringement of registered trade mark 'urban ale' by use of the words 'Urban Pale' on respondent's label and website etc.] '[70] Having considered the evidence to which we were taken, we are satisfied that the primary judge's findings as to the descriptive and laudatory meaning of the word "urban" in relation to beer were open to him. We do not see any appealable error in his Honour's fact-finding. There is, therefore, no basis on which we should interfere with those findings.

'[71] The corollary of the primary judge's findings is that the meaning of "urban ale", when used in relation to beer, is not allusive or metaphorical (as the appellant contended them to be). His Honour so found at [141]. As his Honour put it, the evidence established that the word "urban", in its relevant context, has a tangible meaning — beer produced in an inner-city craft brewery. Had the primary judge found that the Word Mark was an allusive or metaphorical use of the words "urban ale" then this would have indicated that the mark was inherently adapted, or at least inherently adapted to some extent, to distinguish the appellant's beer from the beer of other traders.' *Urban Alley Brewery Pty Ltd v La Sirène Pty Ltd* [2020] FCAFC 186, (2020) 384 ALR 230, BC202010786 at [70]–[71], per Middleton, Yates and Lee JJ

USAGE

[For 32 Halsbury's Laws of England (5th Edn) (2012) para 50 see now 32 Halsbury's Laws of England (5th Edn) (2019) para 50.]

USER PRINCIPLE

New Zealand '[12] It was common ground that damages for infringement were to be assessed by the application of the user principle which is a technique for assessing damages in circumstances where the right holder neither sells nor licenses production of its work. As the Judge explained:

[379] It is plain from the authorities and the parties' positions that the user principle is the approach to be adopted in determining relief when it is not possible to establish a normal synchronisation licence fee. The threshold has been met for the user principle to apply, because Eight Mile Style would not have licensed *Lose Yourself* for use in the National Party's election advertising and the National Party was unlikely to have negotiated a licence with Eight Mile Style.

(Footnote omitted).

...

[26] The object of damages is to compensate for loss or injury. The general rule in relation to economic torts is that the measure of damages is to be, so far as possible, that sum of money which will put the injured party in the same position as that party would have been if it had not sustained the wrong. Where intellectual property rights relating to a product are infringed, the measure of damages will vary depending upon the manner in which the holder of the right chooses to exploit the right.

[27] Hence, where the benefit of the right is realised through the sale of a product and infringement results in a diversion of sales, the measure of damages will normally be the profit which would have been realised by the owner of the intellectual property right (IPR) if the sales had been made by him. By contrast where IPRs are exploited through the granting of licences for royalty payments, and an infringer uses the right without a licence, the measure of the damages for infringement will be the sums which the IPR holder would have received by way of royalty. Those alternative modes of exploitation comprise the first and second scenarios identified in Lord Wilberforce's well-known analysis in *General Tire & Rubber Co v Firestone Tyre & Rubber Co Ltd* [[1975] 1 WLR 819, HL, at 824–825].

'[28] If neither of those scenarios applies, recourse is generally had to the approach known as the "user principle." This involves the assessment of a notional licence fee or royalty, being the price that the IPR holder would reasonably have charged for permission or authorisation to carry out the infringing act. ...

...

'[38] Mr Arthur argued that the user principle is not restitutionary. User damages are compensation for loss, albeit not loss of a conventional kind. He contended that by classifying the user principle as partly restitutionary the Court inappropriately invoked an unjust enrichment concept and a notion of forcing a defendant to disgorge wrongful gains.

'[39] Mr Williams for Eight Mile did not contest the substance of that criticism. He pointed out that user principle damages have sometimes been said to be restitutionary in the sense that they compensate the owner of a valuable right for the loss of the value of its exercise. However he accepted that the orthodox view is now that user damages are compensatory in nature, a view we share.' *New Zealand National Party v Eight Mile Style, LLC* [2018] NZCA 596, [2019] 2 NZLR 352 at [12], [26]–[28], [38]–[39], per Brown J

V

VALUE, IN MONEY OR MONEY'S WORTH

See also **MONEY'S WORTH**

[Finance Act 1997, s 11(10).] '[38] … In my view, the expression "money or money's worth" in s 11(10)(a) emphasises that in determining the value of the stakes staked it is the actual and real-world value of the stakes in the hands of the banker which matters. Section 11(10)(a) is concerned with stakes which are or represent money (as cash chips do) or which can be converted into money. Similarly, in working out the value of the prizes provided by the banker, it is the actual or real-world cost to the banker of providing the prizes that must be brought into account, subject to the operation of s 20 of the BGDA [Betting and Gaming Duties Act 1981]. I would reject the submission made by HMRC that s 11(10)(a) is concerned with the role the stake plays in the game and the value it carries for that purpose. In my view, the UT [Upper Tribunal] was right to say that this goes too far and attaches insufficient weight to the expression "money or money's worth" and the context, which requires a focus on the economic substance of the stake and the real financial contribution that stake makes to the banker's profits from gaming and in turn to the gross gaming yield from the premises. So too, the Court of Appeal was correct to say that the calculation of stakes staked involves a conventional accounting of the real-world value of the stakes which have been staked in any given accounting period.' *London Clubs Management Ltd v Revenue and Customs Commissioners* [2020] UKSC 49, [2021] 2 All ER 333 at [38], per Lord Kitchin JSC

VALUER

[For 6 Halsbury's Laws of England (5th Edn) (2023) paras 488, 499 see now 6 Halsbury's Laws of England (5th Edn) (2023) paras 588, 598.]

VARY

[Immigration Act 1971, s 3(3): limited leave to enter or remain in the UK may be varied.] '[71] Fourth, it is common ground, and I agree, that the meaning of the term "vary" in this context "can in principle", or does, include "cancel". The two words are not "interchangeable", however; nor does the Secretary of State submit that they are. "Vary" means "change". "Vary" is a broad term. Its precise meaning depends on the context. In particular, "vary" can mean different things when applied to limited LTR (leave to remain) and to ILR (indefinite leave to remain).

(i) As I understand her argument, Ms Weston accepts that the word "vary" can in principle include reducing the length of leave to nothing, which is the same as cancellation.
(ii) "Varying" can also mean reducing the length of leave so that some period remains. That meaning could apply, as a matter of language, both to limited LTR and to ILR. Because ILR has no conditions and its length is indefinite, the only way it could be varied is by reducing its length, either to a finite period, or to nothing. Neither side contended for the former possibility.
(iii) The intrinsic characteristics of limited LTR and of ILR are different. Limited LTR, to which conditions are attached, can be varied by changing or removing those conditions. That meaning of "vary", for obvious reasons, does not apply to ILR.'

R (on the application of C1) v Secretary of State for the Home Department [2022] EWCA Civ 30, [2022] 3 All ER 1082 at [71], per Elisabeth Laing LJ

VEIN

[For 76 Halsbury's Laws of England (5th Edn) (2013) para 14 see now 76 Halsbury's Laws of England (5th Edn) (2019) para 14.]

VERDICT

[For 61 Halsbury's Laws of England (5th Edn) (2010) para 847 see now 61A Halsbury's Laws of England (5th Edn) (2023) para 256.]

VEST

[For 102 Halsbury's Laws of England (5th Edn) (2010) para 413 see now 102 Halsbury's Laws of England (5th Edn) (2021) para 414.]

VIOLENCE

See also DOMESTIC VIOLENCE

[For 60 Halsbury's Laws of England (5th Edn) (2011) para 553 see now 60 Halsbury's Laws of England (5th Edn) (2018) para 530.]

[European Convention on Human Rights (as set out in the Human Rights Act 1998, Sch 1), extent to which the use of violence against property during protest was sanctioned.] '[87] The ordinary meaning of violence includes "the exercise of physical force so as to cause injury or damage to a person, property, etc" (*Shorter Oxford English Dictionary*). Violence is not confined to assaults on the person but may include damage to property; and neither is the concept of "peaceful assembly" defined by an absence of violence to the person or property. Indeed, it is not difficult to envisage a demonstration at which no violence to the person or property occurs, but which could not be characterised as peaceful, not least if it is intimidatory or causes alarm or distress. …' *Attorney General's Reference (No 1 of 2022)* [2022] EWCA Crim 1259, [2023] 1 All ER 549 at [87], per Lord Burnett CJ

VIOLENT DISORDER

[For 26 Halsbury's Laws of England (5th Edn) (2016) para 551 see now 60 Halsbury's Laws of England (5th Edn) (2020) para 689.]

W

WAIFS

[For 29 Halsbury's Laws of England (5th Edn) (2014) para 285 see now 29 Halsbury's Laws of England (5th Edn) (2019) para 290.]

WAIVER

Express waiver

Australia [Foreign States Immunities Act 1985 (Cth), s 10(2).] '[23] There is some ambiguity about what these numerous statements mean by their insistence that a waiver of immunity in a treaty be "express". Part of the difficulty is a lack of clarity in legal discourse generally about what is meant by "express" meaning. Properly understood, express meaning can include implications, which constitute the unexpressed content of a statement or term and which are identified by inference.

'[24] An express term of an agreement involves words that are "openly uttered" either orally or in writing. The meaning of an express term is derived primarily from the content of the words expressed. It contrasts with an implied term, the meaning of which is derived primarily by inference from the conduct of the parties to the agreement and the circumstances in light of the express terms. There can sometimes be difficulty in distinguishing between the two types of terms, because often the imprecision of language means that inferences are required to understand an express term. Even the words of the most carefully drafted international instrument are built upon a foundation of presuppositions and necessary implicatures and explicatures. The international authorities that insist upon express waiver of immunity in a treaty should not be understood as denying the ordinary and natural role of implications in elucidating the meaning of the express words of the treaty.

'[25] The insistence that the waiver be "express" should be understood as requiring only that the expression of waiver be derived from the express words of the international agreement, whether as an express term or as a term implied for reasons including necessity. …

'[26] In this sense, the insistence by international authority that a waiver of immunity in an international agreement must be "express" is an insistence that any inference of a waiver of immunity must be drawn with great care when interpreting the express words of that agreement in context. It does not deny that implications are almost invariably contained in any (expressed) words of a treaty. As senior counsel for Spain rightly put the point in oral submissions: "[T]here must be implications that surround every textual passage. The question is: what are those implications, and what level of clarity about the implication is required?" Accordingly, if an international agreement does not expressly use the word "waiver", the inference that an express term involves a waiver of immunity will only be drawn if the implication is clear from the words used and the context. In words quoted by Lord Goff in [*R v Bow Street Metropolitan Stipendiary Magistrate; ex p Pinochet Ugarte (No 3)* [2000] 1 AC 147; [1999] 2 All ER 97] from the International Law Commission's commentary upon (what were then) the draft articles on jurisdictional immunities of States and their property, there is "no room" to recognise an implication of "consent of an unwilling state which has not expressed its consent in a clear and recognisable manner". And as Rehnquist CJ said, delivering the opinion of the Supreme Court of the United States in *Argentine Republic v Amerada Hess Shipping Corp* [(1989) 488 US 428 at 442–443], a foreign State will not waive its immunity merely "by signing an international agreement that contains no mention of a waiver of immunity to suit in United States courts or even the availability of a cause of action in the United States". This reflects the "political principle that those who are independent and autonomous cannot, except by consent, exercise authority over, or establish an external source of authority over, others of independent and autonomous status.

'[27] Against this background of international law, there is no basis to interpret s 10(2) of the Foreign States Immunities Act as requiring a novel approach to interpretation that would exclude the possibility of a waiver of immunity being evidenced by implications inferred from the express words of a treaty in their context and in light of their purpose.

'[28] A high level of clarity and necessity are required before inferring that a foreign State has waived its immunity in a treaty because it is so unusual, and the consequence is so significant. Hence, s 10(2) makes clear that the mere fact that a State "is a party to an agreement the proper law of which is the law of Australia" is not sufficient to waive immunity from jurisdiction. But s 10(2) expressly refers to submission (and thus waiver) "by agreement".' *Kingdom of Spain v Infrastructure Services Luxembourg Sarl* [2023] HCA 11, (2023) 408 ALR 658 at [23]–[28], per Kiefel CJ, Gageler, Gordon, Edelman, Steward, Gleeson and Jagot JJ

WAR

[For 3 Halsbury's Laws of England (5th Edn) (2011) para 6 see now 3 Halsbury's Laws of England (5th Edn) (2019) para 6.]

WARD OF COURT

[For 9 Halsbury's Laws of England (5th Edn) (2012) para 264 see now 9 Halsbury's Laws of England (5th Edn) (2017) para 301.]

WARRANTY

[For 22 Halsbury's Laws of England (5th Edn) (2012) para 557 see now 22 Halsbury's Laws of England (5th Edn) (2019) para 348.]

Insurance generally

[For 60 Halsbury's Laws of England (5th Edn) (2011) para 114 see now 60 Halsbury's Laws of England (5th Edn) (2018) para 91.]

Marine insurance

[For 60 Halsbury's Laws of England (5th Edn) (2011) para 114n see now 60 Halsbury's Laws of England (5th Edn) (2018) para 91 n 2.]

Sale of goods

[For 91 Halsbury's Laws of England (5th Edn) (2012) paras 64–65 see now 91 Halsbury's Laws of England (5th Edn) (2019) paras 63–64.]

WASTE

[For 91 Halsbury's Laws of England (5th Edn) (2012) para 887 see now 91 Halsbury's Laws of England (5th Edn) (2019) para 776.]

Equitable waste

[For 62 Halsbury's Laws of England (5th Edn) (2016) paras 324–325 see now 62 Halsbury's Laws of England (5th Edn) (2022) paras 354–355; and for 91 Halsbury's Laws of England (5th Edn) (2012) para 898 see now 91 Halsbury's Laws of England (5th Edn) (2019) para 785.]

Meliorating waste

[For 91 Halsbury's Laws of England (5th Edn) (2012) para 894 see now 91 Halsbury's Laws of England (5th Edn) (2019) para 781.]

Permissive waste

[For 91 Halsbury's Laws of England (5th Edn) (2012) para 896 see now 91 Halsbury's Laws of England (5th Edn) (2019) para 783.]

Voluntary waste

[For 91 Halsbury's Laws of England (5th Edn) (2012) para 888 see now 91 Halsbury's Laws of England (5th Edn) (2019) para 777.]

WATERCOURSE

[For 87 Halsbury's Laws of England (5th Edn) (2017) paras 917–918 see now 87 Halsbury's Laws of England (5th Edn) (2022) paras 911–912.]

WAYLEAVE

[For 76 Halsbury's Laws of England (5th Edn) (2013) para 335 see now 76 Halsbury's Laws of England (5th Edn) (2019) para 332.]

WHĀNGAI

New Zealand '[32] [An expert witness] also swore an affidavit of 11 September 2019. … At para [7] of his affidavit he stated:

Whāngai is a means whereby social and or kin groups or whānau structures were strengthened. In Māoridom, a child is not the child of the birth parents, but of the family, and the family was not a nuclear unit in space, but an integral part of a tribal whole, bound by reciprocal obligations to all whose future was prescribed by the past fact of common descent.

…

'[41] The literature does not contemplate the possibility of a sexual relationship in the context of whāngai, which is unsurprising given the parental nature of whāngai. I also refer to the article "Whāngai: remembering, understanding and experiencing" by Karyn Okeroa McRea and Linda Waimarea Nacora [(2006) MAI Review]. At the commencement of the article it states:

> The Māori customary practice of whāngai is often equated with adoption or foster care. There are, however, significant differences between the institutions. Adoption or foster care, tends to be mainly focused on the interests of the child. The institution of whāngai, while being cognizant of the interests of the child, is weighted more towards establishing, nurturing and cementing relationships between individuals, families and broader relational networks. …

'[42] In the introduction to that article, it states:

> Within Māori society the customary practice in which a child is raised by kin members other than their birth parents is termed whāngai, atawhai or tamaiti whāngai (for the remainder of this report the term whāngai will be used). The term whāngai literally means "to feed or nourish" (Mead, 1994). The meaning of whāngai implies that the child is being nurtured in the fullest sense including instruction, cultural and affection as well as food (Bradley, 1997). Carroll (1970) provides a working definition of adoption as, "any customary and optimal procedure for taking as one's own, a child of other parents." The expression "*taking as one's own*" under the whāngai institution does not require the child to relinquish all claims to his/her birth identity. That whāngai occurs within the child's own kin group means that, whakapapa (geneology) is acknowledged and maintained to affirm birth lines, and placements were arranged to secure and strengthen whanau and kin links (Bradley, 1997).'

Sears v Franks [2020] NZFC 7474, [2020] NZFLR 763, BC202064156 at [32], [41]–[42], per Judge Cook

WILL

[For 102 Halsbury's Laws of England (5th Edn) (2010) para 1 see now 102 Halsbury's Laws of England (5th Edn) (2021) para 1.]

Informal or nuncupative will

[For 102 Halsbury's Laws of England (5th Edn) (2010) para 81 see now 102 Halsbury's Laws of England (5th Edn) (2021) para 82.]

Mutual wills

New Zealand

'[17] Section 30 of the Wills Act 2007 has codified the equitable doctrine of mutual wills. However, Lorraine's Will and the Second Will were executed before the Wills Act 2007 came into force. This case is therefore to be determined by applying the equitable doctrine of mutual wills as set out in *Lewis v Cotton* [[2001] 2 NZLR 21, CA]. In that case, the Court of Appeal observed that while a will can always be revoked, where non-revocation has been contractually promised, the executors and trustees of any replacement will may be required to hold affected assets upon a constructive trust in terms of the revoked will. The origin of this doctrine is in cases of joint wills, that is, a will signed by two testators. Such a document would ordinarily be read as two wills with the mutual intention that neither should be revoked.

'[18] The relevant promise for the purposes of the doctrine of mutual wills may be either to not revoke a will at any time whether secretly or openly, or to not revoke a will secretly during the other will maker's lifetime and to not revoke it at all after the other will maker's death. However, the crux of the matter is not the non-revocation promise but rather the obligation to not deal with property contrary to the agreement or understanding.

'[19] The Court of Appeal in *Lewis v Cotton* held that the courts are "very slow" to find mutual wills simply because two parties have made corresponding or mirror wills. More is needed to satisfy the doctrine. …

…

'[27] Thus, the equitable doctrine of mutual wills recognises that the executors and trustees of a will may be required to hold affected assets upon a constructive trust in terms of a revoked will. The doctrine applies where:

(a) there is an underlying consultation and coordination between two testators which resulted in an agreement or an arrangement as to how they would make their respective wills;
(b) the two testators made wills consistent with their agreement or arrangement;
(c) there is a contract or mutual understanding (intended to bind each testator to a future course of action) that neither testator would deal with the property in a manner inconsistent with the agreement or arrangement (and therefore the provisions of the corresponding wills); and
(d) one of the testators has died without revoking their will.'

McNeish v McArthur [2019] NZHC 3281, [2020] 2 NZLR 287 at [17]–[19], [27], per Doogue J

WINDRUSH GENERATION

'[40] The name "Windrush generation" and related terms derive from the ship HMT Empire Windrush which arrived in the United Kingdom from the Caribbean in June 1948 carrying around 1,000 passengers. This passage is said to symbolise Caribbean migration to the United Kingdom starting in the late 1940s.' *R (on the application of Mahabir) v Secretary of State for the Home Department* [2021] EWHC 1177 (Admin), [2022] 1 All ER 895 at [40], per Tim Smith

WITHOUT ISSUE

[For 102 Halsbury's Laws of England (5th Edn) (2010) para 442 see now 102 Halsbury's Laws of England (5th Edn) (2021) para 456.]

WITNESS

[For 12 Halsbury's Laws of England (5th Edn) (2015) para 793 see now 12 Halsbury's Laws of England (5th Edn) (2020) para 785.]

WORD

[For 102 Halsbury's Laws of England (5th Edn) (2010) para 247 see now 102 Halsbury's Laws of England (5th Edn) (2020) para 247.]

WORKER

[Delete the entry for *Gilham v Ministry of Justice* [2017] EWCA Civ 2220, [2018] 3 All ER 521 and substitute the following.]

[Employment Rights Act 1996, ss 191, 230(3): whether district judge was a 'worker' and thus able to claim whistle-blower's protection.] '[1] This case is about the employment status of district judges, but it could apply to the holder of any judicial office. The issue is whether a district judge qualifies as a "worker" or a "person in Crown employment" for the purpose of the protection given to whistle-blowers under Pt IVA of the Employment Rights Act 1996 ("the 1996 Act"). If a district judge does not on the face of it qualify for whistle-blower protection, the further question is whether this is discrimination against her in the enjoyment of her right to freedom of expression under the European Convention on Human Rights ("ECHR"). And if it is, what is the remedy?

...

'[11] On appeal to this court, the appellant continues to argue that she is a "worker" within the meaning of s 230(3)(b) of the 1996 Act. She also raises for the first time a new argument, that she is in "Crown employment" within the meaning of s 191 of the 1996 Act. If she fails in each of those, she continues to argue that her exclusion from whistle-blowing protection is a breach, either of her rights under art 10 or under art 14 read with art 10 of the ECHR and that either s 230(3)(b) or s 191 of the 1996 Act should be read and given effect so as to bring her within that protection.

'[12] It is not in dispute that a judge undertakes personally to perform work or services and that the recipient of that work or services is not a client or customer of the judge. The issue is whether that work or services is performed pursuant to a contract with the recipient of that work or services or pursuant to some different legal arrangement. Nor is it in dispute that judges hold a statutory office.

...

...

'[21] Taken together, all of these factors point against the existence of a contractual relationship between a judge and the executive or any member of it. Still less do they suggest a contractual relationship between the judge and the Lord Chief Justice.

...

'[23] Section 191(3) provides that "In this Act 'Crown employment' means employment under or for the purposes of a government department or any officer or body exercising on behalf of the Crown functions conferred by a statutory provision". Clearly, "employment" in this section cannot mean "employment under a contract" because it would then add nothing to the definition in s 230(3). The predecessor to s 191 was inserted into the Industrial Relations Act 1971 because historically Crown servants had not been seen to be employed under contracts of service and had not been able to complain of wrongful dismissal. The object was to enable them to complain of unfair dismissal and enjoy the other employment rights listed in s 191(2). Thus, argues the appellant, s 191 is apt to give her the protection of Pt IVA even if she is not employed under a contract.

'[24] The definition in s 191(3) has two limbs: employment under or for the purposes of a government department; and employment under or for the purposes of an officer or body exercising on behalf of the Crown functions conferred by a statutory provision. For the reasons given earlier, it is impossible to regard the judiciary as employed under or for the purposes of the Ministry of Justice. They are not civil servants or the equivalent of civil servants. They do not work for the ministry. It is slightly more plausible to regard them as working under or for the purposes of the Lord Chief Justice, who since the 2005 Act [Constitutional Reform Act 2005], has had statutory responsibilities in relation to the judiciary: under s 7 of that Act, he is responsible for the maintenance of appropriate arrangements for the welfare, training and guidance of the judiciary of England and Wales (within the resources provided by the Lord Chancellor) and for their deployment and the allocation of work within the courts. As already noted, he also shares some responsibility for appointments, discipline and removal with the Lord Chancellor. But it is difficult to think that, by conferring these functions upon the Lord Chief Justice, the 2005 Act brought about such a fundamental change in the application of s 191. Judges do not work "under and for the purposes of" those functions of the Lord Chief Justice but for the administration of justice in the courts of England and Wales in accordance with their oaths of office. Mutatis mutandis, the same reasoning would apply to the identical definition of crown employment in art 236(3) of the Employment Rights (Northern Ireland) Order 1996, SI 1996/1919.

'[25] It is perhaps worth noting that s 83(2) and (9) of the Equality Act 2010, passed since the 2005 Act, defines "employment" as covering "Crown employment" as defined in s 191 of the 1996 Act. But it also makes express provision, in ss 50 and 51, prohibiting discrimination in relation to, among other things, appointment to public offices. These are defined to include officers appointed by or on the recommendation of a member of the executive (such as the Lord Chancellor) or by the Lord Chief Justice or Senior President of Tribunals. Thus judicial office-holders are clearly protected by these provisions, which would have been quite unnecessary had they already been protected as persons in Crown employment. Sections 50 and 51 do not apply in Northern Ireland, but this does not affect the force of this point.

...

'[37] As no legitimate aim has been put forward, it is not possible to judge whether the exclusion is a proportionate means of achieving that aim, whatever the test by which proportionality has to be judged. I conclude, therefore, that the exclusion of judges from the whistle-blowing protection in Part IVA of the 1996 Act is in breach of their rights under art 14 read with art 10 of the ECHR.

...

'[46] I would therefore allow this appeal and remit the case to the Employment Tribunal on the basis that the appellant is entitled to claim the protection of Pt IVA of the 1996 Act.' *Gilham v Ministry of Justice* [2019] UKSC 44, [2020] 1 All ER 1 at [1], [11]–[12], [21], [23]–[25], [37], [46], per Lady Hale P

[Trade Union and Labour Relations (Consolidation) Act 1992, s 296; European Convention for the Protection of Human Rights and Fundamental Freedoms 1950 (as set out in the Human Rights Act 1998, Sch 1), art 11 (collective bargaining rights).] '[11] ... By a decision dated 14 November 2017 ([2018] IRLR 84) the CAC [Central Arbitration Committee] declined to accept the application [for compulsory recognition for collective bargaining in respect of a group of riders delivering food] on the basis that the riders were not "workers" within the meaning of the 1992 Act because the terms under which they provide their services did not require them to do so personally but permitted the use of substitutes.

...

'[76] ... I think it can safely be inferred that the Panel concluded that the riders in question were not in an employment relationship with Deliveroo for the purpose of art 11: that is the only issue to which its reference to "the unfettered and genuine right of substitution that operates both in the written contract and in practice" would be material.

'[77] I believe that that was a conclusion to which the CAC was entitled to come. The particular feature on which it relied was its finding that riders are, genuinely, not under an obligation to provide their services personally and have a virtually unlimited right of substitution. That is on any view a material factor in the decision whether they are in an employment relationship with Deliveroo. Paragraph 13 of ILO R198 [International Labour Organisation Recommendation No 198 concerning the employment relationship (15 June 2006)] refers to the fact that the work "must be carried out personally by the worker" as an indicator of an employment relationship (see para [57] above); and it follows at least that the absence of such an obligation must be a contra-indicator of worker status (as it was treated in *Yodel* [*B v Yodel Delivery Network Ltd* (Case C-692/19) EU:C:2020:288, [2020] IRLR 550, ECJ)]. However, in my view the CAC was entitled to regard it as decisive. I do not think that the position taken in English law that an obligation of personal service is (subject to the limited qualifications acknowledged in *Pimlico Plumbers* [*Pimlico Plumbers Ltd v Smith* [2017] EWCA Civ 51, [2017] IRLR 323; affd [2018] UKSC 29, [2018] 4 All ER 641)] an indispensable feature of the relationship of employer and worker is a parochial peculiarity. On the contrary, it seems to me to be a central feature of such a relationship as ordinarily understood, and I see no reason why its importance should be any the less in the context of art 11.

...

'[85] For those reasons I would hold that the riders do not fall within the scope of the trade union freedom right under art 11.' *R (on the application of Independent Workers Union of Great Britain) v Central Arbitration Committee (Roofoods Ltd t/a Deliveroo, interested party)* [2021] EWCA Civ 952, [2022] 2 All ER 1105 at [11], [76]–[77], [85], per Underhill VP

[Employment Rights Act 1996, s 230(3); National Minimum Wage Act 1998, s 54(3)(b).] '[1] New ways of working organised through digital platforms pose pressing questions about the employment status of the people who do the work involved. The central question on this appeal is whether an employment tribunal was entitled to find that drivers whose work is arranged through Uber's smartphone application ("the Uber app") work for Uber under workers' contracts and so qualify for the national minimum wage, paid annual leave and other workers' rights; or whether, as Uber contends, the drivers do not have these rights because they work for themselves as independent contractors, performing services under contracts made with passengers through Uber as their booking agent. If drivers work for Uber under workers' contracts, a secondary question arises as to whether the employment tribunal was also entitled to find that the drivers who have brought the present claims were working under such contracts whenever they were logged into the Uber app within the territory in which they were licensed to operate and ready and willing to accept trips; or whether, as Uber argues, they were working only when driving passengers to their destinations.

'[2] For the reasons given in this judgment, I would affirm the conclusion of the Employment Appeal Tribunal ((2017) UKEAT/56/17, [2018] IRLR 97, [2018] ICR 453) and the majority of the Court of Appeal ([2018] EWCA Civ 2748, [2019] 3 All ER 489, [2019] ICR 845), that the employment tribunal ([2017] IRLR 4) was entitled to decide both questions in the claimants' favour.

...

'[119] On the facts found in the present case, and in particular those which I have emphasised at paras [94]–[101] above, I think it clear that the employment tribunal was entitled to find that the claimant drivers were "workers" who worked for Uber London under "worker's contracts" within the meaning of the statutory definition. Indeed, that was, in my opinion, the only conclusion which the tribunal could reasonably have reached.

...

'[130] It follows that the employment tribunal was, in my view, entitled to conclude that, by logging onto the Uber app in London, a claimant driver came within the definition of a "worker" by entering into a contract with Uber London whereby he undertook to perform driving services for Uber London. I do not consider that the third condition identified by the tribunal that the driver was in fact ready and willing to accept trips can properly be regarded as essential to the existence of a worker's contract; nor indeed did the tribunal assert that it was. But it is reasonable to treat it, as the tribunal did, as a further condition which must be satisfied in order to find that a driver is "working" under such a contract.' *Uber BV v Aslam* [2021]

UKSC 5, [2021] 4 All ER 209 at [1]–[2], [119], [130], per Lord Leggatt JSC

WORKING TIME

[Working Time Regulations 1998, SI 1998/1833, reg 2(1).] '[132] For the purpose of the Working Time Regulations 1998, "working time" is defined in reg 2(1), in relation to a worker, as "any period during which he is working, at his employer's disposal and carrying out his activity or duties".

...

'[134] On the facts of the present case, a driver's place of work is wherever his vehicle is currently located. Subject to the point I consider next, in the light of this case law the tribunal was justified in finding that all time spent by a driver working under a worker's contract with Uber London, including time spent "on duty" logged onto the Uber app in London available to accept a trip request, is "working time" within the meaning of the Working Time Directive [Council Directive 93/104/EC] and Regulations.

'[135] The point that – like the majority of the Court of Appeal and Judge Eady QC in the Employment Appeal Tribunal – I have found more difficult is whether a driver logged onto the Uber app in the area in which he is licensed to work can be said to be "working, at his employer's disposal and carrying out his activity or duties" if during such times the driver is equally ready and willing to accept a trip request received from another PHV operator. It was argued with force by counsel for Uber that a driver cannot reasonably be said to be working for and at the disposal of Uber London if, while logged onto the Uber app, he is also at the same time logged onto another app provided by a competitor of Uber which operates a similar service.

'[136] I have concluded that this question cannot be answered in the abstract. I agree with Judge Eady QC when she said in her judgment dismissing Uber's appeal to the Employment Appeal Tribunal (at para 126) that it is a matter of fact and degree. ...' *Uber BV v Aslam* [2021] UKSC 5, [2021] 4 All ER 209 at [132], [134]–[136], per Lord Leggatt JSC

WOUND

[For 25 Halsbury's Laws of England (5th Edn) (2016) para 142 see now 25 Halsbury's Laws of England (5th Edn) (2020) para 201.]

WRONG

[M'Naghten Rules (see *M'Naghten's* Case (1843) 10 Cl & Fin 200); insanity as a defence.] '[41] We endorse this analysis of the authorities [in *Blackstone's Criminal Practice*, 2022 edition at para A3.33]. In order to establish the defence of insanity within the M'Naghten Rules on the ground of not knowing the act was "wrong", the defendant must establish both that (a) he did not know that his act was unlawful (ie contrary to law) and (b) he did not know that his act was "morally" wrong (also expressed as wrong "by the standards of ordinary people"). In our judgment, "wrong" means both against the law and wrong by the standards of ordinary reasonable people. Strictly a jury must be satisfied that the defendant did not know that what he was doing was against the law nor wrong by the standards of reasonable ordinary people. In practice how the jury is directed on this issue will depend on the facts and issues in the particular case.

...

[48] ...[W]e conclude that under the M'Naghten Rules, the defence of insanity is not available to a defendant who, although he knew what he was doing was wrong, he believed that he had no choice but to commit the act in question.' *R v Keal* [2022] EWCA Crim 341, [2022] 4 All ER 83 at [41], [48], per Lord Burnett CJ

X

'X' MARKER

'[11] In due course, several countries introduced "X" to indicate gender "unspecified" (referred to as an " 'X' marker" in this judgment) to their passports, including Australia (2011) and New Zealand (2005).

'[12] It should be noted in this regard that, although the substantive judicial review was heard in April 2018, this court has, at the invitation of all of the parties, been brought up to date as to subsequent developments. The present position is that 11 countries world-wide allow for "X" markers in their passports. As of 2019, there are only 5 countries within the Council of Europe making such provision.' *R (on the application of Elan-Cane) v Secretary of State for the Home Department (Human Rights Watch intervening)* [2020] EWCA Civ 363, [2021] 1 All ER 25 at [11]–[12], per King LJ

Y

YEARLY INTEREST

[Income Tax Act 2007, s 874; Insolvency (England and Wales) Rules 2016, SI 2016/1024, r 14.23(7).] '[1] … The short question, which has generated different answers in the courts below, is whether interest payable under r 14.23(7) is "yearly interest" within the meaning of s 874, so that the administrators must first deduct income tax before paying interest to proving creditors.

…

'[8] … There is no definition of the phrase "yearly interest" anywhere in the 2007 Act. Nonetheless there is this deeming provision in s 874, added by Sch 11 to the Finance Act 2013:

> "(5A) For the purposes of subsection (1) a payment of interest which is payable to an individual in respect of compensation is to be treated as a payment of yearly interest (irrespective of the period in respect of which the interest is paid)."

'[9] This is unfortunately another case in which the full meaning of an apparently innocent-looking simple statutory phrase can only be addressed by reference to the historical deployment of that phrase, or equivalent phrases seeking to express the same concept, in early legislation

…

'[19] At first instance, Hildyard J was persuaded that the absence of any accrual over time (prior to the identification of a surplus and its quantification after payment of all proved debts in full) was fatal to the categorisation of statutory interest as yearly interest. By contrast, the Court of Appeal could discern no requirement from the authorities that yearly interest should accrue due over time. Since it was compensation for the proving creditors being kept out of their money for a substantial time, the interest had the requisite long-term quality sufficient for it to be categorised as yearly.

…

'[51] It is true, as the administrators submitted, that some of the second group of cases were primarily concerned with the question whether payments described as interest were truly interest at all for income tax purposes, rather than whether they were yearly interest. … By contrast in the present case it has been common ground throughout that statutory interest under r 14.23 is interest for the purposes of income tax.

'[52] But those cases nonetheless provide the answer to the conundrum: what period of durability is to be identified for interest payable in a single lump sum as compensation for the payee being out of the money in the past, for the purpose of deciding whether it is to be treated as yearly interest, under the *Hay* principles [*IRC v Hay* 1924 SC 521, (1924) 8 TC 636]? The simple answer, supplied by all the second group of cases, is that it is the period in respect of which the interest is calculated, because that is the period during which the loss of the use of money or property has been incurred, for which the interest is to be compensation.

'[53] This appears also to have been the assumption made by the drafter of what is now s 874(5A), quoted above. It deems payment of interest to an individual in respect of compensation to be yearly interest "irrespective of the period in respect of which the interest is paid". This suggests that, but for the deeming provision (introduced, so the court was told, to deal with compensation for mis-selling of Payment Protection Insurance), the question whether the interest would or would not have been yearly interest would have depended upon the duration of the period in respect of which the compensatory interest was calculated.' *Revenue and Customs Commissioners v Joint Administrators of Lehman Brothers International* [2019] UKSC 12, [2019] 2 All ER 559 at [1], [8]–[9], [19], [51]–[53], per Lord Briggs JSC

Z

ZOONOSIS

'Zoonosis' means any disease and/or infection which is naturally transmissible directly or indirectly between animals and humans; and 'zoonotic agent' means any virus, bacterium, fungus, parasite or other biological entity which is likely to cause a zoonosis. (European Parliament and Council Directive (EC) 2003/99 art 2(2)(a), (b))